Dear EVELYN

WAIT FOR ME

KATHY CARROLL

ISBN 978-1-0980-7430-2 (paperback)
ISBN 978-1-0980-7432-6 (hardcover)
ISBN 978-1-0980-7433-3 (digital)

Christian Faith Publishing, Inc.
832 Park Avenue
Meadville, PA 16335
www.christianfaithpublishing.com

Printed in the United States of America

To Debbie, my sister…
This book would not have been possible without you.

PREFACE

My father, Paul Fogel, was a young Marine during World War II, having joined the USMC on August 7, 1942. He met my mother, Evelyn Wells, at a USO dance in Pensacola, Florida, in February 1944. At the time, she was in a three-year nursing program at the Pensacola Hospital School of Nursing run by The Sisters of Charity. Within a year of their meeting, he was sent to the war in the Pacific, first transported by train to California, and then put on a ship to Maui, Hawaii. He was one of the thousands of men to do battle in Iwo Jima. By the time my mother waved goodbye to Dad at the train station in Pensacola, they were engaged to be married. She was in her last year of training, and the nurses were not allowed to be married while in training nor until after they passed state board examinations. Their first letters to one another begin in March 1944 when Evelyn was sent to Chattahoochee, Florida, to do her required three months' nurse training in the state psychiatric hospital. Their letters picked up once again a few months later when Paul was sent overseas.

My sister, Debbie, and I were going through some drawers with our mom sometime around the year 2002. Along with a couple of her early nurse caps from the 1940s (which she had kept in pristine condition), we discovered an old beat-up box full of letters. Her face flushed, and she explained that these were hers and Dad's love letters from World War II. I was immediately mesmerized. Old things are *my* thing...not antiques necessarily, unless they have sentimental value, but old stories, old houses, old cemeteries, old letters... So I asked her if I could have the letters to keep for "posterity." She couldn't believe that I wanted them.

Through the ensuing years, life happened in a big way. No sooner had we celebrated Mom and Dad's fiftieth wedding anniversary in 1996, they both became very ill for quite a long time, having suffered severally (and together at times) strokes, heart disease, heart attack, cancer, diabetes, and all the accompanying debilitating side effects: high cholesterol, high blood sugar, high blood pressure, lack of mobility, and the like. My family lived in Texas, and during that same period of time, my husband was diagnosed with Parkinson's disease. I would fly to Florida each year, when I could take off work, to see Mom and Dad and make some home-cooked meals for them. Oftentimes, I would just sit by them and enjoy staring at their faces as they held hands across their wheelchairs. I'm telling you, these people were precious!

Our daughter, Holli, was attending law school at Baylor University, and one of her law professors encouraged her to think about having the letters published. While awaiting results of her bar exam, she carefully organized and put the letters in acid-free inserts and placed them in binders. We have four four-inch binders; two are full of my father's letters, and two are full of my mother's letters. I always envisioned transcribing them and one day possibly publishing them—that is, if I ever had time. That time came when I found it necessary to quit work to take full-time care of my husband. In 2014, I began a six-year journey of bringing this vision to life. It wasn't an easy journey, friends. I would stay up nights after securing my husband in bed, and as his care needs increased, I found myself spending less time on my laptop.

Because I have a court-reporting degree, in college I practiced writing transcripts verbatim (in court reporting vernacular, it's referred to as "writing" on the stenograph), so Holli and I thought it would be a great idea to do the letters (and Dad's envelopes that were also kept) this way. It took me twice as long to proofread them as it did to type them. Why? Because my father had terrible handwriting, terrible spelling, and terrible grammar/punctuation (or lack thereof). German was his family's first language. He didn't know any English until he started school. As you read, you will find that many compound words are separated, many contractions do not have apostrophes, and punctuation is omitted many times. So every misspelling, every run-on sentence, every…oh, I could go on and on and on. It's all in there!

The letters found within these pages are worthy of your reading. Presidents Franklin D. Roosevelt and Harry Truman, the storied battle on Iwo Jima, V-J Day, the Yanks and White Sox, Pensacola's San Carlos Hotel, Gabriel Heatter, and specific movies of the day are among the many things of historical significance mentioned. Paul even talks about a parachute silk that he intends mailing to Evelyn so that she can make a garment with it. That was notable because silk was rationed at that time as no imports were coming in from Japan, and soldiers were known to send these parachute silks back to the States. You will also discover some letters from family and friends interspersed, which will help "round out" the love story of Paul and Evelyn. As a reminder, *all* of the letters and envelope information in this book have been entered *verbatim*. More than anything, these words will touch your heart with the telling of young romance and war as a backdrop. And when you get to the end, there might just be a surprise waiting…

Mother passed away in 2005, and Dad passed away in 2010. I heard my dad give his faith testimony many times about coming to Christ in a foxhole in Iwo Jima. My parents were devoted Christians, and they were committed to teaching me and my siblings about Christ. Dad and Mom were both service-oriented and mission-minded folks. Both taught Sunday School classes in our home church, and Dad served as a deacon. He was also a Gideon. He led worship services at our local waterfront mission and county jail, where I used to play piano for him as a young girl. Mom served in the Women's Auxiliary of the Gideons and also served as resident nurse on their mission trips. Once, on a church mission trip across the border in Mexico, she helped deliver a baby, and the parents named the child after her. As you can see, we have a rich legacy of faith in our family, which I value very much.

Of special note, our country has just celebrated the 75th anniversary of Japan's surrender, which officially ended World War II. I want to thank my family for encouraging me to continue this project, especially during times when it seemed overwhelming. To my husband, Terry, thank you for your unwavering faith in me. I love you with all my heart. To our daughter, Holli; son, Adam; son-in-law, Josh; daughter-in-law, Ciarra; and granddaughters Maya and Elaina… I appreciate your support more than I can express. I pray that for generations to come, this part of your family history will serve to inspire you, as well as all our extended family.

Paul James Fogel, U.S. Marines, 1943, 18 years old

The only thing we have to fear is fear itself.
                            —Franklin D. Roosevelt
            March 4, 1933, Inaugural Address

Evelyn Wells & Paul Fogel, 1943 (first began dating)

Postmarked Mar 19 1944 from Cpl Paul J. Fogel, M.B.N.A.S., Pensacola, Fla. to Miss Evelyn Wells. S.N. (Senior Nurse), Fla. State Hosp., Chattahoochee, Florida (envelope marked "free" postage; also marked "Missent to Cottondale, Fla.")

On United States Marine Corps letterhead:

Dear Evelyn:—

Stood me up again eh. Well may be I deserve it. A person can't be certain of any thing in this world. Don't take me too serious. One of these days my kidding quality, will probably get me in trouble. Untill than I guess I'll just continue. I was really disapointed when I didnt see you get off that buss. I was sort of expecting it thought. It might have been women's intuition, but it was there. Some thing just told me you wouldn't be on the buss. In one sence I didn't want you to be either. It was drizzling and trying to rain all day.

The U.S.O. had a formal evening party last night, for the second annaversity of it. All the girls had evening gowns. I stoped in for a few minutes on my way back to the base to look around. They all were looking pretty, but I think you could have shown them a few pointers if you were there.

I was at the hostipal the other night to see some girl that Mrs. Capt. Grebe knew. Her neice arived. Well it isnt exactly her neice. Its a refugee her sister took care of till she grew up. So he called me up and asked me if I would be so kind as to take her to see this friend in the hospital. Shes Finish. She still talks with a slang. I saw Nellie at the U.S.O. on the way home. She told me what she had planned for you. She made big eyes when she saw this girl. I thought she might be getting ideas. I thought it wise for this letter to arive before of hers, or you might get ideas too. And I wouldn't like that.

I got in town last night about eight oclock. I saw Miss McClain for a while. I also had some thing for you I thought you might like. I'll save it till next week though. Dont disapoint me this time. This will be all for now you'll have to spend all next week trying to translat it any way. "Be good," thats what my mother all ways says. Don't misunderstand me. I dont want to be your mother. Ha. I'll see you.

Keep Smilling
Paul

Postmarked Apr 2 1944 from Cpl. Paul J. Fogel, M.B.N.A.T.C., Pensacola, Florida to Miss. Evelyn Wells, Florida State Hospital, Chattahoochee, Florida (envelope marked "Free" postage)
On United States Marine Corps letterhead:

3-1-44

Dear Evelyn:—

I'm not threating you, but don't mention any more of those facts of yours to me. I'm not used to them and they might be taken the wrong way. I guess I'm not like other fellow. I just dont like to be talked about. I guess that could be held against me in one respect. I hope you won't though. I'm no good in letter writting. Perhaps thats my greatest fault. I just seem to cherish in "reading some one off" as we say. in the Corps.

Any thing I say is purely coincedential. or some thing.

I received your letter today. You had it come pretty fast. It was post marked the 31ˢᵗ of March, 1 P.M. And I received This morning at 10. It doesnt seem posiable, but it is.

I just came from town a few minutes ago perhaps thats why I was so angry in the beginning of this letter. I hope I'm forgiven.

O yes; before I forget to tell you. I called Nellie up last night and she says she can't plan on any week ends off in this month but the first week end in next month she might have a chance. That would be May 7ᵗʰ. I know what you are thinking now. If you want to wait that long OK. If you dont let me know and I'll come alone and perhaps Nellie and I can come In May some other time. Now I'm being selfish. I know you dont want to stay in that place all the time. Or perhaps you would like to come to Pensacola again. this month. If you want me to come I can get the 15-22-29 off If I want them. Let me know which one of the three and I'll be hoping down there. Let me know what you plan or isn't it any of my business? Ha. OK. you. can start putting off your glasses now! this is

<u>THE END</u>

<u>Keep Smilling</u>
Paul

Postmarked Apr 6 1944 from Cpl Paul J. Fogel, M.B. N.A.T.C., Pensacola, Fla. to Miss Evelyn Wells, Florida State Hospital, Chattahoochee, Florida (envelope marked "Free" postage)

On United States Marine Corps letterhead:

4-6-44

Dear Evelyn:—

    Well today I got out of bed on the right side. so don't expect me to get angry at any one. Yep it certainly is a lovely day. You ought to send me that last letter I wrote you, back to me. Id like to have it. I'd tear it up into so many peaces no one could ever put them to gether again. I can't imagine how I could ever get angry at <u>you</u> any way. It must have been your Imagination, any way I didn't mean any harm. You know what you said about people that always fight. I'm afraid I don't fight enough with you. Of course than I guess I haven't got the chance. One of these fine days I'll take the chance. **Wo. Wo.**

    Say you know that was a cute little picture you send me with the letter. Although you did take advantage of me when I said I wanted a small one of you for my wallet. Now that is to small and you know it. But I fixed you. Yep I have that portrait that you gave me to frame right here on my desk. Right were every one can see you. And don't think they don't eighter. If some boot Lt. comes up to you and asks you weather you know some Cpl in the QM. departments in the Marine Barracks. You'll know he saw you here. Every one of them seems to ask me if its my girl. Then I say, "Yep ain't she a beauty." The funny part about it is they all agree. It makes me sprout wings some times. I feel them comming out right now. Just a minute till I push them back in. OK. that did it.

Evelyn Wells, HS Senior, 1942
(Paul carried this picture overseas in his wallet;
he placed four-leaf clover sticker on it)

Say you know I think you'd make a good WAAC. If your name wouldn't be Miss Evelyn Wells. If you ever joined the WAAC's, I'd <u>Wack</u> you. If you know what I mean. You made chills run up my back just saying that. Brrr I'm cold right now. I ought to put more cloth on huh. O yes by the way if you have any more trouble you'd like to unload. Well I have sort of broad shoulders. I think I can carry them. If they're not to heavy. You know I'm not very strong. My knees are wobbling now from my own but I can always carry a few more.

I thought you had better bring ing up than to swipe things. *Tut Tut* you better lay off. I'd hate to visit you in the county jail. By the way I'm not in the brig yet. Lucky arn't I. Well If this letter cheers you up. Keep Smilling all day. If it doesn't lay on your bed and cry your eyes out. They say it helps.

THE END.

Paul

Arn't you glad I ran out of paper

Postmarked Apr 10 1944 from Cpl Paul J. Fogel, M.B. N.A.T.C., Pensacola, Florida, to Miss Evelyn Wells S.N., Florida State Hospital, Chattahoochee, Florida (envelope marked "Free" postage)
On United States Marine Corps letterhead:

4-10-44
3:00 P.M.

Dear Evelyn:—

A wee bit late, but except my [illegible] wishes for Next Easter. May they all be as happy as this one wasn't. I had a fair Easter but didn't enjoy it knowing that you were in Chattahoochee. And I know darn well that you didn't enjoy. Thats the way the world rotates I guess. I didn't care much for Pensacola either when I first came here. You begin to like the things in Pensacola and than you begin to like the city; "until the things leave Pensacola again?"

I hope you can have this weekend off. I'll get it off I know. Do your best and I'll be what can be aranged. I hope you arn't wishing for rain. If you want to call me Wednesday evening it would suit me to the tee. Or if you can't get me on Wed. try Thursday. I won't be doing anything. either nights. I usually go to the show across the street or go bolling but I won't do any thing those two nights so don't worry.

I have to move two people this afternoon. so I'm cutting this letter short. Our number on the base is 9454 on city line.

Lots of Kisses
Paul

Postmarked Apr 15 1944 from Cpl Paul J. Fogel, M.B. N.A.T.C., Pensacola, Fla. to Miss Evelyn Wells S.N., Florida State Hospital, Chattahoochee, Florida (envelope marked "Free" postage)

On U.S. Naval Air Training Center, Pensacola, Florida letterhead:

4-14-44

Dear Evelyn:—

Yes! I slept quite well "thank you" hope you did also. Its a fine thing you called me at that time, because if you had not you would have probably run into some resistance. That phone didn't have a breathing period from about four oclock in the afternoon till about ten when taps blew. It must have been like the dormitory at Pensacola Hospital. I remember; it was when you were here. I was forth in line on the waiting list to get to talk to you. That's past I hope.

I haven't seen Nell lately, but when I do I shall tell her to cast aside the social life a wee bit. to let you know more about what you would like.

hear. I just blab. It goes in one ear and out the other.

I'm pretty angry tonight the boss made me get to town at 3:15 tonight with a load of boxes. I had already secured my working detail and he comes along and pulls that stuff. I had quite some running around to do, but I did it and kept my mouth shut. They're were alot of things that were in my mind that I could have told him. O yes his wife sends her regards. The one that was in the Hospital.

I had very little to do during the day so I made my self a dager. I hope to use it someday on a on a jap gisard. Thats one part of the human body I have to look for. I'm not so familiar with. Don't ask me what school I went to. I'll tell you. I learned to spell in a country school. The teacher never could pound spelling in my head. Of course I believe you found that out already.

O yes! You probably thought you saw my age on that promotion data sheet that I let you see. That was incorrect so disregard it. I just don't want you going around believing in an age that I'm not. It probably won't be known to you for some time.

It's raining terriably out side, and I'm soaking wet from that trip I just made so I'll close now and wait for the return letter.

Keep Smilling
Paul

Postmarked Apr 18 1944 from Cpl Paul J. Fogel, M.B. N.A.T.C., Pensacola, Fla. to Miss. Evelyn Wells S.N., Florida State Hospital, Chattahoochee, Florida (envelope marked "Free" postage)

On United States Marine Corps letterhead:

2 P.M.
4-18-44

Dear Evelyn:—

Dont worry about when I'll arrive, rather worry about getting off. I'll not be suprised if the answer is "no" again. When I arive I'll call the Hospital and ask for you, and than we can arange to meat. I'd rather come and form my opinion of the place my self. Of course if you don't agree let me know and I'll set the time. I'll probably leave Friday night or Saterday morning.

O yes it wouldn't hurt my feels if you would write my mother and ask her my age. If you wish her address is Nazareth Route 1 Pennsylvania; Mrs. Leidy C.

I heard from my sister yester-day. My twin sister she tells me she can hardly talk. They still have damp weather there. And she has gone and caught a cold. They were expecting me home on Easter. I don't know why I never said any thing about it. At least some one misses me any way.

So Pitts has her self laying on her back. I think thats an ideal place for her. Give her my regards and sympathy. I know from experience what it's like. I didn't think it was too back. I was up and jiging a dance in seven days. I'll have to leave now. This is no time to write letters the boss tells me.

Keep Smilling
Paul

Postmarked Apr 24 1944 from Cpl Paul J. Fogel, US MARINE BARRACKS, NAVAL AIR TRAINING CENTER, PENSACOLA, FLORIDA to Miss Evelyn Wells, Florida State Hospital, Chatta-hoochee, Florida (envelope marked "Free" postage)
On United States Marine Corps letterhead:

4-24-44

Dear Mary (I mean Evelyn):—

O what a beautiful trip I had. It rained all the way, but the way I felt I could have been soaked to the gills and still would be happy. I hope you didn't get too wet. The first buss that passed was full but the driver said there were four following, so I waited about thirty min-utes more and had a comfortable seat all the way into Marianna. We had to wait about thirty more minutes there to get a buss into Pensacola. I had a seat all the way and made very good connections I thought.

I'm terriably sorry I didn't get to see Mr. Dean. I would have liked to see him again before I I left. He's a wonderful man in my estimation, and I'm sure you think so too. There might have been times yesterday when I wasn't quite a gen-tleman in your presence. Now is a fine time to ask forgiveness I know; but just the same. My conscounce bothers me.

I'm afraid Pitts won't have the pleasure of having sunshine on her trip either. I wish I could have aranged some how, to be along with her on the back. I arived in to base three oclock this morning and didn't get to sleep till four. And had to hit the deck at six so you can see I didn't make it by any to much time to spare. I came into the office this morning and I never saw as much work to be done. I'm just letting it pile up though. Your comming first. We have 150 cruse boxes to ship out to day. That means three trips to town in my language.

The boss is yelling at me now. He claims the trip effected me. Perhaps it has. It was well worth it. I'll see you. Keep Smilling,

Paul

Tell Slim I'll be expecting to see him in the Corp in Pensacola some day, and well go Turkey hunting together. Ha.

Postmarked Apr 28 1944 from Cpl Paul J Fogel, M.B.N.A.T.C., Pensacola, Fla. to Miss Evelyn Wells S.N., Florida State Hospital, Chattahoochee, Florida. (envelope marked "Free" postage)
On plain, lined stationery:

4-27-44
7 P.M.

Dear Evelyn:—

This letter won't be one like you are expecting. Why? I'm in the hospital and am beating my gums about it. Of all the places to be in they have to stick me here. I'm just about foaming out of the mouth. If I wasn't sick when I turned in I sure am now. I guess your wondering why Im here. Well its nothing to discus with a lady but I think you'll understand. I have a cyst at the end of my spine. Its never bothered me until Saterday morning in Chattahoochee than it began to give me a wee bit of pain; now I can't sit, sleep or eat.

If it wasn't that I was in as much pain as I was I would have left it go. They are going to operate as soon as the imflamation is out. I'm glad I had the oportunity to visit you when I did. I would have been terriably disapointed if I would have been layed up the week end you had off. If any one would have been bored I know it would have been you. I know how I would have felt if I were a beautiful girl and had some sap like myself taging about me all week end. I enjoyed the whole thing though including the strole in the hills. I don't believe you need saving. I'm fast on the way to the hot place. I'll be right in the groove for Chattahoochee after I get out of here. I don't believe I hated any place on earth as I do in here.

Please excuse the paper, spelling, writting etc. etc. Hope Pitts doesn't feel like I do. Keep Smilling

Paul

Postmarked May 2 1944 from Cpl Paul J. Fogel, M.B.N.A.T.C., Pensacola, Fla. to Miss. Evelyn Wells S.N., Florida State Hospital, Chattahoochee, Florida (envelope marked "Free" postage)
On United States Marine Corps letterhead:

5-2-44
9:30 A.M.

Dear Evelyn:—

This is the third time I've began a letter for you and I'm not going to stop till I've finished this time. If it were for any other person I would have forgotten about it. The first one was started at 6:45 AM and the second at eight.

They havent started to operate yet, and they wont for another two or three weeks. Why? They think there is still too much inflimation in it. So They are giving me a breathing spell. I'm tired of talking about my self already. And another thing, why waste your pity on me. I'm still the black sheep of the world. Thats the same wise crack I told my mother. Wow. did she blow. I didn't save the letter but I would have liked you to read it. She read me off in a big way.

Slims a good old boy. He ought to be able to take care of him self. I hope I'll get to see him again some time. Maybe he'll want some advise some day. I hope I'll be able to help him.

Today is election day. I supose I ought to go to the poles and vote for Caldwell as Mr. Sheapard recommanded. That was some family. All they seemed to care about was there son. I cant say I blame them.

Mr Dean is a fine man but you knew that already. Any thing he should say could be taken as advise from experience. He's one man I'd like to be like. He has a sense of responsibility about him. Its a good thing to model after.

I can imagine what your night duty is like. I was in the 1ˢᵗ Guard Company for sixteen months before I began driving trucks. That duty was all night duty. From mid night till six in the morning. That was quite easy compared to what you have to go though. I know.

I agree with that last statement you made about taking care of me. Some day I hope you'll have the chance(.)!!

Before you fall asleep from the monotany. I close and get started with my work again.

> Keep Smilling.
> Love and Kisses.
> Paul

Postmarked May 6 1944 from Cpl Paul J. Fogel, N.B. N.A.T.C., Pensacola, Fla. to Miss. Evelyn Wells S.N., Florida State Hospital, Chattahoochee, Floida (envelope marked "Free" postage)
On United States Marine Corps letterhead:

5-6-44
3:30 P.M.

Dear Evelyn:—

This is another one, of my off days. I must have gotten out of bed on the wrong side. This first thing they had me doing was scrubbing the "heads" for "field day." Well I didn't like the Idea so I told them so. Than they didnt like it so they told me so. So before I knew it I was being lead to see the "big boy." I had to do some fancy talking to get out of a restriction. The whole day seems to be against me. I can blame the weather because it's really beautiful out there. The suns out and every one seems to be going to the beach swimming. I feel almost tempted to go to the beach my self this after noon. Its a wee bit too late. I just came from sending a shipment off in town. We don't have very many cadets graduating any more.

Sgt. Maceluch, my boss, is having a birthday party tonight. It ought to be a pretty nice gathering. Every one is suposed to bring a partner. My partner isn't here right now. It seems she's in Chattahoochee. So I guess they won't miss me too much.

If by any chance you would like to be troubled when you have your week end. Let me know and I'll see what I can do about arrang ing to be with you.

Your room mates sure do like to get into trouble. O yes there is another thing. About Pitts. I thought she was come home to Pensacola. She seems to have gone over the hills. I can't seem to locate he or didn't she come? This will be all for to day. This last letter sure arived late. It must have been the mail service. I was beginning to walk the floor. I'll see you.

Love and Kisses.
Paul

Postmarked May 22 1944 from Cpl Paul J. Fogel, Ward G, U. S. Naval Hosp., Pensacola, Fla. to Miss. Evelyn Wells S.N., Florida State Hospital, Chattahoochee, Florida. (envelope marked "Free" postage) On United States Marine Corps letterhead:

5-22-44

Dear Evelyn:—

Was it every compulsory for you to write letters on your stomach. At this moment it is by me. I can't see where my words are going but they look pretty straight. I had the operation on Saterday. It was no picnic for me. In fact I haven't slept yet. I had seven needles thus far. They gave me a spinal injection for the operation. It was really simple. Enough griping about my self.

The ways I feel right now. If I could get a squint at you now. I'd get up and dance a jig. So its good your not around. I'd be mighty dis-apointed if you didn't come to see me. If you don't come home here soon I'll be out before you get here and thats OK by me. I don't like to be looked at in bed anyway.

This is about all for today Sis. Excuse all the mistakes. My Stomach doesn't like to be layed on so long.

Love and Kisses.
Paul

Postmarked Jun 10 1944 from Cpl Paul J. Fogel, U.S. Naval Hosp., Ward G., Pensacola, Fla. to Miss Evelyn Wells, Mary Ester, Florida (envelope marked "Free" postage)
On United States Marine Corps letterhead:

6-9-44
7 P.M.

Dear Evelyn:—

It took me six hours to get your last letter. That was pretty quick service. Wasn't it? I was glad to get it though. I was sleeping and some one put it in my hand so I woke up, with it where they had put. It sort of scared me. I don't know why.

I'm afraid they did catch up me on Tuesday. I don't mind though. I was put on a few hours extra police duty. I'd do it again though if I had the chance. This place is like Chattahoochee in lots of ways. It has me half crazy already. I was down in the Main Station today. I had to put some money in the bank. So while I was there I picked up your picture and brought it up here I where I could look at you. It wasn't any good standing in my wall locker and you wouldn't give me a smaller one.

Yesterday I moved my sack out on the porch in the ward. Its a lot cooler out here. Some times its too cool.

No I don't miss my watch. You may keep it as long as you want, and if that is forever that is OK with me too.

Tut-tut now you know you girls shouldn't down Chattahoochee the way you do. I'm sure some of the patents there like it any way.

Well this is all for now. Hope to see you soon. Let me hear from you again. Alright. now you can put your magnifining glass away. The rest I promish you will be able to read.

Love and Kisses
Paul

Postmarked Jul 25 1944 from Cpl Paul J. Fogel, M.B., NATC., Pensacola, Fla. to Miss. Evelyn Wells, 1101 E. Gadsden St., Pensacola, Florida (envelope marked "Free" postage)

On Office of the Post Quartermaster, Marine Barracks, Naval Air Station, Pensacola, Florida letterhead:

July-25-1944

Dear Evelyn:—

O you need not be suprised. I do get crazy notions once in a while. O my goodness that was an understatement wasn't it. I should have said I get them all the time.

Well how does my Chattahoochee Queen feel today. I certainly hope no one ever felt like

I did yesterday. I could have kicked my own mother. I have to be pretty hard up to do that.

That darn show I saw last night was no darn good. And I do mean no good. You know the one with all the bands in it. I had a good notion to walk out in the middle of it. I got out of there and bolled a few games untill I was soaked to the gills. Than I took a shower and hit the sack; rather bunk. Wonderful evening, well spend wasn't it. Grrr.

I bet your sister is angry at me for making all those things up to put on the report I had to fill. It was the only thing I could think of at the moment. The way I had her was she was born June 7, 1912 that would make her 33. She has brown eyes blonde hair and is 5'7". I didn't know her middle name is I said it was Wells. Let me see that was just about all I guess. O yes she's a house wife I hope. Every thing will work out OK though. This is all for now Hon.

Love and Kisses.
Paul

Postmarked Sep 5 1944 from Cpl Paul J. Fogel, M.B. N.A.T.C., Pensacola, Florida to Miss Evelyn Wells S.N., 1101 E. Gadsden St., Pensacola, Florida (envelope marked "Free U.S.M.C. postage)
On plain, lined stationery:

Sept. 5-1944

6:45 AM.

Dear Evelyn:—

Well if I can't talk to you today, I might as well write. I'm sorry now I didn't come to see you last night. I went bolling with two sore fingers and came back with the third. It seems to me when ever I go against my better judgement it turns out for the worst.

I wish you could have been with me Sunday afternoon. I had so much fun while it lasted. Of course I don't know weather you would have enjoyed being with five boys. May be you would have.

I hope you wrote my mother. I do want you to you know. I guess you think Im sort of crazy. You ought to if you don't. I do want you to get to know my mother. She's a wondeful woman. She's as wondeful as you are. They have to go plenty far to beat you.

You should be ashamed of your self. You kept me awake, half the night, last night. I just lay there thinking of what you might be doing. I can hardly believe, your going to be my wife. I can't get it though my thick skull why a lady like you, would say yes to an ignorant fellow like me. I guess you could call it nature.

Its 7:45 and the boss walked in. I guess I'd better close now. Excuse the writting please.

Lots of Love.
Paul

Postmarked Sep 14 1944 (from Mrs. Fogel, Cpl. Fogel's Mother) to Miss. Evelyn Wells S.N., 1101 E. Gadsden St., Pensacola, Florida. (with 3 cents postage stamp)

Nazareth, Pa. Route 1.
Sept. 13, 1944 9.30 p.m.

Dear Evelyn:

I hope you will not mind if I call you Evelyn, but I just feel I have met you and know you very well. Paul has send us your photo home, and we all fell in love with you. I hope it will not be to long before we have the pleasure of meeting you personally.

I know you will miss Paul when he will be transferred to Cherry Point. and I am sure he will miss you. I often wonder why he wants to be transferred, but I guess its mostly to be close to his brother. It is a wonder but he did write about the engagement. You know he tries to keep things from me. just because I am a mother, but you know I always find out one way or other. I am worried about Pauls health. I wish he would see that he is really healed up. before going in on heavy duty. Polly says to tell you she will write real soon, as just now she is kept quiet busy she leaves home 6.20 A M. and returns 6.30 P. M., then most of the time she and her fiance go out yet.

Sincerely
Mrs Fogel.

P. S. If you have spare time you may write.

Paul's Grandfather, Charles Fogel; his Aunt Maysie;
his Uncle Paul; his Father, Leidy; his Aunt Hester;
and his Grandmother, Helia Fogel; 1904

Paul and his twin sister Pauline, 1927

Paul Fogel's family, Nazareth, Pennsylvania, 1935
[from left: Meda Lilly Fogel (Paul's Mother);
Maysie Fogel Barthold (Paul's Aunt); Charles Fogel
(Paul's Grandfather); Helia Woodring Fogel (Paul's
Grandmother); Leidy Fogel (Paul's Father); Paul and his twin
sister, Pauline, are sitting in the upper right-hand corner]

Paul's family, 1941
Standing: Roy Fogel, Sheldon Fogel, June Fogel,
Charles Fogel, Francis Fogel
Sitting: Paul Fogel, Leidy Fogel (father),
Meda Fogel (mother), Polly Fogel
(Siblings, oldest to youngest: Charles, Roy,
Sheldon, Francis, June, Paul and Polly)

Postmarked Sep 25 1944 from Polly M. Fogel (Cpl. Fogel's twin sister), Nazareth, Pa, R. #1, to Miss Evelyn Wells S.N., 1101 E. Gadsden St., Pensacola Fla.

Sept 25, 1944
Nazareth, Pa
R. #1.

Dear Evelyn,

This letter was intended to arrive to you long before this, but there was always something to hinder it. Before I go to far I want to interduce myself. I am Polly Pauls twin. You proberly heard a lot about me in Pauls conversations. Paul claims we resemble each other and since we do I hope we can be very good friends.

I am very sorry I haven't written any sooner but I really didn't know a thing to write about, and the things I could write about would be very uninteresting I thought. So if you find my letter very boresome I am sorry.

Mother was very happy to receive your letter. In fact we were all thrilled when she received it. We we looking forward for it after Paul wrote to us about your engagement. I felt so glad to hear that Paul was engaged. Because I felt I did something awful when I became engaged. I felt as if I hurt him, but now every thing is alright. And we can all rejoice together.

I am working in a defence plant. and enjoy it. I am a coil finisher. that sound very important, it isn't don't let me fool you for I am one of may be fifty on the very same job. But I dare say it is an interesting job.

My hours are very long ones from seven A M to six P M. I enjoy every minute of it.

I had alway wanted to become a nurse but I guess I am not good enough for such work any way they didn't want me that is way I am in a defence plant. Nursing seems to be a very educational and interesting kind of life and I would certianly would like it. Would you tell me some things about it sometime. Paul tells me you know a lot about it.

I wish you could be here just now and enjoy with us the autum weather with us. The trees are all in full color just now and it is about time to go mutting which if you ask Paul about he would say we hated to do. It was more as a duty to us then enjoyment.

I hope we will become better acquainted through these letters. And I am looking forward to meeting you very soon. The whole family and myself are very found of you.

I will have to close and get ready to go to church. We are having a Luther League program to night and I am in the program so I may not be late.

Sincirly
Polly.

P.S. Please excuse the pencil writing for my pen is dry and am to lazy to refill at the time being.

Postmarked Oct 20 1944 from Cpl. Paul J. Fogel, 16th Repln't Draft., Infantry Training Regt., Training Command, F.M.F. Camp Lejune, North Carolina. to Miss. Evelyn Wells. S.N., 1101 E. Gadsden St., Pensacola, Florida. (envelope marked "Free/U.S.M.C.")

On Marine Barracks Camp LeJeune New River, N. C. letterhead:

10-18-1944

Dear Evelyn:—

I said I'd write when I got into Atlanta, I honestly thought so, too. I did have a lay over there for nearly four hours. I knew a fellow in Pensacola who lived there so I proceded to look up his parents. I was sucessful and also was a wee bit lost in that city. They really treated me like a king. Perhaps you know the fellow. He was the one who married a nurse in the Atlanta hospital. His name is Young. I might have mentioned him to you once or twice. Any way I got too involved in there questions and didn't get the chance to drope a card than. Here I am always making excused and all the time none of them are worth the satisfaction of knowing that I went down on my word.

I know you don't like a mushy letter so I'm going to try and elimate all the thing you don't like. I am going to say, I do miss you alot, and its just been a few days I've been from you. Just knowing that I'll not be able to see you now for quite some time is enough to make me home sick for 1101 E. Gadsden. I'm not sorry, or singing the blues because I left. I'm sort of proud of my self for haveing the nerve to leave for some thing like this. Knowing what I was getting into. They can't do any thing to me down here I'm not expecting.

I came in last night at 5:00 and was put up for the night. This morning was spend in checking in and this after noon we practiced walking down rope ladders. It wasn't to difficult.

Well I've written half the letter so now I might as well let you in on some thing. We were given the word that we are well on the way to foreign duty. Don't tell my mom because she's begged me time after time not to ask for it. I try and keep it from her as long as I can and that will be sooner than you expect. By the time you get this letter I'll probably be well on my way to the west coast. We are the next out fit to leave here and I'm expecting us to leave either the last of next week or the 1st of next. If you give me Frank's address I'll do my best to look him up. If I ever get near to him.

I just now [illegible] from the second chow I had down here. It wasn't bad. In fact it was pretty good. Perhaps its the change in food. Yesterday I hadnt eaten in one who day. You know how it is on a train don't you. I was on the blasted thing two days practically.

I'm not entirely the only one in here that is new, I noticed that they seem to come in every hour. They are in a terriable hurry to get this command completed.

This will be all for now. I'm all ways think-ing off you. Don't ever doubt that I'll be back. A man as crazy as I would have to be dead to stay alway from Pensacola after I get back. I have sort of a lengthy address. Don't let it scare you. I'll be expecting to here from.

This bunch of fellows are pretty good eggs. They believe in having fun while they can.

I haven't seen much of the base but what I did see is as pretty as Pensacola. OK now let me see you desipher this letter and answer it in a hurry. All letters will be transfered to me so I'll be waiting for one. Don't worry about me.

> All My Love
> Paul

W.F.M. [Wait For Me.]
[Paul inserted a worship bulletin dated Sunday, October 15, 1944, US Naval Air Station, Pensacola, Florida.]

Postmarked Oct 21 1944 from Cpl. Paul J. Fogel, Co "C" 16th Repln't Draft., Infantry Training Reg't, F.M.F. Camp. Lejeone, Hadnot Point., N.C., to Miss Evelyn Wells S.N., 1101 E. Gadsden, St., Pensacola, Florida (envelope marked "Free/U.S.M.C.").

On Marine Barracks Camp LeJeune New River, N. C., letterhead:

10-20-44
7:30 AM

Dear Evelyn:—

I can't write every day, but I'll do my best to write every other day. The way I hear my letter is still up in the mail box. I hope not. The mail is very slow in getting out of here. I just waiting around to fall out for some more drill. We had a terriable wind storm during the night. It would have liked to blow me out of my sack. No they didn't put me in a tent but I would have prefered it. I guess I would make for a better house wife than a husband. They have field days every time you turn around. The place looks spotless but still they find some thing wrong.

We have to be at the west coast by the 1st of Nov. so don't stop writing to me during the time I'm on the train. We were expecting to leave this week but. I'm in doubts in. If it were left to me, it would be the sooner the better. I'm getting tired of this place alread. All I have to do is step out side of the door and I'm lost. This is the largest base I've ever seen in my life. It takes up half the Atlantic sea board. Well not quite I guess. Its about 40 miles square I guess. You can't tell one building from the next. Maybe thats just my imagination. You know my imagination, you beautiful red head.

1100 AM.

Sorry honey chil. I didn't get time to finish your letter this morning. I'll finish it before chow. They had me drawing equipment and drilling my head off this morning.

There are three truck drivers with me here, in the whole barracks. We are all specialists in our own field.

A few of the boys went over the hill last night. The way I hear they are pretty tough on them if they catch up with them. They gave the last fellow the way I hear 5 years in the brig with a dishonorable discharge. That is pretty severe.

I accumilated to much cloth at Pensacola. I'm beginning to wander what I'm going to do without. Yesterday I send my green blouse home by accident. I don't hope they make me buy another. Maybe they won't miss it I know I won't. I won't want to go out on liberty any way. Its pretty easy to get in trouble here. I'll have to watch my self a little closer. I'd rather think of you

any way. It keeps me occupied. This is all for now.
O yes If My language doesn't sound right to you,
read between the lines. After I read the letter over
I realized it wasn't up to power. Yep I'm ashamed
of me, and me a Fogel too imagine that. Of couse
I can't say the Well's are much better. Ha.

You have all my Love
Paul
W.F.M.

Postmarked Oct 23 1944 from Cpl. Paul J. Fogel, Co. "C"
16th Repln't Draft., Infantry Training, Reg't, Infantry Command.,
FM.F. Camp LeJeune, Hadnot Point, N.C. to Miss. Evelyn Wells.
S.N., 1101 E. Gadsden, St., Pensacola, Fla. (envelope marked "Free/
USMC.")
On Marine Barracks Camp LeJeune New River, N. C. letterhead:

10-21-44
Noon

Dear Evelyn:—

Good morning my little woman. How are
you this cold beautiful morning. Not so hot eh,
well take off and go for a cup of Joe now. I'm
waiting to go for chow now. We'll probably have
stake. Doesn't that make your mouth water. Mine
is watering and I know we won't have it. They
drilled the devil out of me this morning and my
legs say, they know about it. Any way they are
grumbling about all the exercise they have been
getting lately. One knee told the other he refuses
to bend. So I just lay here thinking of you. Last
night I had a good notion to call you but I didn't
know wheather you had night duty or not so I

decided not too until I knew for certain I doubt weather we will leave this week end because a few of the boys got week end passes. So that means we stay here the rest of the week. Last night I went to a U.S.O show about a mile down the road and I went with two other fellows. When the show was over I turned around and lost both of them. So I had to walk home along. Rather I ran because it was pretty cool and all I had on was a shirt. When I got back they were here waiting for me. They decided it was too cold to wait for me to find them. I didn't have much chance any way. There were about a thousand fellows there. This is all for now.

With all my Love
Paul
W.F.M.

Postmarked Oct 23 1944 from Cpl. Paul J. Fogel, Co. "C" 16th Repln't Draft., Infantry Training Reg't., Infantry Training Command, F.M.F. Camp. LeJeune., Hadnot Point, N.C to Miss. Evelyn Wells S.N., 1101 E. Gadsden St., Pensacola, Fla. (envelope marked "Free/U.S.M.C.")

On Marine Barracks Camp LeJeune New River, N. C. letterhead:

10-22-44
9 A.M.

Dear Evelyn:—

Today is Sunday, no I didn't go to church. I just lay here on my sack wondering which way is the church from here. Poor excuse I know but its just one of those things. Last Sunday is one day in my life I never forget. I guess it meant more to me than it did to you. When I left you on the station plat form. I was thinking of all kinds of things to do in order to stay there with you. None of them seemed sensable, so I didn't do anything but look at you. The more I looked the more I felt like crying. I'll have to admit it was in my heart if it wasn't in my looks. I've just been thinking this bulldogs is taking a beating with all this scribbling over him.

Are you still cooking? Well you ought to be if you arn't. I can't tell about your cooking but some thing tells me a little more cooking experience wouldn't hurt you. I thought I had trouble. A fellow that bunks beside me here just handed me a telegram. It read some thing like this. "Dear Bill. Bob is sick. Not feeling well my self. Your presence at home is needed. Love"—This is the second telegram this week from her. The first one he took to the commanding officer. He can't let him go The red Cross can't do any thing so he is stuck with a sick wife and four kids. and leaving for the west coast this week. I ought to be jumping for joy Im not in that shape. This will be all for now. By the way here are some negatives I think you would apreciate more than I if I threw them a way.

By the way I send Mamie's picture home in my wooden box don't worry its locked and no one but me has the key. I think some pictures of you are in [illegible] to so I cant suprise Mamie now the way I would have liked to.

With all my Love.
Paul

Postmarked Oct 24 1944 from Cpl. Paul J. Fogel, Co. "C" 16th Replnt. Draft., Infantry Training Regt, Infantry Training Command., Camp LeJeune, FMF., Hadnot Point. N.C. to Miss. Evelyn Wells S.N, 1101 E. Gadsden St., Pensacola, Fla. (envelope marked "Free/U.S.M.C.")

On Marine Barracks Camp LeJeune New River, N. C. letterhead:

10-23-44
12 Noon

Dear Evelyn.

Well we had a pretty good chow. I was wondering weather we were going to eat this noon. We fooled around all morning till about 11.30 AM and than had to walk a mile or two to the chow hall. We were drawing equipment all morning. I'll have to get a set of dogtags again. I was foolish enough to forget and take them out of my little wooden box so it looks like every thing I need is in the boxes I send home. If I can do with out them I feel as if I did some thing worth while getting rid of some excess equipment. I'll have to find that out when the time comes. We were given a mattress and cover and half a tent, a rain coat, a helmet and belt.

They were talking about leaving some time during the night. I don't know what to believe, there are so many roomers floating around. I hope we do leave soon though. We might not even go to the west coast we might board ship here at Norfolk navy yard. No one knows for certain.

We had doenuts today and I was thinking what a difference there was between the one's your dad made and those I ate. Maybe we could use him as a baker. Yum Yum. This is all for now.

Love and Kisses
Paul

Postmarked Oct 25 1944 from Cpl. Paul J. Fogel, 16th Repln't Draft., Co. "C TC. FM.F., Camp Lejeune. N.C. to Miss Evelyn Wells. S.N., 1101 E. Gadsden, St., Pensacola, Fla. (envelope marked "Free/US.M.C.")

On Marine Barracks Camp LeJeune New River, N. C., letterhead:

10-24-1944
10 A.M.

Dear Evelyn:—

This will be the last one for quite some time so I try and make it as lengthty as possible. We pull out tomorrow and we are not to write while traveling to the next post. You under stand don't you. We were broke out of our sacks at 5:00 AM this morning not unushal, but what made me so mad was, I was cold all night and could have done with a little more sleep. We had to make a transport pack for traveling and that took my other blanket from me. We must have fallen out about fifty times this morning just for the practice. We did a wee bit of exercise and my shoulders and legs feel like they are knotted up like string. The packs weigh 50 lbs or more and they had us running with them.

Before I forget to mention it I wouldn't write any more till I give you my next address. I'll have to wait long enough for the others untill they arive here and put new address on them to be send to my next base. I do hope you are getting my letters alright. I wouldn't want you to think I was disowning you. That would be a terriable thing, wouldn't it?

Dont you forget to send me those pictures. I'm practically lost with only one picture of you to look at. I think you ought to open your heart and send me one of you alone. I don't like this one that you took some time 2 or three years ago, and thats the only one I have. I should have swiped one off of your sister before I left. All the rest of those picture I send home. After all my mom whould like to see her daughter in law too. Very thoughtful of me wasn't it. I should say so.

Tell Nellie that it wasn't my fault I didnt get to see her. I tryed to see her twice by my self, and twice you were with me. So tell her to put it down as her error.

Give my little red headed honey my regards and tell her to write also some times. Maybe you better not. I'm just mean enough to forget you. What a woman.

I'll have to go for chow now. I'll write as soon as I can.

Love and Kisses.
W.F.M.
Paul

P.S. Just got this letter from mom a few minutes ago It was addressed to Pensacola. Just got the word. We are leaving on train tomorrow morning at 7.

Love again.

[From Mrs. Fogel (Cpl. Fogel's Mother) to Cpl. Fogel; Paul inserted this with above letter.]

Nazareth. Pa. Route 1
Oct. 16. 1944
9. P.M.

Dear Paul:

Last week I missed writeing you and I am very sorry, but I am trying to make up if I can. I am still going strong, but have the blues very much. I hope you are well and happy. I know by your last letter you are in the dumps to because it looks as if you might stay here. <u>Pray</u> so you can.

Do you think you can manage to come home for the wedding I honestly hope you can. and I know Polly is just praying you could be here. I did not hear from the boys accross last week. but Charles wrote and said he was well & very busy. He also said like you the weather is very cold. I hope you lost the cold you had. I was fortunate so far I did not have a cold. Yester day I was freezing when I was picking beans for dinner from the garden. so I just picked half and was going to pick the rest today but over night the frost got them it was 20 above. Every thing is frozen so now I must clean the garden for the winter. Today we started husking corn, we have a man with a husker they husked 10 loads. It does not make a nice clean job it lets to much husk on. The potatoes are still in the ground. I hope it will not get to cold before we get them dug. Well dad came back from Chicago and is gone again to organize counties. On Sunday afternoon Charlotte & I were out hunting nuts and I was telling Charlotte I was wishing Evelyn & June were with us. We did not find many nuts as the gray squirrels carried them away. Its full of squirrels but it seems not many pheasents are around rabbits are plentiful especially <u>white</u> ones. You see Francis bought a lot of rabbits for the butcher shop then there were 10 small ones so he put them in the entry to fatten now they have young ones and running all over.

Polly is sitting on the floor polishing her shoes and Earl just came in from helping Francis unload his corn. Earl's brother Daniel came home from Australia and is home for 21 days. Bertine Keifer is in New Gueina. And Daniel Ritter is missing in action he was a Scout do you remember him? I have not heard from Norman since he left. Tomorrow nite the Mothers will have a Masquarate party. I dont know if I will go or not. as I will have little Andy. because Charlotte works in her daddies office. Remember me to Mrs. Grebe. and Evelyn. so Good nite and God bless you always

Always loving you.
Mother

P.S. Aunt Hester says I love you too

Postmarked Oct 27 1944 from Mrs. Leidy C. Fogel. (Cpl. Fogel's mother), R. #1. Nazareth. Pa. to Miss. Evelyn Wells, S.N., 1101 E. Gadsden, St., Pensacola, Florida.:

Nazareth. Pa. Route 1.
Oct. 27. 1944.

Dear Evelyn:

If you feel as blue as I do this morning I wish you could be up here with me in Penna. then we could have a good cry, because I think it would make our hearts feel just a wee bit lighter. dont you think so? I have had two letters from Paul this week and know that he feels as bad of going accross as we do of seeing him go. But I will try and take it on my chin as he wants me too. It was always his wish to go so I will just keep on praying, hopeing he will return to you and me. I really wished he could be home for Polly's wedding but you know duty comes before pleasure. It will be so hard to think when she gets married he will be on the high seas some where. Do you think you could be here? I wish you could? I wish Paul could see his brother Charles before he leaves but his letter says he may not. I wrote Charles and told him I hope he can go to see Paul. Dad is not home he will be shocked when he reads Paul's letter. Well I must get busy and set my bread and make butter as this afternoon I want to help dig potatoes, but it looks as if we will not pick potatoes as its very cold & a few snow flurries are falling. Lots of Love to you from us all.

Paul's mother.

P.S. If you find time write.

American Red Cross Canteen Service postcard postmarked Oct 30 1944 (McLean Tex.) from Cpl. Paul J. Fogel, M.B.NATC. Pensacola. Fla. to Miss. Evelyn Wells. S.N., 1101 E. Gadsden St., Pensacola, Fla. (marked "Free/U.S.M.C."):

Dear Evelyn

This is against the rules but I'll try it anyway. I'm in Ok. and just passing through a city. This train ride is drying me crazy ought to be on the west coast some time day before tomorrow. I'm feeling fine. Dirtyer than a pig. You can imagine. My regards to all I'll write as soon as I can again.

Love and Kisses
W.F.M
Paul.

Postmarked Nov 2 1944 from Cpl. Paul J. Fogel, US.M.C.R., 17th Repln't Draft. Co. D, Ranch Househouse Area, Camp Pendleton, Calif. to Miss. Evelyn Wells, S.N., 1101 E. Gadsden, St., Pensacola, Fla. (with 8 cents air mail stamp)

On Marine Barracks stationery (with Camp LeJeune New River, N. C., crossed out):

Nov 1–1944

Dear Evelyn:

Got in to Camp Pendleton, California at noon today. I wish you could have made the trip with me. It didn't rain until we arrived here, than it began to pour. It was all beautiful to me, perhaps that was because I read about most of the things I than saw. We traveled within twenty miles of the

Grand Caynon and didn't get to see it. I would like to describe all I saw but I'm afraid I can't. I'm not good at writting long letters any way. It took up to five days to get. here and I'm tired and dirty. I'm pretty well established now though.

This base here is like floating though heaven Its way up in the clouds. Our barracks is on a hill and there are mountains all around us. Some of the larger ones have there peaks, peaking out above the clouds Its the most beautiful thing you ever saw. We traveled along the ocean and the waves came in some thing like Pensacola beach. There are quite a few Mexicans around and all they seem to speak is Spanish. They are certainly a strange sight to see.

Most of the people around here make their living by orange groves. There are orange trees all over the place.

We wont be here long so don't use this address to get in touch with me. We ought to be aboard ship some time next week. I'm just hoping these letters don't get censored. I droped you a card in Ok. some place. Right after that two fellows got caught passing mail out of the window. Now they are in the brig. I guess I was lucky again. I guess you know this is the 1st of Nov. so you better send me those pictures as soon as you can. I'm home sick to see you and can't do a thing about it. Im trying to imagine the red head on my arm is you. It isn't too hard, You red head you. This will be all for now.

Love and Kisses.
Paul

Postmarked Nov 5 1944 from Cpl. Paul J. Fogel (435156), 17th Replacement—Draft, c/o Fleet Post Office, San Francisco, Cal. to Miss. Evelyn Wells. SN., 1101 E. Gadsden, St., Pensacola, Florida. (with 8 cents air mail stamp)

On Marine Barracks Camp LeJeune New River, NC, stationery:

Nov–4–1944
1300 P.M.

Dear Evelyn:—

For a minute there I didn't think we would be here over the week end. It seems to be a wee bit different now. Boys are going out on week end liberty. I'm taking the watch for a few of them. I'll be on duty probably leave Monday evening some time I'm just guessing at it but I know for certain it will be some time next week. We have stenciled all our equipment and turned all our green clothe in. Yesterday we had another physical examination. I was mighty easy. They looked for hemrodes, I my goodness what spelling, they looked at the throat and felt the heart. If I would have been any healthier, I'd be walking around on my hands. Can you imagine my mom thinks Im sick. They said some thing about talking our sea bag aboard ship. They already took our bed rolls aboard. Roomers can certainly be started in a hurry here. We were suposed to get paid the day we arrived. We still haven't seen any money. I'm not forgetting the last of this month. You didn't think I would did you. You may receive something a wee bit late but you can depend upon it. It will be what I promised you.

Oh yes. If all that junk of mine is in your way. Let me know and I'll send you the money to send it home to my place. I thought of my self I guess at the time I never though It might be in your way.

The other day I met a fellow who was like your sister. Yep. He didn't like chicken. Can you imagine that. I thought your sister was the only one in the world who didn't like chicken. We sure do meet some funny and peculiar people on the world. Where is J. C. I remember he is some where here in California but I can't seem to remember where your sister said he was located or did he pull out already? (Pardon me, slight interruption. Had to put my sea bag on the truck. You'd think an important fellow as the duty N.C.O. would have some one do those things for him, wouldn't you?). I hope I run into him and if posible pull duty near him That would be some thing worth while looking forward to, wouldn't it. Jimmy ought to be in Chicago by now eh. I hope he'll like his work when he gets to it.

Some of the boys tell me here it takes from five to six days to get a letter here I won't be here this long. That reminds me. You'll probably get a letter after this one that will have my new change of address on it. They are going to save them till we get there, but I tell you what it is before time, if this letter goes though. I can't be sure of any of this mail. Perhaps they are even keeping the rest of the letters I send you. I don't hope so.

How is Kelly and her operation? Give her my regards and tell her even a letter from her once in a while could remind me of the swell time I had knowing her. I guess I shouldn't have kidded her so much. She might concider me an evil character. Of course maybe you do too. In that case I concider my self in the dog house.

I wrote to Pauline yesterday. It was about time I guess she thought I had just about forgotten her. In her last letter at Pensacola she seemed all fussed up about the wedding. I hope she's not making a mistake. I don't think she is. I hope when your time come you won't either. I know I won't. I can feel it already. The futher from Pensacola I get the worse I feel so I wish you could have come on the trip out here. You would have enjoyed it. The Mississippi was pretty near dry and most of the other rivers were dry. No water what so ever. We passed over caynons that where hundreds of ft deep. We were only 20 miles from the Grand Canyon and didn't get the first look at it. Some places we went hundreds of miles with out seeing a house. I was only about ten miles from Brownwood Texas. That is where my brothers wife lives. I told you about her she's married to Roy the Capt. in Italy. Excuse me again. There was just an assambly. The old Lt. seemed to be pretty mad, It seemed to me like some one swiped some one elses sea bag while they were being stenciled and now if it is not placed on the porch within the next five minutes no one goes on liberty. It looks bad for every one. He hasn't got any thing to put his clothe in and the seabags are leaving for the boat in a half hour.

There are quite a few boys here from Pennsylvania. I was suprised to see as many as I did The majorities of them here in my Co. are from there. One fellow lives within seven or eight miles of my place. He's a big fellow though, goes well over six foot. Its three oclock now and they are loading the last of the sea bags on the trucks. Every body is waiting for me to check them out on libery here. The Lt. hasn't still given me permission.

Camp Pendleton too here isn't a bad place to be at, doing duty. The only trouble is if you want to go any place you walk. We are fifteen miles from the main gate and busses run every hour. Los Angeles is about 300 miles from her and most of the boys are headed in that dir-rection. A few of them are going into Mexico that is only a few miles from here. Sixty at the most. The hills are all barren, all you can see is ground. Not a tree in sight. When boys go walk-ing from hill to hill they look like ants walking around. There are quite a few airplanes flying around. Small fighter planes. Not big ones like in Pensacola.

1900 P.M.

Here it is seven O clock and Ive checked every body out on liberty. They have to be Monday morning eight o clock. What a job that was. I should have taken up booking in school my risk is so tired I can hardly write. We won't leave for two or three days so the Gunny Sgt says. They took our sea bags away I guess they expect to grow beards from now on. Well I guess I can do that too. I'm in a little office here by my self and right in the next squad room there are a few fellows who are amusing them self by playing a few string instruments. It sounds much like a cowboy band. They are really good. They have collect quite a crowd in the past few minutes There are about four and each playing something different. They are singing and having a good

time Wow, even a few Lt came up now. This letter will read funny to you I know. Its just the way
I see it though. I haven't any thing else to do so I
write the one I think will try and read my writting. I guess this letter is getting boreing any way.
I'd better sign off for tonight. Good night. Here's
hopeing you sleep good.

Love and Kisses
Paul

Postmarked Nov 8 1944 to Miss. Evelyn Wells. S.N., 1101 E.
Gadsden St., Pensacola, Florida. (with 8 cents air mail stamp)

Wedding invitation of Paul's twin sister, Pauline (the original
of this invitation was given to Pauline's daughter, Donna, and one of
her sons, Richard in March 2019, Sarasota, Florida):

Mr. and Mrs. Leidy Fogel
request the honor of your presence
at the marriage of their daughter
Pauline May
to
Earl Norman Acker
on Sunday, November nineteenth
Nineteen hundred and forty-four
at 3:30 P. M.
in the
Dryland Lutheran Church
Hecktown, Pennsylvania

Postmarked Dec 5 1944 from Cpl. Paul J. Fogel 435 156,
H&S Co. 23 Mars. 4 Div., c/o F.PO. San Francisco, Cal. to Miss
Evelyn Wells S.N, 1101 E. Gadsden St., Pensacola, Florida (stamped
"PASSED BY NAVAL CENSOR" with initials; with 6 cents air mail
stamp)

On plain, unlined stationery, written in pencil:

Nov-5-1944

Dear Evelyn:—

I'm not trying to complain, but these dehydrated spuds and eggs are making me very hungry here of late. I don't know why but I don't seem to like them and never will. O yes but the coffee they make. Yum yum. I didn't tell you before I'm becomming a coffee feine. The Marine Corps says to use every thing at your disposal. Since coffee is the only thing worth while drinking. I made a habbit of it. Arn't I bad. I'll let you punish me.

There are six men in this tent. Three are mess men and three are Q.M. men in which Im included. Slavock is one; Polish is another and me of course you know what I am, Duchy. Once in a while we like to argue and when its starts you ought to hear the results. Its one for Ripley. It sounds like a cat and dog fight. We can all speak our languages quite well and when we start it usually ends in about five minutes. By that thing everyone has called everyone else everything they knew.

I had a letter from Jake the day before yesterday he send me sixty cents worth of dimes in an envelope. He put a little note on it "Lets shoot some crap." He likes to joke quite a lot. I miss seeing that bunch of fellows. Kupsky and I were always arguing just like you and I. I'd never agree with you. He'd never agree with me.

I wrote your sister a letter last night. I tryed to make it interesting The only thing may be wrong with it is my writting which you can vow to that. Now don't you go sticking your nose in other people's mail. You like to I know.

I'm going to make out an allotment today. I've been sending my money home by money order. I've decided to do it the easy way now. I'm getting lazy. I always was you know.

I write tonight after I get finish working or playing as the case may be. So be expecting me.

Love and Kisses
Paul

Postmarked Dec 7 1944 from Cpl. Paul J. Fogel 435156, H & S Co. 23 Marines, 4 Div., c/o F.P.O. San Francisco, Cal. to Miss Evelyn Wells. S.N., 1101 E. Gadsden, St., Pensacola, Florida. (stamped "PASSED BY NAVAL CENSOR" with initials; with 6 cents air mail stamp); front of envelope imprinted with Marine logo sticker: Semper Fidelis U S Marines 4th Division, * Roi-Namur, * Saipan, * Tinian

On plain, unlined stationery, written in pencil:

Nov-6-

Dear Evelyn:—

Every one else seems to be writting so why should I be an exception Its nine PM. and I decided that rather than stand in the rain and see some corney picture I'd stay in the tent and let a drip hit me now and then. I don't believe I've ever been so homesick in the last two years as I am now. I feel like going out and run around the tents shouting "I want to go home to my mom." A lot of good that would do. Besides its raining.

I saw a few swabs today for the first time and asked them if there were any Construction Batt. on the island and they named two. Neither of them were the out fits your brother is in. I guess there position is pretty well concealed too.

I was given a rifle again. It seems just like old times again. Keeping the thing clean. Friday I think I'll be able to fire it. It will be the first time since I joined the Marine Corps. Ill have to teach you to fire one too. Remind me.

Love and Kisses
P.J. Fogel Paul

Nov–6.

Dear Evelyn,

Tut tut now. I know I didn't write last night but that was excuseable. You see we had another one of those unexpected inspections so we a had a little field. Of course you know what they are. That is the day you clean all the corners instead of only a few. Its raining pitch forks out side and the inspection isn't due till later this morning. Maybe it will drown the old Col. out. I'm hoping so. Some thing makes me dislike inspections Its slowly getting light outside.

Argueing is the only thing that seems to make me happy these days and man these fellows are hard to lose a point. They are never wrong and I'm not either so most of the time I'll give in on a draw.

I wrote mom yesterday right after I wrote you and send the majority of my pay home. I wish I could have gone deer hunting with my dad this year again. The deer wouldn't have pulled any thing on me this year.

I was just thinking if you think you have my permission to cut your hair. You have a nother guess comming. You would better let them alone. Do you understand? You ought to be able to sit on them by the time I get back. Than I help you sit on them. Any way they are the most beautiful hair I have ever seen. Well maybe not. But than of course the others I've seen, were not on your shoulders.

If you would get them I cut I'd love you just as much. One of these days one of these wise-cracks of mine will backfire wont they? I'm waiting to hear what you think of our prophile. O not very much eh. I love the one with your eyes close. I think you have a cute little grin when you laugh. You must practice keeping your eyes open when you laugh. This is enough nonsense for today. Heres some more love for you.

> Love and Kisses.
> P.J. Fogel Paul

Postmarked Nov 17 1944 from Cpl. Paul J. Fogel (435156), 17th Replacement Draft., c/o Fleet Post Office, San Francisco, Calif. to Miss Evelyn Wells, SN., 1101 E. Gadsden, St., Pensacola, Fla. (stamped "PASSED BY NAVAL CENSOR" with initials; postage marked FREE/USMC.; envelope addressed in pencil)

On plain, unlined stationery, with some content actually cut out (with scissors) of the letter:

Nov-9-1944
1200 P.M.

Dear Evelyn:—

I've done quite some traveling since you saw me last. At this moment the Marine Corps has me on a large boat. I'm not alone as you can imagine. There are plenty of other fellows with me. We are still sitting in port. (Next sentence completely cut out) Its all pretty exciting to me. Every thing works mechanical, like in a hospital. Since I know already this letter is going to censored I might as well athear to the rules and let things out that I'd like to put in. So far I don't think I've put any thing unlawful in.

I've kept my health pretty well under controle although I have had a cold and never did get rid of the one I accumelated at Pensacola. It seems to have stayed with me. We haven't cussions to sit on so sitting on iron decks all day makes your seat a wee bit sore for the first few days. We eat chow standing and its a pretty good idea. It keeps you from eating too much. The drinking water and chow is very good. We have a few inconveniences due to being crowed pretty well.

Most of the boys seem to be from Texas and Pennsylvania. Some are no good and others are as good as you can find any where. Of course thats just my opinion. It gets pretty boresome around here when all you do is sit and stand around all day wondering what will happen next. I nor any one else knows where we are headed.

Nov-10-1944 [same letter; next sentence completely cut out]

Everyone seems to be enjoying them-self by giving each other hair cuts. Some of them need it mighty bad, including me. I got my last, about a week before I left N.C. I've decided to grow banks though, by the time I see you, I ought to have pig tails down my back.

There is quite a lot of gambling going on and I've been praising my self; because I've not drawn any money for two month. When one has no money he is not tem pted to spend it so easyly. I'll have to watch my money spending any way. I'll have to save quite a bit to set up good house keeping.

Have you heard from Jimmie since he's gone. I'd apreciate his address if you received it yet. I'm sure he'd like to keep up with the Pacific or maybe he would rather forget it.

I hope you don't get all these letters the same day. I'll break some ones neck if they hold on to them till we get where we're going. Did you go home lately? I'm terrably sorry I didn't get those pictures out of that box, the ones of Mamie, I would have liked to see the expression on her face when she opened the letter with them in. It might have been a bloody battle.

This will be all for now. Give your red-headed mother my regards also Kelly and Nellie and Elizabeth. That ought to be all.

Love and Kisses.
Paul

Postmarked Nov 17 1944 from Cpl. Paul J. Fogel (435156), 17th Replacement Draft., c/o Fleet Post Office, San Francisco, Cal. to Miss. Evelyn Wells, S.N., 1101 E. Gadsden, St., Pensacola, Fla. (stamped "PASSED BY NAVAL CENSOR" with initials CEM; postage marked FREE/USMC.; in pencil)

On plain, unlined stationery, written in pencil, with date and other content actually cut out of the letter:

Dear Evelyn:—

My mother told me there would be days like this. This is the (cut out) out it isn't quite as bad as the rest. Yesterday and the day before,

I was laying around wish I could die. I got so darn sea sick. Well I guess if you've never been sea sick you wouldn't know what I'm talking about. It reminded me of the time I took you to the carnival across from the U.S.O. I got sick from the farris wheel. This had the same effect only a wee bit more so.

I'm getting used to it now and getting along much better. I'll probably get land sickness now when I get off of here. I wasn't the only one so I didn't feel alone. the whole ship, except the Capt, seemed to feel the same as I did. I was Thanking my lucky stars I didn't become a sailor.

The first day every meal I ate was in the ocean and the second day only two were in the ocean. Now it has come to the point where I keep every meal to my self. Shareing it with no one.

One fellow caught his finger in a hatch and pretty near tore it off this morning. It was a job for you had you been here.

We have Corp men aboard who go with us where ever we go. They are the same as was Jimmie. When he was with the Marines.

This is the worst ship to get lost on I ever saw in my life. Maybe my head is still rolling like the ship but every time I go for chow. I have to look around a half hour for my sack. We have very good chow. You won't mind if I get a little thiner will you? My wrist watch begins sliping back and forth on my wrist Same with your ring. I'll have to get it made smaller if I don't put, on a little meat.

Inspection in the compartment was just held. I promise it was OK but what I was comming to is that I got your first letter today it was dated the 27 of Oct. Man was I glad to get it.

Already the words look blurr from reading it so often.

We have already set our clocks back (cut out) one hour. Our first stop will be (cut out). I can tell you that I guess because this mail won't leave the ship till we get there, and you'll probably get it for a Christmas present. This will be all for Today.

Love and Kisses
Paul

Postmarked Nov (date marked out) 1944 from Cpl. Paul J. Fogel (435156), 17th Replacement Draft., c/o Fleet Post Office, San Francisco, Cal. to Miss. Evelyn Wells S.N., 1101 E. Gadsden, St., Pensacola, Fla. (stamped "PASSED BY NAVAL CENSOR" with initials COV; postage marked FREE/USMC.)

On plain, unlined stationery with some content actually cut out of the letter:

Dear Evelyn:—

A good. morning to you. And how would you be feeling this fine morning? Personally I am crowed into one uncomfortable position. The old sensor seems to be pretty tough on us, the way I hear. I can just imagine how you received those last two letters. They are even cratching the dates out now. I guess it won't make too much difference. There are more things we can't put in letters than what we can so if you find these letters a wee bit bore some you can make a few deductions. Maybe you noticed I finally found me some ink. Man was that a job.

We are still paddling around out here in the Pacific. Sort of injoying it now. I'm getting more used to it by the day. I wouldn't mind being a sailor now so much.

I just figured it out. It ought to be just about Christmas now in Pensacola so hear's wishing you a Very Marry Christmas and may I spend the next one with you.

I guess you know I don't go much for reading books. I've reformed a wee bit in that respect. I've averaged about one a day, since we left dock. Thats quite a record. The red cross has been might good to us so far. They gave us a carton of cigrettes and about 10 bars of candy a piece. I still haven't developed the habbit of smoking and never will. I must have to admit though that the first week of sitting around at Hadnot Point N.C. I was tempted to take it up. I decided I felt better if I didn't so I abandoned the idea.

Drinking hasn't apeared on the ship yet due to the sea sickness of everyone I suppose. It wouldn't supprise me if there would be an over express of it when we hit shore again. Some of the men are getting mighty thirsty. They usually do.

I'm sitting on the main deck here and facing in ward to ward the ship. I can see on the deck above me that some officers are out with their shorts on trying to get a sun tan. Can you imagine that in the (cut out). Its quite a sight.

It was raining a wee bit last night and this morning going to break fast, the rain bow was out. It was quite bright. Just now the weather reminds me of an ideal Sunday. Its getting warmer by the day. I guess that is due to us (cut out). I understand below that it will be quite warm.

I guess this will be all for now. Chow is just about to go. I seems that, that is all I live for. One chow to the other. That isn't a very nice way to put it is it.

> Love and Kisses.
> Fogel-P.J.-Cpl.
> Paul

Postmarked Nov 22 1944 from Navy Department, Headquarters U. S. Marine Corps, Washington 25, D. C., Official Business to Miss Evelyn Wells., 1101 E. Gadsden, St., Pensacola, Fla.

Postcard (pre-printed form on back with underlined information Paul filled in):

> Dear <u>Evelyn</u>

> I have been transferred overseas and have safely reached my destination.

> Please address all mail for me exactly as follows:

> (Name) <u>Cpl. Paul J. Fogel (435 156)</u>, USMC,
> (Organization) <u>17th Replacement Draft.</u>
> c/o Fleet Post Office
> San Francisco, Ca.
> ~~New York, N. Y.~~ (Cross out one)
> <u>*Cpl. Paul J. Fogel*</u> (Signature)
> (This card was prepared prior to departure, held and mailed in the United
> States upon receipt of information of writer's arrival).

Postmarked Nov 24 1944 from Cpl. Paul J. Fogel 435-156, H-S Company, 23 Marines, 4 Marine Division, c/o Fleet Post Office, San Francisco, Cal. to Miss. Evelyn Wells—SN., 1101 E. Gadsden, St., Pensacola, Fla. (stamped "PASSED BY NAVAL CENSOR" with initials; 6 cents air mail postage stamp)

On plain, unlined stationery; envelope and letter written in pencil:

Nov. 23–1944

Dear Evelyn,

Just got finished moving again. We didn't go far. Seems to me they put us up in the hills futher. It's a wee bit cooler up here but it isn't too bad. We have all the conviences of home. Beautiful tent, cold and more cold running water Can you imagine me pulling my beard off with the help of cold water. I not only can but did. We scrape the dirt off with knives than rince with cold water. Very ifficient. Try it some time.

I told you I'd send you my pen home. It dosn't look like I'll be able to now. Some how some one gave me the bum rush and swiped it or rather the other one I had so I'll have to keep it till I get another.

We have been put in some what a perniment out fit now. So this will probably be the last time I'll have to change my address.

I wrote you a letter yesterday and didn't mailed it. I read it to-day It didn't sound too hot so I tore it up.

I wrote you a letter the nineteenth and forgot to tell you to keep that Stamp it was a pecular type. It ought to be worth some money. I bought some six cent stamps just before I left about half of them stuck together. You know its been over about a month since I heard from you last. I guess I haven't stayed in one place long enough to get mail. How did you like the pictures you were to get from the San Carlos for me. Didn't eh. Its the best I could do. You have my sympathy.

I sure would like to see, the good your muscles did in getting me to pose, as you say, for that picture. I don't believe too many pictures of me is good for you.

How is Kelly and Nellie? Still kicking huh. Give them my regards

This will be all for now.

Love and Kisses
Paul

Postmarked Nov 25 1944 from Cpl. Paul J. Fogel 435156, 4 Marine Division, 23 Marines., H-S-Company., c/o F.P.O. San Francisco, Cal. to Miss. Evelyn Wells. SN., 1101 E. Gadsden, St., Pensacola, Fla. (stamped "PASSED BY NAVAL CENSOR" with initials; 6 cents air mail postage stamp; envelope addressed in pencil)

On plain, unlined stationery:

Nov. 1944–19

Dear Evelyn:—

It looks like the Marine Corps likes to do things the hard way. Yep we got payed today. Sunday a day of worship and rest, they break us out and pay us. It was a bad pay day at least it was the largest I ever received in the Marine Corps. $55; You can't consider that equal to a civilian's pay but it does make you think you're not doing some thing for nothen.

Yes, Yes Yes, I want you to save this letter. and all the rest of mine till I tell you to throw them away. I'd like to read them my self when I get back.

I'm still waiting for your letters to catch up with me. I know where they are but I can't seem to get my hands on them. You see there is a nother Fogle in the 17th Draft and while at Camp Lejeune and Camp Pendleton, they were trying to give him my letters because while I was still at Camp Lejeune I was in the 16th Draft, C-Company. Now that they put me in the 17th Draft. D-Company they still send my mail to the C company in the 17th Draft. A wee bit fouled up but if you can figure it out you'll be able to understand it. It will finally land up in my pesessions.

Goodness I had a letter from Pauline yesterday and was she burned up. She was of worried about the wedding and she seemed to be against the whole idea of a church wedding. She told me she invited you and if you showed up it would be worth every part of her troubles to organize it. I know it is as imposible as it is for me to get a six month leave.

We live in tents just now. I guess I won't be able to have my own quarters, as I did in good old Pensacola. I don't mind it too much. We are pretty crowed though. Eight to a tent. Four would be just about right in here.

I guess by the next time you hear from me it will be from some where else. We won't be staying here long any more. That remains to be seen. I haven't missed very many days have I. I'm trying hard not to. This will be all for now.

Love and Kisses.
Fogel—P.J.—Cpl. Paul

P. S. I have my Parker-51 I'm going to send you. You probably can use it. Its a little too expensive

for me to carry around. I want to get you some
thing else so I'll send it all at once.

Paul.

Postmarked Nov 27 1944 from Cpl. Paul J. Fogel 435-156, 17th
Replacement Draft., c/o Fleet Post Office., San Francisco, Calif. to
Miss Evelyn Wells S.N., 1101 E. Gadsden, St., Pensacola, Florida.
(stamped "PASSED BY NAVAL CENSOR" with initials; 6 cents air
mail postage stamp)
On plain, unlined stationery:

Nov–1944

Dear Evelyn:—

We have arrived at our first destination. I
don't believe we will stay here long though long
enough to look around I supose. I won't be able to
tell you any thing about this place except maybe
that it is plenty hot. I don't know for certain but
they way they talk they censors really murder the
contense of a letter. I guess they have to though.
We were given the rules so I'll have to abide by
them. That was certainly some boat ride. I'm even
trying to keep my self balanced on dry land. People
when they look at me walking think I'm drunk.

I just received a letter from my brother
Sheldon. I'd like you to read it. He thought I was
still in Pensacola, I've never kept anything from
you, and I don't intend to start now. I haven't
forgotten what you said in the hospital when you
had your tonsils removed. I'll never forget it in
fact. I don't know how long I'll be over here. I'll
try to do my best, not to make it longer than is
posible but in the mean time. If you do figure the

way Sheldon expresses in his letter, Please tell me about it because if you think you can turn your thoughts to some one else more than to me, there would be no point in comming back. I honestly mean what I say. By the way he would like to hear from you. He isn't kidding I no. If you find time you can get aquainted with him. also. I thought he would be comming home by this time.

I saw a pecular bird while on my way to chow. We have to walk a mile for chow so I look at the senery on my way. It looked something like a turtel dove or quail. Only it was blue instead of brown. Maybe it got in a rain storm or some thing. It looked funney to me. I'll have to go to the P.X and do my Monday washing now.

Love and Kisses.
Fogel—P.J.—Cpl. Paul

Daddy inserted this letter from his brother Sheldon, referenced above (on plain, unlined stationery):

Italy
Oct 13–44

Dear Brother

Don't you think it is about time I give you another breafing:

Mother informs me that you want to be sent on over seas duty.

I dont know how often I have told you to keep your self in the states untill they decide to shanghi you over seas.

Take it from a fellow who knows, but two or three years in some strange country is not what

I would call advanture at least when you are pay-ing with your life and health.

The thing is that I have been over here going on my 30th month and it looks like may be I will see my three years over here too.

Beleave you me when and if I get back to the good old U.S.A. they will have a hard time to sent me back over seas Again.

And by the way, I understand that you are engaged to some nice looking young red head nurse. Mother said she wrote a very lovely letter to her. How about me getting a nice long letter from a future Sister if she will be my future sister. That is a nother reason for you to remain in the states.

You see when you are away for two or three years at a stretch you loose all conections with what you might call your future prospects for a wife. I know because if I had remained in the states I would have been married, but since I am away so long, things changed that now I don't know who would have me if I wanted to get married.

You might say to me, just what is wrong with Electra, well she writes to me about once or twice a month, She use to write every week but you know, too longer Absence makes one forget.

How ever if you are still foolish enough to ask for over seas duty after this breefing all I can say you ought have your head examined.

What does your girl friend think about you going away?

Well you are your own boss I guess??

Bye now

write soon Your Brother
Sheldon

Postmarked Nov 27 1944 from Cpl Paul J. Fogel 435-156, H-S Co., 23 Mar., 4 Div., c/o F.P.O. San. Francisco, Cal. to Miss. Evelyn Wells S.N., 1101 E. Gadsden, St., Pensacola, Florida. (stamped "PASSED BY NAVAL CENSOR" with initials; 6 cents air mail postage stamp)

On plain, unlined stationery, written in pencil:

Nov-25-1944

Dear Evelyn:—

I've finally been put to working. Yep they made a mechanic out of me. Considering I haven't done such work in practically 3 years, I not doing bad. To-day they made a painter out of me, tomorrow I'll probably be driving trucks. I'm a jack of all trades. Its a wee bit hard to go from truck driving to mechanic work. Im willing to do anything to keep my mind occupied. The hardest thing so far is trying not to think of you while I should be thinking of some thing else. Thats about all I can tell you about my self.

I haven't had liberty since I left Pensacola and don't intend to get till I see the states again. It wont be a disadvantage to me. Some of the fellows say that I'm not missing any thing on this base. I would like to get some thing for a certain little woman and my mother for Christmas. I think she's going to be disapointed though. The PX's here haven't got a thing that I'd like to see you wear.

I trust by this time that picture is in the mail. I'm going to keep mentioning it untill I get it. I miss seeing you so darn much I didn't think it could be posible. I can't have every thing

I want. But if I could it would be you, the first on the list, the way I left you.

How is Elizabeth? I hope she is in better health than I. I caught a cold the first night here and forgot to loose it. That was my fault. I'll have to write her some time. Do you think she would bother reading my writting?

How did your cooking lessons turn out? By this time you ought to be telling the Sisters how to prepare diets. I wouldn't try it, they might fire you.

I guess Kelly is back on duty now. Going as strong as ever, eh? She's a wonderful woman! She has all my best wishes.

Havent had a letter from you yet. Supose they got lost? Could be. Here's hoping I hear from you soon. I'll have to seign off for today.

Love and Kisses.
Paul

Postmarked Nov 29 1944 from Cpl. Paul J. Fogel 435 156, H-S Co. 23 Mars. 4 Div., c/o F.P.O., San Francisco, Cal. to Miss. Evelyn Wells S.N., 1101 E. Gadsden, St., Pensacola, Florida. (stamped "PASSED BY NAVAL CENSOR" with initials; 6 cents air mail postage stamp)

On plain, unlined stationery, envelope and letter written in pencil:

Nov-26-1944

Dear Evelyn:—

To-day is Sunday. I got out of bed this morning with every intention of going to church. So I did but it seemed to me I was the only one with that intention. Church services were to begin at nine and I arrived a wee bit last to find no one was around, not even the minister. I went back to the tent not wanting to sleep, cleaned my sea bag out. Right now, I'm in the midst of clothing on either side of me and was about to put them back in when I spied a groupe of letters tied up in the pail on the bottom of my sea bag. Nope you guessed wrong. They were the letters you wrote while at Chattahoochee, Fla. There were twenty three and I read every one including the one or two you wrote at Mary Esther.

They were cute. Some times you were scolding me and other times you were advising me. What a woman I caught for my self. They can't come any better. I never forget the times went spend Especially the Chattahoochee trip I made, and Naval Hospital when you and your sister walked in on me in pajamas. Then to top it off when you and I were at Elizabeth's place and up walk your folks and I looked as if I had come off the truck for the day. I can imagine I turned as red as I have ever been.

Don't forget to mention your brother's address, the one thats across sea. He may well be on this island. I hope I may get the chance to meet him. In a few weeks my letters wont be comming so regular but you keep writting anyway. I'll get them and be the happiest man in the Pacific.

I just came from chow. It wasn't to bad. We had all the rice we wanted to eat.

Yesterday one of my teeth chiped off. I went to get it fixed and the dentist said that a decay had started underneath an old filling. He just about ground the tooth apart. in fact there isn't much of it left, but he put in a temperary filling and told me to be back tomorrow.

Love and Kisses
P.J. Fogel—Cpl. Paul

Nov-27-1944

Dear Evelyn:—

That ring of yours darn near took my finger along yesterday. Some how it hooked in one of the trucks and didn't have sense enough to stop, so it took the bark off.

They are giving us shots again. It seems to be a regular rutine. I don't mind those as much as having that tooth filled yesterday. I told you about it cracking off. He just about ground the thing out. He might as well have pulled it. Any way he filled it again and he claims its as good as new.

It looks like rain again today. We were all wet yesterday and the day before. This is certainly a wet country for being so high up on a mountain. The clouds hang right into them. The rainbow stays out all day rain or shine.

We have the chance to see a show every night and I usually take advantage of it. Last night we were sitting in the rain and injoyed the picture just as much. Some nights we work till ten o clock or later other times we secure at 4 o clock.

My buddy and my self seem to be the only unexperienced men who have never seen action. It might be be a little hard to keep up with the rest. I think we can keep up with the best of them though.

Yesterday one of the cooks that sleep in the same tent as I, brought some ice cream in and layed it over my chest. I was sleeping and it began to melt and driped down though the box. I didn't tast any for so long I didn't care how I received it. It was very good only it didn't tast like the kind

Wagg's has. I'll have to be going to work now. I write again tomorrow morning.

Love and Kisses
Paul
P.J. Fogel—Cpl

Nov-28-1944

Dear Evelyn:—

If you were here now you would agree that a day like this is only weather for the ducks or some such weather that we should find in Chattahoochee. Remember that night we took a walk to the beach and you found you had the wrong dress on for the weather. Thats what I'm thinking of right now. Most of the boys are out getting soaked looking at the show. I don't think its worth getting wet for though. I got soaked once already today. Thats plenty for me.

I dont know where I'll be on Christmas but my thoughts will be with you. That letter I received from you two weeks ago was the first and the last. I'll really be happy when the rest of them catch up with me. I can imagine how Jimmy and the rest of your brothers felt now also my brothers. I hope that war will be over in Germany soon. I'm sure my Mom would like to see both my brothers safe in the states again. I'd feel better to if I knew I was the only one in the family sticking my neck out. This is all for now.

P.J. Fogel—Cpl. Love and Kisses, Paul

Postmarked Dec 1 1944 from Cpl. Paul J. Fogel 435 156, H-S Co. 23 Mars, 4 Div., c/o F.P.O. San Francisco, Cal. to Miss Evelyn Wells S.N., 1101 E. Gadsden, St., Pensacola, Florida. (stamped "PASSED BY NAVAL CENSOR" with initials; 6 cents air mail postage stamp)

On plain, unlined stationery, written in pencil:

Nov-29-1944

Dear Evelyn:—

I just came from a show I saw while I was still in Pensacola. I can't remember the name of it. It wasn't bad. Reminds me of every time I took you to a show. Either I had seen it in the station before I came to town or some thing else had come up. You never enjoyed a picture because you knew I had seen it already.

I received your letter that you mailed on Oct. 23.—Five weeks is a long time to wait for a letter. I was beginning to get impatient. I could work all nigh now though and would mind one bit. You wrote exactly what I want to hear and I feel much better. I don't want you to act like an old maid like you put it. I want you to go out and have a good time while Im not around. I know how I feel siting around here not being able to get out and associate with people. You have the oportunity so take it, only let the male wolves bark at them self.

I wrote to Kupsky day before yesterday. I hope he answeres as soon as posible. I'd like to know what are happening to the fellows at the barracks. I miss the whole groupe especialy him. He's a good man. Most of his buddies are gone now. He is just about the only one left that came down with me.

The boys in this tent are cooks and we were mixed with them so tonight they are have a small party. Quite a lot of drinking, and eating. They brought quite a lot of shmall things down from the mess hall.

I noticed you had nine cents on that letter that took five weeks to get here. You can send air mail letters for six cents not eight. Maybe you knew that but I thought I'd tell you. You need not answer all my letters. I just injoy writting you. I know you will read my letters. This will be all for now.

Love and Kisses.
P.J. Fogel—Cpl. Paul

Postmarked Dec 21 1944 from Cpl. Paul J. Fogel 435 156, H-S Co. 23 Mars. 4 Division, c/o F.P.O. San Francisco, Cal. to Miss. Evelyn Wells S.N., 1101 E. Gadsden, St., Pensacola, Florida. U.S.A. (stamped "PASSED BY NAVAL CENSOR" with initials; postage marked "Free/USMC.")

Christmas card imprinted with "Season's Greetings" on front, and imprinted inside with:

Semper Fidelis
From his post on the battleline,
In places far away—
A Marine kneels beneath the sign,
That lights the World on Christmas Day.

MARINE 4 DIVISION
[signed] *Cpl Paul J. Fogel*

Postmarked Dec 4 1944 from Mrs Earl N. Acker, Nazareth, Pa, R.P.D #1. (Paul Fogel's twin sister, Pauline) to Miss Evelyn Wells, 1101 E. Gadsden St., Pensacola, Florida (3 cents postage stamp)

On plain, unlined stationery; the original of this letter was given to Pauline's daughter, Donna, and one of her sons, Richard in March 2019, Sarasota, Florida:

Dec 1, 1944
2:45 PM.

Dear Evelyn,

Was so glad to receive your wonderful letter and also that beautiful gift you send. Thanks a million. Both Earl and I were quit thrilled to receive a gift from Fla. It is quit odd which sets of the beauty to every one who saw it so far. You see we received so many gifts that people from other towns come in to see them. It reminds me of open house at high school. I was soary that you couldn't come I was planning on having you. In fact all of us were. Do come when you have leave we will always be glad to have you.

I hope you understood why I couldn't write for such a long time. The wedding took up all of my time.

We had a beautiful day for our wedding and I was quit happy. In fact every one remarked that both Earl and I were so interested in one another that we simply ignored them for a while.

I missed my brothers terribly though and thought of them all as I was entering the alter. I almost had to cry but when I looked at Earl he gave me a beautiful smile which made very thing alright. He always does that to me when he see somethings is bothering me.

I hope when you and my brother get married you will be as happy as I am. I don't want to bradge but Paul is a wonderful person and I am sure he will make a good husband.

To day mother took a little vacation from the farm I am glad, it was beginning to annoy her. She left this morning with my brother Fran to go to the mountians for deer hunting. We have friends up in Strougsburg were she stays while the men hunt. I do hope they get a deer.

This morning we had our first letter from Paul I was so glad to hear from him. He says he is well and says he can't tell us where he is, but if we ask you you would tell us because your guess was correct. Please do tell us if you will. It will do mother an awful lot of good to know. She to will proberly want to know and ask you. Please don't think we want to [illegible] in you letters from Paul because we don't. We both do a lot of worrying of him and it would put our minds at ease if we knew where he was.

Well I will have to close and get my cleaning out of the way. Write soon.

Love
Polly.
(Address now)
Mrs. Earl N. Acker
Nazareth, Pa
R #1.

Postmarked Dec 4 1944 from Cpl. Paul J. Fogel 435 156, H-S Co. 23 Mars. 4 Div., c/o F.P.O. San Francisco, Cal. to Miss Evelyn

Wells S.N., 1101 E. Gadsden, St., Pensacola, Florida. (stamped "PASSED BY NAVAL CENSOR" with initials; 6 cents air mail postage stamp)

On plain, unlined stationery, written in pencil:

Dec. 1-1944

Dear Evelyn,

Time is sure passing fast. This morning I went to work at 7 instead of eight. It was worth while though. We took a little truck ride. It was just time for children to start to go to school. They were on either side of the road and none had dark collors on them. They were dressed as brightly as you would expect to see in a circus. It was really beautiful. Most of the people here are Japanese as on practically any other island. They are the most peculiar people you ever saw. I have to say one thing for them. They are more cleanly than the rest of the native population. Seem's to me every one good barefooted.

That letter yesterday sure came in at a good time. I was wondering if you had forgotten me, but I find you do think of me once in a while, you wonderful woman you.

Man O man was I tire this morning I was laying there thinking of the time when you wouldn't let me sleep. They wouldn't let me sleep this morning either. I never forget that. You know thats the way I like to remember you. You were pure white and you had a silly little grin on your face and were just poking fun at me. I pretended I didn't like it but if you had done any thing else I wouldn't have as much fun. Then I used to comb your hair out and what a job that was. I'd do it the rest of my life though just to be with you. A fellow with as many brains as I, you would expect him to do some foolish thing as I did.

I have a buddy that also comes from Pa. He's been with me ever since they made a mechanic of of me. He's sort of crazy, just as I am. We like to make fun at each other and he likes to tell me all of his trouble. It seems to me I'm a very good chaplin and adviser. He's a wee bit wealthy and likes to throw money around more than I. I convinced him to save a wee bit.

I wonder if I told you that it rains every day here and that the only time you can't see a rain bow is at night. Thats a fact and not a fable. This is all for now.

Love and Kisses
P.J. Fogel Cpl. Paul

Dec. 3-1944

Dear Evelyn:—

Was suposed to yesterday off. What a day it was to spend in a tent. It was raining and blowing practically all morning. I bought a few Christmas cards and mailed them out. I never knew I had so many relatives. After all morning of doing nothing I decided I'd work in the afternoon, and so I did. Most of the boys had off to go to football games etc so I think I was quite welcome in helping out.

I went to a show last night in the rain. You can imagine I'm cracking up when I do that. But I wasn't the only one crazy. There were at least a few hundred of us. "Thats my baby", was playing and I had already seen it. The majority of the pictures are old ones, but I seem to injoy them just the same. As soon as it started raining I dove under a wash table and watched it from there while every one else was soaked I was fairly dry. All but my seat.

You send that last letter airmail and it took five weeks to arrive it must have made a few. trips around around the world, before I sat down long enough to catch it. I did and was certainly glad to get it or else it might still be flying. Some boys say they received letters from the east coast in five days. Most have made good connections eh.

You ought to start to go for board exams soon. You would better pass them all. I'd hate to see you take a few exams over. Ah but I know you won't. You always were a clever woman.

My mom wrote and told me you couldn't make Paulines wedding. My, my. I wonder why. Ha. You'll make mine though, and you won't have any thing to say but "yes." O yes where would you like to get married Pensacola or Pennsylvania? You decide that and I make in my bussiness to be there as soon as possible. This is all for now.

Love and Kisses
Paul
P J. Fogel

Postmarked Dec 4 1944 from Cpl. Paul J. Fogel 435 156, H-S Co. 23 Mars—4 Div., c/o San Francisco, Cal. to Miss Evelyn Wells— SN., 1101 E. Gadsden St., Pensacola, Florida. (stamped "PASSED BY NAVAL CENSOR" with initials; 6 cents air mail postage stamp); front of envelope has sticker imprinted with Marine logo: Semper Fidelis U S Marines 4th Division * Roi-Namur * Saipan * Tinian.

On unlined stationery with same Marine logo as above, written in pencil:

Dec. 3-1944

Dear Evelyn:—

I received the letter you wrote on Oct 24. I was a wee bit late, but that didn't make any difference to me. O yes, that speech you gave me. You ought to do it more often. I'm serious. It makes me feel good to go told off once in a while. I need it. I'm not perfect. Far from it. Every once in a while my mother gets in an angry mood, and then you should see the sparks fly. You ought to do the same. I'd feel right at home then. I don't want you to agree with everything I say or suggest. I'm wrong most of the time and want to be corrected. So if I say any thing in these letters you don't aprove off, don't think I'll get mad or angry, because I understand and do my best to correct them.

You should have read the letter your sister wrote, or perhaps you did already". It was a honey. Her letter way "newsy" alright and I was sure glad to hear from her. You don't have to tell me about her. I found out by my self. J. C. made a good decision. I am a fair judge of charter. I bet she makes a good chicken dinner dispite her dislike for them. We'll have to impose on her for one when I get back. I won't know how chicken tastes when I get back, so it will taste just as good raw or other wise. I can't say that I've eaten any kind of bird in two month. Pretty long eh.

I'm slowly losing faith in these "red heads" I thought that had more spirit than most girls but I'm afraid I've changed my mind. You would better not think of quiting or I'm liable to come back and whale the tar out of you. Yes now tell me I can't do it. I did it before. I can do it again. Well I'd make a good try at it any way.

About my mother I told her when I left North Carolina that I was heading oversea's. I couldn't keep if from her if I wanted to. She knows me like a book, and she really took wonderful. Her letters sound so cheer ful but I know she crys quite alot. Even when I was home she would sit and think about Sheldon and Roy and you could see the tears come. Once in a while I get a letter from Pauline reminding me to write more often, that she worries about me too much. I guess being the youngest in the family has some thing to do with that. She can depend upon one or two a week and sometimes more. Paulines tells me all about mom and mom then turns around and tells me all about dad and Pauline. You see none can keep any secrets from me. You either, Elizabeth will tell me yours. Ha.

I wish I would have received your letters earlier and could have seen J.C. and Jimmy at Deigo. I would have injoyed seeing them. I left the port of San Deigo. I'll have to write them both.

This is all for now.

Love and Kisses
P.J. Fogel Paul

Postmarked Dec 9 1944 from Cpl. Paul J. Fogel 435156, H&S Co. 23 Mars. 4 Division, c/o F.P.O. San Francisco, Cal. to Miss. Evelyn Wells. S.N., 1101 E. Gadsden, St., Pensacola, Florida. (stamped "PASSED BY NAVAL CENSOR" with initials; with 6 cents air mail stamp); front of envelope imprinted with Marine logo sticker: Semper Fidelis U S Marines 4th Division, * Roi-Namur * Saipan * Tinian

On plain, unlined stationery, written in pencil:

Dec. 7-1944

Dear Evelyn:—

Pearl Harbor day and no excitement. I went
for a wee bit of a ride this afternoon and passed
through a few towns. None of them are very
large. They reminded me of a small place like
Warrington. You can imagine how it looks with
the whole 4 Division walking around in them.

Having no wife and no laundry makes it
very difficult for me to keep up with my Monday
washing. I just finished it a few minutes ago and
I can't imagine why a woman is always calling it
work. All you do is rub your fingers to the bone.
Small matter. Isn't it.

Its still raining and I'm beginning to wonder if I can dry it any time. I just saw the most
beautiful rainbow I have ever seen in my life up
to this date. You still haven't send any letters that
I received from Camp Pendleton.

[Written in pen.]
Dec. 8-1944

Dear Evelyn:—

Just came in off liberty for the first time. It
wasn't any too good. Had off from the morning
till 6 in the afternoon. I came in early because I
had some more washing to do and also because
I bought every thing I wanted to. O yes, how do
you like the pen. I paid every bit of $1.25 for
it. Not a bad buy. Of course I had to adjust it

a wee bit. I bought a few other things for you. The most important I'm going to send as soon as possible. That will probably be tomorrow if I can get them cencored by that time. The others if I would send now would pretain to this place so I wouldn't be able to send those.

The thing that intrested me most was the way every man had his shirt tail hanging out. You sould have seen it, all dressed up ready to go to church and than show up with out shoes and there shirt tails hanging out.

O yes I had a snapshot taken of me. Its a honey so don't make fun of it. I just had it taken because I remembered that you were complaining in one of your letters about only having one. I only have one too so I expect you to follow suit.

There is only little object I want you to hang on too as tightly as posible so when I get back I won't have to run around and waste time on things of that nature.

I just now received that letter you wrote on the 25 of Nov. A wonderful letter if I should say so my self. My mom is a wee bit hard to understand now and than. I'm ashamed to say so but that was one factor that helped me come in the Corps. She's still the best mother a fellow ever had and I can apreciate it now more than ever. Pauline also wrote and told me every thing about the wedding. It must have been some affair. She seems to be very pleased with her decision. So am I.

This is all for now so Ill go for chow now and hope you are not eating what I have too. I'll always love you.

Love and Kisses.
Paul

Dec. 9-1944

Dear Evelyn:—

I just came from the best chow I have eaten here yet. Beef stake, what do you think of that. I'm just wondering what I'll have for Christmas. I think you'll have to send me a chicken leg. Don't think much of that idea eh. I don't blame you.

I just finished a letter to J.C. and I intend to start the next one to Frank. I'd like to find out about where he is located. I know about where I am heading from here and I can tell him than wheather I'll get to see him or not. I don't believe it will be worth while though. I going to try though.

I still couldn't get those few things censored yet so hang on your hat. I'll try again tonight. I'll see if I can get them out tomorrow.

Your sister Elizabeth claims you need a spanking. I agree to the full extend, just on general principal. She says you should not have given me her picture. I fooled her though. I'll have two of her if she sends me that one of her she promished. I'm still anxiously waiting for yours so don't disapoint me. This is all for now.

Postmarked Dec 11 1944 from Cpl. Paul J. Fogel 435156, H & S. Co. 23 Mars. 4 Division., c/o F.P.O. San. Francisco, Cal. to Miss Evelyn Wells SN., 1101 E. Gadsden, St., Pensacola, Florida. (stamped "PASSED BY NAVAL CENSOR" with initials; with 6 cents air mail stamp); front of envelope imprinted with Marine logo sticker: Semper Fidelis U S Marines 4th Division, * Roi-Namur, * Saipan, * Tinian.

On plain, unlined stationery, written in pen (all letters following written in pen unless noted otherwise):

Dec. 10-1944

Dear Evelyn.

I sure received that last letter of yours mighty fast. One week exactly. You won't have to worry about changing my address again. I think this will be perminent for a while at least.

You need not criticize your self any more because I'll just skip those lines and go on to the next. Your the most perfect women I have met and your going to stay that way, no matter what you or any one else thinks. I'm sure my mother will love you as much as I do, if any one could, when she meets you. Don't worry about your so called faults. I haven't noticed any yet and when I do. You shall hear about them.

I had a letter from Mamie Lou about a day ago. She talked about every thing in general, and after she finished the letter, I sat down and apolized to her for going to try to pull that trick on her. She would have really been imbarrassed and I didn't want that to happen. I told her if was all my fault I had the negs. It was too, and I realize now. I should not have taken them from you, I am forgiven I hope.

She also send me the most beautiful picture of you. You always do take beautiful pictures. I'd much rather hold you in my arms than look at you in a picture. Since I cant, I just dream about you.

I know how you are going to miss Elizabeth and I can't blame you. She's a wonderful person.

You can't help but like her. It must run in the Wells family.

That letter you wrote on the 4 Dec was what I was waiting for you to say all my time knowing you. I'm in a much better state of mind now, and if and when I hit a little action, I'll be right in the front punching, without a fear in the world.

I wasn't expecting any thing for Christmas from you and if you had forgotten me. It would not have made any difference. I'm happy as I am knowing what I know is from the heart and not from the lips. An old doctor, while I was going to a Boys camp in N. Y. once autographed my book in that manner and I never for got it. He told me to leave the book with him and told me since I was young and had my life time before me he wanted to think of some thing real good to remember him by. He used broken language to talk to me and I'll never forget I asked him at the time what caused pimples, and he told me I got to know him farely well by the time the week was up. Any way his theme went some thing like this. "Look at the heart and not at the lips" He than told me to think. I never saw him again, but will aways remember him. He's probably dead by now. He's was about 70 then.

There is a buddy of mine, a polock. He has all kinds of trouble. Hes twenty one, old enough to know his mind any way. He's been asking me advise. It so happens he is ingaged to three girls at the same time. He's a handsome fellow and these girls are crazy over him. He reads his letters to me and askes my advise. Hes so involved now that one of the girls are going to announce the ingage-ment of her to him in some big paper and he's scared to death about. I can't say I blame him. I told him to explain it to the rest of them, but he hasn't figured a way out yet. He's still scratching his head. I find it enough to think of one little blonde but he has to think of three. He should be shot be pulling some thing like that on either one of them. Every thing he gets he deserves. They have a good suit of preacher promish on him.

I wrote to Frank and Mamie Lou yesterday and also J.C. Tomorrow I'll probably write to Jimmy.

Here is that picture I promised you. Tare it up if you want but dont go letting it lay around where all can see it! They would be ashamed of you have some thing like me. Signing off wish all my love.

Paul.
Cpl. P. J. Fogel.

Postmarked Dec 13 1944 from Cpl. Paul J. Fogel 435 156, H & S. Co. 23. Mars. 4 Div., c/o F.P.O. San Francisco, Cal. to Miss. Evelyn Wells. S.N., 1101 E. Gadsden, St., Pensacola, Florida. (stamped "PASSED BY NAVAL CENSOR" with initials; with 6 cents air mail stamp); front of envelope imprinted with Marine logo sticker: Semper Fidelis U S Marines 4th Division, * Roi-Namur, * Saipan, * Tinian.

On Marine stationery with same logo as above:

[No date]

Dear Evelyn:—

I just came from taking one of those tropical baths. The water couldn't have been colder, if it had contained ice. That's my version of it at least. It can't be far from wrong. It does make you feel better though. I still have that blasted cold and my head feels as if it contained lead instead of saw dust.

I'm the first one up in the morning. I ought to be the buglar. From about four oclock on I seem to lay waiting for him to blow his brains out. He usually does.

These past few nights seem to have me here on my sack writting to you rather than seeing that show a few feet away. I can hear them shouting there heads off out side there must be some thing good on the screen tonight. I think I'll go see the last part of it later on.

It gets pretty cool during the night. I've had to use a few blankets the past few nights. I can imagine Pensacola is getting chilly too. It usually does in Dec. I'm sure glad I'm not pulling guard duty down on the beach, there.

This water around here makes you loose hair. I've noticed it a few times. In fact every time I take a shower and wait till my hair dry. They seem to fall out. Don't be suprised if I become bald headed. That would be a joke. Wouldn't it?

We have a few cooks in our tent here. Its in favor of us because once in a while they come in quite late and bring was some cakes or cookies or some thing on that order. We make quick work of them. Some time the chow we get, well it isn't exactly what I'd judge a club stake. So we are thankful for little odds and ends in that manner. We hardly eat candy because we can get practically all we want. When we want it we get a supply to last a month and then eat it in one day. Aboard ship we could get candy for $.80 a carton. Everyone had plenty. I got sick of the sight of it personally.

I've received the address of all your brothers and wrote to Jimmy this morning. I thought he was heading for Chicago but, I guess the Navy changed its mind.

Listen. If you cant read this writting, which I cant blame you for. Tell me and may be I can take a little more time in writting the next letters. This will be all for now.

Lots of Love
Paul
Cpl. Paul J. Fogel

Postmarked Dec 13 1944 from Cpl. Paul J. Fogel 435156, H & S Co. 23. Mars. 4 Div., c/o F.P.O. San Francisco, Cal to Miss. Evelyn Wells S.N., 1101 E. Gadsden, St., Pensacola, Florida. (stamped "PASSED BY NAVAL CENSOR" with initials; with 6 cents air mail stamp)

On stationery imprinted with Marine logo: Semper Fidelis U S Marines 4th Division, * Roi-Namur, * Saipan, *Tinian

Dec. 12. 1944.

Dear Evelyn:—

My head is just about breaking in half tonight. I wondering what you would prescribe for it if you were here. Symptoms are mainly a head cold. It would probably say in some book "Go see your physician." Not me though. I love to sit here in agony. It makes me feel smarter than the next man. Isn't that just like me. I knew you would agree to that.

There are times in the future when my letters won't be comeing in as frequent as they do now. We aren't as busy as we could be these days and I have quite a bit of time too write. Once in a while we work at night. Keep writting just the same and I may be able to explain every thing when I get back. We aren't in any danger here as yet as yet. Don't worry about me. I have shoulders large enough to carry both our troubles, so if you have any. Get busy and start unloading.

I met a few boys from Pensacola that were transferred over sea's a bout a year ago. I didn't [scratch outs, and then] recognize them at first. What a word that was; but they did me and was happy to see me. All of them saw action already and most of the ones that came with them are either shot. or injured, they tell me. I guess by now you think this letter is in code. I asure you its not. I'll finish it in the morning I may feel a wee bit better. Good night.

Good morning:—I feel as though I can stager through this day again. I never had such a variety of jobs to be done, as I did yesterday. It even amazed me. I was putting a battery in a battery box and just about took two fingers off. If I would have done it my self I would not have taken the bark off of me. Some other fellow had to be there pushing around. I learn to take care of my fingers. I was in bed mighty early last night. I think it was seven thirty when I stop writting you. I didn't wake all night, till this morning around five. One of these gooffy pals of mine just told us what he dreamed. You should have heard him. It was the longest dream I ever heard of. He even remembered things shaking. Remarkable, ay what.

Ive got a lot of work to do to day so I might as well end this terriable letter. I will have to wash day again. Then I'll have to stencil some cloth, clean my sea bag and a few other odds and ends.

I certainly hope Elizabeth will arrive in California safely. I envy her, I wish I had the chance to do what she is doing. I miss you alot. I'll write you tomorrow.

Ending With all my love
Paul
Cpl Paul J. Fogel

Postmarked Dec 15 1944 from Cpl. Paul J. Fogel 435 156, H & S. Co. 23 Mars. 4 Div., c/o F.P.O. San Francisco, Cal to Miss. Evelyn Wells S.N., 1101 E. Gadsden, St., Pensacola. Florida. (stamped "PASSED BY NAVAL CENSOR" with initials; with 6 cents air mail stamp); front of envelope imprinted with Marine logo sticker: Semper Fidelis U S Marines 4th Division, * Roi-Namur, * Saipan, * Tinian.

On Marine stationery with same logo as above.

[No date]

Dear Evelyn:—

This is the first experience I've had writting by candle light. I guess I'll be in [illegible] by the time I hit the states. I'll be able to write blind folded. I received your last letter you wrote on the 7th. Six day service isn't bad to be comming way out hear. It isn't like rail way.

So some one swiped your letter huh. You ought to look into that. Its a courtmarshal offence, you know. Thats right you nurses don't get courtmarshaled. Thats the Marine Corps blood in me. They are always threating some one around here with that story. The truth to it is, they could do it.

We live out of our sea bags and the only thing that makes me angry is, every day there seems to be some thing I want at the bottom of it. I have it so neatly packed now and tomorrow if I have to un pack it. Some boys around here are going to hear some fancy languages. Naughty me.

Its drizzeling outside again. I can't remember a single day we didn't have rain sometime or other, during it. We are just about sitting on the top of a mountain and we get more rain than the people down along the seashore. I can't understand it but I guess the Lord knows how to regulate this wheather.

You mentioned you hadn't heard from Kelly yet. I didn't even know she had gone. You'll hear from her don't give up hope. She's not that kind as to let a friend down.

I saw an old cow boy picture the other night and enjoyed it more than one of the new pictures the roll out. I guess everyone else though as I did because they felt like yelling too.

I was sort of disapointed with the breakfast this morning. We had sunny side up eggs and they were fried to a crisp. Then the only gave me one. It wouldn't have filled my mouth up with one gulp. The coffee was pretty good though.

Don't you just like to hear me complain about something? I enjoy it. I can't complain with any one around here but these two polish eggs and they always agree with me.

I'd like to know what kind of work Iris is going to do. The Marine Corps too was tough for the first couple weeks but I could it quite. That makes a difference I suspect. I would have tried to talk her back into it if I were you. You were right though. A person cant make a success out of some thing they don't injoy doing.

I'll have to go to work now. I'll write tomorrow again. I just came back from chow. Not bad either. I'll close now and mail this letter. I forgot to this morning.

Loving you always
Paul
Cpl Paul J. Fogel

Postmarked Dec 16 1944 from Cpl. Paul J. Fogel 435156, H & S. Co. 23 Mars. 4 Div., c/o F.P.O. San Francisco, Cal. to Miss Evelyn Wells. S.N., 1101 E. Gadsden, St., Pensacola, Florida. (stamped "PASSED BY NAVAL CENSOR" with initials; with 6 cents air mail stamp); front of envelope imprinted with Marine logo sticker: Semper Fidelis U S Marines 4th Division, * Roi-Namur, * Saipan, * Tinian.

On Marine stationery with same logo as above:

[No date]

Dear Evelyn:—

I've got about a half hour before I go to work. Might as well write you. Got to do some thing to occupy the time. Had a letter or rather a beautiful Christmas card from Mamie Lou— yesterday. What a sister-in-law you have. I hope she didn't find too many mistakes in that letter I wrote her. School teachers always pick out mistakes before you yourself would. I hope you run over them and when you finish the letter burn it so it won't remind you how ignorant I am.

One of those polocks worked in a place like Chattahoochee. He's tells of all his experiences. Some of them are pretty raw you would probably know it to be true by experience, but it all sounds pretty silly to me.

It rained all day yesterday and it was colder this morning than ever before. I couldn't gather enough cloth to go to chow. I finally managed to dig some thing up. It wasn't worth while. The chow wasn't any to go. I'll have to close now. Closing

> With all my love.
> Paul
> Cpl Paul J. Fogel

[Same envelope; same stationery]

Dec. 15-1944

Dear Evelyn:—

I wrote my dad a letter yesterday. As far as I know I'm the only one of his sons that ever wrote him a letter. I don't know if he will answer it or not. If he does I'll let you read it. It ought to be interesting. I can imagine he would like to know what I have planned for the future. That depends upon you though.

I have the day off, if you could call it that. I had quite a lot of washing to do this morning. I'm not finished yet. I also had to do some more stenciling. I finished that up now and and sitting down to take advantage of the rest of the day writting to you. I had my hair cut short again. If you remember I had them short the first time

I met you, in fact I always kept them short. I'm glad you don't have to look at me now.

There is a little matter of haveing my picture plastered around in public, I object. And it isn't over ruled. There isn't much I can do about it, I supose, but I still object.

It's raining again out side. Its not unusual as you know already. I was at chow and when I came back all my wash on the lines had been soaked again. They will probably be on that line two or three days before they are dry enough to wear again.

I just won another one of those arguements from these polocks with me here. They both think they have a better woman than I have, but they soon give up when I let them take a squint at my nurse. They may have the rest of the arguements but when it comes to that one, [illegible], they haven't got a chance.

They are always doing some thing to annoy me. They just painted my slippers white with some paint I had left. This morning they turned my sack up side down. Tonight they will probably carry me under the shower. Never a dull moment when they are around. They were debating wheather to write you a letter or not. I don't think you would like to read it if they did. They don't like to write nice things especially of me. It stoped raining now so I'll close now and do some more washing.

All ways Loving you
Paul.
Cpl Paul J. Fogel

Postmarked Dec 17 1944 from Cpl. Paul J. Fogel 435 156, H & S. Co. 23 Mars. 4 Division., c/o F.P.O. San Francisco, Cal. to Miss Evelyn Wells S.N., 1101 E. Gadsden, St., Pensacola, Florida. (stamped "PASSED BY NAVAL CENSOR" with initials; with 6 cents air mail stamp)

On Marine stationery imprinted with Marine logo: Semper Fidelis U S Marines 4th Division, * Roi-Namur, * Saipan, * Tinian.

Dec. 15-1944

Dear Evelyn:—

Ten more days till Christmas. What wouldn't I give to be with you on that day. Every thing in the world. Every thing I own. Just to be with you. I miss you more than you know. More and more each day. Tonight they are playing Christmas carrols over the loud speakers and it's echoeing all over these many tents. It really sound beautiful. I wish you could hear it. I can remember last Christmas. It rained and I got soaked to the gills. I spend the day at the barracks because I was disapointed at certain things mainly my self. I had planned on going to church, but one thing and another turned up and I was unable. I wish I would have known than that, that would have been the last Christmas I could spend in the states. I would have headed home so fast my head would still be spinning. I had just returned from a 15 day leave on the 6 of Dec of 43, but that would not have made any difference to me. I would have gone over the hill any way. I just wish I would have known you at that time. I would have spend the entire day with you, had you wanted me to. We would have done any thing you wanted to do. Its different now. I won't even be able to look at you and tell you "I wish you a very Merry Christmas." Wish that beautiful red headed mother of yours a Merry Christmas for me also. I wouldn't worry about her hair turning gray if I were you. Once a red head always a red head. I can just see another little Evelyn running around with a few beautiful red curls down her back. I can just see her now. She'll have a few freckles and two dimples just like you. Every time she laughs she will shut her eyes and she will be the prettiest girl in all the world.

A few minutes ago I decided to go to bed because I was sort of cold. Then I began to thinking about you and remembered I hadn't written you yet today. Here I am, half of me outside of the cover and the other half of me inside, keeping me warm.

I haven't had a letter from you for two days now and it seems like a year. Later on when I wont be able to receive any mail for some time it will seem longer than that. I decided to write to my mom and ask her to send my sheep lined vest. I could use it these chilly mornings.

I send that box to you three or four days ago. I send it air mail so you should have just about received it by now. I can only hope you like it. My mother wears one exactly like it. When I left home she couldn't take it off. I don't know wheather she can now or not. She didn't care wheather she could. Its not too expensive and it does come from a foreign country so if you like another, when I hit the states again we shall get one you like. You have a very large finger the man said to me when I gave him the size. I couldn't get a thing fancy in your size or I would have. I was in four towns and only saw this one small shop. I supose when we leave here I'll be able to tell you the name of this place. I have a few things I'd like to send you but they all petain to this locality. So I'm not permitted to send them. I can't hardly wait till those pictures arrive. I'm anxious to see how the real pictures turned out. Pauline said when we had our pictures taken, when I was home on foulough in 43, that the negitives didn't turn out so well but the pictures were not too bad. In any case they would have to do a lot of fixing on my face to make it worth looking at.

I have only received one letter from Elizabeth and was very happy to get it. I'll be looking for the rest though in the future. She will be with J.C. over Christmas. She is [illegible]. I'm glad she could be with him the remainder of his time in the states. It will mean a lot to both of them. It will also be some thing they will never forget. I'm only hoping he won't be send over here. I hope he has the sense of mind to keep out of it if he posibly can. I know what you are thinking now. You are perfactly right too. I stuck my neck out and I'm not sorry to an extend but I would<u>not</u> have done it again for any thing. I'd be satified, at letting people talk about me banging ears, as we say, just to stay in the states with you.

I hope you receive this letter before Christmas because I want you to do something for me. I want you to go to church and pray for me. I know it sounds silly, but I'm going to need all the help the Good Lord can posibly give me to get through this year of 1945 I'm not the only one. There are many more feel as I do and and not ashamed to admit it. We are all afraid to an extend. No one talks about it though, except perhaps me, and then I'd only mention it to you. I believe you understand me better than any one else I know. I hope so. I'd rather talk to you then a chaplin. I'd rather talk to you than any one in the world I guess. This is the longest letter I've ever written you and I'd tear it up now if I were you. Its a lot of nothing ness. I'll have to weak one of those Polocks to go to Mass tomorrow morning. If I don't get up no one else in this tent will. So they depend upon me to weak them each morning. I'm pretty realiable. Closeing with all my love, Wishing you a Merry Christmas, Hoping that I will be with you in 45.

Lets make our resolutions now.

Love and Kisses.
Paul
Cpl Paul J. Fogel

Postmarked Dec 20 1944 to Miss Evelyn Wells S.N., 1101 E. Gadsden St., Pensacola, Fla. (3 cents postage stamp; no return address on envelope)

Christmas card from Paul Fogel's twin sister, Pauline:

Front of card:
Joy at Christmas (with Nativity scene pictured)
Inside left of card:
Behold, what manner of love the Father hath bestowed upon us…1 John 3:1
Inside right of card:
May the Babe of Bethlehem
In His great love and goodness bless
Your heart, your home,
your dear ones all
With golden hours of happiness!
"Polly and Earl"

Postmarked Dec 20 1944 from Cpl. Paul J. Fogel 435 156, H & S. Co. 23 Mars. 4 Division, c/o F.P.O. San Francisco, Calif. to Miss Evelyn Wells. S.N., 1101 E. Gadsden, St., Pensacola, Florida. (stamped "PASSED BY NAVAL CENSOR" with initials; with 6 cents air mail stamp); front of envelope imprinted with Marine logo sticker: Semper Fidelis U S Marines 4th Division, * Roi-Namur, * Saipan, * Tinian.

On Marine stationery with same logo as above:

Dec. 18-1944

Dear Evelyn.

I guess I can write this letter in peace. I'm trying to write and try to explain to one of these eggs how to get a package censored for mailing. He understands OK only he likes to disturb me. I bet you couldn't guess from who I received a Christmas card yesterday. I guess you could at that. She wrote me a little note in it. It sort of surprised me. I didn't know what to expect. It made me feel wonderful to get it. It made me feel as if I were forgiven for that first time at Elizabeth trailor, where I was with my sleeves and [illegible] out of place. I'll never forget that as long as I live. I bet I turned all colors. If you ever do a thing like that to me again so help me I'll… I don't need to tell you. You know already, and I can do it too.

I doubt if we will have Christmas off but if we do the boys here have made plans for a small party. There are six in this tent and we are all going to chip in a little money to have some thing to eat and drink. The majority of them feel happy at the fact that I don't drink. About the time when every one gets drunk I think I'll take a walk. I hate to be around where any one gets into a state they won't know what they are doing. I don't believe you have ever smelled liquor or beer on my breath, and you wont if I can help it. I have started smoking a pipe though and I'd probably be lost without it now. It made me sick for a while but I had to do something beside widdling my fingers. I believe I've worked harder these past few days than I've ever in the whole time in Pensacola. I've noticed my self getting nevious. When you and I were talking about Jimmy being that way, I didn't think that this type of life would do it. I've changed my mind now and found the only way not to feel that way is to work and Im trying to work my self out of it. What is your remidy? Most of these fellows here think I'm banging ears. I need not tell you what that is. I don't mind working half as much as standing around doing nothing.

The colors are comming down again. Soon it will be dark again out side. Some of the fellows are still playing football out side. I just finished washing again. In Pensacola you could hang clothe out over night and by the next morning they would be dry. That isn't the case here. You let them out over night here and by morning it will have rained on them again. This is the only place it rains seven days a week. Well just a bout any way. This is all for now.

Loving you always.
Paul.
Cpl Paul J. Fogel

[Same envelope; on plain, unlined stationery]

Dec. 19-1944

Dear Evelyn:—

I forgot to mail that last letter I wrote so I'll inclose this small note to the same envelope. We all received our pay today and most of the boys are injoying a nice peace ful game of poker. Not unusual around this place. They will play until they are broke and than they wait for the next pay day to roll around to do the same thing all over again. Money is just another useless material to them. They live today, and don't think of what tomorrow may bring.

I have a pair of terrably sore hands. I must have swiped off skin in a dozen different places. It seems the more care I take of them the sorer they get. I was just on a special job and had to untighten bolts and nuts quite a bit. Most of them were a little tight and when the wrench sliped off you can imagine the next thing. It was a good thing ladys weren't around. They would have thought I was the devil himself.

You must have very nice patients to send you roses. I envy them. Why? because I can't send you some my self. Here I am and can't even send you a decent Christmas present.

I Love you very much,
Keep Smilling Cpl. Paul J. Fogel

Postmarked Dec 23 1944 from Cpl. Paul J. Fogel 435156, H & S. Co. 23 Mars. 4 Division, c/o F.P.O. San Francisco, Calif. to Miss Evelyn Wells. S.N., 1101 E. Gadsden, St., Pensacola, Florida.

(stamped "PASSED BY NAVAL CENSOR" with initials; with 6 cents air mail stamp); front of envelope imprinted with Marine logo sticker: Semper Fidelis US Marines 4th Division, * Roi-Namur, * Saipan, * Tinian.

On plain, unlined stationery:

Dec. 21-1944

Dearest Evelyn:—

New title. My mom likes to call me that in her letters to me. If my mother thinks of me enough to call me dearest, I think of you even more only it can't be expressed in the salutation. I guess the only place it could be found is in my heart.

I received that last letter you send dated Dec. 12. I enjoy reading any of your letters and during the course of a day they have been read over so often that the letters become blur. I had a letter from Pauline dated Oct. 27. It took practically two months to reach me. She was telling me how Earl acted when he asked my dad to marry her. It was a funny discribstion. She said he paced the floor fifteen minutes till at last Pauline said to dad that he wanted to ask him something. He was so excited that he could hardly talk. My dad than told him to calm down and then received his answer. I can just imagine how he felt. I would have felt the same way if I had a [illegible].

I told you about all my troubles and cryed upon your should too often. I can't do a thing about it because there isnt any thing else to talk about.

I have part of the day off tomorrow. I shall go into one of these small one horse towns and see what I can get for you. Now don't tell me you don't want any thing because thats the only pleasure I get out of going on liberty in a place like this. Besides any thing I get for you wouldn't be half good enough any way. It has to be little things. I like to keep you in suspense. I did when I was in Pensacola and I haven't changed. I hope you like the things I send you. I could send you another grass skirt but you dont look to well in one so I pass that by. We can't send any thing pretaining to the identy of this place so we have to be very careful of what we attempt to send home.

I haven't received those pictures as yet and I'm terriably axious to see them.

There may be a posiblity that I'll be able to see Frank. Not soon but perhaps later on, that is of course if he isn't home by that time. I hope he does get home soon. I also hope on his way he may run across me.

This will be all for now.

Loving you always
Paul
Cpl Paul J. Fogel

[In same envelope on plain, unlined stationery]:

Dec. 21-1944

Dear Evelyn:—

I just received a letter from my mom and Pauline today. They seem to be in a happy mood. So, I'm the way and intend to stay that way. My mom says she is missing your letters too. I guess she hasn't received your last. She seems to be as excited as Pauline over the wedding. Pauline wrote and told me all about it. It must have been quite large. I would have like to see it. Pauline is probably going to ask you where I am. She said she would. Thought perhaps you would know. You ought too. She also told me what you send her for her wedding present. You wouldn't tell me would you. I found out. Any way. She said it was the nicest present she had received. She will be sending me her wedding picture. She must have been beautiful. She had nothing on you how ever she looked. You are still the most beautiful woman in the world. At least I think so and aways will. I'll send you the picture as soon as I get it. I want you to keep it for me or rather us.

I was on liberty to day. I and another fellow went together. We ate noon chow in a small town and then went window shopping. shopping. I bought a few things for you. After you get them I'll tell you a little about the trouble I had in regards to them. I hope you'll like them.

The polock just came in and told me that one of my buddies commited suicide. I knew the fellow quite well. He came across with me in the seventeenth draft. A swell fellow.

Every one else is playing poker and I'm the the only one writting letters. I guess I'll close now and and go to the show again. Its going to be quite a picture they tell me. I guess the name of it is Mirage is a private affair." This is all for now. I love you very much. Keep Smilling.

Love and Kisses.
Paul.
Paul J. Fogel Cpl.

Postmarked Dec 23 1944 from Cpl. Paul J. Fogel 435156, H & S Co. 23 Mars, 4 Division, c/o F.P.O. San, Francisco, Cal. to Miss.

Evelyn Wells. S.N., 1101 E. Gadsden, St., Pensacola, Florida. U.S.A. (stamped "PASSED BY NAVAL CENSOR" with initials; with 6 cents air mail stamp); front of envelope imprinted with Marine logo sticker: Semper Fidelis US Marines 4th Division, * Roi-Namur, * Saipan, * Tinian.

On plain, unlined stationery:

Dec. 22-1944.

Dear Evelyn:—

I never knew a candle gave off as much light as they do. Perhaps I'm just getting aquainted with this candle light writting. It isn't as bad as one would imagine. I see by your last letter that you are on night duty again. I can remember how I hated it. I had to come to see you in the hospital, and then didn't get to see you but for a few minutes. I won't ever complain again. So help me. I still have that mask I took from you one night. Its too me like candy would be to a baby. It brings back a lot of memories. Thats all I'm living on over here. Wonderful memories.

I asked you where you would like to get married. You came back with an answer which I received today. Perhaps you don't want me to agree with you. I do though. For this reason I'm agreeing with you. No one here knows if they will ever see the states again. We all want to, and especially me. I've got a great deal to come back too now, and so have alot of other fellows. You stated in one of your last letters you wanted to come out west. You will injoy out there, I'm sure. You won't regret it. If you are there when I hit the states I won't have to look very far for you, will I? It doesn't make any difference to me where you are, Florida, California

112

or Maine. It will be my first stop on the way home. Of course every man has a few confessions to make to his future wife and if mine are acceptable in your sight we can decide there and then. Now that I've explained how I felt. It isn't too one-sided as you put it. Is it?

I wouldn't worry about that State Board. You are a very smart girl. You will get through it OK. When one of those hard questions come up, do exactly the opposite of what I would have done in that case, and with out a doubt you'll get it correct.

I went to a show last night again in the rain. The name of it was "Since you went away." It was sort of lengthy. Some thing like two hours long. It was getting tiresome during the end. I didn't wait to see the finishing touches. Tonight there is another good one. I have already seen it. "Going My Way." We saw that one together. Bing was playing a chaplin in it, remember.

I started this letter last night. Its six in the morning now and high time I went to chow. It will probably be French toast and bacon again. It usually is. Most fellows go for a cup coffee and come back.

I'll have to close now. How was New Year day by you? I hope you spend a wonderful time have fun.

Always Loving You.
Paul.
Cpl Paul J. Fogel

Postmarked Dec 25 1944 from Cpl. Paul J. Fogel 435 156, H & S Co. 23. Mars. 4 Div., c/o. F.P.O. San Francisco, Cal. to Miss. Evelyn Wells. S.N., 1101 E. Gadsden, St., Pensacola, Florida. U.S.A.

(stamped "PASSED BY NAVAL CENSOR" with initials; with 6 cents air mail stamp)

On plain, unlined stationery:

Dec. 23-1944

Dear Evelyn:—

It's nearly seven P.M. now. I just broke up one of these bull sessions. It seems we get in one every night. Everyone here has a different opinion on a subject that is brought up, and no one gives up until someone walks out. Most of them are pretty lengthy. I haven't admitted defeat yet and if I have any thing to say. I think I won.

I received the letter you wrote on the 14th of Dec. today. You mentioned some thing about snooping into Elizabeth's letters. That is very bad manners. Nope, I wouldn't advise. You might find some thing out. You know we have little secreds. It would never do if you found out. You would just better stick to the letters I write you. I should not go as far as to call these letters. They do ressemble a form of one though.

I can hear the rain drops on the roof out side. I hope its nice Christmas. I'd like to go to church and take communion. I have had it since I left Pensacola. I would better get busy don't you think?

Its surprising how long this pen has lasted me. I consider my self well rewarded for buying it. The same way with that wrist watch of mine. For a wrist watch that thing has gone through more abuse in the past two years than I would have liked too. I was throwing someing the other day and it losened from my arm and must have flown ten feet or more up against a building. Its still running and keeping better time than ever before. I guess if I tried to break it, I could. I got in while I was up in the hospital, at the base of [illegible], in Nov of 1942. I've been wearing it ever since. Had it repaired twice.

The loud speaked has Christmas carols comeing over it at present. It sort of makes me homesick. You blame me? You must have very mean Sisters not to let the best nurse in the hospital have Christmas off. I'd give them a peace of my mind.

Pauline wrote and intresting letter the other day, her first sentence was, "How does your belly feel now?" I told her I got a little sea sick. I had to laugh at the way she put it.

I hope Elizabeth wrote you by this time and told you she has arrived safely. I only received one letter from her so far. I hope she keeps writting. I enjoy hearing from her. I told Mamie Lou to tell your mom to tell me the bad points you have. You don't mind do you? Ha. I'd laugh if she would. This is all for no.

Always Loving You,
Paul.
Cpl Paul J Fogel.

Postmarked Dec 26 1944 from Cpl. Paul J. Fogel 435156, H & S Co. 23 Mars. 4 Div., c/o F.P.O. San Francisco, Cal. to Miss Evelyn Wells. S.N., 1101 E. Gadsden, St., Pensacola, Florida. (stamped "PASSED BY NAVAL CENSOR" with initials; with 6 cents air mail stamp)

On plain, unlined stationery:

Dec.-25-1944
5:30-AM.

Dearest Evelyn:—

It's still in the wee hours of the morning. I got up especially to see what Santa had left me in a pair of socks I had hung up. They weren't hung beside a chimney perhaps that was why were so empty. They did have a good smell. Perhaps he didn't like the kind. Any way I believe he had good intensions So I'll let him off lightly. The true reason I got up so early is that I wanted to wish you a very Merry Christmas where ever you are at, and I wanted to be the first to do it. You are probably still in bed. I hope so and I also hope your ears are ringing reminding you that I love you with all my heart. I won't be able to mail this letter today. I'll just save it till tomorrow.

Yesterday I received these Bonds as they call them at Tooley Myron Studios. Maybe you can make use of them. I know Ill never be able to. I still haven't received the ones you send me. I hope to get them any day.

Last night wasn't as bad as I had expected. The boys were a wee bit dazed but they didn't bother me so I was quite content. I went to the show. Stage Door Canteen. Before the show the Commanding Office gave a talk and wished us all a Merry Christmas. Then I went to bed about ten. I go to bed now and finish this letter this afternoon. It's light now. I'd better wash a few cloths.

Its just about time for noon chow now. I took communion this morning and attended the whole church sevice. It was a nice way to spend part of Christmas day. Don't you think so. I never injoyed a sevice more in all my life. From Majors on down to buck Privates were waiting in the same line to take Holy Communion. Its a good way to feel, when you know that in every thing else except the worship of the Lord, officers have the top hand over enlisted personal. It made me feel as if the were part of us instead of always feeling we were part of them. The saying "all men were created equal" stood out there than any where I have ever seen it. I'd better cut it out. They'll be looking me up to peach next Sundays sermon.

I'll go to chow now and then tell you what we ate. How would that be?

Goodness it's terriably hot today. The water is pouring off of me. This is a freakish day. I can't imagine this happening ever day. We will probably have a cloud burst tomorow. Old Santa was disapointed if he expected snow.

What a chow we had. I'll send you the Menue. This is all for now.

Love and Kisses
Paul

Postmarked Dec 26 1944 from Cpl. Paul J. Fogel 435156, H & S Co. 23 Mars. 4 Division, c/o F.P.O. San Francisco, Cal to Miss. Evelyn Wells S.N., 1101 E. Gadsden St., Pensacola, Florida. (stamped "PASSED BY NAVAL CENSOR" with initials; with 6 cents air mail stamp)
[Items included in this envelope]

TWENTY-THIRD MARINES - FOURTH MARINE DIVISION

0900 - Christmas Day, 1944

-o-

Call to worship

1. O come, all ye faithful,
   Joyful and triumphant,
   O come ye, O come ye to Bethlehem;
   Come and behold Him born the King
     of angels;
   O come, let us adore Him, (Repeat)
   Christ, the Lord.

2. Sing, choirs of angels,
   Sing in exultation,
   Sing, all ye citizens of heaven above;
   Glory to God, all glory in the highest;
   O come, let us adore Him, (Repeat)
   O come, let us adore Him,
   Christ, the Lord.

Scripture Reading and Prayers

1. Joy to the world! the Lord is come; Let earth receive her King;
   Let every heart prepare Him room, And heaven and nature sing,
   And heaven and nature sing, And heaven, and heaven and nature sing.

2. Joy to the earth! the Saviour reigns; Let men their songs employ;
   While fields and floods, rocks, hills and plains Repeat the sounding joy,
   Repeat the sounding joy, Repeat, repeat the sounding joy.

Address - The Regimental Chaplain

Prayer and Benediction   (If you are not going to stay for the Communion
                          service, you may leave during the next carol)

1. The first Noel the angel did say Was to certain poor shepherds in fields
     as they lay;
   In fields where they lay keeping their sheep On a cold winter's night
     that was so deep.
   Noel, Noel, Noel, Noel, Born is the King of Israel.

2. They look-ed up and saw a star, Shining in the east beyond them far,
   And to the earth it gave great light, And so it continued both day & night.
   Noel, Noel, Noel, Noel, Born is the King of Israel.

The Communion Service

   THE CONFESSION - Almighty God, Father of our Lord Jesus Christ, Maker of
all things, Judge of all men: We acknowledge and bewail our manifold sins
and wickedness, Which we, from time to time, most grievously have committed,
By thought, word, and deed, Against thy Divine Majesty, Provoking most justly
thy wrath and indignation against us. We do earnestly repent, and are heart-
ily sorry for these our misdoings, The remembrance of them is grievous unto
us; The burden of them is intolerable. Have mercy upon us, Have mercy upon
us, most merciful Father; For thy Son our Lord Jesus Christ's sake, Forgive
us all that is past; And grant that we may ever hereafter serve and please
thee in newness of life, To the honour and glory of thy name; Through Jesus
Christ our Lord. Amen.

Christmas service, North Pacific, 1944 (pg. 1)

118

SURSUM CORDA – Chaplain. Lift up your hearts.
               Answer.   WE LIFT THEM UP UNTO THE LORD.
              Chaplain.   Let us give thanks unto our Lord God.
               Answer.   IT IS MEET AND RIGHT SO TO DO.

Chaplain. It is very meet, right, and our bounden duty, that we should at all times, and in all places, give thanks unto thee, O Lord, Holy Father, Almighty, Everlasting God; Because thou didst give Jesus Christ, thine only Son, to be born as at this time for us; who, by the operation of the Holy Ghost, was made very man, of the substance of the Virgin Mary his mother; and that without spot of sin, to make us clean from all sin.

Therefore, with Angels and Archangels, and with all the company of heaven, we laud and magnify thy glorious Name; evermore praising thee, and saying, (All together) HOLY, HOLY, HOLY, Lord God of hosts, Heaven and earth are full of thy glory: Glory be to thee, O Lord Most High. Amen.

COMMUNION HYMN –

1. How silently, how silently
   The wondrous gift is given!
   So God imparts to human hearts
   The blessings of His heaven.
   No ear may hear His coming,
   But in this world of sin,
   Where meek souls will receive Him
   The dear Christ enters in. (still,

2. O holy Child of Bethlehem,
   Descend to us, we pray;
   Cast out our sin and enter in,
   Be born in us today.
   We hear the Christmas angels
   The great glad tidings tell;
   O come to us, abide with us,
   Our Lord Emmanuel.

GLORIA IN EXCELSIS – Glory be to God on high, and on earth peace, good will towards men. We praise thee, we bless thee, we worship thee, we glorify thee, we give thanks to thee for thy great glory; O Lord God, heavenly King, God the Father Almighty. O Lord, the only-begotten Son, Jesus Christ; O Lord God, Lamb of God, Son of the Father, that takest away the sins of the world, have mercy upon us. Thou that takest away the sins of the world, receive our prayer. Thou that sittest at the right hand of God the Father, have mercy upon us. For thou only art holy; thou only art the Lord; thou only, O Christ, with the Holy Ghost, art most high in the glory of God the Father. Amen. (Be seated).

FINAL BLESSING and Response, with silent prayer

1. Hark! the herald angels sing
   Glory to the new-born King;
   Peace on earth and mercy mild,
   God and sinners reconciled!
   Joyful all ye nations rise,
   Join the triumph of the skies;
   With th' angelic host proclaim
   Christ is born in Bethlehem.
   Hark! the herald angels sing
   Glory to the new-born King.

2. Mild He lays His glory by,
   Born, that men no more may die;
   Born to raise the sons of earth,
   Born to give them second birth.
   Risen with healing in His wings,
   Light and Life to all He brings,
   Hail, the Son of Righteousness!
   Hail, the heav'n-born Prince of Pea
   Hark! the herald angels sing
   Glory to the new-born King.

The Chaplain would be glad to send word to your home minister or to your family, that you were at church on Christmas Day and received Communion. Come up to the stage after the service and put your name on the list.

A BLESSED CHRISTMAS TO YOU ALL

Christmas service, North Pacific, 1944 (pg. 2)

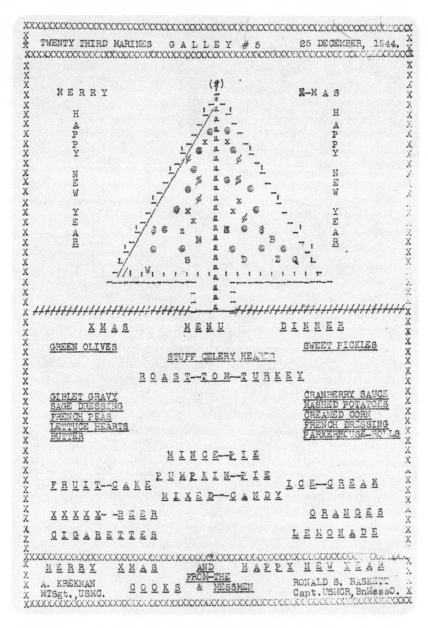

Christmas menu, North Pacific, 1944

Pre-printed service:

TWENTY-THIRD MARINES—
FOURTH MARINE DIVISION
0900—Christmas Day, 1944

Portrait coupons for one-dollar portraits
(referenced in previous letter)

Postmarked Dec 28 1944 from Cpl. Paul J. Fogel 435156, H & S. Co. 23. Mars. 4 Division, c/o F.P.O. San Francisco, Cal. to Miss Evelyn Wells. S.N., 1101 E. Gadsden St., Pensacola, Florida. (stamped "PASSED BY NAVAL CENSOR" with initials; with 6 cents air mail stamp)
On plain, unlined stationery:

Dec-27-1944
630 A.M.

Dear Evelyn:—

I wrote you a letter yesterday and after look-ing at the writting and spelling. I decided I could do much better if I told a wee bit more time. I have the day off, if you can call it that. It's a beautiful morning and we are walking in mud up to our necks. Yesterday it seems to me we had a cloud burst. I told you Christmas we had very hot wheather. We paid the price yesterday.

Yesterday was my brothers birthday. Roy. I don't know wheather I've told you any thing about him or now. I told you if I remember right that he married a girl in Texas and shorty after was shipped to Italy. He made Capt while he was a cross. My mom wrote and said he was in the states on a special mission a few months ago and

121

had the chance to see his wife. He must have been a happy man. I wish I could get on some sort of mission. I'd like to get to see my woman too. It would help my moral. I think I'll have to suggest it to the Gen or some one. I doubt wheather he would consider it. If I can't see you I ought to be thankful I can write anyway. Your letters mean alot to me so don't stop writting what ever may happen. I'll write as often as I can. That won't be too often in the future. I'm going to have a lot more work to do.

I had a letter from Charles my oldest brother. yesterday he was home on fourlough for a few days in the first part of the month. Lucky fellow. I hope Jake got back safely. My mom is like you, she said she liked that boy. Every one likes him He's a wonderful fellow. He's not like the majority of the Marines in Pensacola, so if you had any chance of getting aquainted with any of them you know what I mean. He likes to have fun.

The fellows in this tent are getting more batty by the day. Peace is what I like, only they won't give it to me. They go from one foolish conseraction to another. I managed to get rid of them, maybe I can finish your letter now. After I get out of this place perhaps I can tell you more about it. It really is interesting. Maybe its just because I think different from the rest of the people. One has to get used to living in this sort of place. Ha I don't think you'd like it though. I prefer to think of you in the states. You are safe there any way. That means a lot.

I miss you. You can be glad I'm not in Pensacola. I'd probably come to see you every night instead of every other night. I'll make it up to you when I get back. I'll be with you all of the time.

Lots of Love.
Paul.

Postmarked Dec 29 1944 from Cpl. Paul J. Fogel 435156, H & S. Co. 23 Mars 4 Div., c/o F.P.O. San Francisco, Cal. to Miss. Evelyn Wells. SN., 1101 E. Gadsden, St., Pensacola, Florida. (stamped "PASSED BY NAVAL CENSOR" with initials; with 6 cents air mail stamp)
On plain, unlined stationery:

Dec-28-1944

Dear Evelyn:—

If this isn't a letter of usual composition. You'll know I'm in a bad mood. We had to work to night. We usually work till four but not tonight we work till seven thirty and then—knock off. I suppose I shouldn't complain. What really gets me is, I'm as filthy as a pig puddling around in the mud all night and its inky black out side. Besides that there is cold. water. Should I mention any other reasons why I shouldn't take a bath tonight. I could go on all night this way.

I hope I'm excused for not sending that last package any sooner. I was sort of occupied, if you know what I mean Its probably the last you will get from me. Its not because of me.

I have a note book exactly like the one I send you. Probably the only place you could get one like it is in N.Y.C. same place Mrs. Grebe gave it to me. I had lots of use for mine. Maybe you can make use of yours too eh:—You are worth fighting for.

Don't go putting holes in your ears for those ear rings I bought you. Its sort of a Catholic custom here that a married cupple should wear them. The girl wears one and the boy wears the other. Only wealthy familys will wear them. As for the handerchiefs I thought you would like some thing color ful. Every one down here dress that way in very bright colors. Thats about all for that.

The picture Mamie send of you is a beaut. You were dressed in an evening gown. You would be the most beautiful woman in the world in any dress. I think you take wonderful pictures. I hope I'm the only one who thinks so. I know you don't. You are very lovely. Your mother can be proud she has a daughter like you. I proud of you my self. Me being so stupid and all I can't see how I could rope a girl like you. Some times I wonder why you like me. All you would have to do is bat your eye at another fellow and he would be eating out of your hand. You would better not. I hate to fight over the woman I love. I never really got angry at any one yet. That is enough to fight with them I don't hope too.

This will be all for now.

Always Loving you.
Paul.
Cpl Paul J. Fogel.

Postmarked Dec 30 1944 from Cpl. Paul J. Fogel 435156, H & S Co. 23 Mars. 4 Div., c/o. F.P.O. San Francisco, Cal to Miss. Evelyn Wells. S.N., 1101 E. Gadsden, St., Pensacola, Florida. (stamped "PASSED BY NAVAL CENSOR" with initials; with 6 cents air mail stamp)

On plain, unlined stationery:

Dec. 29-1944

Dear Evelyn:—

'No letter today.' The man who thought up
that there, ought to be shot. It does hold true in a
great many case. I don't lose faith so easy so here
I am again bothering you. I wrote you a letter just
a few minutes ago I hope you will never have to
receive.

I had a letter today from one of your family.
It was quite interesting. Why? Hmmm. I supose
it could have been because it had a great deal to
do with you. Nothing I didn't know already. I
doubt if any one could tell me any thing about
you I didn't know already. Brilliant aren't I.

It didn't rain today. Nope it was as clear as
the nose on my face. You know how clear that is.
Its going to rain tonight I can tell. They might
as well put me in the wheather bureau. This
wheather is no mystry to me. Rain, Rain, Rain.
I could only be wrong once a week. I have it all
figured out.

If you ever get the chance to see Mrs.
Reynolds, the old lady in the U.S.O. I always
called her mom. Remember. She's a grand old
woman. Tell her I asked about her. Give her my
best wishes. I supose Miss McLain is still in New
Orleans in the hospital yet. I guess she will never
be back in Pensacola. She was alright in her way.
Only no one liked her way to well.

I hope Elizabeth made the trip safely. I
hope she realized that it would be a few thousand
instead of a few hundred. I'm sure she thought it

was worth it. I cant say I blame her. I would have probably done the same.

Abbot-Costello are playing tonight and I can already hear the rain drops on the tent roof. I'm starting to growl. Can you hear me? I'm not very pleased at the situation. I hardly go to a show any more. Tonight I had planned on it and I go and if we have a cloud burst.

You really aren't as bad looking as you imagine so don't class your self so low. Your looks don't mean a thing to me. Its you, and all of you, that I'm in love with. Of course, I don't want you to look different when I get back. You are beautiful as you are so don't change.

This is all for now.

Always Loving You.
Paul.
Cpl Paul J. Fogel

Postmarked Dec 31 1944 from Cpl. Paul J. Fogel 435156, H & S Co 23. Mars. 4 Division, c/o. F.P.O. San Francisco, Cal to Miss Evelyn Wells S.N., 1101 E. Gadsden, St., Pensacola, Florida. (stamped "PASSED BY NAVAL CENSOR" with initials; with 6 cents air mail stamp).

On plain, unlined stationery:

Dec. 31-1944

Dear Evelyn:—

This is going to be a big day for me so I'll not be able to write as long a letter as I had planned. I don't know how to begin this letter. In the first place I want to scold you and then again I want to thank you. I did ask for one [illegible] beautiful picture in that groupe I had remember. Poor memory eh. I don't believe a word of it. You did it on purpose. I'll fix you just you wait. It came at an operotune moment. I would have never received it if I had not received it yesterday. Thanks also for J. C.'s and Elizabeths picture. I wouldn't part with them for anything.

If you only knew what I was thinking last night when I received those pictures. I'm sure your ears were ringing. They would have if I had any thing to say about it. Every thing told me I was angry with you. I went to bed last night and just about frooze my ears off, so I guess now the angry ness has left me.

I received a letter from you from the first of Dec. It took a month to get here. Excuse please for short letter. Keep Smilling I must go now.

Always Loving You.
Paul
Cpl Paul J. Fogel.

Postmarked Jan 6 1945 (*Spoiler alert:* as an aside, they married exactly one year later from this date) from Cpl. Paul J. Fogel 435156, H & S. Co. 23 Mars. 4 Div, c/o. F.P.O. San Francisco, Cal to Miss. Evelyn Wells., 1101 E. Gadsden, St., Pensacola, Florida. (stamped "PASSED BY NAVAL CENSOR" with initials; with 6 cents air mail stamp)

On plain, unlined stationery:

Jan 1-1945

Dear Evelyn:—

The old year went out mighty silent last night. The New Year didn't come in with a bang. Every one kept there thoughts to them self. This is one New Year morning I'll never forget. When I return I'll probably tell you why. If I don't it will probably be because I don't wish to remember it.

Its been very nice for the past two days. Something unusual around here. The sun is just coming up and makes the clouds reddish around the edges. They are hanging mighty heavy we will have our share of rain by the time the day is over. I'd rather be in Pennsylvania right now looking at the clouds than sitting here thinking of thing to tell you. You'll find out how pretty they are as soon as I get back.

I have already simmered down from that picture deal you pulled on me. I can't see what your girl friend wanted with that one. But since she has it, I guess it will be of no harm. I did want though. I like to remember you with a big smile on your face. You could smile about any thing. Thats more than I can say for my self. When I get angry you are lucky if you can pry my mouth open with a crow bar. Its like have lock jaw. I guess if I got mad at you. I'd probably spank you.

Love and Kisses
Paul.

* * * * *

[The following V-Mail letters were kept together, so the dates Paul wrote them will be out of sync with the document as a whole.]

Postmarked Jan 12 1945 from Cpl. Paul J. Fogel 435…, H & S Co 23 Mars 4 Div., c/o Fleet Post Office, San Francisco, Cal to Miss.

Evelyn Wells SN., 1101 E. Gadsden—St., Pensacola, Florida (envelope imprinted with: WAR & NAVY DEPARTMENTS, V—MAIL SERVICE, OFFICIAL BUSINESS; stamped "PENALTY FOR PRIVATE USE TO AVOID PAYMENT OF POSTAGE, $300"; no postage); letter stamped "PASSED BY NAVAL CENSOR" with initials

On very small paper (marked "V-Mail"):

1/3/

Dear Evelyn:—

Haven't received your package yet and don't intend to for a while yet. Your last letter was dated Nov. 29. I was sort of wondering why you had not written me in the month of Nov. I'm getting them a wee bit late but I love em just the same.

I decided to cut my pig tails off. I thought you might get jealous or some thing. So now I'm as bald as a pineapple. I need not be ashamed as no one looks at me except a groupe of fellows. I don't supose Id care anyway because I only want to look attractive to you. Thats hard to do in my position.

I'm hoping Elizabeth got to California in time to spend Christmas with J.C. I had a letter from Mamie Lou and she some times thinks she won't. This is a long enough period to find out in. I do hope she made it alright. Write and tell me about it. I've been wondering about her every day. I guess I should be satisfied wondering about myself. I'm afraid I like to poke my nose in other peoples business too much. I don't regret poking my nose into yours though.

I might go on liberty tomorrow again for a short time. I'll have to see what I can dig up for you. These places aren't like New York City you know. Heres a hug and a kiss. Got it? Good.

Always Loving You.
Paul.

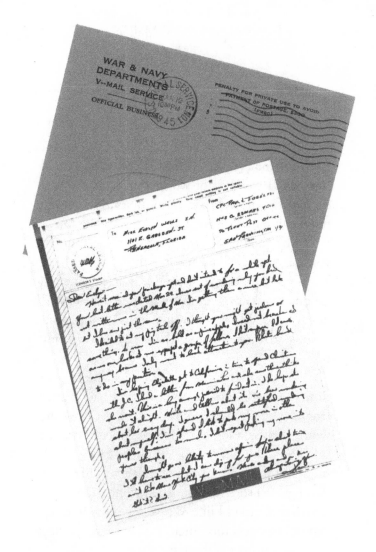

Paul's V-Mail to Evelyn, postmarked January 12, 1945

Postmarked Jan 12 1945 from Cpl. Paul J. Fogel 435..., H
& S. Co. 23 Mars. 4 Div., c/o F.P.O. San Francisco, Cal to Miss.
Evelyn Wells S.N., 1101 E. Gadsden St., Pensacola, Florida. (enve-
lope imprinted with: WAR & NAVY DEPARTMENTS, V-MAIL
SERVICE, OFFICIAL BUSINESS; stamped "PENALTY FOR
PRIVATE USE TO AVOID PAYMENT OF POSTAGE, $300";
no postage); letter stamped "PASSED BY NAVAL CENSOR" with
initials

On very small paper (marked "V-Mail"):

1/4/45

Dear Evelyn:—

Received two letters from you dated some
time before Christmas. I was so anxious to receive
them. I guess I was walking in circles. It was the
first I had in about a week. O no. It wasn't your
fault. It wasn't mine either. We'll blame it on
some one else. I'm not mentioning any names,
but I'd like to murder him. Its not good for my
constitution.

I wish I had not received those letters or
rather pictures you send me. Don't mis understand me. I truely wanted them at that time.
Right now they are in my way. Id much rather
have you in a picture alone. Now that I see my
self in a picture beside you. I can redially see how
ugly I am. Don't send me any thing besides you
lone anymore. Thats all I'm concerned about.
I probably couldn't tell you why because of the
censor. I do want that picture of you in the worst
way. Not to big because I'll have to carry it with
me. Say some thing around a 3"–4" or any one
you think I would like. I do want to look at you
often. I'm crazy but if I look at you I feel I could

talk with you as if we were together again. I can't tell you how much I wish that were true. I had the chance and left it past. I guess I really wouldn't have known how much I loved you if this would not have happened. Admitting a mistake is one thing and trying to correct it is another. I will when I hit Pensacola again, so help me I will. I'll murder the first fellow who looks at you. I'll write tomorrow. I'll probably have some thing to talk about then. Lots of kisses

Always Loving You
Paul.

Postmarked Jan 18 1945 from Cpl. Paul J. Fogel 435156, H & S. Co. 23 Mars 4 Div., c/o. F.P.O. San Francisco, Cal to Miss. Evelyn Wells. S.N., 1101 E. Gadsden, St., Pensacola, Florida (envelope imprinted with: WAR & NAVY DEPARTMENTS, V-MAIL SERVICE, OFFICIAL BUSINESS; stamped "PENALTY FOR PRIVATE USE TO AVOID PAYMENT OF POSTAGE, $300"; no postage); letter stamped "PASSED BY NAVAL CENSOR" with initials.

On very small paper (marked "V-Mail"):

1/7/44 (was actually 1945)

My Dear Little Honey Bun [illegible]:—

Hmmmmmm, Sounds good, doesn't it? It is to me. The best in all the world. I can hardly wait and I supose you too, in order to take that SN. off the last part of your name. Perhaps you would prefer it taken off already. If so, say so. It would be no trouble in my part. I'll do the changing of the last name my self. So don't worry about that. That will come later.

So Nellie joined the Nurse Corps eh? I'm shure she would injoy it. I'm so happy a certain Marine had some influence on your will power concerning that matter. I'm sure you would make a very good nurse in the sevice. Besides I need a nurse to take care of me. I'm very sick. Love sick. There is only one cure for it. O yes, I supose I could think of a lot more reasons. I won't take the time at present. Talking about present. Oh yes yes yes. I was in a fairly large city yesterday and was able to purchase a gift in your behalf. Some thing you will injoy. "I hope." It is an indentfation bracelet with your name ingraved. I hope you haven't one already. It has my personal touches on it. You see there are very few times in a course of a day that my thoughts don't follow you around. I bet you feel haunted at times.

If my writting is half as readable as yours my mother or any one else can say a word against it. I'll have to admit I wrote your mother at little letter. I glad she received it. I don't know when I'll be able to send that bracelet to you. You'll get it sometime though.

All ways Loving You.
Paul

Postmarked Feb 3 1945 from Cpl. Paul J. Fogel 435156, H & S. Co. 23 Mars 4 Div., c/o F.P.O. San Francisco, Cal to Miss. Evelyn Wells S.N., 1101 E. Gadsden, St., Pensacola, Florida. (envelope imprinted with: WAR & NAVY DEPARTMENTS, V-MAIL SERVICE, OFFICIAL BUSINESS; stamped "PENALTY FOR PRIVATE USE TO AVOID PAYMENT OF POSTAGE, $300"; no postage); letter stamped "PASSED BY NAVAL CENSOR" with initials

On very small paper (marked "V-Mail"):

January 24-1945

Dear Evelyn:—

I was going to write you a letter last night. I try to write every night. I was sort of busy last night and didn't get the chance. Don't blame me if you can't read this. I'm used to writting small and can't get out of the habit. I don't like to write a [illegible] mail anyway. Can't help it though. Writting paper is all [illegible] gone. Yep some one swiped my $1.50 pen. What any one would want with it is beyond me. I had to borrow this one. I'll have to see if I can't get another soon.

It gets pretty cool night times. No one knows that better then I. I was up all last night and just about froze. I was dressed like an eskimo and froze any way. This afternoon I have to sweat the drill out of me.

The moon was out bright as day. One could see every tonight. Reminds me alot of Pensacola.

I should have waited till tonight to see if I had any letter from you. If there is one I'll answer it tonight. I'll close for now.

Love Always.
Paul.
Cpl. Paul J. Fogel.

Postmarked Jan 10 1945 from Cpl. Paul J. Fogel 435156, H & S Co. 23 Mars. 4 Div., c/o. F.P.O. San Francisco, Cal to Miss. Evelyn Wells S.N., 1101 E. Gadsden, St., Pensacola, Florida. (stamped "PASSED BY NAVAL CENSOR" with initials; with 6 cents air mail stamp)

On plain, unlined stationery:

Jan 8-1945 4 P.M.

Dear Evelyn:—

Whats a good remedy for indigestion? I'm in a hurry. I'm afraid I can't wait on your precribetion.

I supose you poke your nose in your mothers letters too. Huh? Just like you did mine. But I wanted you too so it didn't make any difference to me. After we came back from that trip to Panama City and I really found out the kind of woman you were, I doubt if hell or high water could have kept me from loving you. A person only finds one of you in a life time. I'm glad I found you before I left. I'll never let you go unless you want me to. I did mean what I said that night in that cabin. I meant it with all my heart. I know you will remember it.

If you can't read this letter, throw it a way now because the rest of it will be the same way. I supose I could blame it on the position I'm in and then again it could be the pen I'm using. I'm not good at making excuses so I'll not try to make any more.

We play quite a bit of peonackle. What a word to spell. Any way it reminds me of the time we didn't get the chance to play the game you said you were so good at. I would have liked to have taught you a lesson in it. I'll have to cancel that till I get back too. We'll have a lot more time than.

I might be able to get to send that bracelet to you today. I'm going to try. I can't tell how sucessful I'll be.

I was able to go to church yesterday. It wasn't a large gathering only about twenty-five to thirty people could attend. An open air service. I enjoyed Rather different but to the point. I'm sure you could have smiled at the place it was held. I tell you about it later on. If you remind me.

Have you heard from Kelly lately? What is she doing for a living. I hope the operation had good affects on her. I still have a few after effects on mine. No one knows about it but me. Tendons are still stretching.

Last night I dreamed I was home and was working on the farm and all of a sudden like, both my operations were infected. It scared me so I immediately woke up and felt around to see if it were true. Isn't that some thing to dream about?

You won't believe this but I'm writting this letter waiting for a haircut. Yep the curles have to be cliped off. The wind is blowing the hair all over the place.

This will be all for now.

Aways Loving You
Paul.

Postmarked Jan 10 1945 from Cpl. Paul J. Fogel 435156, H & S. Co. 23 Mars. 4 Div., c/o. F.P.O. San Francisco, Cal. to Miss. Evelyn Wells, SN., 1101 E. Gadsden, St., Pensacola, Florida. (stamped "PASSED BY NAVAL CENSOR" with initials; with 6 cents air mail stamp)

On plain, unlined stationery:

Jan 8-1945

Dear Evelyn:—

   You probably couldn't read those V mail I wrote you because I wrote to small. I shall, the next time I get in that fix and have to use Vmail, try to write a wee bit larger. Did you ever write letters laying on your stomach up four decks high. Its some experience. You ought to try it some time. I'm having the time of my life. Last night some one let something fall and it was so late at night I thought someone had fallen out of there sack. If he had, the person would probably be in the hospital by now. Its quite a distance to the floor.

   I was finally able to send that bracelet to you. I hope you receive it soon. I send it air mail so it shouldn't take too long. I'm only hoping you like it.

   Did Elizabeth reach Cal. safely. I hope she didn't have too much trouble. I'd hate to think she was stranded any place. The U.S.A. is a fairly large country to cross. I seem to know some thing about it.

   My Brother Roy was home for Christmas. I guess I told you about him before. The Lucky stiff. I guess I'll have to wait my turn.

   February is going to be an anniversary month for me but I'm afraid I wont be able to celebrate. Next year if I can posibly arange it. We'll celebrate together. It will only be a year but it feels to me as if it were a life time. I feel as if "time" cheated me. Perhaps I was expecting to much. You may consider your self a lucky woman. For if I would have remainded in Pensacola or rather the U.S. for ten more months your last name would not remain Wells. May be it is better the way it turned out. I'd probably feel more indepted to you if I had you as a wife instead of a wife to be. I wouldn't want you to become a widow or feel like one. In any case don't worry about me. If I'm able I'll be in Pensacola before you know it.

You mentioned that Smitty's sister had another baby. I knew her only was disapoined because she lost the red hair she had, if she had any. To bad. Smitty has beautiful hair. Only once in a while she gets them cut. Our children will all have red hair. I'm not woried about that. Your mom has some thing to do with that. Bless her. I miss your not blessing me all the time. I always felt much better after you blessed me a few times.

I just picked up my moms letter yesterday before I mailed your letter and though you might enjoy reading about some snow. Might as well get used to it. I think maybe you would like to go slay riding. Its fun.

I'll close now and go back to work again.

Always Loving You.
Paul.

[Paul enclosed his mother's letter referenced above.]

Nazareth. Pa. Route 1.
Dec. 30. 1944.

Hi there my pet:

This will be the last letter you will receive from me in this year so try not to feel hurt as

New Year is just around the corner. Well how is your old self and did you have a good Christmas dinner? We had a very pleasent surprise on nite before Christmas when Roy came in and Charles was here. only my big handsome son that want to see the world were not here. I missed you and Sheldon very much. Grandma & pa could not be with us either as Grandma had a very bad cold and Aunt Hester was in bed also with a heavy cold so, Robert was here in the afternoon he is an ensign now and is stationed at Asbury Park N.J. for a while. Wayne is out somewhere. Yes Paul I received your money order for $15. and thanks for it. That was not nescessery you need your money too. I have put your other three money orders in the bank. Yes Paul I am getting you a sheep lined jacket and send it as soon as possible. You say you don't see snow well we have snow sleet and ice and some more snow. the kids that are left in the comunity are all out skiing and sleighrideing, the moon was out nice and bright and the hill was full of sleighs.

Francis went home early and said he and Charlotte were going sleighing on Kemels Hump. so you see he still is as funny as ever. Polly and I deceited we would go too (ha ha). Did you receive the boxes for Christmas and were they all spoiled. we heard so many packages were spoiled. I hope not. well this letter finds us all well, so hope you the same. will close now and clean ducks for customers that are coming to get them so Lots of Love

Mother & Dad.

P.S. I send Evelyn two nice hankies for Christmas. hope she likes them.

Postmarked Jan 16 1945 from Cpl. Paul J. Fogel 435156, H & S. Co. 23. Mars. 4 Div., c/o. F.P.O San Francisco, Cal. to Miss. Evelyn Wells. S.N., 1101 E. Gadsden, St., Pensacola, Florida. (stamped "PASSED BY NAVAL CENSOR" with initials; with 6 cents air mail stamp)

On plain, unlined stationery:

Jan 10-1945

Dear Evelyn:—

I just came from another open air show. Kay Keiser played in it I think the name of it was "Swing Time" If I remember correctly I saw it in Pensacola while I was still there. I enjoyed it just as much as the first time. I thought it was worth while staying awake to see. Its the first one I saw in over a week now.

Had a letter from my mom to day. They say the snow is two feet deep. I would like to see you experience a winter in the north. You probably wouldn't like the first one but one gets used to it. I'm sure you won't have any trouble. All you have to know is how to use a shovel. Ha.

I'm hoping you received the handerchiefs by this time. I'd like to tell you where I bought them but I can't just yet. These places around here have very funny names. It seems to me you would have to be native born to pronounce them. You speak about one town and it, turns out you mean another. They sound just about a like.

You were speaking about final exams in Urology. Does that mean you won't have to take that exam in June? I guess these exams are just leading up to the big day. I supose it isn't comming soon enough for you. I certainly wish I could be there for your graduation. I bet your mother will be poud of you getting your diploma. I can't get over that cousin of yours. Never though a red head was any one to back out. I'll have to give her a fatherly talk when I get back. That's a laugh.

I had quite a time last Tuesday. We went to different camps on some business. Had a swell time looking at the senery. We didn't get back till late.

I miss sitting on the circle in the park with you and also the times we went down to the beach and got full of sand. What memories they are. If it were only that I could live them over again. Especially the time we got caught in the rain. Wasn't that some thing.

This will be all for now.

Love and Kisses.
Paul.

Postmarked Jan 16 1945 from Cpl. Paul J. Fogel 435156, H & S. Co. 23 Mars. 4 Div., c/o. F.P.O. San Francisco, Cal. to Miss. Evelyn Wells, S.N., 1101 E. Gadsden, St., Pensacola, Florida. (stamped "PASSED BY NAVAL CENSOR" with initials; with 6 cents air mail stamp)

On plain, unlined stationery:

January 12-1945
6:30 A.M.

Dear Evelyn:—

Just now came from chow. Scrambled eggs. The best chow we have had now for quite some time. You don't hear me braging about it do you? I never did taste any of your food or did I. It

was so little! Can't remember. You tasted some
of mine. I know. Weren't those hot dogs good
that I roasted. Yum. I can taste them way over
here. O thats right, you did help make the fire,
didn't you. Have to give you credit for some
thing. That was a swell day wasn't it? I had the
most fun watching Kelly. I believe she enjoyed
her self. John Collins the fellow I brought alone.
I'm afraid he was used to drinking and haveing a
good time in that manner. Remember I told you
he had been shipped out before I did. He's still
in Camp Lejeune N.C. In fact all those boys that
were from Pensacola were shipped there and as
far as I know they are still there. I believe I mentioned to you before that I had ran across one of
my old buddies that first came to Pensacola with
me. We were both glad to see each other. He has
just about been all over the Pacific already. We
had a great deal to talk about. A few of the other
older fellows are over here too.

Remember a fellow I was nearly always
talking about. His name was Paul Bird. He used
to be my first bunk buddy. I've gotten in touch
with him and expect to see him at any time. He's
around here some place.

I haven't heard from Kupsky yet. The last
letter he wrote, he inclosed $.60 which some fel-
low had owed me for some sort of business trac-
tion I never knew about. We were always shooting crap together and had some fun in that way.
He told me I should use them for shooting crap
also. Evelyn!!! Now don't get any funny ideas. I
haven't made a habit of it. I haven't come to the
point when money is my God, and never hope
to. It does help occupy the time and if you play

for pennies and nickles you can't win or lose more than a dollar a day.

Penockle is the principle game as that is the I know most about. Yes sir I'm a shark at that game. I'm also a hard loser.

Those buddies of mine have been threating to write you a letter and give you a few pointers on the things you should know about me. If you get a letter, I'll know nothing about it. They have cooked up quite a few stories to tell you. They ought to be honeys by the time they get them to sound right. How they could come true is beyond me. I wouldn't hold it against. If thats what they call fun, it OK with me. This will be all for now.

Loving You Always
Paul.

Postmarked Jan 16 1945 from Cpl Paul J. Fogel 435156, H & S. Co. 23 Mar. 4 Div., c/o. F.P.O. San Francisco, Cal. to Miss. Evelyn Wells. S.N., 1101 E. Gadsden, St., Pensacola, Florida. (stamped "PASSED BY NAVAL CENSOR" with initials; with 6 cents air mail stamp)
On plain, unlined stationery:

Jan. 12-1944

Dearest Evelyn:—

These goones crowded around me here just now are trying to teach me how to write a letter. They found fault with every thing. They first claimed I had January spelled wrong and then you always put a coma after the saluation, and you always begin a letter to your woman with

"Dearest." You always write distantictly. They are right in every respect. I don't know how to write a decent letter. I hope you over look the mistakes, and the ones you do notice, you won't hold against me too much. Will you. There will be a day I won't have to write letters I can tell you what I wish from my mouth. That will be a joy ful day for me. I won't let you out of my sight.

You have your nerve, trying to get my New Years, resolutions out of me. You will have to tell me yours first and then perhaps you won't be able to pry them out of me. I'll tell you this. They all concern you. And if I reach the states I'll do all I can to make them come true.

The wheather is alot worse at present and we walk around most of the time striped to the waist. I can imagine Pensacola is quite different. Mom says they have quite a bit of snow in Pennsylvania. Perhaps you will also get to go sleigh ridding in Pensacola.

I haven't heard from Kupsky yet. I'm wondering if he had the time to stop in up home. My mom like him too. He must be a Pomino or something. I ought to hear from him any day now I suspect.

I just caught one of my buddies washing his teeth in the water fountain. I called him out about it. He didn't feel as if he were doing much harm. It was filthy in one respect. I saw worse things than that committed. He was just too lazy to go to the head. I must have got plenty angry, any way a Sgt had to quite us down.

Yesterday I received a letter from a Bain, a W.R. of a Woman Marine. What ever you want to call her. I met her in Camp Pendle ton the two days I was there. I was in a P. Keating some thing and heard her say some thing about Pensacola. She told me she knew a few fellows I knew, that were at Camp Pendle ton and since I didn't have the time to look them up she would, and give me there addresses. I guess her letter was miss layed or some thing any way it was still dated in Nov. Don't worry about her. Her nor any one else could talk your place. It seems that every one likes to get out of the states. Most of the boys from Pensacola and comeing the way here. Lets hope not.

Always Loving You
Paul.

Postmarked Jan 16 1945 from Cpl. Paul J. Fogel 435156, H & S. Co. 23 Mars. 4 Div., c/o. F.P.O. San Francisco, Cal. to Miss. Evelyn Wells, S.N., 1101 E. Gadsden, St., Pensacola, Florida. (stamped "PASSED BY NAVAL CENSOR" with initials; with 6 cents air mail stamp)
On plain, unlined stationery:

January 13-1945
12 Noon.

Dear Evelyn:—

I'm still waiting for that letter from you, telling me that Elizabeth arived in California safely. Mamie Lou wrote and told me she might have had tire trouble in Miss some where. You wrote than and said she went as far as Texas, than had some more trouble. I'm afraid she's having more trouble than she expected. Lets hope she has made it, far before this time, safely.

Since Dec.-1 I have received from you seventeen letters. Go and ask me how I know now. Simple Arithmatic. One and one makes two and so on. I enjoy keeping them. I read them over and over. I guess that sounds pretty silly. To me it isn't silly because its the only way I know how to speak with you.

I still haven't received your package. I wouldn't worry about it if I were you. It will probably find me some day. I hope you received mine by this time. I don't hope you tried to put on those ear rings. I'd laugh at you if you even wore any. I can't picture you wearing ear rings. I dont want to either. You are beautiful as you are. You don't need any cheap, [illegible], Let me try that word again, jewelery, to improve your looks. Besides I don't want too many people looking at you. I should have reserved that privilage.

I told you about the day I bought that bracelet any while I was getting that my buddy somehow slipped away and got tatooed. I told him before I left, I was going to keep him from it. I never thought he'd do it. The poor fellow when he gets back to the states he'll realize the mistake he made. He thought he was pretty tough to get one. When people begin to laugh at him and stand around and look at him like a freak. He will than realize what a worm he was. He has to learn like I had to learn. There wasn't any one to prevent me from getting mine. I wish now there would have been. I purposely removed my shirt that day on the beach so that you could see them. I didn't want to be told later that you didn't know about them. I am ashamed of them. You won't see any more decorations on me.

How is that red head mom of yours. I bet she is as different as day and night from Iris. I can't make my self believe all red heads are the same. Your mother did a fairly good job of bringing you up. I'll have to congradalate her the next time we get in a conversation. I'm a little doubt ful wheather I was brought up correctly. That remains to be seen.

I'll have to close now. No one but I can read these letters. So if your not to successful, don't let it worry you. Throw them away and hope the next may be better.

Aways Loving You.
Paul

[Mailed with letter above:]

Jan. 14, 1945
8: P.M.

Dear Evelyn:—

To day is Sunday. One wouldn't know it if they were around this place. It was treated as any other day. I went to church this after noon at about 4:30 and missed chow because of it. It was worth while. I don't regret it one bit. I wish you could have heard the talk he gave. It was only about five minutes long he said plenty within that time. The topic was something on this order. What good is your soul if you gained the whole world. In some way he brought women into the subject and I'm sure most of the fellows absorbed what he tried to bring out. Perhaps you have noticed that sermons being preached to service men are on a different bases as those taught to civilians. Even more so here, than in Pensacola. Perhaps that is due to the absence of women. We sing quite a few songs. More than usual.

I think I'll have to write to my mom yet tonight. I haven't answered her letter yet. I received it on the 11ᵗʰ. She will probably think I have lost my self in the Pacific some where.

I read a fairly good western story. It took me all day. It was only a short story. My eyes blur out on me once in a while. I just had to sit and look in to space a few minutes before they came back to normal. I guess I'm not used to it.

It did my heart good to receive those pictures. It doesn't satisfy my selfishness though. I'll be expecting the others very soon. You have no right to feel as if those pictures ought to be hit. I can asure you that they won't. They were but few, I have ever seen you smile on. I was also happy to see you still had your long hair. I can't picture you haveing them cut. They do belong to you. Just as much as fingers belong on my hand. I would hate to see them cut.

I had a letter from my sister today. She seems very happy. I hope she remains that way. She says they have quite a bit of fun sleigh riding. Makes me sort of home sick.

Haven't heard from Mamie Lou for quite some time now. She does write an interesting letter. I'm glad she wasn't to angry. She did say she wouldn't forgive me unless I returned the pictures. She'll have to stay that way till I return I'm afraid. Lets hope not.

I'll close now and answer the rest of the mail I received. I still have to answer my Grand father and my Brother in N.C. Than if I have time I'll answer Paulines.

> Always Loving You
> Paul.
> Cpl Paul J. Fogel
> H&S Co. 23rd. Mars.
> c/o F.P.O. S.F. Cal.

Postmarked Jan 28 1945 from Cpl. Paul J. Fogel 435156, H & S. Co. 23 Mars. 4 Div., c/o. F.P.O. San Francisco, Cal. to Miss. Evelyn Wells. S.N., 1101 E. Gadsden, St., Pensacola, Florida. (stamped "PASSED BY NAVAL CENSOR" with initials; with 6 cents air mail stamp)

On plain, unlined stationery:

Jan 16-1945

Dear Evelyn.

Sorry old girl. Was sort of occupied these past few days. Wasn't anywhere near writting paper. That excuse will have to do for the time being. By this time you can imagine Im better at making excuses than any thing else. I'll have to break my self of that habbit. If there was any way I could tell you the real reason for it I would. Right now I belong to a groupe of fighting men and not to a groupe of 4F. The kind that were in Pensacola.

I'm hoping I get a letter from you today. I haven't received mail for nearly a week. I miss your letters terrably and you worse yet. Absence makes the heart grow lonely. It's doing a good job in holding true in my case.

I'll close this letter and wait till the mail comes in. Well my assumption was correct and I did receive not one but two letters from you. I was especially interested in finding out wheather Elizabeth arrived in California safely. I sorry to hear she didn't. Perhaps the next letter will be of more injoyable news.

You did receive my handerchiefs eh. That's a good thing. I'm afraid your Christmas presents are a wee bit late for this Christmas. Don't be dis-apointed for I shall get them before next.

[This letter had no sign-off at the end.]

Postmarked Jan 21 1945 from Cpl. Paul J. Fogel 435156, H & S. Co. 23 Mars. 4 Div., c/o. F.P.O. San, Francisco, Cal. to Miss Evelyn Wells. S.N., 1101 E. Gadsden, St., Pensacola, Florida. (stamped "PASSED BY NAVAL CENSOR" with initials; with 6 cents air mail stamp)

On plain, unlined stationery:

Jan. 17-1945
12 Noon

Dear Evelyn:—

Every body but you, has asked me the meaning of H. & S. I took it for granted you knew but just in case you may be interested it stands for, and you may quote me, "Headquarters and Service." There are quite a few branches to it, but the Quartermaster Department is of the most importance.

I received two letters this morning that were a wee bit late in arriving. One was post marked the 6th of Dec and the other the 11th. They were both Christmas greetings so I wasn't too disturbed about it. One person I never even heard off and the other came from my Aunt.

I'm waiting for chow call to sound off. In the mean time a few fellows across from me are argueing about some simple card game. It looks to me as if they will be at each other and pulling hair in a few more minutes. That ought to be some fun to watch.

I certainly met a great number of people since I left Pensacola. Most of which I can't understand. Some are selfish, foolish, afraid to talk advise, big mouths, and most of them think they know every thing about every thing. Than too you will find some swell people to be around. I guess you will find that to be true in any large organization. Some times its fun to just sit and listen, not saying a word.

Right now I'm sweating like a hog. It's not a comfortable feeling I assure you. I can just about stand my stink. After I finish this letter I think I shall indulge in taking some of the scum off. It's a good thing I'm not the only one in this fix.

We may have liberty again tomorrow. I hope you. I'd do practically any thing to get out of this rut I seem to be in. The last time I was on liberty my buddy and my self spend one whole after noon playing pool. I hadn't played since I let Pensacola. It was sort of fun. Than we proceeded to buy a decent meal. They had fairly good meals. Slightly better than the Navy puts out. I doubt if they are as bothered was [illegible] rationing here as you people are. It doesn't apear to me they are missing very much.

Have you been home lately? Still haven't received Mamie Lou's letter. It ought to be quite interesting. Hope by this time Elizabeth has reached her distanation. This is all for now. Give my regards to your parents.

Keep Smilling
Always Loving You.
Paul.

Postmarked Jan 21 1945 from Cpl. Paul J. Fogel 435156, H & S. Co. 23 Mars. 4 Div., c/o. F.P.O. San Francisco, Cal to Miss. Evelyn Wells S.N., 1101 E. Gadsden, St., Pensacola, Florida (stamped "PASSED BY NAVAL CENSOR" with initials; with 6 cents air mail stamp)
On plain, unlined stationery:

Jan: 18-1945
6 P.M.

Dear Evelyn:—

This is another one of those days I should have stayed in bed. I would have been feeling better if I had. This morning we were doing a few odds and ends and I had to step on the side of my foot. Right now the old ankle is swollen up like an orange. I probably told you my ankles were weak once or twice before. I didn't have any trouble with them for nearly two years now and today the tide turns against me. It isn't too bad. Just enough to iratate me.

I had liberty today but decided to stay in. I could not have spend a great deal of time on liberty any way. I'm sure I wasn't missing any thing.

A pecular thing happened to me. I was reading a book all by my lonesome in some ceculaded spot when I hear some one speaking Pennsylvania German. I listened to them for some time, then thinking he may live near me I asked him from what parts of the state he was from. He came from Montana. You could have blown me over with a feather.

Jan 19. 1945

I purposely am finishing this letter today because I had a feeling I might receive a letter from you today. I did and I can ashure you I'm by far the happiest man in the world today. I received four of your letters today and have set out to answer them.

I bet you well be surprised to hear this. I received one from your Mother, brother Frank, Mamie Lou, and my mother. Than you toped it off. I read yours first and am answering them first. I had to laugh at Mamie Lou's letter she said she likes to write small notes. That letter must have contained at least four pages. I hope she continues to write small notes to me if it is but once a month. I'd rather read your letters and I would any one elses. I believe I'm more concerned about what you do, than I am about this war. Some one has been talking too much again. Your brother Frank tells me that he has heard quite alot about me and thats not good. I know I'll be looking forward for letters from your mother. I wish you could have read the one she send me. I'll always remember it. The meaning that was in it really stuck to the strings of my heart. Perhaps she wouldn't want me to tell you so I'll not inde-ver to. I'll have to answer that letter in the very near future. Frank thinks he might meet me on the way home but I doubt it very much now. He mentioned some thing to that effect.

My mother says they are have some sort of snow storm up north. lets hope they keep it in controll. I know what they are like.

I still received a few Christmas cards. Better late than never. One from some one at home. I never even heard. I'm just wondering how they received my address. Its a freak of nature to me or perhaps I'm becomming absent minded.

Good old Kelly I knew I could depend upon her to keep tabs on you. Shes a realiable woman if I ever knew one. I'll have to appoint her as my special blood hound.

That relative of yours sure told me alot of interesting things about you. O, just to think of what I didn't know about you. My My. Ha. I don't believe any one could tell me any thing about you I don't already know so have no fear. I like suprises so if you have any after we're married you may pull them on me one at a time.

Tell Bennett not to worry about the bed siduation. I have it all figured out. It will have to be double deckers. I'd never feel comfortable any other way. I'm so happy Elizabeth arrived in California safely. Lets hope she injoyes her stay.

It must have been quite ordeal to go though. I know I would not have liked to make the trip. Even with some one with me. It certainly is a realief to know she is with J.C. again. I'm hoping he will never have to come over here.

I never expect Bennett would want to get in the Nurse Corps too. If you can talk her out of it I wish you would. I'm sure she would like it, but I'm also sure she would never be happy after this war is over. I'm foolish to predict some thing like that I know. I knew a little about it though and there is a chance I'm right. I hope she's not trying to convince you to do the same. I'll have to close now. I wish I were with you next month to celebrate that anniversary of ours.

I love you very much. Hope you'll over look my writting. I know its the poorest written.

Always Loving You.
Paul.

Postmarked Jan 23 1945 from Cpl. Paul J. Fogel 435156, H & S. Co. 23 Mars 4 Div., c/o. F.P.O. San Francisco, Cal to Miss. Evelyn Wells S.N., 1101 E. Gadsden, St., Pensacola, Florida. (stamped "PASSED BY NAVAL CENSOR" with initials; with 6 cents air mail stamp)

On plain, unlined stationery:

Jan: 20-1944

Hello Honey:—

How are you? Me? Not the least bit refreshed. Right now I feel like you must feel when you just come off duty. A little sleep wouldn't do me one bit of harm.

O by the way you let Mammie do what she pleases. If you think you can convince her not to send me anymore pictures. Your mistaken by a long shot. I didn't like that crack you made about "teen" age, and besides I think you didn't change too much. You need not be ashamed of them. I never get tired of looking at pictures of you so the more the marier.

I answered Mammie's letter today. I hope she won't be too disapointed in me. I also had a letter from Elizabeth. She told me she had to get

J.C.'s permission to write me. I'm glad he let her have it. He's a good man letting me correspond with his women this way. I thought he would be angry at me for taking you away from him. I'm so glad he had no objections that amounted to any thing.

I have quite a bit of time for writting and reading these days. I'm reading a book by the name of "A Tree Grows in Brooklin" Its quite lengthy and doesn't hide the facts of nature. It's very true to life. After reading a few sentences I was ashamed to admit that could remember my self doing the same things. It's all about how poor people try to sirvive in New York. We Fogel's arn't exactly rich rich. In fact we are far from it. I hope you knew that when you said "yes." We always do manage to make a living though.

Polly also wrote me a letter yesterday. It had me puzzled for a second. She signed it "Sis." It didn't look like her writting or June's all until the last sentence. All though the letter she was talking about one thing and another and then she mentioned some thing about Earl. This will have to be all for now. I'll have to write a buddy in M'd. now. Haven't written him in quite some time.

See you tomorrow.

Always Loving You.
Paul.

Postmarked Jan 22 1945 from Mrs. Leidy C. Fogel., Nazareth. Pa., Route 1. to Miss. Evelyn Wells. S.N., 1101 E. Gadsden St., Pensacola., Florida.

On plain, unlined stationery:

Sunday afternoon 1/21/45.

Dear Evelyn:

Dad and I are hugging the stove as it is very cold here in Penna just now. We were snow bound for almost a week, but the country roads are open once more for traveling. We did not have mail for 4 days then some neighbors close to the highway got it there and came through fields to deliver it. I was very anxious to hear and get news from our boys. Paul wrote two letters but onely very few words as he says his letters and writeing are limited, but we very glad to get the few lines he writes. He has as yet not received his Christmas package. I onely hope and pray he gets it. He says its still very cold and he could use more cloathing.

Yesterday my heart was almost broken. Two of Roy's Christmas packages came back marked "<u>unknown</u>." We are writeing every week but none of his letters came back yet. Dad & I are very lonely and are thinking and praying for our boys and every body else's boys in the service. We both hope it will not be to long before we can all be together again. We believe Paul is in Leyete as its always cold there. Polly & Earl are out sleighriding with the youngsters in the neighbor hood. its grand. I wish you could be with them. I know you would enjoy it. Our two grand children just love to be outside all the time.

We are in the best of health and hopes this letter finds you the same. All our love and best wishes to you.

Paul's Mother & Dad.

Postmarked Jan 26 1945 from Cpl. Paul J. Fogel 435156, H & S. Co. 23 Mars. 4 Div., c/o. F.P.O. San Francisco, Cal. to Miss. Evelyn Wells S.N., 1101 E. Gadsden, St., Pensacola, Florida. (stamped "PASSED BY NAVAL CENSOR" with initials; with 6 cents air mail stamp)
On plain, unlined stationery:

Jan. 22-1945

Dear Snooky:

Olo,—Ho. So you are again interfering in my corespondance with other women eh. Well, well, well. I'll have to look into this. I disaprove of it whole heartally. I haven't written Elizabeth an answer to her letter yet but when I do, Look out. The results might be faital.

By the way if I don't find your letters boresome why should my mother? Now don't go and get flusterated, or some thing. I haven't let any one read my letters "<u>yet</u>," but if something doesn't happen about you reading other peoples letters. Ahem, that is all together different. To talk seriously, which is hard for me to do. My mother never reads any of my letters from you because I preserve that privilage to my self, and no one shares it. Why should they? It's none of there business.

What we did in Panama City concerns only you and I. Let's not let it go any futher. I am highly satified with the results and love for just what I expected you to be. You have a good name. You can hold your head high with the best of people. Some of those nurses at Pensacola Hospital can't. Not trying to down the nurse corps of course. There are always some decayed apples among a bushel. It holds true in any case. Lets forget about it. My concern is at the moment trying not to lose you. That thought that fortune teller told you about two husbands. The first one might be purely imagineary. I hope not. Time will tell.

It looks like you will have to celebrate our anniverity by your self. I hope you don't go out and get drunk as would be the custom of a man. I couldn't get drunk any way and if I had the chance I wouldn't. You can readilly see what a poor sport I am. I'd much rather be with you to spend it. Maybe next year we will be able to spend it together.

I had another letter from Sheldon my brother today. This letter seems more cheerful now that he knows he can't talk me out of comming over sea's. He still insists in wanting you to write him. I send him your address and warned him not to get to serious about you if he want to write you. Maybe he'll never write to me again Ha. He's a good fellow as much as I ever knew him I can't remember much about him other than I aways sat on the bench in back of the table beside of him. When we seven kids were all home to gether and still going to school. Don't tell him that though. I was pretty small at that time. He is the third in the family from the top. You will have to meet them all some day. We are a bunch of happy people some times

Always Loving You
Paul

Jan. 23-1945

Dear Evelyn:—

To me it sounds as if I'll have to murder me a white man, especially if they try to draft my nurse into the Army. I knew I should have never left you in the states. I should have put you in my sea bag and brought you along. Come to think about it I guess I wouldn't want you over hear anyway. No this isn't the place for a woman, besides that I wouldn't trust you for one second around these fellows. You tell Pitts I'd rather see her in the states and if she has any brains at all she'll stay there.

O, ho, so you have been out kissing girls again. I had you fooled that time. Yes I guess no one knows better than I how I caught all the colds I did. They must have been from you. I can't think of any one else I caught them from. Ha. They might have come from the times we sat out in the park on that cold cement. It was never really cold, so that isn't a good excuse.

Last night I should have gone to bed early. The only thing that stoped me was that I just had to see a picture over again that I saw in Pensacola. I always say the second show is always better than the first, you know me. Paul [illegible] and played in it. I forgot the name of it.

Its getting a wee bit chilly out side to night for some reason. It looks as if I'll have to put a swetter or some thing.

Schotch tape is a little hard to get. I managed to get some today. Don't ask me what I wanted that for. Ill tell you. I put all your pictures on a card board and placed them over my sack so

I could see you every time I pass by. I had to cut a few of them down. It made them much nicer. More of you to look at when not all the senery is present. For instance that picture of you and I together. I had to cut me off. I found out that you are much prettier with out me so I threw me away. I'm not much good any way. I ought to have a few more to fill the card board up. You know the corners. Do you think I could talk you out of another. I'll have to go to bed before the lights go out. Good night. I love you.

Always Loving You
Paul.

Postmarked Jan 28 1945 from Cpl. Paul J. Fogel 435156, H & S Co. 23 Mars. 4 Div., c/o. F.P.O. San Francisco, Cal. to Miss. Evelyn Wells. S.N., 1101 E. Gadsden, St., Pensacola, Florida. (stamped "PASSED BY NAVAL CENSOR" with initials; with 6 cents air mail stamp)
On plain, unlined stationery:

Jan 26-1945

Good morning Miss Nightingale:—

A very beautiful flowering morning. I'm hoping the day stays this way. What are you trying to do drive me crazy. Haven't heard from you for four days now. Each time mail call sounded I received mail from every one but you. I was beginning to believe some one was playing tricks on me. I know its not your fault. I had to blame it on some one though. The trouble with me is I think of you too much. It seems to me the only reason days pass is to live from mail call to mail call. Then to be disapointed by not receiving the letter you were waiting for...

I haven't received your package yet. Are you sure it was a Christmas package. O I see, you wanted it for 46 (Paul means 1946). Well thats OK too. It has a good start now.

I was swimming yesterday for the first time since I left Pensacola. I haven't forgotten how. It was fun, the time time it lasted. It did'nt last long enough.

I had a letter from my mom today. She said she is snowed in. What fun she must be having. I wish we could be there to injoy it. Can you imagine snow being five ft. high. It's not very hard too. I saw when it was higher than that. When it gets that deap. You walk on top of the snow. Some times you fall through and dig your self out.

I wish I could be in church the day you receive your diploma. I'd really like to see that. I'll never forget when I and Sinclair went to see Smitty graduate. Smitty was so full of smiles, she was beaming all over. You will be the same way. I know. Let me be the first to congradulate you. I hope Im the first. Am I? I like to tell people you aren't any ordanery woman. You are my lovely little nurse. Im a lucky fellow.

I'll close now and write you tonight. I might have a letter from you then. I'll always love you.

Paul

Postmarked Feb 6 1945 from Cpl. Paul J. Fogel 435156, H & S. Co. 23 Mars. 4 Div., c/o. F.P.O. San Francisco, Cal. to Miss. Evelyn Wells S.N., 1101 E. Gadsden, St., Pensacola, Florida. (stamped

"PASSED BY NAVAL CENSOR" with initials; with 6 cents air mail stamp)

On plain, unlined stationery:

Jan. 30-1945

Dear Evelyn:—

Well, my boy Val decided that his woman would have to change her religion to his. I sort of agree with him. Of course I'm not the one to say. I'm sort of glad we don't have that dispute to settle between us. In as much as I'm a Lutheran. I think just as much of you being a Baptist as I do of my self and more so. We both have one thing in common. We are both Protestant. In this Marine Corps we haven't got any special demonations as we would have if we were civilians.

It must have quite windy last night. This ship was rocking like a top. Its a wonder I wasn't rolled out of my sack. Quite a fall. Four deckers high. How would you like to get in a [illegible] sack ten feet off the deck. It takes some sort of skill. I mange to do it once a day.

How is Kelly? She ought to be feeling like a new woman now. I hope so. She has had enough rest for both of us. I hope she is still keeping an eye on you. ha. My secred agent you know.

This is pretty monotous, receiving no letters. I'm afraid you feel the same way by this time. I'm wishing I could be with you. I miss you terriably. I'm ashamed of this writting. It's the best I can do. It does prove my igorance.

Jan. 31–1945

Dear Snooks:—

There is going to be a busy day comming up so I'll have to write this letter early. You can already see I must have got out of bed on the wrong side. I'm writting all over the page.

I have picture I had made when I was still at my last camp. I though perhaps you would like to have a squint at it. You see I'm not half as had to get along with as you think. That is the one and only and that will be the last one until you become Mrs. Fogel.

Were you home lately. How is your Mother and Dad. I'm anxious to get some mail. I can hardly wait to get mail from you. There ought to be quite a few waiting for me. I hope so.

Do you still see Nellie around? Or did she leave for the Corps already. Give her my regards and tell her I wish her lots of luck if you still see her, She will sure need it.

Had a Valentine from Mamie Lou before I left. It was very thoughtful of her. Don't you think. She is very nice. She understands me like a book and thats bad. This is all for now.

Love and Kisses,
Paul

Postmarked Feb 5 1945 from Cpl. Paul J. Fogel 435156, H & S. Co. 23 Mars. 4 Div., c/o F.P.O. San Francisco, Cal. to Miss Evelyn Wells S.N., 1101 E. Gadsden, St., Pensacola, Florida. (stamped "PASSED BY NAVAL CENSOR" with initials; with 6 cents air mail stamp)

On plain, unlined stationery:

[Date torn off of next three letters which were mailed together.]

Dear Evelyn,

At last I'm able to tell you more about what I'm doing. I'm aboard ship and am on my way to combat. I've been aboard ship for quite a while now as you no doubt could have guessed. You will have been wondering where my letters are. When you receive this one you will know. I'm beginning to get used to this Navy life. It doesn't affect me as it did once before. Its a lucky thing for me. That is a terriable experience. One that you will have to try to avoid. They say you only get sea sick once in a life time. I know for a fact that is an untruth.

I was to church again this morning. I'm becoming quite a church goer. I haven't got much of any thing else to do. It's a good way to spend your time. It's better than laying in your sack at least. The chaplin has quite a schedual worked out. Thuesdays and Thusday, are donated to Bible Study. Every morning at 8:15 Prayer Meetings and Sundays 1 hour of church.

I do quite a bit of card playing and reading. I must have read every book in this place, not that I've learned any thing from them.

Good morning Chick:

I'm glad you arn't with me now. I'm so hot I'm about to burn up. This is the stuffiest room I've ever been in. I just about smothered last night. I wouldn't have felt worse and I would have stood guard twelve hours. Complaining is the only way I can spend my time. I hope you don't mind listening to it. There hasn't been a letter I've ever written you I haven't complained about some thing. This one is no exception.

The wheather is quite different that it was at my last station. The sun shines through the clouds here once in a while. Back there it always rained.

My mom doesn't have to know I'm going into action if you don't tell her. I I rather keep it from her till I get back from the first one. I'd rather you kept it too your self. Perhaps by the time you get these letters I'll be on my way back. I'm hoping so any way.

We don't hear much about the outside but the last report sounded very good. The Germans seem to be folding up. Maybe thats means we will be able to get home sooner. I'm waiting for the day.

I was just thinking. The past few months I thought if I'd ever reach California. I'd be just about home. If I reach the middle of the Pacific I'll feel lucky now.

I was put in charge of a working party today to clean this joint up. Did a pretty good job of it. If I do say so my self.

I was just in a discussion with these Polocks here. They are in an argument about the Catholic religion. They are both Catholics. Each of them have different opinions. This buddy of mine is a Russian Catholic and he's marring a girl who is Roman Catholic. Each celebrate holidays on different days. One of them will have to change, he says. This other fellow thinks each should stay with his ow religion. I'll tell you tomorrow what he's going to do. Its' interesting to listen too. I think of you often. I love you very much. Keep Smilling

Love and Kisses
Paul.

Postmarked Feb 6 1945 from Cpl. Paul J. Fogel 435156, H & S. Co. 23 Mars. 4 Div., c/o. F.P.O. San Frans. Cal. to Miss. Evelyn Wells. S.N., 1101 E. Gadsden, St., Pensacola, Florida. (stamped "PASSED BY NAVAL CENSOR" with initials; with 6 cents air mail stamp)

On plain, unlined stationery:

Dear Evelyn:—

This and probably others will be late in arriving. You will know I've been thinking of you always. That is the best thought I can repeat. I try to write a few lines each day.

Gosh Im hot. I'm nearly sweating all the water I drank in the course of a day, out in one two minutes. I hope it gets cooler tonight. If it doesn't I'll probably lay awake all night.

I think I told you yesterday that I had a letter from Kupsky. What a fellow. He told me quite a few fellows were getting ratings. He also told me that Capt Grebe made Major. It's that wonderful. You remember we were talking about it the night we went visiting them. I bet Mrs Grebe is happy. Sgt Maceluck, that boss of mine whose wife was in the hospital there for a while, has been transfered to Phila. and then he was send to California. I'll probably meet him some time out here. I hope so. He was a regular fellow. He did alot for me in a small way. I'll never forget it. They had good neighbors. When ever I stoped there on business. The lady next door would throw me some fruit. She must have been in her late thirties.

Postmarked Feb 6 1945 from Cpl. Paul J. Fogel 435156, H & S. Co. 23. Mars. 4 Div., c/o. F.P.O. San Francisco, Cal. to Miss. Evelyn Wells. S.N., 1101 E. Gadsden St., Pensacola, Florida. (stamped "PASSED BY NAVAL CENSOR" with initials; with 6 cents air mail stamp)
On plain, unlined stationery:

Feb. 4–1945

Dear Evelyn:—

It certainly is hot today. It's not my imagination. The sweat is pouring off of me in pales full. Today is Sunday. Attended Church this morning and took communion. I wasn't a service one would expect in a church. It was just an informal gathering on the deck. A Short cermon was taught and as every one came from the alter they left to other parts of the ship. There must have been nearly a hundred and fifty who participated in the service.

The sun is about to set and it will get dark quickly. The sun shining against the clouds makes a beautiful picture. I can remember we used to watch it many times. There are quite a few dark clouds around. The darker they are the prettier they look. Havent seen a drop of rain in weeks. Seems strange. I ought to injoy the sun shine while I can. Quite a few of the boys received sun burns from laying on the decks all afternoon. I heard them complaining at chow tonight. Marine Corp and Navy chow doesn't vary. We can still expect chicken Sunday dinners and some sort of boloney at night for supper.

They have a very up to date hospital aboard here. I'm sure you would be right at home in it. I'm going to try to stay well until I hit the states. I'd rather have you talk to me than one of these Corp men. I'm certain you would do a better job of it any way. I'm expecting a letter from you tomorrow. I heard we might receive some mail. I hope so.

A few officers and men received medals and citations yesterday for galentry on Siapan. I'm sort of glad I wasn't in that operation. I've heard alot of the boys talking. It was no easy matter to take that island.

Ill finish this letter tomorrow when I receive a letter from you. Good Night.

Feb. 7–1945 [Paul wrote the wrong date here; from the sentence above, I believe he meant Feb. 5]

I did receive three letters from you today. I need not tell you how much I enjoyed getting them. So Pensacola is still on the map. I'm beginning to wonder if the United States hasn't changed. It seems to me I've been out of the states a terriably long time.

You mentioned you didn't know what you would do after you finished training. May I make a suggestion. Remember this is just a suggestion. You told me you liked the operating room. If you injoy that work why not do it. The truth of it is I'm afraid for you. I've read a few papers and every one has had some thing about drafting women into the Nurse Corps. I dont like it. I supose they need all they can get but I don't want them to get you. You don't know how much I mean it. I want you to be there when I get back. I don't want you to be tied down by regulations. The way I am. I want you to go where you please, when you please.

I ought to be called a heal now. I just asked my intended wife to go to work again. It would have been different if I would have been kept in the states till this June. I will be different when I return. You won't have to do any thing but cook for me. I don't care where you enter a hospital. Pensacola, Pennsylvania, Kansas, or California. I know you don't want my opinion. And I'm ashamed now for giving it. You do what you think is correct and I'll know it is the right thing. Your mother is going to miss you if you leave her right after finishing training. There is something about your mother a peson can't help but marvel at. I can't explain it. In fact I haven't yet figured it out. I haven't talked to her but once in my life and yet she can read me like a book. She talks to me as if I were her son and I like it that way. It must be her "red hair." Untill I figure it out, we will dismiss that subject. I always said two mothers are better than one.

It's mighty hot up here on deck today. There is a slight breeze though. It feels very nice. Before I knew you I went to the beach on the station. There I layed around a receive very nice sun burns while the sweat was pouring off of me. This reminds me of the very same thing. The only difference is the steel deck instead of the sand. A negro fellow has a fishing line over the side of the ship. I haven't seen him pull up any thing yet. They must not be bitting today. I promised to take you on a fishing trip on the Montezuma while I was still at Pensacola. I never did get the chance. Perhaps when I return I get the chance.

I see your lipstick is still getting in your way. I remember it got in mine a few times too. In summer it was on my kaki. In winter it was on my greens. I didn't mind the kaki but the greens I used to fuss about, didn't I? That was because the dry cleaners, nine chances out of ten would let it on when it was returned. I'd have to take them back three times before it would be removed. I didn't mind and never will. The reason I brought it up, part of your paper was smugged.

I'll have to answer Pauline's letter today and also my mothers. So I'd better close this letter, untill tomorrow then. I have received a letter from Elizabeth. That was the last I received from your family. Haven't heard from Jimmy yet. This is all for now. I love you very muchalis. Keep Smilling

> Love and Kisses.
> Paul.
> Cpl Paul J Fogel.

Postmarked Feb 14 1945 from Cpl. Paul J. Fogel 435156, H & S. Co. 23 Mars. 4 Div., c/o. F.P.O. San Frans. Cal. to Miss. Evelyn Wells., 1101 E. Gadsden, St., Pensacola, Florida. (stamped "PASSED BY NAVAL CENSOR" with initials; with 6 cents air mail stamp)

On plain, unlined stationery:

Feb. 8–1945—

Dear Evelyn:—

This is absolutely the last time this letter is going to started. Maybe I shouldn't be so discouraged. This is only my third time at it. Every evening an swab come around washing the decks down for over night. Than in the morning the same rutine goes on again. They just splashed water all over me, and have gone away feeling greatly amused. I can't say I blame them. I needed a bath.

I'm hoping these letter don't arrive to late. I know you are wondering by now where they are. It's not I that is keeping them from you. Uncle Sam seems to think its safer.

Today it rained for the first time while aboard her. Beginning to think it was a mircle, I was. It did have a good feeling to it. Nice and cool against the skin. It didn't last long. Two or three minutes, than the sun shone and I began to sweet as always.

I was listening to some Philipino talking this afternoon. We have a few aboard ship. To me they sounded like crowing roosters. Well not as bad as that perhaps.

I was reading an interesting book yesterday and before I realized it, I had my self scorched a wee bit. Nothing that kept me from loosing sleep. Maybe that is another queer thing about this Pacific. Perhaps you can't get sun burned. I don't want to find out. I'll let some one do that for me. Isn't that a wise idea?

I'll probably be able to see my Uncle on this operation. I hope so. I'm getting mighty tired of seeing strangers. There ought to be some one from the states I know here in the Pacific. I'll probably run into them all at the same time.

I was playing cards practically all afternoon. I can't see why I was sitting down there in that stuffy hole when I could have been sitting here in the air. To interested in the game I guess.

The sun will be going down soon and again darkness will set in. To day must have been

Friday. We had fish for noon chow. Not a bone in them. You will have to remember that I like boneless fish. Ha. I'll write tomorrow and put an ending to this letter. Good night how. I'll be dreaming of you.

Feb. 10 1945.

Fresh air. Nothing can compare with it. You can usually tell the mood I'm in can't you? I'm not too happy today. They had me working. Very unusual. Ha. I was again put in charge of a clean up detail. We arn't near land and where so much filth comes from is beyond me. Three large trash cans were full in my compartment alone. It's one of those unexplainable happenings.

Well well so Iris had her tonsils removed also. That is a pleasant thought. I wouldn't ravish the idea. The day you had yours taken out was a day to remember. It was a day I'll never forget. You wouldn't make it one bit easier. It was a good place to have you. Didn't give you much opportunity to talk.

I must have sounded as if some thing were choking me. The truth of it was my heart must have been in my mouth.

Pauline thinks I'm in Alaska some where. I can't see where she came to that conclusion. Here I am sweating all my energy and hoping a freeze blows my way and she thinks I'm there. I'm sure if I were I would be much more comfortable. I guess I'd be grumbling at any rate. Tomorrow I hope we received some mail again. I'm hoping so. This mail rationing is about to get me angry.

We had hot dogs again for chow. Every time we have them it reminds me of the time at

Pensacola beach. Remember the time we had to push the car, had sand [illegible] and hot dogs mixed. Besides a few other mishaps. Those were the days. Days to be remembered eh. We will have to do those things the right way some day. This is all for now Sis. I'll always be loving you.

Lots of Love
Paul

Feb 12. 1945

Dear Evelyn:—

Today was another one of those tiresome days. Isn't much of any thing to do. Lay around until its time to go to lectures or have exercises. We try to loosen our muscles every morning. I haven't felt stiffness set in so far. Am expecting it any day now.

I washed cloth again today. Bet you couldn't guess how I did it. It was my first experience in doing it. I made made my self some rope out of a few outs and ends and tied my cloth on to them. Than I hang them over the stern of the ship. Free laundry service. It didn't last long. I just about finished when an order came out to cease doing it. I was quite lucky. Our ships laundry is out of order for the time being.

It seems strange to see no rain out here. I supose it never does rain out here though. What would the ocean want with rain any way. Nature has it all figured out.

Every one seems anxious to get back from this comming operation. The majority of them will probably leave for the states. The forth Marines have been in four operations already. I can't blame them for wanting to get a rest. This is all for now How is that red headed cousin of yours progressing. What kind of work is she doing? She disapointed me I'm sorry to say. I have to lay down the rules to my red headed children. None of them or going to be quiters. I was sleeping up on deck last night. Kind of cold. It was better than sufficating in the hole. I was mighty dark. It didn't take long to fall asleep.

This ship rocks and bounds like a runaway house. Some times I wonder what keeps them from turning over. They have to tie every thing to the deck or else it would be flying all over. Most of the time I find my self with wings trying to grab for some thing.

I hope you didn't feel crowed the other night. Some how your picture worked loose and landed on top of me and I sleep on top, of it all night. I didn't squeeze you too much.

I'll have to close now. I'll write again soon. I'll always love you. Hope you knew what you were saying when you said yes to me. I'm a devil arn't I?

Love and Kisses.
Paul.

[No envelope] From J. F. Wells [Evelyn's brother, Frank] to Evelyn Wells

feb.21.19.45.

Dear Sis:

Just a note to let you hear from me I am not getting along so well now I am having trouble with my back.

175

I hope I will be able to go back to work soon I have been off duty for three weeks.

Evelyn I am glad in a way that you are a navy nurse and in another way I am sorry you are.

I am afraid you will have to come overseas I had just about as soon see you in the red light distract.

There is one thing I don't want you to do and that is to volinteer to go overseas. They don't realy need nurses over here the corpsman can do all there is to do except one thing and you know what that is. Don't let any one talk you in to going overseas. the enlisted men resent the nurses any way.

Evelyn you are a nice girl and a nice looking girl and I [*don't*—inferred] want you to be looked down on to the lowest.

Well I hope you remember this and my advise.

by With love your budd J. F. Wells

Postmarked Mar 6 1945 from Cpl. Paul J. Fogel 435156, H & S. Co. 23 Mars. 4 Div., c/o F.P.O. San Francisco, Cal. to Miss. Evelyn Wells., 1101 E. Gadsden, St., Pensacola, Florida. (stamped "PASSED BY NAVAL CENSOR" with initials; with two 6 cents air mail stamps)

On plain, unlined stationery:

Iwo Jima
March 6–1945

Dear Snuggs:—

Sorry old girl I have'nt been writting lately. There has been a reason for it. You have proba- bly read about it and also heard about it on the radio. They have given you a pretty good account of it I hear. I'm still well and happy. No need to worry. Most of the heat is over. We can still hear the buzzing of bullets over our heads at times. The Lord was with me on the nine teenth of February. If he would not have been I'm afraid the future you and I had planned together might never have been posible. It may yet be imposible I'll never give up hoping. I hope you won't either. I probably won't want to remember all this when I return. Personally I can't figure all this killing and spoil ness of this war out. I've seen things I've thought imposible. I've decided every thing is posible in war. I'll change the subject now.

I've received quite a few of your letters here on the island. You'll never know how much they have meant to me. This isn't just another line. I've never tried to string you along. This is one place you can do your confessing freely with out the least bit of hesitation. I've re read your letters so often I've just about memorized them and am continueing to do so. You were always a good listener and now I can talk to you just the same although I would enjoy have ing you answer in your own tone of voice.

I'm glad spring time is setting in. I can imagine it was plenty cold there this winter. We have a very comfortable climate around here. It is quite different from any of the other islands I've been on, in the respect that we dont have as much rain as they do. It doesn't get very cold although the first few nights on the beach I nearly froze. I didn't sleep much any way so it didn't have an effect on me. There is quite a bit of sulfer around and if you happen to bunk near a deposit of it you would probably wake up feeling dizzy.

I've had that experience a few times. The sand at some places became very hot.

I've had a letter from Kupsky the other day from Little River. Evelyn you must be slipping. I got a kick out that when you mentioned it in your letter. Remember you wrote me a few letters while I was at <u>New</u> River. I had the same trouble the first time I heard of it. Ill probably be seeing him over here shortly. I hope so. I would really like to see him again.

My Uncle is some where on this island and can't be more then two or three miles away. I can't seem to find him for love or money. I've looked from him twice. No one seems to know a thing about him. I'm hoping he will look me up now. He's my mother's youngest brother. He must be nearly forty. Has four children For the life of me I would like to know what he's doing in an out fit like this. I guess we Fogel's can't keep our nose out of things like this.

The Marine Corps has taught me one thing for certain. I must own my own home and if posible build it. Those are just a few of my plans for the future. They are a fairly large order to fulfil.

I wasn't too far from where your brother was stationed when we were on our way to this marodge of a place. We were unable to leave ship or else I probably would have met him. He must be a swell person. Of cours how could the Wells family tree be any different Ha. "Ain't I awlful." If we return to any place near him you can bet your toe nails he'll be seeing me.

Had a letter from J.C. yesterday. He seems to be happy. I sencerely hope he can stay with Elizabeth longer than he expects. He told me he is subject to be called any day. Let's hope its a long time off. He also mentioned that Elizabeth eats like a horse. I can't imagine that. Comming from J.C. though I can understand that.

Haven't heard from Mamie Lou for some-time now. She really has plenty to say when she gets time to say it. I look forward to reading her letters. She is a lot of fun Frank did a good job of picking a woman. So did I.

So you went to a formal the other night huh? Stepping out on me. I'm glad you did. I only wish I could have been with you. I wish I could have walked with you to let people know what a wonderful woman I had. You must have looked beautiful dressed in formal. You allways did. I'll never forget the night I brought my boss in to the hospital to see his wife. You were just comming out of the door. I must have been all smiles and you must have been suprised. I guess it when them I made up my mind to have you as a partner. That was about the best move I've ever made in my life.

My advise to you young woman is to go see your parents more. You'll never realize how fool-ish you are until you are in the position I'm in. You would give your right arm to see the people you love then. When you go to Pennsylvania with me, we will have to make some sort of arrange-ment to visit your parents as often as posible.

I haven't quite decided in which manner to suport my wife yet. I have plenty of time to think about it over here. I'll have enough money to start out. Perhaps you could suggest what you would want me to do, and I could fit it in with my plans and perhaps invent some thing.

That's very kind of Iris to think of me. I don't exactly know what to think about her. She puzzles me. She should have never become a red head. She disapointed me. A person can't help having a soft spot for her though. I must have been quite a pest around 1101 East Gadsden to be remembered so readily. I tried not to be but I can imagine I was. Its late for apoligies now. Tell the girls it shall not happen again.

So you have been transfered to the operation. I bet you are injoying your self. There were a few hospital ships in the harbor a few days ago. If you would have been on there I'm sure you would not have injoyed it quite as well. None were ill from normal causes if you know what I mean. I hope I shall never have the chance to be put on one. They certainly looked beautiful standing out among all the other ships in the convoy. They were painted all white. Stood out like sore thumbs.

So Nellie has received her physical and left Pensacola. I'm wondering where she will be headed for next. She will probably get to see part of this ugly world too. Lets hope she enjoys it more than I. Personally I'd rather be back in the U.S. Of course that again is just my opinion.

If Bennett hasn't left yet. Wish her all the luck posible for me. I'm sure she deserves all she can receive. I used to get tickled watching her. She just about came to your shoulders. Same with Pitts.

You and Pauline were the first persons I received letters from on this island. Pauline seems a wee bit worried because she send a packet to me and put N.Y.N.Y. on it and was afraid it might have gotten lost. I won't need it here any way so it didn't make too much difference to me.

I can remember last year at this time I was also writting you. That was because you had gone to Chattahoochee. I was also a sad case then as I am now. Im hoping the next year this time will become a wee bit more happier for me.

So you are becomming an Aunt, again. I can't believe that you can feel your age creeping up on you. That would never do. I feel as young as a chicken with phummonia. Ha. I'm ashamed to admit it. I can just picture Jimmy now. He will be a proud father. I can't blame him. As for David he is building him self quite a family. Proud of himself too I bet. More power to him. I'll be an uncle to all his children too so I shall share with you feel age creeping up.

O ho!!! So Elizabeth is cheating on me huh. Well I'm glad to know that. I can see right now where Ill have to do all my corresponding is J.C. personally. This has gone to far. I should think I write you enough letters. with out having to read your sisters too. I'll have to write her a fancy let-ter sometime soon. Give her a piece of my mind. That was a very bad habit you developed. "Very bad." I like Elizabeth alot. She can't keep any thing too her self. I don't remember now if I put any thing of importance in her letter or not. It really doesn't make any difference. I don't believe there was any thing in it you already knew.

You wrote some thing in your one letter that I'll never forget as long as I live. You told me to take care of myself now and when I return you would take care of me. I'm still laughing. That sounds funny to me. I might even hold you too it. Arn't I mean. I'm also hoping you won't have to wait a number of years for me. This was a good step when we landed here lets hope it will shorten the years of this war.

I would not have mentioned losing sleep over a certain little Marine. Perhaps some day you may have too. The joke would be on you then. One you could not laugh at.

I'm sure I couldn't feel any different toward taking you home than I would at going home my self. I'm sure every one there knows you and I'm sure they like you as much as I do. Well!!! no I wouldn't say that. That would be rather hard for them to do. When they do meet you in person I'm sure they will agree with me, that you are one in a million.

If I have been "swiping" your thoughts so often. All I can say is that it serves you right. You have just about disabled me as a Marine. Thats bad for the Corps you know. They will soon have me doing close order drill soon to quicken my senses. If there was any thing I hate it was that.

How is Earnestine and her off spring. Still kicking high steps eh. You are mighty greedy not sending me any of that candy she made. Truthfully speaking we have plenty of candy and we are usually kept from getting a sweet tongue.

O yes I meant to tell you in a few preceding letters that any thing I've ever given you do [*not*— inferred] hesitate to make use of. My Parker 51 is yours now. You do what ever you like with it. I would advise that you use only Parker 51 ink in it. It was especially made for the pen in fact not only the pen every thing I've ever given you is now yours. Do what you think ought to be done with it. Throw away what you dont want of it.

I'm glad the radio is comming in handy I thought it would.

I'm going to be looking for more pictures of you in the future. It keeps me up to date with you. I stuck one of them in my helmet D day so if all the rest of my gear was lost I'd still have you to look at. You are all I want any way.

I'm put on a gas dump here. Part of my job is to keep vickles gased up. The first few days we worked practically all night. It isn't quite that bad now. I'll start writting regular after I get back aboard ship again. That won't be too long. This will be all for now. I'll always be loving.

Love and Kisses.
Paul.

Paul's letter, March 6, 1945, Iwo Jima

184

Postmarked Mar 8 1945 from Mrs Leidy C. Fogel., Nazareth. Pa., Route 1. to Miss. Evelyn Wells. S.N., 1101 E. Gadsden St., Pensacola, Florida.

On plain, unlined stationery:

Nazareth. Pa Route 1.
Mar. 7. 1945.

Dear Evelyn:

I just finished a letter to Paul so now I am writeing you. I guess you must be thinking I forgot all about you. but no I always think of you, but am slow in writeing because I was waiting for Paul to write. Well I finally got two letters from him last week after waiting four weeks. I was almost frantic because of what the papers & radio said what the third <u>fourth</u> and fifth divisions were doing on "Iwo" and you know Paul is in the 4th Division.

He tells me in his letters he is well and on board ship and that he has not seen land for over four weeks. He also says he receives your letters and is very happy but did not receive his Christmas packages. This really was a long and hard winter for every body includeing our service men. I only hope and pray they will soon be back. I had a letter from Paul's brother Sheldon and he writes he is very tired and working day & nite. Roy & Charles his other brothers do not find time to write very often either. Hope my letter will find you in the best of health. Dad Fogel was sick with a cold but is back at work again. We are both in good health. Polly & Earl are well too. I will try and not make you wait so long for your next letter.

Sincerely Mother Fogel.

Postmarked Mar 10 1945 from Cpl. Paul J. Fogel 435156, H & S. Co. 23 Mars. 4 Div., c/o. F.P.O. San. Francisco, Cal. to Miss. Evelyn Wells., 1101 E. Gadsden, St., Pensacola, Florida. (stamped "PASSED BY NAVAL CENSOR" with initials; with 6 cents air mail stamp)
On plain, unlined stationery:

March–8–1945
Iwo Jima

Dear Evelyn:—

I start this letter now and put the end on it later I'm expecting a letter from you to day. You would better not disapoint me. [Illegible] you too don't know where I was or I should say still am. I'm quite a few miles from the Philippines as you already know by now and in the heat of battle a little wave perhaps. It is slowly becomming civilized around here and one becomes less insufficient each day. You would probable laugh if you saw my housing quarters. It isn't exactly a palace but it keeps the rain out. Im dug in on a side of the first air strip you probably heard so much about the twenty ethy of February. I built up sand bags all around and it looks some what coosey. The only thing wrong when it rains my feet get wet. Who am I to grummble about that. The first few nights I was under the stars when there were any. I'll be glad to get off of here, but fast. There is still too much sniping to suit me.

We have all had narrow escapes and Im sure the who division feels as I do.

A good shower would feel like a Christmas present to me now. I'm glad you don't have to look at me now. I'm enough to turn a person's stomach. I don't believe I have lost any weight.

I found out about my uncle. I was scared stiff that he would be on here. I located his out fit and they claim he was left back with the rear troops. They said they were the only ones of his out fit left and that he was in the hospital for some sort of trouble. Some thing to do with the stomach. It started to rain a little as you no doubt have noticed.

My lips have been so japed I could hardly eat. They have begun to heal now. My lower lip was split in half. I had some G.I. lipstick. I finally finished the tube so I'll have to do with out.

Mail Call—no mail. Slipping arn't you. You better get busy. I guess I'm expecting too much. You write when ever you get the time I'll be well satisfied.

I doubt wheather I have told you this or not but the first letter your mother wrote me had a statement to this effect in it. I had never heard it before in my life "If you believe in the Lord with all your heart. All the bullets in the world would land about you and you would never be touched." I guess I thought more of what she had said all D day and all that night than I did of any thing else. I really did some fast thinking. Every thing rushed to my mind at one time. This will be all for today hon. Goodnight Snuggs!

Always Loving You.
Paul

Postmarked Mar 14 1945 from Cpl. Paul J. Fogel 435156, H & S. Co. 23. Mars. 4 Div., c/o. F.P.O. San Frans. Cal to Miss. Evelyn Wells, 1101 E. Gadsden St., Pensacola, Florida. (stamped "PASSED BY NAVAL CENSOR" with initials; with 6 cents air mail stamp)
On plain, unlined stationery:

March–11–1945
Iwo Jima

Dear Evelyn:—

I was in hopes of hearing from you today. No letter so I'll just pretend I heard from you. I just finished rereading some of the old letters you wrote though January and February. I find it good pass time. Your letters are always so interesting. Good thing I saved them. You always commend on your poor hand writting. I haven't had any trouble reading your letters yet. I don't ever expect too. You write as well as my mother. That was a compliment! I think alot of my mothers hand writting. If I should ever reach her peak, I would consider my self a ledgiable letter writter.

I don't know wheather you read Mamie Lou's letter while you were with her, the one she send me, she mentioned that she was scared that I might be on Iwo Jima. I got a big kick out of that. It made me laugh untill I heard bullets whistling over my head, than the smill droped from my face.

It almost looks as if it might rain tonight so I might as well sign off for now and prepare for the worse. We could do with some for it has been terriably dusty these past few days. I write tomorrow and finish this letter. Good night Cookie I'll be thinking of you.

March–12th

Hello again:—

This is P.J.F. trying to disturb you! A few fellows just came back from salvaging. They found a few beautiful Jap flags and some other Jap gear. I don't wish to go out for such sport. Risking one's life for such things so near the end of this operation, isn't using one's head. What is your opinion? I'm sure you will agree with me. I'm hoping we leave here mighty soon for I am already tired of this place. I'd have two letters from you today. I was beginning to wonder where they were. I'm terriably sefish. Arn't I? I do miss your letters so bad when I have to wait a week for them.

I also wish I could be there in Pensacola with you. I hope some day to wake up and find out this has all just been a dream. You would better not wait on me to be Instructor in cooking and mopping decks. I may know a little about it but not enough to satify my self especially in cooking. We have had alot of training here on the island but that was only basic. You know add water and heat!!! Than if you can't smell it because of a cold you have. You can attempt to eat it. No it isn't that bad. I have a tendency to build a story up too much. I would better controle my imagination. At least some of it.

Gosh that's right. I'm due for congradulations. I'm one year older today. Don't fell a day over thirty. O no I'm not losing my teeth yet. Give me a little more time. Still no bags under my eyes either.

I'll have to find time one of these peaceful nights to write your mother and Elizabeth. I'm not atall sure I should write Elizabeth. She may let someone read her mail. What do you think??? I know what you are thinking. I can just hear you saying, "Whats wrong with that." Nothing, I guess I should never put in letters what I would not have any one else heard.

I really dont know what I'd do if it were not for you, I'd probably walk into something with my [*eyes*—inferred] close. When ever I'm about to do some thing foolish, you come into the picture and some tells me you would never do it, so I turn my back on it and walk away. You are with me though out the day. You probably don't realize it. Some thing keeps telling me theres a cute little nurse waiting for me in the states and I keeping wanting to return to her. This war wont end to soon for me.

I've found some thing for you on this island. I though it "kinda" cute. It is some silk from a parashute. Perhaps you can make your self some pantie out of it. Ideal meterial. This is all for now hon. See you in that dream tonight. Can't see how I could get myself to love anyone while on this place. Always remember I'll always Love you.

Huggs and Kisses
Paul.

Postmarked Mar 15 1945 from Cpl. Paul J. Fogel 435156, H & S. Co. 23 Mars 4 Div., c/o. F.P.O. San Frans, Cal. to Miss Evelyn Wells., 1101 E. Gadsden, St., Pensacola, Florida. (stamped "PASSED BY NAVAL CENSOR" with initials; with 6 cents air mail stamp)

On plain, unlined stationery:

Iwo Jima.
March 14–45

Good morning Snuggs:—

Beautiful little breeze blowing this morning. Comfortable enough to go swimming I'd
say. I could do with a good swim. Get some of
this grime off of me. I'll soon need some steel
wool to take the crust of dirt off. I try to take a
bath every day or as near a possible. It doesn't
do much good though. It does make you feel
clean for at least thirty minutes. I should have
become a doctor. I'd know what it means to
keep clean.

I hope you injoyed that week end you mentioned. Bet you went home. How far wrong am
I. I can imagine what I would have done if I had
that week end even in Pensacola. I would have
probably went over the hill and persuaded you to
do the same.

Those three buddies of mine are still with
me. Two of them don't get along with each other.
Right now I expect they would rather fight than
look at each other. Its a hard job at times to keep
neutral. It's an easy thing to take sides. They
arn't in the same vacinity as I so don't get to see
them too often. I have been shareing a [illegible]
with another fellow. We get along Ok too. We
sit up lots of nights and talk about what we left
back in the states. He was married and had a
child. Now he devorced, and is sorry for it. He
is always talking about his ex wife. He still loves

191

her alot. They will probably get together again some day. He drinks sort of often and that was the principal, or part of the reason for the seperation. He is quite a bit older than I. I'm trying hard not to let him put ideas in my head about married life. I'd like to find out myself. I might find it to be a very interesting subject, especially with you.

Haven't heard from any of your family lately. I hope they haven't had a job of writting as I had. I've had to find a pen, borrow some paper and than find the time. To try to work all three in at the same time is quite a job.

I don't remember but I think it was Pitts that wanted me to reserve an island for her. I can't promish this is what she would like. I know she wouldn't want this many service men on it. It's a wee bit beat up. She's welcome to it if she can take the U.S. out of it. Shouldn't be too hard after the war. Give her my regards. She can move in any time she pleases. I'll have to close now and do some work again. Send me a few more pictures of you. I have lost a few old ones. I'm not selfish! Am I?

I have'nt received that package yet. Getting me concerned.

> Always Loving You.
> Paul

Postmarked Mar 18 1945 from Cpl. Paul J. Fogel 435156, H & S. Co. 23 Mars. 4 Division, c/o. F.P.O. San Francisco, Cal. to Miss. Evelyn Wells., 1101 E Gadsden, St., Pensacola, Florida. (stamped "PASSED BY NAVAL CENSOR" with initials; with 6 cents air mail stamp)

On plain, unlined stationery:

March–17–1945

Dear Evelyn:—

We have just about finished our job here on Iwo Jima. We had not counted on as much trouble as we ran into. We pulled though it. We had a very good meal yesterday. Pardon, <u>me</u>, that was to have been a new paragraph. Well to get on with it. We had turkey. Some thing I bet you didn't have. All we wanted. Uncle Sam opened his heart. All the trimmings you could think off. It was a wee bit better than a Christmas dinner. I'm sure every one stuffed themself. That was beside the point! The point is we all injoyed the meal very much. Wish you could have been there.

I'm hoping I receive a letter from you today. Haven't received mail for quite some time. Getting lonesome for a letter from you again. If Ive read your letters more than ten times, I begin memorizing them. [Illegible] that would be bad.

I feel in a very happy mood today. Haven't felt this way since I was in Pensacola. Pen sliped there. I suppose no one could have felt worse than I did when I left you with your sister at the train station. I realize I couldn't have left you in any better company. I wish and I suppose you do too, that you were with her yet. I'm hopeing that J.C. will (*not*—inferred) have to come into this reckless kind of war over here.

I'll know what to expect on the next operation. Perhaps I'll be a little more prepared. This should have been the worse I'll ever have to go though. If its not. Ill not be suprised. If it is I'm lucky. Im selfish Evelyn, and I'm depending upon you for alot of help. You were right when you said my mother isnt any different than the rest of the mothers. She does as much worring and maybe more than the next. She won't mention it to me. But Pauline tells me once in a while. Pauline likes to give me little lectures once in a while. Especially when I miss a week in writting home. I can depend upon a little letter from her then. I don't want you to worry about me either. That was easy to say, I know. I'll always love you no matter where Ill be, or no matter how badly Ill be in need of care. Remember that saying, No news is good new. It certainly held good this past month. Hasn't it? Trying to keep some thing from my mother is like pulling teeth. Especially if she finds out. It hurts me then for trying to keep it from her. She will probably try and find out a lot of things from you about me. You see you already know more about me then my mother. Well almost. Thats beside the point. I'll have to stop now. I can just hear you say, "Well its about time". Here's a hug. Got it?

Always Loving You.
Paul.

Postmarked Mar 22 1945 from Mrs. Fogel (Paul's Mother), Nazareth, PA to Miss. Evelyn Wells., S.N., 1101 Gadsden St., Pensacola., Florida. (with 3 cents stamp)

Easter card:
He is Risen
May the risen Prince of Peace
Grant these gifts to you—
Faith—in Heaven's guidance,

Hope—that's deep and true,
Courage—when the road is hard,
Cheer—to light your way
And His strong abiding Love
To bless you every day
[Signed:] Mrs. Fogel

Postmarked Mar 23 1945 from Cpl. Paul J. Fogel 435156, H & S. Co. 23 Mars. 4 Div., c/o. F.P.O. San Frans., Cal. to Miss. Evelyn Wells., 1101 E. Gadsden, St., Pensacola, Florida. (stamped "PASSED BY NAVAL CENSOR" with initials; with 6 cents air mail stamp)
On plain, unlined stationery:

March 19–1945

Dear Evelyn.

I'm going to look forward to those pictures you promised me. I can hardly wait. As you doubtless can see already. I'm writting in a very uncomfortable position. If you will wait a second I will shed a few cloth. That feels a wee bit better. Perhaps you will be able to read every other word now. Lets hope so. I've have just about been freezing. The more cloth I could put on the better I felt. That was exactly what I did. It seems to be getting colder by the day. I think winter is just about to set in.

I told you about my grandfather liking to collect flowers. I did gather a few speciments upon this island for him. He will get a great kick out of it when he finds out. I'm just hoping I'll be able to send them by mail. If I can't I'll just keep it till I reach the states personally. Without a scratch. I wonder if you have ever examined that letter I wrote on Nov the nineteen of forty four. I told you some thing in that letter I thought you may be interested in. I put it down in my little book here and for the love of Mike I can't think what I said. It will probably come to me later. I was supose to remember it I know. I'm slipping.

We have playing pinochle again. It's been quite a game here of late. It's also a habit in my spare. We haven't had too much to do. Enough to keep us occupied. Chow is improving quite a bit. I remember the first week after D day. All we had than to eat was cold cheese that were in K rations. We liked it to an extend. We do enjoy hot chow better. That was living to much cave man style. We sleep in fox holes four and five feet deep. Half standing. Was quite an art. I wasn't in practice than. In right up among the best of them now. You probably heard about the men of the twenty third marines. If you didn't it wasn't our fault. To me, we did the best job there. There was one man responsible for our success. I can't help admireing him. He is a Lt, and in charge of us in the [illegible]. He has no favorite men and no man seems to like him too well. Just the same a lot of men can contribute a great deal to there being here today. Lucky things he doesnt sensor my letter, eh. I wouldn't have mentioned it if he had. This is all for now, so keep smilling. Think of me once in a while. I'll always be loving you.

Love and Kisses.
Time to get your Easter bonnet.

Postmarked Mar 27 1945 from Cpl. Paul J. Fogel 435156, H & S. Co 23 Mars. 4 Div., c/o. F.P.O. San Frans, Cal. to Miss. Evelyn Wells., 1101 E. Gadsden, St., Pensacola, Florida. (stamped "PASSED BY NAVAL CENSOR" with initials; with 6 cents air mail stamp)

On plain, unlined stationery:

March–26–45

Dear Evelyn:—

Last night I was out laying under the stars;
most of the night. Didn't feel much like sleeping, Did alot of thinking instead. Mostly about
you. If you imagined some one speaking to you
it was probably this sadsack. He does quite a bit
of talking to you. Enjoy every word of the con-
servation. You don't put up much arguement I
must say. So far you have agreed to every thing
I suggested. I know that wouldn't be so if I were
to talk to you personally. You would probably
argue your point till I would have to give in.
Isn't that correct. Days are draging along. I'm on
my reading rutine again. Average about a book
a day or every two days. Not many good books
left. Most of the fellows hang on to them. I get
more enjoyment out of a Western story than one
of these blasted dectative novels. Days pass into
weeks and weeks into months and the longer I'm
away from you makes me miss you that much the
more. If I were a pilot I'd probably be over the
hill far before this. I would have wasted no time
in heading my plane for the states. You don't realize it but I haven't had a letter from you for three
weeks. Such poor mail service must cease in the
future. I know its not your fault. I don't feel to
bad for no one else has received any either. It has
a feeling as though we were snow in, in Penna.
You will probably experience it someday. It won't
be my fault if you don't.

I picked some thing out of a jap store here I though you may be interested in. Of course you will have to learn to read japanese or else use your imagination. It is part of a cook book. Illustrators, resepes, even chop sticks. I had to pick up the "sticks" in a pill box. I always wanted to see how they used them. Mighty interesting. When we settle down again I'll send you those articles. O yes, I'll send that parachute silk along too.

Florida ought to be budding at this time. Green leaves should be showing up. A person can sure note the change over night when spring hits Penna. That is one season every one enjoys to see. New Life. I'm afraid there won't be a plant on Iwo Jima that will be able to bring forth a bud or flower. There wont be enough flowers gathered to place one on every ten graves. I had a look on the grave yard before I left that part of the island. It was really layed out beautiful. If you have ever seen a picture of Flanders Field. It had a slight resemblence. Crosses row on row. I doubt wheather I'll ever forget this island. Neither will the jabs. This will be all for now. Not very long till you graduate eh. Haven't any doubt that you will. Don't let it worry you too much. I'll see you later. Bye now.

Love and Kisses.
Paul.

March–27–45

Dear Evelyn:–

These rain squalles arn't doing me any good. Was soaked to the skin twice today. If I were at home my mom would lecture me on catching cold and I would say, "Yes mom." That would be all I would be able to say. Mothers know best. I have no doubts you will be the same way. Ha. I shouldn't laugh at you should I?

Was at church Sunday. Stood in the rain a few minutes. Washed me clean. Duel purpose service. Had a different chaplin preach the semon. Did a good job.

Received mail yesterday. Yep. Three letters from you. One could not ask for more. I did receive another suprise though. Also received one from your mother. She made me blush a wee bit. Her letters are some what different than any I have ever received. Perhaps that is the reason I enjoy reading them so often. Don't get any idea's now that I might let you take a squint at them. Your off your course. She has some what changed my mind about a few things. She does agree with me on a great many things. I can just hear you say, "stop beating around the bush" Thats all I'm going to tell you, so you need not ask me.

You mentioned you were doing quite a bit of sewing. Sounds to me as if a hope chest were being created eh? If that be so I might have descovered some things that you may injoy adding to it. I haven't layed my finger on it yet. But when I do I'll have to figure a way to send it too you. When it arrives you will know from who it is. It won't be any time soon. I mean real soon.

I'm certainly glad that Bennett still "Loves me" I was getting sort of worried for fear she might have forgotten me. I can set my mind at ease now.

I had a letter from Pauline. She claims the first year of married life is the hardest. She is haveing all kinds of trouble. Perhaps the comming year will be happier for every one. Let's hope so.

I still haven't come in contact with any of the boys from Pensacola. I sure would like to meet up with a few of them. We could sure find lots of things to talk about. A Great many of the boys do come from Ga and Ala. I'll have to close now. Get back to work you know. Keep Smilling

Always Loving You
Paul.

Postmarked Apr 2 1945 from Cpl. Paul J. Fogel 435156, H & S. Co. 23 Mars. 4 Div., c/o. F.P.O. San Francisco, Cal. to Miss. Evelyn Wells., 1101 E. Gadsden St., Pensacola, Florida. (stamped "PASSED BY NAVAL CENSOR" with initials; with 6 cents air mail stamp)
On plain, unlined stationery:

March 29–'45'

Dear Evelyn.

Just been talking with one of the boys. From the south. Was sort of suprised to hear I knew his uncle in Pensacola. In fact I was my self. We knew of quite a few places both of us had visited. He worked in the ice plant down there. I've been with him all this time I never struck upon me. He is from out of Atlanta, some place. That reminds me. Remember while I was still in New River I mentioned stopping in to see one of the fellows' parents, that worked in the office there in Pensacola. I'll have to write to them. I haven't done that yet. I should by all means. They really treated me fine. I ate dinner at there place and had a wee bit of a rest there. I'll have to write them next. I should have written them sooner. I'm slipping. Arn't I. I'll have to write your mother today some time too. Haven't heard from Mammie Lou lately. She is some person. Alot of fun. Your mother tells me Frank is more of the serious type. Thats hard to believe. A serious husband and a happy wife. Quite a combination. I'm sure they would enjoy the combination if they were to gether. I surely hope she won't have to wait too long for him. I'm hoping you won't have to wait to long for me. Of course it's hard for uncle Sam to decide about how long to keep us here.

I'll be anxiously waiting to receive those pictures of you. the sooner the better. You asked me why I wanted so many pictures of you. I can't answer that and you know it. All I can say is every one I get is more valuable to me than any other possessions I own. That was a terriable explanation, but it just about summs up the feelings I carry with me. This [illegible] took out some foolish Ideas I might have had.

I took Easter Communion yesterday. It wasn't Easter but he held it any way. It did me good. Had Good Friday Church Service today. Couldn't attend. Was occupied at the moment. I'll have to close now and write to the Young family.

Always Loving You.
Paul.

Postmarked Apr 5 1945 from Cpl. Paul J. Fogel 435156, H & S. Co. 23 Mars. 4 Div., c/o. F.P.O. San Francisco, Cal. to Miss. Evelyn Wells., 1101 E. Gadsden, St., Pensacola, Florida. (stamped "PASSED BY NAVAL CENSOR" with initials; no stamp)

On plain, unlined stationery:

March–30–45

Dear Evelyn:—

 It's all your fault. No one else's. What? Yesterday I sat in the sun writting you a letter and last night I suffered the concequences. Its a honey. Covering the hole back and shoulders. I was sitting out in the air all day trying to cool it off. No help. It will probably be there a couple more days. See what I get for thinking of you so often. I can't see why I love you so much. Look at all the misery you are bringing me. I love it though. Wouldn't have it any other way. There is another worry you are giving me. I see where a bill was past to draft you people. It certainly affects me. If there was any thing I could do about it don't think for one moment I wouldn't. Frankly it has me worried.

 I can hardly write. The wind is just about tearing this paper to shreds. Next thing I'll have my feet on it trying to keep it down. All I seem to do at the time is write letters and read books. I read on the average 1 every two day. Slow reader arn't I. Its getting mighty dark now. I can [*can't*— inferred] see what my writting. I write tomorrow again. Bye Bye now. Keep Smilling.

 Heres a kiss for you—Got it?—

Lots of Love.
Paul

April–1

Dear Evelyn:—

A Very Happy and Joyes Easter to you. May you have many more. Not by yourself. Had a pain full night last night. This sunburn doesn't want me to forget how foolish I was to get it. I sure am paying the penalty. Just finished a letter to my mom. I don't really know how long it has been since I've written her. I'm getting worse by the day. As long as you don't mind me being too bad once in a while. I won't mind it too much. I sort of enjoy laying down thinking of all the things we did together. All the arguments we had I always gave in to. Small things like the time I presented you with the ring, and you said to me when I reached for the right hand, "Not that hand." Its still tingling in my ear. That was what I wanted you to say. I was a devil. Wasn't I! The time we went to Panama City and got wet and Mobile where I saw the same picture twice, and the time when I wanted to see you so bad that I snug out of the hospital and went to town to meet you at Doc's office. Than you had to go to a funeral, and I turned right around and bumped into one of the people in charge of me. Lucky thing I got to know him pretty well. The time you brought Mamie Lou with you right after you came from Chattahoochee. And I was arguing over a game of monopolly with only a ward robe on. Then came the time you introduced me to your parents. If there was any time I felt murder in my heart it was then. Strickly a suprise attack. A below the belt blow.

I can think of all those things now a laugh to my self. Wishing I were back and knowing its imposible. You can bet your last cent if your in Florida when I return that will be my first stop on my way home. I do miss you so much. I can't explain in a letter I'd have to hold you in my arms and perhaps pinch you to see if you weren't just another moradge or some thing. I'd have to feel your hair. I'd think I was dreaming. It would be to good to be true.

You don't really know how much I hope and pray we can some day be to gether for always. I was dreaming about you last night. Woke up to quick though. Didn't finish it. It sort of made me laugh. It was some thing to this effect. You were looking for me and when you didn't find me. All you said was Paul. I was watching you all the time from behind some thing. There you stood saying my name over and over. I must have been laughing before I woke up, because there I was on my bunk all smiles. I will be back for you sis. Keep your chin up and Draft Board off of your heals. Keep Smilling, Think of me some times.

I'll always be loving you no matter where I'll be.

Love and Kisses,
Paul.

Postmarked Apr 5 1945 from Cpl. Paul J. Fogel, H & S. Co. 23 Mars. 4 Div., c/o. FP.O. San Frans., Cal. to Miss Evelyn Wells, 1101 E. Gadsden, St., Pensacola, Florida. (stamped "PASSED BY NAVAL CENSOR" with initials; with 6 cents air mail stamp)

On plain, unlined stationery:

April–2–'45

Dear Evelyn:—

This is a very pecular day. I'm sitting hear yawning my head off. I ought to back and hit the sack for a few more hours. Not that I need the sleep. More or less on general principal. Had a good eight hours sleep. Thats enough of any one. Except me of course. Wait till I get back. I'll let you see how much sleep a fellow can really consume in a days time. I'll stay in the sack for a week. No worring about being disturbed by some one (I hope) unless it would be you. And you would disturb me just because you like to see me squarm Like the time I tried to get a few winks in Panama City. I guess I deserved that. We had so much fun that day.

I just about finished catching up with my answering letters. I just hope by the time I hear the next mail call there will be a few more letters from you in it. I do injoy your letters very much. Durning those long days on Iwo Jima. I'll not try to tell you how much I did appreciate getting your letters. I couldn't write but you wrote just the same, that made me feel as if I really had to do some thing, to come back sooner. If there were any doubts about you in my heart. They vanished now. I certainly know how to pick a wife. I couldn't have made a better decision and if I had a grand stand filled with judges. I do love you with all my heart and always will. I want you to remember it because I don't want to mention it too often in a letter. Due of course to the censor. Some how

I'm always consicious of some one else reading my mail. I'd like to take to you about things I couldn't in these letters. I don't expect you to understand that last statement. I guess only I could.

I mentioned that Polock named Valantich, we all call him Val. We allways chum around together He's a swell fellow. He also comes from Pennsylvania. He likes to drink a wee bit. I can keep him from it when I want too. I, for some reason; mainly your reason; dont want to get into that habit. I usually chum around with people that dont drink. He is also ingaged to a girl in Ohio. We usually write letters at the same time. That is mainly why I'm discribing him now, because he is constantly disturbing me. No dont get the wrong opinion, he isn't causing all these mistakes. That is of course my fault. The other fellow of the trio is named Zarach. What a fellow he is. He is all ways admiring himself. He is quite a handsome fellow in fact they both are. He come from N.J. Married a girl in Virginia. In my opinion of course that is only my opinion. He is pretty filthy. I mean in keeping him self clean. We have quite a bit of fun reforming him. He was pretty lazy but we got that out of him. Arn't we all at times. He is also a constagater. Dont ask me if that is spelled right. You get the idea dont you. He likes to see people get in trouble. So much for them. Now you know what kind of people I associate with. You should hear some of the conversations we get into. Anything from ___ to ___. I know you won't be able to do any more work after you get through trying to translate this letter, so I'll not write any more. Keep Smilling Sis.

All my Love
Paul.

Postmarked Apr 8 1945 from Cpl. Paul J. Fogel, H & S. Co. 23 Mars. 4 Div., c/o F P.O San Francisco, Cal. to Miss. Evelyn Wells, 1101 E. Gadsden, St., Pensacola, Florida (stamped "PASSED BY NAVAL CENSOR" with initials; no stamp)

On plain, unlined stationery:

April 6

Dear Evelyn:—

Here I sit eating fruit cake and for the first time in month enjoying myself. You see our Christmas presents finally arrived and I can asure you it came at an oportune memoent. Im sort of glad they didn't arrive for Christmas. It makes me feel much more thank ful. O yes I also received that swell gift of yours. I feel as if I should send it back. That's exactly what I would do if it had not my name put on it I know what you are thinking. You think I don't appreciate it. I do and I think you were very thought ful. But, such a gift is not for me. The first place its too beautiful. The second place I wouldn't think of wearing it. Perhaps if I worked in an office on a typewritter I would but the kind of work I do was not meant for rings and jewerly. I know you don't know what I mean so I'll not try to explain. Later I'll try again. I'll have to put it away till I hit the states again may be I wont have to crawl around on my stomach then. I can lay down in peace then. We finally arrived in rest camp if you could call it that. We started out with that rutine of washing in ice cold water and things I've mentioned before about this place.

I received quite a few letters yesterday also. In fact I received 8 from you alone. Dont think they weren't welcomed with alot of sincerity. I was never so glad to received a thing in all my life. Had quite a few from home also. One of these days I dig up your letters and answer all the question you asked. How will that be. We are kept quite busy trying to square away things. I have so many things to do. I'll take time out to write to you though.

I had a letter from Jimmy also. I remember in one letter you mentioned that I might have misunderstood you about reading Elizabeths letters. I didn't, take my word for it. I must have kidded you too much in that letter you received from me. I'm sorry I did. I realize Elizabeth is a person to confide. If I said any thing that you think reflected on her in any way. Believe me it was far from being done on purpose. I'll have to write him as soon as I get the first chance.

I also received those pictures I've decided the reason for the pictures is the cemera. Not the person. You are much to beautiful to take a bad picture, I would still like that inlarged picture of you alone. That would be the nices present I could receive. So if you get the chance do it for me will you? I like zoo, as you say. And if my zoo was filled with no one but you I would not be disapointed. I wrote this letter in five minutes. A good excuse eh.

Love and Kisses
Paul

Postmarked Apr 8 1945 from Cpl. Paul J. Fogel, H&S. Co. 23 Mars. 4 Div., c/o. F.P.O. San Fran., Cal. to Miss. Evelyn Wells, 1101 E. Gadsden, St., Pensacola, Florida. (stamped "PASSED BY NAVAL CENSOR" with initials; with 6 cents air mail stamp); imprinted on front of envelope: Par Avion, Via Air Mail, Correo Aereo!

On stationery imprinted with Marine logos and with "Roi-Namur, Saipan, Tinian, and Iwo Jima" in color:

April. 7

Dear Evelyn:—

Getting stylish eh? Thats the Marine Corps for you: One sided; ha (describing the letter-head). Looking over your letters again I see where you mentioned where I might get a letter from Bennett. I hope so. She was one of my spies. I'd like to have a report from her. O my goodness are you in for it. Jimmy told me about the blessed event to take place. He seems to be very happy over it. I can imagine how he would feel. I hope to be as happy as he, one day. Perhaps not soon, but in the future. I can hardly wait. I'm writting by candle light again. I mentioned that once before a few month ago.

I told you to remember News Day in the letter I send that date. Now I can tell you why. We left for Iwo Jima than. We didn't start the year out to good. Do you think so. I would have rather been peacefully in the states some where to begin the new year. You know what I had planned if I would have stayed in the states that long. I would have taken you out to the most expensive place in Pensacola and we would have eaten chicken legs intill they hung out of our ears. On the stroke of twelve I would have kissed you three time. Than you would have turned around and looked at me with suprise. O yes I would have had a reason. The main one would have been that I love you. Thats a broad statement because I've never loved any one beside my parents. Its a wonderful feeling. I'm glad is was you rather than some people I could have.

April–8–1945

Hello Honey:—

As you can see I'm making use of that practical joke you send me in that last letter I don't need the writting paper now. Perhaps I should send it back.

You talked about Florida being so rainy. The first few days here were really grand. Than last night some thing must have irated the clouds and down comes the whole heavens It didn't leave up until around eleven oclock. Than the sun came out and it began to clear. I was wishing I was a duck also. We could have used some of this rain on Iwo Jima. No that I'm back from that place. I can tell you about the trip there and back The trip there was made as comfortable as can be expicted we were sitting around the middle of the ship. The trip back didn't turn out so hot as we were sick nearly three days. They had no skipping the waves in the bow of the boat. I'll never forget it. Every time the ship went up it lifted us ten or twenty ft hight. I had the darnest time keeping my stomach calmed down. It wasnt too bad often I caught on. Each morning I went to the back part of the ship and sat and read; till noon chow.

Sister Theordora must have taken a liking to you. Who wouldn't. She also knows something good when she see's it. Ill never for get the Father you have in that hospital. We also had a very nice Father, on board ship comming over. He was friendly to every one.

I had a letter from my mother yesterday. I think you might like to read it. It is one of the nices letters I have ever received from her. What a mother she is!! She doesn't forget a thing. Half past twelve, that must have been me. Pauline must have come at twelve. I'll not argue that point I don't know. a thing about it. I'll put it with this letter.

We re living in tents at present. We three are together again. Plus a few new fellows. They are all in the 2M. and that makes it nicer. We all know each other.

I cant help admiring that bracelet. It sure is sweet. I think it is the nices you could have bought. Its nice to look at even though I couldn't wear it.

I'm looking forward to receive a letter from Mamie Lou. She should have gather a great deal of news by this time. Have you ever received a letter from her? I wrote Frank a letter about a week ago. I passed the island he is staying on. It looks to me as if it might be a fairly nice place to be. Pits would like Gaum. That island is really beautful Its a place you dream about. Had a birthday card from Mrs Grebe. She still considers me her son. Mr. Grebe made Major. I'll have to put an end to this letter. Don't study too hard for that exam next month. I know you will make it. Keep Smilling Heres a hug. Got it? Good!

> All my Love.
> Paul

Postmarked Apr 10 1945 from Cpl. Paul J. Fogel, H&S. Co., 23 Mars., 4 Div., c/o. F.P.O. San, Fran, Cal. to Miss. Evelyn Wells., 1101 E. Gadsden, St., Pensacola, Florida. (stamped "PASSED BY NAVAL CENSOR" with initials; with 6 cents air mail stamp).

On stationery imprinted with Marine logos and with "Roi-Namur, Saipan, Tinian, and Iwo Jima" in color:

April–8

Dear Evelyn:—

I started writing yesterday noon, at this time. After writting half a page I stoped and tore it up. I went for Chow and when I came back I was in a better mood. I'm glad I did (*didn't*—inferred) send you that letter I had started. You mentioned some thing I didn't like so I proceeded to "read you off" as the saying goes. It would have been a pretty strong letter if I would not have calmed down. Today is Sunday. We work any way. No time for church. Perhaps tonight I can attend some service. We had a fairly good meal to day. Turkey. I ate my share and am suffering the results of a full stomach. I must feel like you felt the time you went out for chow. You told me about it remember. You will receive your mail a wee bit more regular now. I can assure you.

I am certainly glad you send me a picture of you and your mother together. She looks exactly the way I saw her first. That was the best picture out of the lot that you took. Your getting to pretty. A fact of course. Next thing I know some fellow will be making eyes at you. I wouldn't like that you know. Especially when I'm not around to protect my security. I'd give any thing to be back in Pensacola. I miss that place so much. I could walk around the town with my eyes closed and pick out every house I supose. Especially eleven O one. East Gadsden.

This is quite a job getting settled down. I'm trying hard not to aquire to much gear. That is just about an imposibility. We are going to have inspections very sone. We are to get all our clothes marked. Than of course come the laundry problems again. Get out the old brush and soap and start some motion. The job I'm on now really keeps me dirty. I'm on a grease rack if you know what I me. The general idea is to grease [illegible] of all types and small odds and end jobs. You should see me now. I can asure you I'm not a likely sight to look at. My pants legs are mud up to the knees. I can see where you would come in handy. Ha. Hold your temper sis.

We have a radio in this tent. It sure is a handy thing to have around. At least we can listen to music and hear the news than it dies out for a few minutes. It continues on that way all durnig the day.

I can tell you now. I believe I mentioned before I went to Iwo My boss that is, Remember Sgt. Maceluch. He was built exactly like him. A wonderful person. He was killed the first day on the island. We all miss him a lot. There was also a carpenter I talked with alot a friendly fellow. He was also killed. I miss him too. Its a funny feeling to have people disapear before your eyes Never to see them again. One can't explain it.

I'll have to sign off for today. Till tomorrow than. Bye Bye now. Keep Smilling. I'll always be Loving you.

Love and Kisses,
Paul

Postmarked Apr 12 1945 from Cpl. Paul J. Fogel, H & S Co. 23 Mars 4 Div., c/o. F.P.O. San Frans, Cal. to Miss. Evelyn Wells., 1101 E. Gadsden, St., Pensacola, Florida. (stamped "PASSED BY NAVAL CENSOR" with initials; with 6 cents air mail stamp)

On stationery imprinted with Marine logos and with "Roi-Namur, Saipan, Tinian, and Iwo Jima" in color:

April–9

Dear Evelyn:—

Time out: Do you have time to gander at this letter? If you don't lay it aside because they are the same monotous mess. You were talking about Easter in your last letter. I had quite an experience on Easter this year. Ask me when I get back to the states I'll tell you about it. You know military secreds.

Today I spend a very nice day on liberty. Didn't rain a drop. Suprised me half to death. I first went from town to town. I should say village to village to find a jeweler. No one in this place could fix my watch. I guess I'll have to send it to J.C. I also sat down to a delicious dinner. I really made a hog out of my self. I wasn't along though. Those two buddies went with me. That was good while it lasted After that we went to an Army recreation center where we went swimming on the beach. I again received a light burn. I know. You need not say it. I'll never learn. That was also alot of fun. That was first swim I had since I left this place for Iwo Of course I went swimming at Iwo but that wasnt willfully. You probably noticed in different papers where there was alot of reckage on the beach. I helped to remove in the first couple days. You can imagine what a mess that was. I had to change clothe twice in one after noon. It would have been fun if the Japs would not have thrown so much motar and artillary fire at us. It was like forth of July only not as funny. Im sorry you didn't received that letter I send you in the nineteenth of Nov. For get about it.

This is quite a job writting by candle light. It's fun in one sense. Candle light has some thing to it that makes a person think. My head is so solod it takes more than candle to sink through.

I should receive a letter from my mom one of these fine days. She's a diller. How did you like that last on she send me. I though that was cute.

Had quite a time last night. Was eating turkey. Some guy swiped some out of the mess hall and we had quite a feast I'll have to stop now so. Keep Smilling. I hope you get time to take that picture one of these days.

Lots of Love.
Paul

Dear Evelyn:—

Had to just take a radio apart. The darn thing was quacking like a squarrel. It sounds better now. I poked my screw driver around the works here and there. I must have hit the trouble some where. Its playing its head off now. Clearer than ever. Jack of all trades, thats me. The only thing Im not able to do is get to the states and stay there. Thats a mighty broad statement. Its the way I feel tonight though I wish you could hear the music I'm listening to. Can't understand a word of it. It sounds good so I'll just take it for granted he's saying nice things about me and every one also. Once in a while they put a few English words among there songs. We don't have it too bad around here. I'd much rather be here than any where I know. I wish I could say where I'm located. You would understand than.

A church service has just come on the air. I doubt wheather I'll be able to go to church very often now. Why? Mainly because we work Sundays and its hardly like what we had aboard ship. There, we didn't have to far to go and we also had the time.

Did you hear from Bennett yet? She is probably so busy getting into the rutine of military life she has quite a time find time to write. I remember while I went though boot camp. I was so tired nights after all day drilling. I fell on the sack, not brother to undress and slept till the next morning. The next morning we got up at half past four and scrubbed the heads till eight oclock. Than went back to the old routine (amazingly, spelled right) of drilling again. What a time that was. I can't see that it did much good. I wouldn't want to take that training over again but I'm not sorry I took it.

Yesterday I was trying to figure out which one of your pictures was the best. I was going to take it along to town to get it inlarged. I had decided upon the one of you in the evening gown. The one Mamie Lou send me. I think that is the best one I have of you over here. He wouldn't enlarge it for me because he claims it would fade more that it is already. Remember the one I have in my [illegible]. It was taken when you first came in training. You were standing on the hospital campus. I had it in my pocket the first few days on Iwo and it to gether with my mother and days pictures were practically ruined. Every thing was soaked. I still have it though. I still have one of you in your swimming suit. It also got wet Ha. Had to give you a bath in the Pacific. How did you like it???!!!

The longer I'm away from you the more I miss you. I told you once you were worse than a desease. I realize it more than ever now. I doubt if I could ever forget you even if I wanted to. I found you much to likeable to ever forget you.

Have you heard any thing more about that draft the President seems to enjoy signing his name too. I don't know what I'd ever do if you came in the service I only know this is no place for you. I praying the Lord will keep you safe in the States till I return. I'm trying to get back and when a fellow trys, he succeeds sooner or later. Perhaps not in the near future but later on.

I'll always love you. Keep Smilling
Always Loving You
Paul

Postmarked Apr 13 1945 from Cpl. Paul J. Fogel, H & S. Co. 23 Mars. 4 Div., c/o. F.P.O. San Francisco, Cal. to Miss. Evelyn Wells, 1101 E. Gadsden, St., Pensacola, Florida (stamped "PASSED BY NAVAL CENSOR" with initials; with 6 cents air mail stamp)

On stationery imprinted with Marine logos and with "Roi-Namur, Saipan, Tinian, and Iwo Jima" in color:

[No date]

Dear Evelyn:—

I'm receiving your mail quite regular now and to prove it, I received two letters from you and one from Pauline. Gosh, I certainly was glad to receive them. It's like a spark within me some where. Its like a refueling. What an example!!

There were quite a few things happened today. Mainly the death of President Roosevelt. It's hard to believe. I see quite a few other people find it hard to believe also. It's going to be strange changing Presidents.

Than another thing has happened. My uncle I told you about while I was on Iwo Jima also arrived in the states. He is on fifteen days leave now. My brother Sheldon is also on his way home. In fact they expect, he is in the states right now. They seem to be all excited about it. Thats sounds good to me.

I was lifting bar bells last night and not being used to it. Well!! You can guess the rest. I thought I was carring a horse around on my back. It was sure sore. Perhaps I ought to go back for some more. I'd be just that foolish. Can never tell about me.

We have had beautiful wheather here of late. Sun shining all day. I was preparing for the rain. We put cinders all around the ship. We won't have to walk in too much mud now.

I had an interesting letter from your mother yesterday. You wouldn't be interested in it. I just now came form chow. It was alright. You can easily see I'm not hard to please. Hamburgers and spuds.

Hodges is the same old girl she was when I left. I personally can't see how you stand her. I formed my opinion while at Chattahoochee. It wasn't a pleasant opinion. If you want to keep a friend, dont be the way she is. I know you won't. I'm not afraid of that.

These boys playing crap in front of me while Im trying to write you. Very annoying, also very tempting. Can't aford to be involved. Got to think of the future.

You should be ashamed of your self going around sticking small children in the arm with a needle. A very poor policy. I hope you take it easy on the red headed kids. They are the sweetest of all you know. You ought to receive my letters pretty regular by this time. I hope so. I'll close now and go to bed. I hope I can sleep although I doubt it.

I'll always love you.
Paul.

Postmarked Apr 15 1945 from Cpl. Paul J. Fogel, H & S. Co. 23 Mars., c/o. F.P.O. San, Frans. Cal. to Miss. Evelyn Wells, 1101 E. Gadsden, St., Pensacola, Florida. (stamped "PASSED BY NAVAL CENSOR" with initials; with 6 cents air mail stamp)
On plain, unlined stationery:

April–13–45

Dear Evelyn:—

I don't remember wheather I told you before, but your mother also send me some pictures of your home. She doesn't seem to think it does justice to the home. It hides the flowers. It does have a beautiful appearance.

My laundry has just arrived. Reasonable prices. Pensacola I had to pay thirty five for pants and forty for shirts. Here I pay twenty five for all pieces. Not bad eh? I had lots more laundry there in Pensacola.

I'll be having my oldest brother with me in a short while. I hope he will be with me. I certainly hope so. If he has to come over here I want him to be with me. How do you like that me taking care of my oldest brother. Thats a laugh.

I bought myself another wrist watch, a fifteenth jewel Bulova Thats the second Bolova I have I have to get a cristal for it. I don't know what I shall do with all of them. It was a cheap buy. Ten buck. I can sell it for lots more than that. I had to wear the other one on my ancle. The greese and gasoline rubbed my rist so sore I had to bandge it.

April–14

Last night when I wrote that first page. The paper looked white to me. I was writting by candle light again and must have pulled out the wong sheet of paper. No. no, you mustn't think that of me. I was as sober as, well I can't say the boy in the tent because they were quite happy. I didn't have a drop to drink.

It was raining again today. How do you like that Liberty day too. Went anyway. Was soaked as usual. I did some thing very wish though. bought my self a swimming suit. Saving money arn't I. Raincoats cost lost more than swimming suits. I can just picture my self out in the front of our boss at roll call with a swimming suit on. I never would get out of the brig.

I did get some good sunny side eggs also. Say, thats the first thing you shall have to make me when I get back. I can just taste them. Maybe I better make them my self. You might burn tham [illegible].

Well you sweet little chick. I'll have to sign off now. I'll see you tomorrow. [Illegible] seven oclock. OK. Don't be disapointed if I don't arrive. You are a lovely woman to marry. I'll always Love you.

Love and Kisses.
Paul.

Postmarked Apr 16 1945 from Cpl. Paul J. Fogel, H & S. Co. 23 Mars. 4 Div., c/o. FPO. San, Frans. Cal. to Miss. Evelyn Wells., 1101 E. Gadsden, St., Pensacola, Florida. (stamped "PASSED BY NAVAL CENSOR" with initials; with 6 cents air mail stamp)
On plain, unlined stationery:

April–15
Pacific Arer

Dear Evelyn:

How is my honey today, as my mother would say. What a mom she is. She still likes to take care of me. If only I were not so far away. She always reminds me to keep out of trouble. I guess all mothers are more or less the same. She told me to think of you when I was about to do some thing off of the ordinary. Do you think that is such a hot idea? I don't know now. Maybe I should think of a cute little red head, huh? That's an idea. I have to find which one I prefer thinking of must. Perhaps you can help me. Any idea's. One you don't, you better not dye your hair. I'm not worried about your hair. You see all our children are going to have hair like your mother. If they arn't. Than's the time to dye hair.

Had bake beans for chow tonight. That reminds me today is Sunday. Heard the church call go but was too busy to attend. No one's perfect I supose, and I'm far from that goal.

Did you think over that picture proposition? Going to have one made? Wish you would!

I'm sure Pitts isn't as crazy as you claim. I think she's a cute little half pint. Don't take me wrong. That was a compliament. She reminds me of an aunt of mine. You will meet her some day. I can imagine the opinion you will form. She is a tiny as Pits. Sort of soft hearted. In fact the first time I came home on fourlough she practically drowned me in tears. Can you imagine that. Yes, I know its hard to believe. I can't picture my self being cried over by any one. Getting back to he. She'll talk a leg off of a person in less time than it would talk to make eggs. Not referring to Pitts, of course. They own a cabin at a lake in Penna, and one week end invated Pauline and I to visit them there. It was a beautiful place. We went fishing and had lots of fun till one night I was running down to the boats at the edge of the lake, and plop, right into a marsh. You can picture me now. Weeds, mud, dirt and mush all clinging to the front of me. When she saw me she flew into a fit. Pauline only laughed. We were quite young yet and didn't see the harm in it. To her it was like cutting up the furniture. They liked to come out on our farm. to hunt quite a bit. Now he is too old. I'm talking about her husband now. I'll close now and discribe some more of my relatives tomorrow. Perhaps you would like to hear about them. They are quite interesting

Always Loving You
Paul.

Postmarked Apr 18 1945 from Cpl. Paul J. Fogel, H & S. Co.
23 Mar. 4 Div., c/o. F.P.O. San Frans, Cal. to Miss Evelyn Wells,
1101 E. Gadsden, St., Pensacola, Florida. (stamped "PASSED BY
NAVAL CENSOR" with initials; with 6 cents air mail stamp)

On stationery imprinted with Marine logos and with "Roi-
Namur, Saipan, Tinian, and Iwo Jima" in color:

April–18

Dear Evelyn:—

Im in a bad mood this poor morning. If I
start cursing at you! Shut your ears if you can. I
couldn't not have gotten out on the wrong side of
the bed, because the is only one side to my sack.

Yesterday was one of the worst days I spend
in the Marines. It started out with an arguement,
and ended up with nearly taking off three of my
best fingers. It took the back off of them anyway. They are puffed up like balloons. So much
for my trouble. Your trouble looks serious to me.
I'd have a solution to it if it were I Put all the
dresses in a locker and put lock and key on them.
Than loose the key. Very simple eh? No. Just a
suggestion.

Lesten you, you would better write me
today. Havent heard from you for too days now.
Long time. Don't keep me in suspense so long.
I really do look forward to receiving your letters. Practically every song I hear on the raido,
reminds me of some instance with you or someplace we were at while it was being played.

I didn't get a chance to get that silk censored
yet as soon as I do. I'll send them to you. I'm
shure you can make use of it some how.

Had a letter from my mom yesterday. My brother Sheldon still had not made his appearance home. I can imagine the feeling that will run though her when she see's him. My cousin Wayne is over here with me some where. I hope I get to see him some where. He's an Ens. in the Navy. Got married to a girl just before he left. Met her while he was in college. He went to college in Penna. Same with his brother. They are the only two in the family. One is a couple years younger than the other. They used to visit our place for vacations. We had lots of fun together. You would like them. They are all large blone headed men. As blone as your hair. Nothing exceptional though. Should have been red. I'd love you no matter what collor hair you had. You are the sweets thing this side of sugar I have ever tasted. A fact. O, yes one more thing. Dont eat too much. Save a little for me. I'll be hungry when I get back.

> Always Loveing You.
> Paul.

Postmarked Apr 21 1945 from Cpl. Paul J. Fogel, H & S. Co 23 Mars., c/o. F.P.O. San Frans, Cal. to Miss. Evelyn Wells, 1101 E. Gadsden St., Pensacola, Florida. (stamped "PASSED BY NAVAL CENSOR" with initials; with 6 cents air mail stamp)

On stationery imprinted with Marine logos and with "Roi-Namur, Saipan, Tinian, and Iwo Jima" in color:

April–20 45

Dear Evelyn:—

I don't know if I wrote to you yesterday or not. If I didn't it couldn't be helped. I had plenty of time but didn't take it. I've decided that "line" about haveing no time to write is just alot of bunk. Every one has time to spare. They can't go out at night around here any way so every one should write. Im no exception to this. At least I try not to be.

Ah yes, I had a letter from your sister in law yesterday. I'm nearly certain. I told you about it. What a letter. Newsy letter too. And the things she told me. Ah yes the things she told me. The main thing she told me, was that you still Loved me. Not that I doubted it, but it always sounds good to my ears.

Today was my liberty day. I went to town to get a few things in the morning and came home again at noon. Main reason was to eat a good meal.

These people are worse than negroes. They are playing crap and then make noise that one would think they were out of there head. I'll blame that on my writting.

I don't remember wheather I told you or not but this country around here is the most beauti- ful I've ever seen. When you travel though the west though Texas, Arizona, and California. You will think that county is also beautiful. It has no comparence—to the senery around here. In one way I wish you could be here to see it. But I'd rather you not. Do your waiting in the states.

I bought a book for my grand father also. Its on Botany. He should injoy it I'll have to send it to him one of these days. I also bought quite a few snap shots of this island. When I get back I'll have to make a collection. That will be fun. I'll be able to tell you every thing I've seen.

I meet a very nice family last night. I felt
as though I was a wee bit out of place around
people older than I. I have a great deal of respect
for the natives of this island. They dress like you
or I so dont let that word miss lead you. They
were the first civilian I've met thus far. I had a
swell time. There was a lady with three children
on vacation at this home. You wouldn't want any
sweeter children. Dark brown eyes and brown
hair. There eyes were nearly ebony. I never saw
such beautiful children in all my life.

I'll have to close now. Write to Mamie Lou
next. She'll want to hear from me.

I Love you very much sis. Dont forget

Love and Kisses,
Paul.

Postmarked Apr 27 1945 from Cpl. Paul J. Fogel, H & S. Co
23 Mars., c/o F.P.O. San Frans. Cal. to Miss. Evelyn Wells, 1101 E.
Gadsden, St., Pensacola, Florida. (stamped "PASSED BY NAVAL
CENSOR" with initials; with imprinted 6 cents air mail stamp)

On stationery imprinted with Marine logos and with "Roi-
Namur, Saipan, Tinian, and Iwo Jima" in color:

April–23–1945

Dear Evelyn:—

How is my sweet tonight. Well thats good
news I hope you continue to feel fine. I went and
done it again. I bought another watch. This time
It was for you. Its a cute little watch. I think you
might like it. Its not a new one so don't raise your
hopes. You can wear this one on duty and the

other one on social meetings etc. Of course there is always a trash can. Those things you dont like you may deposite there.

Remember I told you Pauline send me a sheep wool jacket with out sleeves. "Some one swiped. Imagine that. I put it into a taylor shop and the next thing I knew the owner was paying me for its disapearance. Was I sore Cant get them around here and in the states either. It sure came in handy while it lasted. Good things can't last forever. I wouldn't mention this to my mother if I were you. She might think I'm careless. I know I am only I don't like to be reminded

I just finished eating part of a water mellon. Yum did it test good Sweetest thing I tasted since I left you. Thats a very broad statement. I can't wait till I get back. I'll stick to you like flies to fly paper. The next war I get into. They will have to dig me out of the hills to draft me. What a sap I was to join up and land up over here.

I just came from a show. Michel OShea was playing I like to see him in a picture. I like the way he talks.

This afternoon we had a beautiful inspection by the Col. Not half as bad as we expected. Hope the rest of them are as easy. We received a new commanding officer. He seems to be a regular fellow. You should have seen the tent. It nearly sparckled.

Did I tell you Mamie Lou wrote me a long letter. She only writes now and then but when she writes She writes.

When you write to my mom again you ask my mother where my cousin, Wayne, is. You might be interested in him.

I'll have to close now and go to bed befoe the lights go out.

I'll write tomorrow.

Always Loving you—
Paul.

Postmarked Apr 27 1945 from Cpl. Paul J. Fogel, H & S. 23 Mars. 4 Div., c/o. F.P.O. San Francisco, Cal. to Miss. Evelyn Wells, 1101 E. Gadsden, St., Pensacola, Florida (stamped "PASSED BY NAVAL CENSOR" with initials; with imprinted 6 cents air mail stamp)

On stationery imprinted with Marine logos and with "Roi-Namur, Saipan, Tinian, and Iwo Jima" in color:

Dear Evelyn:—

Was on duty yesterday. Went into one of the towns and had to walk up and down the streets to see that none of our boys in the 23rd didn't get too drunk to get back. Pretty tire some. I'll have quite an album by the time I get. I've collected quite a few pictures. If I were able to, I'd send them to you.

Had a letter from you and my sister yesterday. So you are wondering what I was so furious about. For get it. Your forgiven. I don't believe you ment to say it any way. Perhaps I took it the wrong way.

As I told you before there are quite a few Japs on this islsand. Its funny how you can tell the difference between them and the other people. Its like telling night and day apart. From the back if you look at a woman she has the most beautiful hair, coal black, and as long as yours. Than the front view suprised you, there face is as flat as your hand. Funny looking people. They all wear long dresses some drag on the deck. The younger girls wear dresses like you.

Practically all the little girls. Have dark brown eyes and black hair. You should see them come out of school in the morning. They are a sight.

I was on liberty today, came back around five oclock. I was just about in the base when it began to pour down You can imagine the rest.

I bet you won't guess who I received a letter from today. Nope, wrong again. Bennett. Lt. Bennett. How do you like that a Lt. writting a Cpl. Hard to believe isn't it. It made me laugh. I did injoy receiving. It was a very nice letter. She told me she just received a letter from my wife. and than went on etc. I'll have to answer it sometime soon.

I told you I bought you a watch the other day. What a deal that was. He came back for it today. The person I bought it from found it and now has located the person to whom it belongs. Im sorry it had to work out that way.

I'll see good night now and go to bed. I'll aways Love you.

Love and Kisses,
Paul.

Postmarked May 2 1945 from Cpl. Paul J. Fogel, H &S. Co. 23 Mars. 4 Div., c/o F.P.O. San Francisco, Cal. to Miss Evelyn Wells, 1101 E. Gadsden, St., Pensacola, Florida. (stamped "PASSED BY NAVAL CENSOR" with initials; with imprinted 6 cents air mail stamp); front of envelope imprinted with Marine logo sticker: Semper Fidelis US Marines 4th Division * Roi-Namur, * Saipan, * Tinian

On stationery imprinted with Marine logos and with "Roi-Namur, Saipan, Tinian, and Iwo Jima" in color:

[No date]

Dear Evelyn:—

So now I've changed to a big brother eh. I certainly would like to be Kelly's big brother. I'm sure that would be exciting. Never a dull moment. Pitts has an altogether different opinion of me. I mean Bennett. In her letter she asked me if I was as mean as ever. Was I ever mean to you. I didn't try to be. Of course there were times I must have wondered off of the straight and narrow. Couldn't be helped. Tell Kelly I do apreciate her comment on my behalf. You may tell her to write and tell me what she really thinks of me. I'm afraid she was trying to make you feel good.

I'm certainly glad I received all my shots for a while at least. I can well imagine the feelings those poor kidds have when you come at them with a needle. I've been stuck so often I feel like a pin cussion. I don't believe I'd feel quite so bad if I'd give them to my self.

I certainly wish that I'd be there for your graduation You can be glad I'm not, for if I were you would not stay single. I'd make sure of you then. I'd take you with me where ever I'd go. I can hardly wait till I get back. This waiting around is driving me nutty. I believe I'd rather be on an operation.

I have off tomorrow I hope. I might do a little fishing. I had an invation to go. They do quite a bit of fishing around here. I'd also like to go swimming again. The surf is a little [illegible] than that at Pensacola beach. It has a teriable under toe. The last time I was in, it caugh me and turned me over four or five times. I was laying up on the beach all out of breath when I finally knew where I was. Some fun. They also do a lot of spear fishing. I'll have to try that one of these days.

I don't know if I answered Elizabeth's letter or not. I'll write her tonight to make sure. I'm neglecting my writting a little I believe I'll have to do some thing about that.

I'll have to go to work now. Keep Smilling. I love you very much.

Love and Kisses.
Paul

Postmarked May 2 1945 from Cpl. Paul J. Fogel, H & S. Co. 23 Mars., c/o. F.P.O. San Frans. Cal to Miss. Evelyn Wells, 1101 E. Gadsden, St., Pensacola, Florida. (stamped "PASSED BY NAVAL CENSOR" with initials; with 6 cents air mail stamp)
On plain, unlined stationery:

April–29

Dear Evelyn:—

I had liberty again to day. Was invited to go to the ocean to do some spear fishing. I never enjoyed any thing so much in my life. That is of course next to being with you. There isn't any thing I'd rather have happen as to be with you. We can't always have what we want. Now to tell you what happened. We took along part of a ham and a case of cokes. We had enough chow to feed an army. You should see the shore where we were fishing. It must have been a hundred feet high. We put on glasses that fitted on the eyes. When you looked at the bottom of the ocean it was as light as day. We had long spears about fifteen feet long. When ever we saw a fish we would jab toward it. We missed the majority of them but we still had the fun of it. The water was pretty rough and every time a wave would come it. It would carry us up on the rocks off shore. Some of them had sharp edges and I was cut up a wee bit till I caught on to it. It was worth it. We got a few lobsters and when we returned back to the man's place. His wife cooked them for us. They were better than I had expected. O yes These people do that kind of fishing for a living so you can imagine the were on to every trick.

I guess I suprise most people around here, mostly because I don't drink. It seems to be a sin not to drink. Every house I've visited so far have offered me a drink. When I refuse they seem hurt. I do drink now and then to be sociable. I don't hope you will hold that against me.

You see I don't keep any thing from you. If I'd hear anything from some one else you wouldn't want me to know. I would not feel so well It could also be visa versa.

One of these fine days I'm going to have my tonsils taken out. Remember one day at the hospital I was going to have them taken out. I didn't succeed than but I am now. What memories a tonsil operation brings back to me. I bet you can also remember that day, for more reasons than one. You were unable to talk and I was unable to talk, "mainly because there was a lump in my throat as large as an egg (no end quotes). I don't know why, I had the advantage on you. Father

Dolan came in then and eased the job a little. Before you leave, thank him for me will you.

I haven't told you yet, but I'm going to be transfered. Its pretty certain now, and I'm quite safe in telling you. I'm being transfered to a regimental weapon company. I'll tell you more of what I'm doing when I get into it. I asked for it. It looks like I'm always sticking my neck out, eh. One of these days I stick it your way. I hope you will grab it. When I get out of this corps I'll have experience in all [illegible]. Jack of all trades and master of none. What a husband you are going to have!!! Disapointed???

I'll Aways Love You.

Love and Kisses.
Paul

Postmarked May 2 1945 from Cpl. Paul J. Fogel, H & S. Co. 23 Mars. 4 Div., c/o. F.P.O. San Francisco, Cal. to Miss. Evelyn Wells, 1101 E. Gadsden, St., Pensacola, Florida. (stamped "PASSED BY NAVAL CENSOR" with initials; with 6 cents air mail stamp)

On plain, unlined stationery:

May–1–1945

Dear Evelyn:—

How is my honey today. Received that letter Iris wrote to you today. What a person she is. I'm sure we could get along splendidly. Don't you? You must send me a picture of her when you send me that one of you I want. Remember! I'm sure you do.

I'll not remind you about my red headed children again. You won't have to worry about them being blondes or brunettes I have it all figured out.!

I'm going to school right now. Its pretty monotous. I've had it all before but its good to get refreshed on it. It's a mechanics course. Only two weeks long. It's almost as if I were back in Trade School. Always waiting for time to pass more readily. I got so terribly sleepy in class today. I just about had to prop my eye lashes open. Its been too long since I've attend class last Thats probably the reason.

You ought to put your watch away if it costs you that much money every time you fix it. I'll send you that Bolova you wore before I got shipped out. It runs good. Its the best souvineer of Iwo Jima I have. It was in the Pacific more the first two or three days then it was on land. Its a pretty salty watch by this time in more ways then one. I wish I could have send you the other one.

I have pretty much to accomplish tonight before I hit my sack. I have to get up at five thirty to wake one of my boys that work in the mess hall. Then I have to eat and get really to shove off at seven We have some sot of M.C.O. meeting tonight. Don't know what its about. Its drizzling a little out side. Just to make the day complete.

I think I write your mother tonight too. Just to let her know I'll be thinking of her on Mothers day. This will have to be all for now. Keep Smilling

Love and Kisses.
Paul

Postmarked May 4 1945 from (Cousin Ernestine) 210 Magnolia St., New Smyrna Beach, Fla. to Miss Evelyn Wells, 1101 E. Gadsden St., Pensacola, Fla. (with 3 cents postage stamp)

On plain, unlined stationery:

Wednesday Night
May 2, 1945

Dear Evelyn,

Your sweet letter came several days ago, and we are all ways so happy to hear from you—I expect you are getting ready for graduation— How many will graduate with you?

This is Wednesday night, and Bill has gone to Lodge meeting—He went to Jacksonville yesterday, and to Miami last week end—I sure do miss him when he is away—

You should see the dresses Bill gave me on my birth-day. He picked them out, and they are a grand fit—I am so proud of them—I hadn't brought any clothes, waiting until I stop nursing Arthur—and that will be in a month or two. He is cutting teeth, and doesn't feel any too good. (or may be he is just spoiled) His right thumb is red where he has biten it—

We went to see a movie Sunday night—saw "National Velvet"—If you haven't seen it, don't miss it! It is the best I have seen in a long time— May be because it isn't a war picture—By the way—the war news sounds good, doesn't it?

Guess I will go to Daytona Beach tomorrow. It is such a pretty place. Mrs. Ulbrych has asked me to go with them—They are so sweet to help me with Arthur—

I imagine you are enjoying Public Health—
you know, that was what I planned to do before
I met Bill—I am glad that you and Paul are not
going to wait so long to be married—(Evelyn, I
can hardly wait to see you—So much has happened since I saw you—) I know that you will be
happy—I havn't met Paul, but I am sure that he
is a fine man—and he is so lucky to get a girl like
you—you have told me very little about him—
what did he do before going into service?

It is almost time for Bill to come home, and
I have to get a bath—Take care—and write soon.

I love you—

Ernestine

May be I will get the right address on this letter—I sent the last one to New Smyrna Beach—
did you notice??!

Postmarked May 5 1945 from Cpl. Paul J. Fogel, H&S. Co.
23 Mars., c/o. F.P.O. San Frans. Cal. to Miss. Evelyn Wells, 1101 E.
Gadsden, St., Pensacola, Florida. (stamped "PASSED BY NAVAL
CENSOR" with initials; with 6 cents air mail stamp)

On stationery imprinted with Marine logos and with "Roi-
Namur, Saipan, Tinian, and Iwo Jima" in color:

[No date]

Hello Honey:—

How are you. Had a letter from you and
mom today. You probably saw some pictures of
Iwo in some magazine. We were just trying to
find the places where we bunked the first night

on the beach. The pictures must have been taken after we left the island. It sure changed plenty.

It's six oclock now and I just ate chow I didn't get the chance to finish this letter last night. I went to a stage show put on by the Army. It was pretty good. Had some raw jokes. They all do. Just about average. Of course every body is interested in the women in the show. Wheather they are good or not. A lot of yelling.

I send your mother a Mothers Day card. You don't mind, do you? I wanted her to know I'd be thinking of her and wanted to be back there. Especally with you sis. They only way I'll be able to get back is to get half my head blown off. What do you think. Is it worth it?

Were you caught in the rain lately! I was yesterday again. I have the hardest time keeping me dry. I have the solution though. I'll walk around with a swimming suit on. Than the M.P.'s will be after me. Anyway I don't feel half as bad as you did the time we came walking up from the beach and you got caught with a shrinkable dress. Let me stop laughing now! That was funny. Bye for now.

Love and Kisses.
Paul.

I'll try to finish your letter now. I just came from school. We have to travel a few miles by truck to get there, on the way back tonight a few children were walking home from school. They sure looked a sight. Bright collors and no shoes. Can you picture that. My mom is some thing like that. She doesn't like to wear shoes often either. Don't tell her I told you now. The older ladys wear big bonnets with bills nearly two foot long.

I was talking today to a person who did duty in Pensacola before I did. He knew some of the fellows there I knew. We had quite an interesting conversation.

I'm listening to the raido now and would injoy it much more if I could under stand what he is saying. It sounds Greek to me. Ha.

Well the boys had liberty today and they are just returning. I might as well give up the idea of writting. Think of me once in awhile eh? Keep Smilling. I'll always love you.

Love and Kisses.
Paul.

Postmarked May 8 1945 from Cpl. Paul J. Fogel, H & S. Co. 23 Mars., c/o F.P.O. San Frans, Cal. to Miss Evelyn Wells, 1101 E. Gadsden, St., Pensacola, Florida. (stamped "PASSED BY NAVAL CENSOR" with initials; with 6 cents air mail stamp)

On stationery imprinted with Marine logos and with "Roi-Namur, Saipan, Tinian, and Iwo Jima" in color:

May–5

Hello Honey:—

Another beautiful day is about to end so here I am about to interupt you with one of these iritating letters. Are you prepared? I'm glad to hear that. I know it must take a great deal of fore thought to even read one of my letters. Even my mother complains. What shall I do??? I don't hope it is that bad but if it is. Crate them up untill I get back. I'll read them to you than Better still throw them away. How is that?

I'm glad you are getting that picture made. Something like you, I shouldn't hide. No sir. You are something valuable. I want everyone to see the person that is waiting for me. If there was any way to make time fly faster Id do it just to get home. That wouldn't be so good either. I'd be getting too old than.

I'm still going to school. Learning some thing every day. Don't see how I do it. You know how hard my head is. It's just a wonder I'm absorbing anything.

Have you decided what you are going to do after the middle of May? I know its none of my business. I just thought I'd ask.

I'll finish this letter tomorrow. I'll have more to say then.

Another sunburn another day. Today is Sunday and I had liberty. So I went on liberty. Had a very delightful day. Was in swimming during the morning and fishing and a little dancing in the afternoon. The Army has a large recreation Center. Its a beautiful place. I picked up a few sea shell along the shore. I'll send them to my Grandpa. He will enjoy having them.

My mom wrote today. She told me she would tell me how starch my shirts in the next letter. I asked her about it in my last letter. You two people cant be beat. I should know.

Tomorrow, back too work. School again. Its somewhat interesting but its the same old classes. Always watching the clock to try to make the hours pass faster.

Tell Smitty to drive slower. She's way ahead of me now. I don't like the idea of being the last married. It looks like I pull up the rear in every thing. Ask her about a double wedding eh? Some fun eh. So you think you would like that name Fogel. Well now. I don't know. Its a gruesome name. If you insist I guess I'll let you have it though. Enough foolishness for today. Night now. You sweet thing you.

Love and Kisses
Paul

Postmarked May 9 1945 from Cpl. Paul J. Fogel, H & S. Co. 23 Mar, c/o. F.P.O. San Frans. to Miss. Evelyn Wells, 1101 E Gadsden, St., Pensacola, Florida (stamped "PASSED BY NAVAL CENSOR" with initials; with imprinted 6 cents air mail stamp)

On stationery imprinted with Marine logos and with "Roi-Namur, Saipan, Tinian, and Iwo Jima" in color:

[No date]

Hello Honey:—

Some good new came in today. Had a letter from my brother Charles. (the oldest) He's in California, Miamar, Right near San Deigo. I wrote and told him if he had the chance to drop in to see Elizabeth. I hope he does. I'm sure he'll agree, you have one swell sister. Maybe he will also meet Jimmy and Doris. That all comes under an "If" If he doesn't get shiped out to quick.

Kupsky is in the 55th Draft. He's over here some where. I hope he come's into this out fit. That would suit me to a tee.

You mentioned about not receiving a letter in four or five days. I've made a habit of writting you ever other day. Don't know what happened to them. Don't worry I write you so many letters, one or two ought to come though sooner or later. Received a pretty good mark in class today. Don't know how I did it. Must have been thinking of you too often.

The mosquitoes are being well fed here of late. They must like the taste in me. Dont know why though I've tried to be mean enough to them. I think I'll put my netting up tonight.

I wrote to Elizabeth yesterday. I wasn't sure if I had answered her last letter so I wrote her again. I wish I were in Calif. Perhaps you would come to see me too eh? I had my time of happyness so now I'll have to like what I have.

I though I was Iris's only boy friend. What is she trying to do two time me. I'll tell her off. Ha.

Where is Nellie keeping her self. She gone to war yet. Just like her. Isn't it. She doesn't know what she likes. Now she has to like what she has. Lots of boys are going to the show I might as well go too. What do you know. "Its not raining." Suprised.

"You still like me??" You sweet thing you.

Nighty, Nighty,
Lots of Love and Kisses.
Hugs too.
Paul

Postmarked May 11 1945 from Cpl. Paul J. Fogel, H & S. Co. 23 Mars., 4 Div. c/o. F.P.O. San Frans. to Miss. Evelyn Wells, 1101 E. Gadsden, St., Pensacola, Florida (stamped "PASSED BY NAVAL CENSOR" with initials; with imprinted 6 cents air mail stamp)

On stationery imprinted with Marine logos and with "Roi-Namur, Saipan, Tinian, and Iwo Jima" in color:

[No date]

Goodmornin, Hon:—

Did you sleep well? I just came from eating breakfast. Pan cakes! I guess I should be thank ful for even getting them. O don't get me wrong I'm not complaining. When I get back you would better not slap some of those in front of me. I'm not worried about your cooking ability. If you dont know any thing of cooking. I'll teach you! How is that. Not that I'm so good! Seriously, if you can cook half as good as that last meal in the trailer. I'll be more than satified. Can't even by a meal as good as that was. (<u>Compliment</u>). I bet you feel good now. Ha. Don't mind me. I only think Im the best cook in the world. May be I'm letting my self open for some thing. I know what you are thinking.

I'll be going to school in a few minutes. I'll only have to go till Saterday. I'll be glad its over.

By this time you may have received your diploma. I can imagine you are aslo glad school is over. I'm glad you stuck it out. I knew you would. All you have to do now is hope that I'll return some day and if I dont, you can always say I was a nice boy. Ha. If I'd get half the chance I'd be back before you could blink an eye lash. Your my pot of gold. If I never become rich with money. I'll be rich with having a wife like you. I'll be happy in thinking that I took a lovely thing like you from some one else. Hang on sis I'll fin-ish this tonight!!

May–10–1945

Just came from School. What a day. You should have seen me. I was the most interested fellow in class (rough drawing of a face) Do you know this fellow? I doubt. It has a good resemblence He is the Polock I told you about. If he must look over my shoulder I might as will draw pictures of him. I'm an artist and didn't know it. How do you like that. Hidden talent. Can't never tell what I'll turn up next.

I don't know wheather to address your letters home now or not. Let me know what you want me to do. I guess it will be hard to believe you are out of training. I know it will be hard for me to believe I'm out of the Marine Corps when the time comes.

Some fellows were out on liberty today. They seem to have visited a drinking place. You know what I mean of course. They haven't located the door way as yet How do you expect me to sleep nights if you insist on me thinking of me? Keep me awake half the night last night. "Arnt you ashamed?" Keep Smilling.

Love and Kisses
Paul

Postmarked May 13 1945 from Cpl. Paul J. Fogel, H & S. Co. 23 Mars, c/o. F.P.O. San Frans. to Miss. Evelyn Wells, 1101 E. Gadsden, St., Pensacola, Florida. (stamped "PASSED BY NAVAL CENSOR" with initials; with 6 cents imprinted air mail stamp)

On plain, unlined stationery:

April–
May–12

Dear Evelyn:—

I had two letters from you today. You don't really think Bennett told me any thing about you now, do you? Well she did. I skipped the lines that were none of my busness and read the rest of the letter.

I've come to the conclusion that sixteen hours is entirely to long to work in one day. When I get back things are going to be different. Me and you are going to take a little rest. You know sleep till noon, on a big bed. One with lots of room. Not like my sack. You have to be afraid to turn over, or else you will find your self on the deck. I'm always picking the covers off the deck. When I get back I'm just liable to have all those things. Like I had them in Pensacola. The Hospital I mean. Im hoping not. I had enough laying both on my stomach and back.

This graduation could not have been as bad as you were discribing it. I'm hoping it wont be

You wanted to know who Wayne is. Hes one of my cousins. My fathers sisters son. That is getting down to it. Hes and, Ensign in the Navy and is stationed near me. Only I cant get to see him because he's on another island. Isn't that a tough break. He was brought up like I was suposed to. Went to collage. So did his brother Robert. They are both married now.

So Mamie Lou left too eh. I dont know what your mother is going to do now. Every body seems to leave her.

I just came from School today and I received that letter you wote on May 6. I feel as cheap as the devil. You havent heard from me since the 23 of last month. I'm sorry you havent been receiving my letters. They are on the way some where. I have the censors word for that. He is probably getting tired of reading all your letters.

As for me feeling OK. I feel as well as any one could. Not even a little finger aching me. Thats a picture of health isn't it.

So Bennett has been transfeed. I hope she writes again. She always writes such interesting letters. [illegible]

Your brother David might also visit me eh? I don't hope so either. We really don't need him. Dont you think I'm doing a good job of winning this war. Not bragging of course. If very many more of my relation comes across here. The whole family might as well pack up and move here.

I miss you more every day. I'm just praying you will stay the way I left you. Not to change even a little. I love you the way you are. Don't ever change. You can bet as soon as I reach the states you will know about it. I can hardly wait. Heres a hug and a kiss for you.

Love and Kisses,
Paul

Postmarked May 14 1945 from Cpl Paul J. Fogel, H & S. 23 Mars. 4 Div., c/o. F.P.O. San Frans. Cal to Miss. Evelyn Wells, 1101 E. Gadsden, St, Pensacola, Florida (stamped "PASSED BY NAVAL

CENSOR" with initials; with one 6 cents air mail stamp and one imprinted 6 cents air mail stamp)
On plain, unlined stationery:

May–12–1945
[numbered page '1']

Dear Evelyn:—

To show you how much I love you. I'll just sit here and write you one of the longest letters I've ever written you. The mosquotoes will have me bodily carried away by the time I'm finished, but I think you are worth the saticrifice and lots more too. I had started to go to the show tonight. I did go I just stayed for some short features. Then the big show disapointed me and beside that I made a remark to a buddy of mine and he didn't like it so I though it best to leave. I have to candles on either side of me. They seem more homely to me. We have electricity and the blulb is on also but there is something about candle light I like. It reminds me so much of the night we had that party at the beach. Remember how beautiful it was when darkness fell and we had that bond fire. This just about gives the same effect. The only thing lacking is you.

I have liberty again tomorrow and I intend to go fishing with another fellow. He is a Jew. He stands for exactly that. If you know what I mean. He injoys collecting things. It doesn't matter much what it is. He will find some thing else to trade off on. You should see the wide assortment he has. Every thing from A. to Z. Hasn't missed a thing. He is in the same tent as I and knows some good fishermen down near the ocean. So

I intend to join some professionals tomorrow. I have been out with them once before and already told you. Its a lot of fun. I wish you were here just to enjoy it also. I'll have to teach you the art when I return. I'll have alot of experiences to tell you then. Some good and some not too pleasant. We usually take some lunch along to eat a wee bit at noon. You would be suprised how hungry a person gets after swimming half a day. I have a huge appetite anyway but after that it just about doubles. I can see where you will have quite a job cooking for me alone.

[numbered page '2']

From the sounds of your letters you do injoys cooking. I'm glad you do. I think I'm the luckiest person in the world to have a person like you. You don't complain much. You are easy to get along with (Thats more than I can say about my self.) I do hope you will like me as a husband. I'm going to try darn hard to be a good one. I'm trying hard already not to do things I know you wouldn't want me to do. So far its helped me keep out of a lot of trouble. It would not have been hard to get into some around here.

We have quite a bit of women running around the towns. Not natives exactly. Most of them try to keep them selves beautiful and respectable. Its not not uncommon for a Marine to marry one of them. It seems to happen every day. Most of the families are very agreeable with service men. They injoy having them drop in on them for dinner. I've meet quite a few people that way. There homes are built much like yours or mine so they not huts as you would have imagined. The Japs especially on this island are very clean. I dont know how to explain it, but its true. The young girls have very beautiful hair and take good care of it while on the other hand there faces are as you would have guessed, flat as brownish collor. Their teeth usually stick out. The yellow you hear so much about the collor of the Jap comes after they are dead. I saw the ones on Iwo and they were pale yellow. (I made an interesting study even down to geting a tooth off of one.) That was cruel wasn't it.

I hear them comming back from the show. It must not have lasted long. I don't believe it was much good.

I don't know wheather I ever told you about that girl I knew in Pensacola that came from Iowa City, Iowa. She found my address some where and wrote me. I guess Jake gave it to her. To get back to the subject she wrote me a little letter yesterday and wanted to know what happened to me. Know where she is now? Somewhere in Italy. How do you like that. She joined the...

[numbered page '3']

the American Red Cross, and they send her across. I though that was nice of her. She was engaged to some fellow in Corry Field and came down to see him. Miss McClain introduced me to her one night. I only remember her slightly. So much for her.

I don't remember wheather I told you about this pal of mine or not. One of us three. He wants to become an under taker when he gets out. He's engaged to a sort of wealthy woman. Any way she has enough money. His parents also has enough money to last a while. I wonder how it feels to be that way. To get back to the story. He thinks hes in love with another woman so if he gives this woman up to get engaged to the other, hes afraid he won't be able to set himself up in business. How do you like that. To me its sounds like "getting married for the money" What do you think? Hes a swell egg though, a little fouled up. Once in a while comes around for advice. I tell him to see a chaplin. If you get down to clear facts. That is exactly what he should do.

Now the other one of the three. The one that is married already. He has a child and his wife writes him not quite as often as you to me. (You sweet thing you) Tonight I went to get our mail and on the back of her letter she had SWACK. You know, for her self than for her son and then she had another for one I guess that is on its way. He didn't tell us about it yet. We are keeping quiete about it until he tells us personally. Then we will jump on him for not telling us. He has been mighty quite lately. He lives in New Jersey and his wife from Norfork, Va. You see he was doing duty there when he met her. Before he came in the Marines he was some thing like Mr. Dean at Chattahoochee. He was working in an insane asylum. Some times I wish he would have stayed they. He gets me too terribly mad some times I could begin to pull my hair out. He sure likes to argue.

[numbered page '4']

Rember Mr Gable—I mentioned him in connection with Iwo Jima. He was also my commanding office—In charge of the Q.M. He was sick again and had to turn in at the hospital Every one seems to miss him He was hard to satify but, he knew how to get things down. We have a Lt, I forgot his name. Hes seems to be a good fellow also.

I finished school today. I was sort of glad I did. I have to learn to keep away while in class. It was hard for me to do but I succeeded. I came though with a fairly good average. I can say I was a wee bit over average. No one had a perfect rating and I had as high as the majority. I really did need the experience. I had forgotten most of what I had learned from Tech High in Bethlehem. While I was going to school there. I only went to school about a year and a half for Auto Mechanics. Than they transfered me to Machinest work. You know working on lathes and drill presses and on that varity. I really wish I knew more about it. I believe Im going to take a corrosponcence course in Welding. I think it may come in handy after the war. I'll be more or less a jack of all trades after I get done doing what I want. The trouble is I wont be master of any.

I wrote and told you about Sgt Maceluck writting me the other day. He gave me quite a bit of information on Pensacola before he left. He says they have a new commanding officer and things are more fouled up then ever. He also wrote and me the address of Maragret his wife. Remember her the person who got her appendix removed. I bought him up to see her. I'll never for get that night when I was comming up the front steps and out came a flock of girls. One of them was in a white gown. I felt very silly standing there no tie, collar open waiting for the...

[numbered page '5']

last to come though the door. You were practically the last and you looked very proud. I smilled and you returned the smill. Then was the time I told my self "yep she is the one for me. So then the next time I had an advantage on you. You had no other choice. Arn't you sorry? I'm sure if you feel like writting to her she would apreciate hearing from you. I guess I mentioned you so often, every marine who ever did duty with me knows you as well as I. She would not have forgotten you. If you are interested her address is. Mrs. Joseph L. Maceluck–25–50–23rd Street, Long Island City New York. I'll never for get their son. He was the cuties thing. Don't you think. I guess I knew all their neighbors too. I miss seeing all those people. (Not near as much as I do you)

My Aunt Mazy send me a box of candy about a week ago. I couldn't eat it but I made an attempt at it. Darn near broke my teeth on it. We had to throw it away. It must have taken six months to reach me.

An Italian just came in with what they call Italian pie. It contains (now listen to this). First comes the does. Like sweet bread. Than they put some sort of dressing on it it looks like jelly. Than comes some tomatoe soup of some sort after that they put plent of pepper on it. (It is still burning my inside of the mouth. After that they throw in some cheese—Put in stove and bake. Don't ask me when to take it out. That comes in on the next lesson. Whooo is that stuff hot.

I believe, I told you about my brother arriv-ing in the states the 8th of this month and arrived home on the 12ᵗʰ That was fast traveling wasn't it? I hope I get to see you that soon after I hit the states. He is back with his old sweetheart. Pauline wrote and said he is thinking seriously about getting maried. I hope so. She also says he needs a new slant on life. Pauline is sort of my home

[numbered page '6']

newspaper. She claims that married life is be comming more agreeable by the day. I'm glad of that. What my mother doesn't want me to know I can depend on good old Pauline She never fails. I'm sure you two will get along OK. I can't see how any one could dis like her. Of course she and June my oldest sister fight once in a while. Of course that is the Fogels for you. Love and Fight comes hand in hand. Are you prepared? I used to have some honey's on the way to school. She used to walk ten paces in back of me. You see now how I used to make her toe the line. Boy, was I rugget. This is the fifth or six page. I'll have to continue its getting on to eleven oclock and it must be time for you also to go to bed so good night untill tomorrow. Don't dream of me tonight because I'll probably be chasing you with a ball bat. Arn't you afraid. I'll aways love you sis Keep Smilling

Paul.

<u>To Be Continued</u>
Chapte 7 Continued From Page 6 Book 1

How do you like that. Just like I was writing a book. I'm sure you would. I've lost all my interest in this letter now. As I was telling you I went on liberty yesterday. I enjoyed my self intill my arm went out of joint. Right at the shoulder. By the way I caught my first fish by spear yesterday. I guess I be came to excited after catching it. It was about twelve or thirteen inches long. Just a mino. You should have seen the one the Jap that we were with caught. It must have been twelve inches in diameter. It was one of the largest I've ever seen. (Some one has the radio running full blast, some cow boy is crying his heart out.) Poor fellow. The way my arm came out of joint was. Now get this. Here I was hanging on to two big bloters see. There was a big wave comming toward me so I caught it OK and when the out tow came I was also prepared for it. But— when it hit me one of us had to give and it had to be my arm. Did you ever have it done to you. What a terrable experience. It feels as if some one tore your arm off. (It still does. Here the trouble comes in. No one knows how to put it back for me so I had to put it back my self. You beat that. All I did was wack the top part that was out and it snaped right back into place. Simple wasn't it. (Just came from chow. Pan cakes) We ate super at there place last night. What do you think was on the menu. Rice—Not forgetting we ate it with chop sticks. Can you imagine me eating with two sticks. I couldn't either. It works though. We also had fish—and more fish. I've just about eaten every thing in my day but this was the last straw. They put sea weed on the table too. I had to taste it and I did. They put some sort of sauce on it. It didn't turn out bad at all. In fact it was sort of good. Now don't you get any funny Ideas in your head.

When I get home I want a nice juicey rare stake. Yum. Wait a minute that wasnt all they had. They put octopus meat in front of me too. You know, those long fingers didn't taste bad either. Don't waste a thing those Japs. I never saw the likes of them. We usually throw the head of the fish away. They think that part is the best part of the fish. In fact they leave the eyes in the fish also. I got a big kick out of trying to pick things up with those chop sticks. While we were at the beach. One of the kids crawled up a coconut tree and broke off a few coconuts. We pealed the shell of the core of them. We puched holes in the top and drank the milk. I never tasted it before. That was also some thing new to me.

This Jap family I was telling you about has eleven children. in it. How would you like a family as large as that. She is like a hen with chikes. She still has four little girls at home and they hang to her like bees to a hive. The rest of them are all either in the service or married some where.

I must have forgotten to tell you some thing I know. I dont know what just now so I'll sign off. You are probably tired from hearing me gab any way. I think I go to sick bay get this arm of mine taped up or some thing. Boy what wouldn't I give to have you take care of it for me. I still think you are the most beautiful wife I could ever have pick. Lucky me I'll aways love you. Keep Smilling. Here a hug and a kiss for you. Got it, Good.

Love and Kisses
Paul.
This is the longest I could write.

Postmarked May 15 1945 from Cpl. Paul J. Fogel, H & S. Co. 23 Mars., c/o. F.P.O. San Frans. Cal to Miss. Evelyn Wells, 1101 E. Gadsden St., Pensacola, Florida. (stamped "PASSED BY NAVAL CENSOR" with initials; with 6 cents air mail stamp)

On plain, unlined stationery:

May 14–1945

Hello my sweet little Sweg gums:—

And how are you this fine evening. May I call for you at seven. O if I want too eh. Same old you. If I don't want to I could go to bed. It wouldn't make any difference to you. How am I? Well what did you want to bring that up for. Stop chang ing the subject. You are so easy to take to you dont even put up an arguement. Thats what I like about you. You are a good listener. Yep I could talk to you all night. I cant though you have to be in at ten oclock.

What dreadful days they were remember. Gone forever. Can only make believe now. By this time you are a ful graduate nurse. You are proba- bly celebrating your victory or self controle. Me. I'm celebrating my having duty tonight. I don't have one single pleasant thought in my mind with an exception of you. You are a very pleasant thought. I hope that graduation wasn't as bad as you seemed it would be. You didn't think much of it the other day. I wish I could have been there to flirt with other girls while you were getting your deploma. Ha. You would have gotten a kick out of that. Wouldn't you. Let me guess what you are thinking now. I would have gotten the kick. Not you eh?

Had a letter from my sister in Law today. The wife of my oldest brother Charles—She a wonderful person. Big and skinny like me. You should see the stomach muscles I have now. This food is agreeing with me. In Eliz abeths last letter she said she may reach 164 after all. It will keep me from becomming a liar you know.

I'm sure you would injoy meeting her. If you would like to write to her, her address is Mrs Charles W. Fogel Tatamy Pa. I know you can't read it. Try reading it anyway. You hear from my mom lately. She said she wrote you not too long ago. She enjoys hearing from you so much.

I hope you are getting my letters OK by this time. You see I'm trying my best. Thats all I can do. How did you like that book I wrote you yesterday. It was a dille. Wasn't it. It will take me another six months before I can do it again.

Love and Kisses.
Paul.

Postmarked May 16 1945 from Cpl. Paul J. Fogel, H & S. Co. 23 Mars. 4 Div., c/o. F.P.O. San Francisco, Cal. to Miss. Evelyn Wells, 1101 E. Gadsden, St., Pensacola, Florida. (stamped "PASSED BY NAVAL CENSOR" with initials; with 6 cents air mail stamp)
On plain, unlined stationery:

May–15–1945

Hello Honey:—

Right now I have nothing to do but write you this boresome letter. I was rereading that letter you mailed me on the 2nd of May. You didn't sound any too happy than. Perhaps I can cheer you up a little, if by this time you are still in the dumps. I you are thinking my next move is that of the states. That is what I call, wishful thinking. Besides that, it is impossible, so to speak.

I had another liberty day, today. Now wasn't that nice of the Marine Corps. Yep they said to go and enjoy your self. I like to disobey orders so I stayed in my sack. Arn't I mean. No that wasn't really the reason. I had to catch up on some work I had to get done. While I'm thinking of it, I send you a present after all, for your graduation. A fountain pen. You see you cant give me the excuse that you have no pen to write to me with. When you get tired of writting to me. I think this is a nicer one than I gave you before. Now you have two. I found that on shotely after I came from Iwo. Beside I could not have gotten one like it around here any way. Some officer wanted to give me twelve bucks for it. You know me. Money means nothing to me. Of ya. I'm as hard to squeeze money out off than an empty bucket. You should know. O yes I also send that risk watch I said I would. The case is a wee bit beat up but it runs like a million dollars. Take my word for it. I don't know why. Its a wonder it wasn't send home already with the rest of my belongings including my dog tags. You know personal effects. Ha. I've been thinking I ought to make me out a will of some sort. What do want beside my love. I haven't got much, so be reasonable.

O my goodness here it comes. Its beginning to rain. I'll have to shut the door. Hold on a second. There.

I'll be loosing another of my officers shortly. A Mr. King. He's a swell fellow. Hell be going home to where I wish I were going. He seems to be plenty happy about it. Cant blame him. He was in charge of the maintance section of the Q.M. here. Reminded me a whole lot of Mr. Grebe.

There isn't too much to talk about. I could have used you today, I was sewing chevrons on my shirts. Man O man am I going to keep you busy when I get back. This is all for now Hon! The End

Heres a kiss too. Got it.

Lots of Love
Paul.

Postmarked May 18 1945 from Cpl. Paul J. Fogel, H & S. Co. 23 Mars., c/o F.P.O. San Frans. Cal. to Miss. Evelyn Wells, 1101 E. Gadsden, St., Pensacola, Florida. (stamped "PASSED BY NAVAL CENSOR" with initials; with 6 cents air mail stamp)

On plain, unlined stationery:

May 16–1945

Listen You:—

Dont be so much in a hurry to please me. If you dye those beautiful blonde hair of yours, I'll do what I've threatened to do. Only harder. You might as well put that idea right out of that pretty head of yours. I'm getting used to your hair now and just as long as Paul Jr. has red hair. Thats all that matters. Now, now cool off. I was just thinking out loud. Well now that we have that subject settled. We might as well talk about some thing else. You haven't told me what you intend to do after you get out for good, or dont you intend too. Want to sneek off on me huh. Bad girl. Don't you know you can't get rid of me.

You know what you were doing to those poor little kidds last week. They are doing the same thing to me. Its becomming quite a habit by me. Are you going to feel sorry for me like I did for you. I'll finish this letter tomorrow. You arn't in any hurry to get it are you?

May 17–1945

Hello Hon:—

How is the wheather today in the sunny south. It looks like rain to me. I did my washing just the same. If it rains I be so angry in the morning I'll be hard to get along with all day. You don't get that way do you. I only boiled my gangarees in some soapy water. It does the same job as scrubbing them only it takes a little longer. I get me self a G.I. can and put some water and start a big fire. Simple isn't it. For a second there the fire seemed a little too big. We finally got it under controle. Its eight thirty and there is some sort of U.S.O dance dirrectly up the field a few hundred yards. I can hear the band and every body seems to be having a good time. A few busses bring the girls in from the towns. You have to get dressed up for such an occasion. I dont think it quite worth that much. Beside I have the duty for this week. It would [*wouldn't*—inferred] do me much good to want to go any way. There are ten boys to every girl so you can see the odds I have against me. I was having the time of my life with a blow torch in one hand and part of a motor in the other. Trying to make the electro magnet on a windshield wiper work. It was sort of fun till I gave up the idea for the night. Thought I'd better get this letter out to you.

You know I often think about the times we came back from were we spend the evenings and sat on that fountain in the park across the street. I spend some of the happiest days of my life there. The majority of time I was floating on air though the clouds. Sort of in a haze. And how we used to drink at our privite little drinking fountain. Little low wasn't it. Got to know exactly where it was located just before I left. Didn't I? What about that night I was sitting on the porch and my pants riped. I really didn't know what to do or say. Most every one else would have flew into some sort of fit, but you didn't and I was glad. I had to walk down side streets with my hands in back of me What a night that was I'll never forget those things as long as I live. Mainly because I lived them with you. I love you so much. Its hard for me to wait to get back to you.

Always Loving you
Paul.

Postmarked May 21 1945 from Cpl. Paul J. Fogel, H & S. Co. 23 Mars. 4 Div., c/o F.P.O. San Frans. Cal. to Miss. Evelyn Wells., 1101 E. Gadsden, St., Pensacola, Floria. (stamped "PASSED BY NAVAL CENSOR" with initials; with 6 cents air mail stamp)
On plain, unlined stationery:

May 19–1945

Dear Evelyn:

I can now see the reason you made that statement about Bennett. She did talk too much Not too much. Just enough. Enough to make me feel like going out and get drunk for the first time in my life. I'll try any thing once. Practically any thing. I'll have to keep her letter so when I get back I can let you read it. It's quite interesting. O so I have you courious. Im going to let you stay that way. I know what you are going to do now. You are going to write our Lt. friend. What a Pal she is.

Had a letter from you yesterday. I thought after you graduated your time was served. I see where I was slightly misinformed. I'm due to learn some thing new every day.

Today I was trying to construck a grease rack. Get what I mean. A place to run trucks on in order to grease them. Quite a job. Had me sweating there for a minute. My hands are becomming a wee bit blistered. Thats me working my fingers to the bone. All for the Marine Corps. Now isn't that patriotic.

Did you get that package yet. Hope so. Wouldn't like to hear that the pen and the watch were removed. That would really get me angry. It was send air mail Thought you may receive it sooner.

I'm not much in the mood for writting. Perhaps if I waited to tomorrow morning I would feel better. I have liberty tomorrow again. I really haven't got a thing planned. Uusually when I haven't got any thing planned I wind up by washing clothe or trying to catch up with things I should have done month's go.

There is quite a breeze out side at the momet Really raising the devil with the tent. The flapps are flapping so loud I can hardly hear any one talk.

There was another fellow came into the out fit not too long ago. Really a swell fellow Been in the Marine Corps for some time. Longer than I hope to be. We often kid each other about thinks. Right now he is teasing me about writting you so often. I don't mind it. It comes in one side and out the other.

Mom says she hasn't heard from you for some time now. Im sure she enjoys getting your letters.

I'll sign off for now. Keep Smilling

Love and Kisses.
Paul.

Postmarked May 14 1945 from Mrs. L. C. Fogel., Nazareth., Pa., Route 1. to Miss. Evelyn Wells, S.N., 1101 E. Gadsden St., Pensacola. Florida. (with 3 cents stamp)
Graduation card:
Front:

Good Wishes on Your GRADUATION

Inside:

Congratulations, Graduate, For studies so well done! May you continue on the road Successfully begun! "Mr. &. Mrs. Fogel."

Postmarked May 14 1945 from Mrs. E. N. Acker., Nazareth., Pa., Route 1. to Miss. Evelyn Wells. S.N., 1101 E. Gadsden St., Pensacola. Florida. (with 3 cents stamp)
Graduation card:
Front:

Best Wishes As You Graduate

Inside:

    May all your plans and efforts, too, Be crowned with real success; The future never dim the glow Of this day's happiness. "Polly and Earl"

Postmarked May 23 1945 from Cpl. Paul J. Fogel, H & S Co. 23 Mars, c/o. F.P.O. San Frans, Cal. to Miss. Evelyn Wells., 1101 E. Gadsden, St., Pensacola, Florida. (stamped "PASSED BY NAVAL CENSOR" with initials; with imprinted 6 cents air mail stamp)

    On plain, unlined stationery (envelope and stationery written in light pencil):

May–21–1945

Dear Evelyn:—

    Forgot to bring my pen so you will have to read pencil writting. Isn't that too bad. Had a letter from mom today. She thinks I'm getting gray hair. Can you beet that. Me with gray hair. [Illegible] an imposibility. No one knows my mom the way I do. If she were half dead she would still say she was OK. By the way How am I supose to know how you are if you don't write.

    Tomorrow we have a big inspection Every one is running around trying to get ready for it. Including me. Never could get out of one of those things. Every one hates them so much and I'm no exception. I hates em too.

    I believe I worked as hard today as I did all though my life time. My bones sure feel it I was "digging a ditch." You know that pit I was telling you about. I had my picture taken in it. During the process If you are a good girl I may even let you look at a working man. Of course I was leaning on the shovel at the time. Than of course the camera was off at the time. It all adds up to a bum picture. Talking about a picture Tarzan is playing at the show tonight and here I am on duty again. I'll be glad when this week is over. This nighty duty over in this place is driving me crazy. I'm crazy already, "mostly about you." It's a good thing I can write to you even if I can't be with you. This war is lasting entirely to long to suit me. The sooner its over the better I'll feel.

I was fishing yesterday again. Thats just about wound up my fishing for a while. In fact my swimming too. Me arm went out of joint again. Didn't put a bit of strain on it. I was swimming sort of fast and very soon I felt a pain in my shoulder and heard some thing snap. I had to get out of the water with one good hand in order to get it back in place. It gives off some pain. I'll have to let it get real well before I do anymore swimming. Met some more nice people. Again the minue was nice and fish. We caught quite a few. We also took some pictures of the beach. If I may I will sedn them too you.

Its raining outside again I doubt wheather I would have injoyed going to the show any way.

This will be all for now.

Keep Smilling. Here's a hug and a kiss for you. Got it? Good.

Love and Kisses,
Paul.

Postmarked May 23 1945 from Cpl. Paul J. Fogel, H & S. Co. 23 Mars., c/o. F.P.O. San Frans. Cal. to Miss. Evelyn Wells., 1101 E. Gadsden, St., Pensacola, Florida. (stamped "PASSED BY NAVAL CENSOR" with initials; with 6 cents air mail stamp)

On plain, lined stationery:

[No date]

Dear Evelyn:—

Your letter sounded quite sad today. I can easily see why? I dont hope that graduation turned out as badly as you had thought it might.

Yes, I think quite a lot of your mom also. I like the way she writes a letter. It sounds sincere to me. I guess I'm the only one who could understand that. It means alot to me. Some people think they are pulling "the wool over my eyes" She doesn't pull any punches. I knew that from the very first letter she wrote. I'll be one proud son of hers

Did you receive that package I send you. I hope you can make use of that parachute silk in some way It looked like some thing that you could make use of.

It's getting pretty late and I'd like to see part of the show. They say it is pretty good. So good night untill tomorrow.

We had a General's inspection today. Some day it was. The first General I had to inspect me. He walked up to me and took my rifle and than asked me what duties I preform in this section. He looked me directly in the eye for at least fifteen seconds. And I just looked him back in the eye so when he saw I wasn't going to look away he took my rifle and looked at it. It struck me funny that he looked at me so pecular. It felt as if he he were drilling a hole clear through me. Most of the fellows were in need of hair cuts. That was the only fault he found. You should have seen our tent it was as clean as a plate. I believe I could have eaten off of the deck.

I'll have to leave my buddies as I have to take charge of another tent. That means I won't have to argue with them any more. I'm going to miss being with them.

I hope you don't mind this type of paper. It's the only thing I found laying around. I try to do better tomorrow. Bye for now.

Love and Kisses.
Paul.

Postmarked May 26 1945 from Cpl. Paul J. Fogel, H & S. Co. 23 Mars., c/o. F.P.O. San Frans. Cal. to Miss Evelyn Wells, 1101 E. Gadsden, St., Pensacola, Florida. (stamped "PASSED BY NAVAL CENSOR" with initials; with 6 cents air mail stamp)
On plain, unlined stationery:

May–25–1945

Dear Evelyn:—

I just came from the show. Was disapointed. Not in the show. In the wheather. Was all indications of rain. I was even prepared for rain. Took my rain coat along. It didn't rain. Ya beat that. Was a cow boy picture Reminded me of that kid we used to see in the show up in that section. You the one who couldn't sit still. I'm reminded of it so very often. We often had rain to escort us home too. Did we not? Those days may be gone for ever In Pensacola at least.

Received your invation to your graduation today along with a letter. Thanks alot. You will have me be present at the next event, I know. Till

Death do we pat It seems to me that will be the happiest event in my life. Just to touch you and be near you would make me happy. I'm so darn home sick to see you. If I don't stop talking this way, I'm liable to convince me to go over the hill. The big hill to the states.

I took another of my bosses to the air port. Getting shiped to the states. Lucky fellow. I would have liked to have gone with him. Got a lot of time to serve over here yet. Too much. Don't be disapointed in the proofs. You know me I'd like you in any position. If I would have only taken those pictures from my little box before I send it home. Im glad they haven't opened it. I'm sure you are too. If they ever saw those pictures of you and Mamie Lou. They would probably never stop laughing. Wasn't that a mean trick I played on you?

The mosquitoes are just about eating me alive. I guess I'll put my net up and hit the sack. It seems to me if I wouldn't get up and get the rest of the fellows up they would always be restricted for missing roll call in the morning. They are all so hard to wake. Have to push them two or three times. I don't know I have to get up at six. I can't sleep after that no matter how much I try. You won't have much trouble waking me in the morning. I just like to lay in the sack because its nice and soft and comfortable when I return. If you were to lay on my sack now. You would probably be stiff in the morning.

Love and Kisses,
Paul

Postmarked May 26 1945 from Cpl. Paul J. Fogel, H & S. Co.
23 Mars., c/o. F.P.O. San Frans. Cal. to Miss. Evelyn Wells, 1101
E. Gadsden St., Pensacola, Florida. (stamped "PASSED BY NAVAL
CENSOR" with initials; with 6 cents air mail stamp)
On plain, unlined stationery:

May–25–'45

Dear Evelyn:—

Just received a letter from you and Pauline.
I want you to read her letter. She's a diller—Isn't
she? I enjoyed reading Mamie Lou's letter. I can
just imagine the feel she possesses. She must feel
very proud to be with him again. I can easily
see why she thinks it untrue. It will seem like a
mircle to me also. I certainly hope she gets her
wish about him being transfered to Pensacola.
That would really top every thing. My mom
said she send you a gift for graduation. You see
she didn't for get you either—She must have a
more wonderful memory than I had though. I
just mentioned it once that you were graduating
in May. That was last Dec. some time. Pauline
mentioned it today in her letter. Mom said she
was going to wait and let you tell me what it was.
They think a lot of you and haven't even met you
yet. I'm afraid when I take you home they might
like you better than they do me. That would be
awkful. They couldn't like you half as much as I
love you. I feel safe.

Before I forget what sort of person is this
chick you talk about so frequently. Perhaps I
could use her as another stuge to look after you. I
think you need looking after. I can't get home fast
enough to do it my self.

I just read an article in the paper of a buddy of mine who was with the fifth Div. on Iwo Jima. He was wounded there and recovered now is back to duty again. I came through boot camp with him. Never got the chance to see him.

How is my picture comming along. I'm still sitting here and looking at the old one. Which doen't suit me. I'm not too patient either. I guess I have to be though.

This place is becomming too quite and becomming too regulation. A place can be that you know:—I guess just about ready for another operation. Things will be a little more exciting— You know what I mean. I must be getting crazy or some thing. I'll close now. Had liberty today. Made myself a locker box and send my grandfather a book on birds. I'll alway love you.

Love and Kisses.
Paul

[Enclosed letter from Paul's twin sister, Pauline. The original of this letter was given to Pauline's daughter, Donna, and one of her sons, Richard in March 2019, Sarasota, Florida:]

May 15, 1945
9:05 P.M.

Dear Paul

Mother just got finish giving me heck for not writing you boys oftener. So now don't you scold me.

I just came back from taking her out to mother's meeting it is her night to serve and she had enough food for an army. ha, ha You know mother. Each month one of the mothers has to treat because it is her birthday. And if there are more mothers with a birthday in a same month they help each other. Mrs Woblert is with mother. And all day they were calling each other up to see what they are bringing.

I also was down at grandparents place but they were both in bed. Aunt Hester said they went to bed at eight oclock already. Poor granny has such a bad cold she can hardly speck loud. And grandpa will defintly take the medicine the doctor gave him.

Yesterday I was with Fran to Lancaster to the stock yards. What a day. That is certianly a stinky place. I enjoyed the trip very much though, but how can you do any different with that silly Fran. There was never a dull moment all the way down and and back.

By the way did you see Wayne yet. Aunt Hester said he knew where you were but never had a long enough leave to go to see you. And some times never could get off board ship. I hope you get to see each other.

Do you know what? Sheldon is talking about getting married. He said he and Electra were going to run away and get married on Sunday but in the end got cold feet.

He got a nifty sun burn today he was on the tractor all after noon disking and tonight he wanted to go roller skating.

Last week we went skating with the Luther Leagues and did I ever fall. Earl and I were skating along so nice and all of a sudden his skates caught mine and thru me very nicely on my left knee and brused it quit a bit. My knee cap still hurts me.

Did you ever hear any thing as silly as this. There was an accident around Easton Sunday that the car was going so fast that when it hit a tree, it thru the man out of the car up on some telephone wires now isn't that something.

Boy are we having a thunder storm just now it is lightling like all get outs. I am glad I am not alone.

Mother send Evelyn a nice gift for graduation on Monday. It is a compact silver with a hand panted pea cock on the lid. It rearly is nice. I hope see will like it.

We also asked her to come up for her vacation. I hope she comes. We all think the world of her. which you proberly know by now.

Well I suppose mother wrote and told you all the new and I am running out so I will close. Except don't be too supprised if you come home and find your self a new neace or nephew.

Love and kisses
Polly. & Earl.

Postmarked Jun 3 1945 from Cpl. Paul J. Fogel, H & S. Co. 23 Mars., c/o. F.P.O. San Frans. Cal. to Miss. Evelyn Wells., 1101 E. Gadsden, St., Pensacola, Florida. (stamped "PASSED BY NAVAL CENSOR" with initials; with 6 cents air mail stamp)

On plain, unlined stationery:

June–2–1945

Dear Evelyn:—

By this time you are gain wondering where my letters are. Don't disturb your self. There was a good reason for my neglect. I was "on the field" all last week. I was firing my trusty rifle. It nearly let me down but on record day it made up for all the days it had me disapointed me. I had to fire a total of 268 for qualifying. 296 was sharp shooter and 306 was expert. I had a grand total of 304, two less than expert. Was I burned up. All I had to do was try a little harder and I would have gotten it. This happened this morning and I'm still burned up. I got a swollen lip out of the deal so right now I am brooding over my troubles. O now dont get the wrong opinion. I wasn't in a fight, yet. Every time the rifle jumped up it hit me on the lip. Don't ask me why. Talk about being dirty. That was the filthiest place on this here side of the earth. Dust all over the place. I had to visit the ocean ever night in under to feel comfotable in the sack. There must have been a crust of dirt on me as thick as an inch. We had movies every night. Saw them all in Pensacola a year ago. You should have seen how they had it hooked up. They had the projector on the hood of a jeep. We had to sit on the deck in order to see the thing. It feels good to get back to camp again. I took a nice peace ful shower and now I feel like a million dollars. You should have seen the wiskers I growed. They must have been an inch long. Had to use a clipper to chop them off before I shaved. Arn't I an awkful liar. It was just a bout that bad though.

I just collected my mail for the week. You are really on the ball. I hope you continue to be. Had four letters from you. I'm glad you received the watch and pen. I'm also glad you enjoyed that story I wrote to you. May be one of these days I'll get into the mood and write another.

I shall not mention again what a good cook I am. I doubt wheather I'd enjoy that as a life time job or not. I hardly think so. These Japs ain't lazy. I'd rather think they are conservative You'll find a great difference in the way they prepare there food. Its not pleasant to look at but its eatable. Thats all they do any way, servive!

I had a letter from my brother Roys wife. The first I've received from her. It was a very interesting letter. She is glad to have you join the family so as she won't feel too lonesome being the only one from the south. She is not the only one. I doubt wheather I could ever find any one else to take your place. I doubt very much if I could forget you if I tried. So I'll not try. I'll only try to get back to you faster.

Why didn't you tell me you wanted to get into the station. I see Smitty's boy friend doesn't have the pull I had. (not to bragg.) No those rules were allways the same. The only reason I was able to get you it was because I knew every one who worked on the gates. I allways had it settled before you arrived.

I doubt wheather any one in the world has been stuck as my times as I have. Before we left for Iwo we took some thing like fifteen shots. I was glad I was through with them.

Your opinion of Miami is very high. I see where I will have to visit that place with you some day, I hope it is sooner then I expect.

Was that a slam in my dirrection about Old Friends?—[girl in Italy]

Now that Mamie Lou is back she can start to write me those chapters. What a person. She deserves all the happiness she is having. I can bet yor mom must feel pretty proud also. There must have been a lump in her throught. I know there would have been in mine. I doubt wheather I'll ever forget Father Dolan In my book, he comes at the beginning. He always had thoughts.

Im glad you are getting plenty pratice with those safty pins. You are going to need it. Maybe not soon, but in the future.

I can hardly wait for that picture of you. I have also some pictures I have to get them censored. I think you may injoy seeing these. Of course they are nothing to show to your friends but they have an interesting point of view.

Yes I remember Smitty. Quite well. I guess she became pretty angry at me at times for taking you from her. You will tell her it wasn't intirly mine.

I'll sign off for now.

> Keep Smilling.
> Love and Kisses.
> Paul

Postmarked Jun 5 1945 from Mrs. Leidy C. Fogel., Nazareth., Pa., Route 1. to Miss Evelyn Wells., 1101 E. Gadsden St., Pensacola, Florida. (with 8 cents air mail stamp)
On plain, unlined stationery:

Nazareth Pa Route 1.
June 4, 1945.

Dear Evelyn:

Please forgive me for not answering your most welcome letter a few weeks ago. But being Paul's brother Sheldon arrived home there was so much to do and so much to talk about that I just

put writeing aside but for Paul. Roy and Charles.
I wrote them regularally. Yes I received a very
nice letter from Paul last Saturday he seems to
be well, but a bad case of home sickness. I know
he wishes he could be home with Sheldon too
as he has not seen him over three years. Sheldon
left Saturday for Camp Dix. N. J. and came back
tonite for another 15 days and then to go to the
South Pacific again. Brother Charles is on his
way over as we had a letter today. Brother Roy is
some where in Northern Italy and has a leg injury
but thinks he will be send down to Paul too. I am
so sorry to know your brother is in the States and
you can not see him. I hope and pray the time
will soon come that you can visit him or he you.
I am so glad you liked the little gift I send you.
I hope you will pass your State Board examination with flying colors. I know Paul is very proud
of you. as he tells me in his letters. He has me
worried because he tells me some of his buddies
from Pensacola came to where he is and nome
knew him. I hope and pray he will look as fine as
Sheldon did when he came back. You say about
the weather well the sun tries to shine but it rains
most of the time. Its very hard on the crops it
makes them rot in the ground. We are all in good
health and must let the weather conditions to the
good Lord he will let the sun shine some day.

> Always loving you.
> Mrs Fogel.

Postmarked Jun 6 1945 from Cpl. Paul J. Fogel, H & S. Co.
23 Mars., c/o. F.P.O. San Frans. Cal. to Miss. Evelyn Wells., 1101 E.
Gadsden, St., Pensacola, Florida. (stamped "PASSED BY NAVAL
CENSOR" with initials; with 6 cents air mail stamp)

On plain, unlined stationery:

June 5–1945

Dear Evelyn

How is my honey today. Elizabeth told me the only time I write her is when I'm angry. She claimed a small tornado burst in side of me the last time. Did you notice anything like that? I didn't feel any difference. Must have been her imagination. I would have known about it, if it would have.

The old heavens are really giving off alot of water these days. A little too much. Sat in the rain at the show again last night. The past month I had seen all the shows that played. Reminded me of the times I had to see two shows with you. I can truthfully say I enjoyed them at that time. Isn't much fun around here. You arn't sitting aside me. Some difference eh? Say I'm jewing some gum. Want a peice? I bet your mouth is watering. I got up this morning and had to walk to show in the rain. Did I complain. You would not have liked to hear me.

So you received three letters from me in one day. Thats too many I think I'll have to start rationing them to you. What you dont like that idea.

You know you are becomming just as I am. Thats not very advisable. Don't ever become like I am. Heaven forbid. You mentioned some thing about Elizabeths present and didn't say what it was. You might forget by the time I get back. Don't you think you ought to tell me now. I do. I'll have to write Elizabeth and ask her. She'll tell me.

So Smitty wants to be one way eh? I thought so. Don't want to wait on us. I ought to wish her bad luck but do to my position I can't hardly do that. You will give her my best wishes. won't you. What would she like from over here for that event. As her and let me know. They have every thing over here. Even wedding rings! Maybe you ought to though that one away. I thought you may like one bought in the states. Any thing you say.

Had a letter from mom today. Got to keep an eye on her. She may get to love you more then I. (Can't be dont.) Then where would I be.

Love and Kisses.
Paul

Postmarked Jun 9 1945 from Cpl. Paul J. Fogel, H & S. Co. 23 Mars. 4 Div., c/o. F.P.O. San, Frans. Cal. to Miss. Evelyn Wells., 1101 E. Gadsden, St., Pensacola, Florida (stamped "PASSED BY NAVAL CENSOR" with initials; with 6 cents air mail stamp)
On plain, unlined stationery:

8–June

Dear Evelyn:—

By this time you should have received those pictures of me. I hope you find something about them that intrests you.

I received a letter from your mother yesterday She seemed to be in a jolly mood. From what she says, I gather you talk to much. Mostly about me. Ha. You know thats a bad thing to do. Talk behind my back. Arn't you ashamed? If you weren't so sweet and if you weren't going to be my wife. I'd spank you. And I can do it too. I know just what you are thinking. Exactly. You know a paddle is what we have to get in our home. So every time you get out of hand. I can put you back in the groove. You know thats a good idea Don't you agree. I knew you would. The rest of our conversation is confindential. Just between she and I.

You are just a brutial as you ever was. Killing those poor defenseless cockroaches. Where is your kindness? They also love to live and multiply.

Bennett told me about that Sgt. She put it this way. "I've finally found some one, I want to like." I believe she was sort of worried about being an old maid. Thats a laugh. You need not be afraid of being one because you are already taken. If the Lord and the Marine Corps doesn't stop working together you may still have a good chance, unless another lucky fellow comes along. We always say if the Lord doesn't get you on the first operation. The Marine Corps sends you on another and if he lets you get home than you really rate in his book.

I went to the show again last night in the rain. I guess you know. I wouldn't give it a second though if I were back in the states. Over here getting wet adds up to a little excitement. It was a fairly good picture "Enchanted Cottage." This is one of the worst letters I've ever written you. You can see what I do with my liberty days. Catch up with my letters. I'll close now.

The sun is out and it raining pitch forks.

Love and Kisses.
Paul.

Postmarked Jun 11 1945 from Cpl. Paul J. Fogel, H & S. Co. 23 Mars. 4 Div., c/o. F.P.O. San. Frans. Cal. to Miss. Evelyn Wells., 1101 E. Gadsden, St., Pensacola, Florida. (stamped "PASSED BY NAVAL CENSOR" with initials; with 6 cents air mail stamp)

On plain, unlined stationery:

June–10–1945

Dear Evelyn:—

I'll never forget those hours we spend at Chattahoochee. I really injoyed. If it were not for that after affect I received. Beyond me what brought it on. It must have been Friday the thir teenth. I'd do it again if I had the chance, although that first week at the hospital was the most painful I have spend to date. By now I guess you know why I picked on a nurse to be my wife. Some day we shall go back to Chattahoochee and look the place over again. Pay our respects to Mrs Shepard. She had her troubles also. She was very good to me while I was there.

Your military secred is as good as kept. Give them both my best wishes Were you bride's maid. They would have had a beautiful one if you were. You don't have to remind me about the regulations of the nurse corps. It interefered with me enough. I think I'll put my foot down. I should have sooner. Right in the middle of a bunch of directors.

How do you like that sleeping in the middle of the day? Arn't you ashamed. Come to think about it. It might be a good idea after all. When I get back I'll keep you awake all the time. I'll be floating in the clouds. What do you mean you are glad I haven't been married. Never had the chance. You seem to be the only one that wants me. I feel sorry for you. Poor you. What about that other fellow you are to marry before me. You met him yet. Better hurry up. I might be back sooner than I expect and I don't want him to be in my way when I get there. There wouldn't be much of him left to marry—or less of me.

By the time this war is over and we have settled down. Some one will have invented a new safty pin or else new diaperts. Ones that dont stick.

I bet Mamie Lou is running around like a young chick. Can't get enough done for Frank eh. She's OK.

I don't know but the way it sounds you have included me in with the house work in our home. We ought to go in a huttle or some thing!

> Love and Kisses.
> Paul

Postmarked Jun 14 1945 from Cpl Paul J. Fogel, H & S. Co. 23 Mars. 4 Div., c/o. F.P.O. San Frans, Cal. to Miss. Evelyn Wells., 1101 E. Gadsden, St., Pensacola, Florida. (stamped "PASSED BY NAVAL CENSOR" with initials; with upside-down 6 cents air mail stamp)

On plain, unlined stationery:

June–12–1945

Dear Evelyn:—

Did you ever have field days in that hospital? It couldn't have been any tougher than the ones we have been having lately. Inspections everyday nearly. Its about to get me down also. A fellow can't have any thing of his own these days. Becomming a real G.I outfit.

Had a letter from you and my history teacher I told you already about. She likes to travel quite a bit durning her vacation. Now she is complaining about not having enough gas to go to Canada. She has some relatives up there she wants to see. She is getting pretty well up in years and wants to get all the travel time in she can. May be she intends to cash her chips in one of these days. She's a swell person. You will have to meet her when I get back. Wouldn't want to let you alone with her she could tell you what an ignorant person I was while she was teaching me.

Every one in the tent seems to be in a very happy mood. You wouldn't want to be in on this discussion. You probably, with out a doubt, know more than I'll ever know about it. Still I hear things I never knew about before. I thought I knew and was taught every thing about sex. Those instructors had nothing on these fellows. What one doesn't know the other one will. What gruesome subjects.

Val had a letter yesterday from his woman and she said her parents were in some small town in Ohio. It just so happens that he has another woman in the same town. Now he is broding over wheather by chance they bump into one another. Engaged to one girl and stringing another along. We are all the same arn't we. I'm glad I can truthfully my stringing days are over. I must have handed you a wicked line. Wish I could remember it. I had to go to extremes for some thing as valuable as you. What a price I paid. You are worth every bit of it and more. I'll be back some day to collect my intrest.

This morning when I woke up it was raining pretty hard so I rolled over on my side and tried to go to sleep again for a few minutes. The next minute it stoped and we all jumped out of our sack and had to stand roll call after all. Talking about weakening one's moral.

By this time Smitty and Smith have become man and wife. Thats a happy thought. You will have to learn all about it from them. our time will be in future. This is all for now.

Love and Kisses.
Paul.

Postmarked Jun 16 1945 from Cpl. Paul J. Fogel, H & S. Co. 23 Mars., c/o. F.P.O. San Frans. Cal. to Miss Evelyn Wells., 1101 E. Gadsden, St., Pensacola, Florida (stamped "PASSED BY NAVAL CENSOR" with initials; with 6 cents air mail stamp)
On plain, unlined stationery:

June 14–1945

Dear Miss Wells,

As my personal physician at the moment, your reaction at the moment would be, "Go to bed and get some rest. I just ran about a mile and a half, over one mountain and down the next. I'm panting like a mare. Sorry, I should have known you were not a farm lady. Any way it all adds up to. "I'm out of wind. I don't know why I'm writing you now. "I must be true Love." I wouldn't even write to my mom in this condition. The sweat is just pouring off of me. You should have been with me I'm sure you could have beat me.

I'm going to school again. Yep started tonight. Its on mines etc. Very interesting, Still I could hardly keep awake during the lectue. I'm becomming a bad as you. I am glad I don't have night duty at least for awhile any way. It was nine oclock before the school left out so I and another fellow ran home in the dark. The meetings were held in a church. Imagine that. It served the purpose.

Pauline wrote me yesterday Made me laugh. I'll send it to you. Perhaps you, can see why. I'm all alone in the tent at the present Every one else has gone to see the show. By the way no rain tonight. You see I wouldn't injoy the picture it I didn't get wet trying to see it. So I stayed in tonight after I got back.

Sheldon went back on duty on the first of the month and is home again on another fifteen days. How do you like that kind of luck. Every one must posess it but me. Don't you feel sorry for me? Not even a little. Woo is me!

I hope you received those pictures by this time. Don't tell me how much you liked them because. You would be fibbing any way. On the one to me you would better put one of your best kisses. To remind me that I still have the Loveliest lady in the world. I feel much better now that I unloaded all my troubles on you. My what broad shoulders you have. When I get back you can make an exchange. I'll have to say good night Snoop. Sweet dreams. They would better be of me. "You chip'per you."

Love and Kisses.
Paul.

283

On very small paper (marked "V-Mail"; Paul Fogel inserted this letter from his twin sister, Pauline):

To Cpl Paul J Fogel 435156, H & S. Co. 23rd Marines 4th Div., c/o Fleet Post Office, San Francisco, Calif. From Mrs Earl N. Acker, Nazareth, Pa, Route #1

June 4, 1945

Dear Paul,

I hate to write with this paper but it so happens that our airmail is all so I won't be able to write so much. We received your package and every thing was in although the things were plenty dirty and smelled terrific. I gave the belts of a thousand stickes as thurow bath in nice clean [illegible]. I said to mother I bet it was the first washing they had in ages. I also disificant the other articals just in case. By the way I wish you wouldn't eat with Jap's it scares me And after I read that letter I dreamed about them three night after each other and gave Earl the worse scratching he ever had, he still has the scabs over his nose. And now he is scared to sleep with me. Now see what you did? ha!ha! We are still having winter here. In Okla. they had to dig themself out of a five foot snow. And it dose nothing but rain around here. Sheldon is home again on a fifteen day leave, he has to go back to N.C. after his days are up and then he will be on his way for the Pacific. He had 130 points and the didn't do him a darn bit of good. He is plenty sick about it.

Love and kisses
Polly and Earl

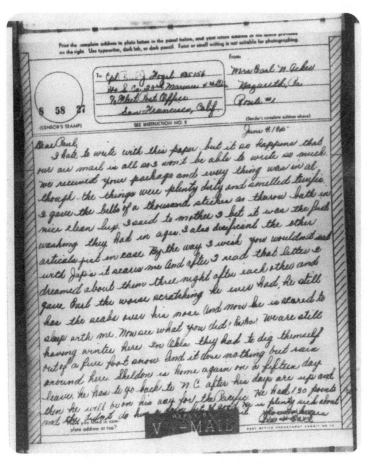

"V-Mail" sent to Paul from his twin sister, Pauline

Postmarked Jun 18 1945 from Cpl. Paul J. Fogel, H & S. Co. 23 Mars., c/o. F.P.O. San Frans. Cal. to Miss. Evelyn Wells., 1101 E. Gadsden, St., Pensacola, Florida. (stamped "PASSED BY NAVAL CENSOR" with initials; with 6 cents air mail stamp)
On plain, unlined stationery:

June–16–1945

Dear Honey—

Just finished my Monday washing. Its far from being Monday. It seems to me that day comes everday. At least its come too many times during the week.

Had four letters today one from you, mom, and my grandpa. Made me feel pretty good too. I don't feel so alone now. Every one else seems to be happy. So I might as well too although I don't feel much like it.

You asked if I needed a special nurse. I sure do. In the worst sort of way. I get some of the worst sort of aches you ever heard of. Mostly in my heart. It feels as if cupit is just about bleeding me to death. I'm sure of what the only cure could be. Only it isn't in this part of the world. O woo is me. Perhaps you know of a cure for it. The pain seems to get worse every night about this time. Don't be suprised if I hug you half to death when I return. In fact you would better have a body guard with you.

You know if Earnestine is half as good as you think she is. I don't know for the life of me why you have been hiding her from me this long. Maybe you were keeping her as a suprise for me. I'm sure she and I would get alone fine. I'm looking forward to meeting her.

I just came from another lecture. Had to hoof it home again. I remember the times you kept me so long as to miss the last buss out of East Hill. You were so mean to me than. But I enjoyed it. Every second.

My boys <u>Val</u> mostly. Came and brought me over to this garage. Hes on duty tonight and doesn't like the idea of being alone. He is preparing something to eat at the present. He's a wonderful fellow. If we ever get the chance we will have to visit him. He has great ideas in store. I have to close for now and help him alittle. I told him I had to finish this letter to my boss. He got a great kick out of that. Don't you get any idea's now. I'm still running the family. Ha.

Love and Kisses.
Paul.

Postmarked Jun 20 1945 from Cpl. Paul J. Fogel, H & S. Co. 23 Mars 4 Div., c/o. F.P.O. San Frans. Cal. to Miss. Evelyn Wells., 1101 E. Gadsden, St., Pensacola, Florida. (stamped "PASSED BY NAVAL CENSOR" with initials; with 6 cents air mail stamp) On plain, unlined stationery:

June–17–1945

Dear Evelyn:—

I have to write you this letter tonight yet. If I waited till morning. I couldn't express myself as I feel at the moment. I just came from a show, "no rain," and I haven't seen a better in my life to express the feelings I carry with me. The name of it was "The Very Thought Of You." You probably have seen it already. Do me a favor and see it

again and when you do think of me because I'll
be in the same state of affairs. The waiting may
be a little lengthy but I'll make it my bussiness
to live to see America and you. I may have wrote
foolish letters once in a while. I supose its all in
the way I feel. To night I feel serious. When I
feel like this I have to tell you I love you with all
my heart and I'll be back to prove it to you. Be
patient. I'll stop for now. In the morning I'll be
in a better mood. I'll finish then.

At the moment I'm yawning my head off.
Lack of sleep? Nope had enough. There must be
some other cause for it.

I did some thing yesterday, I did for the
first time. Ate Pinapples right out of the field. It
seemed to me they tasted a wee bit sweeter. They
were good, though. You slice them into circles
with the outside husk on. Than break an end and
start eating. Really very simple. Its about time I
finish this letter. I started it last night and was
called out twice in the same day.

I met two of my old boys from Pensacola
yesterday. One was Berdan. I must have introduced him to you. Remember that Stage show.
the Air Station put on I took you to see. He was
in it. Hes a great singer. It was good to see him.
The other fellow I came through boot camp
with. We had a long talk. It was like a reunion.
This will be all for now Snuggs.

Love and Kisses.
Paul.
All my Love, Always.

Postmarked Jun 22 1945 from Cpl. Paul J. Fogel, H & S. Co.
23 Mars., c/o. F.P.O. San Frans. Cal. to Miss. Evelyn Wells., 1101

E. Gadsden, St., Pensacola, Florida (stamped "PASSED BY NAVAL CENSOR" with initials; with 6 cents air mail stamp)
On plain, unlined stationery:

June 21–1945

Dear Evelyn:—

You should have had a nice time in Jaxsonville. I'm sure you passed all your subjects. With me on the grand stand cheering for you. How could you help but will. You have come this, and that in itself is more than some people can say. If only I were back there, the day you can say good bye to all those duty hours. I can imagine you are going to feel a strong sensation. Not to be put back on duty the next morning. I wish I could have been with you there in Jaxsonville. Imagine it was as interesting as the rest of the places we visited together. I see you have new names for the Sisters. You called them old Maids. I think you are as bad as we are. If I'd know the truth I think they have inherited worse names than that. Human nature I guess. You find high-strung people around the Marine Corps once in a while also. We have a method thats cures them. I'll tell you about it some time. Very effective.

Did you receive those picture I send you yet. That reminds me. Mine should just about be ready. I'm sitting on pins and needles till I receive it. It means alot to me. I don't care what you think about your self. I think your wonderful. I hope I'm the only one to think so too. I'm very jealous or don't you want me to be.

How is Frank getting along. Mamie Lou ought to move back to Pensacola. She wouldn't have as far to go to see him.

I met some more fellows yesterday that I did duty with in Pensacola Was good to talk with them again. There must be half of them in this outfit now.

Just this after noon had a letter from Mamie Lou. She was so happy she wrote me an eight page letter. Mostly about every thing. Ah She's a lucky woman. She certainly thinks the world of Frank. You Well's must have some thing to attract people to you. How else would I have found you. "You lovely woman you."

All my Love All my Life.
Paul

Postmarked Jun 25 1945 from Cpl. Paul J. Fogel, H & S. Co. 23 Mars. 4 Div., c/o. F.P.O. San Frans, Cal to Miss. Evelyn Wells, 1101 E. Gadsden, St., Pensacola, Florida. (stamped "PASSED BY NAVAL CENSOR" with initials; with 6 cents air mail stamp)

On plain, unlined stationery:

June 23–1945

Dear Evelyn.

I have a busting headache tonight but I'll write this letter if my head splits wide open

I went on liberty today with one of my buddies. We went into a small town and had a stake dinner. It was fairly good. Stake was nice and tender. There was plenty of it too. We paid $2.15 a peace for it. It should have been

good. Dont believe it was that good. We than
went to a U. S. O. where we played card practically all after noon. We bought a large cake
and brought it back to the Camp and we all
enjoyed it.

I joined the Verterns of Foreign Wars, yesterday. I think its a good out fit to belong to. May
come in handy some day. I'm also enroled in the
Marine Corps Institute. I'm taking a course on
Electric and Gas Welding. That knowledge may
also come in handy. If I succeed in that I supose
I'll put in for a corresponce course to finish my
high school education. I'll probably never forgive
my self for quiting. It would have come in handy
many times during the time I was in here. We
can't all be clever so I supose I was elected to be
the stupid one of the family.

We have been having inspection after
inspection. It very tiresome trying to keep up
with them all. We average two a day lately. I had a
letter from you yesterday together with one from
Miss Dwyer my former history teacher.

Yep your mothers secreds still continue,
and I doubt wheather you will hear of them
because when I retire I'll have to destroy the evidence. Ha.

No one knows better than I how much you
do like to read other people's letters. Straight
[illegible]. Right from me.

I hope I receive that letter real soon, telling me the picture is on its way. I'm hoping your
appearance never changes.

I wrote to Mamie Lou and Frank yesterday.
She wrote me another of those books. Each one

gets more interesting. I'm anxious to see what the next ones about.

> Love and Kisses.
> Paul.

P.S. I have no doubt in my mind that Frank does know where I am.

Postmarked Jun 27 1945 from Cpl. Paul J. Fogel, H & S. Co. 23 Mars., c/o F.P.O. San Frans, Cal. to Miss. Evelyn Wells., 1101 E. Gadsden, St., Pensacola, Florida. (stamped "PASSED BY NAVAL CENSOR" with initials; with 6 cents air mail stamp)
On plain, unlined stationery:

June 27–1945

Dearest Evelyn.

Here I am as tired as I've ever been in my life and writting to you. It must be love. I assure you I don't think of any one else as much. You Wells' have some sort of charm connected to you. I can't under stand it. I doubt wheather any one else can. It all adds up to "I Love You very much and think of you always."

I've been trying to built a table for this tent of ours. I'm in charge of it so its up to me to get it don't. There was plenty wrong at inspections this morning. It seems to all pile up at once. Any way it all has to be corrected by morning. Its pretty late now and we have thinks pretty well under controle. It's quite a relief too.

We have one person in the tent that doesnt seem to want to get along. We get alone fine but every body else has some thing against him. The first Sgt was just in and gave me a wonderfull proposition. Either put him on report or I go on report. I never put any one on report yet and dont want too.

Now haven't I got troubles. My heads flooting on air.

My lessons on Welding or going along OK. Have two more lessons to complete before I finish my first period of instruction.

Every one seems to be tradeing jap souvinors so different articles. There sure is some queer trades. Its interesting just to sit and listen.

There must be an interesting show playing tonight every one is shouting. Must be funny. It was raining at the time it began I don't supose many people attend it.

I'll hit the sack now. "Be good." That's what Pauline always says. Ha. I'll always Love You.

Lots of Love.
Paul

Postmarked Jun 29 1945 from Cpl. Paul J. Fogel, H & S. Co 23 Mars. 4 Div., c/o. F.P.O. San Frans, Cal. to Miss. Evelyn Wells, 1101 E Gadsden, St., Pensacola, Florida. (stamped "PASSED BY NAVAL CENSOR" with initials; with 6 cents air mail stamp)

On plain, unlined stationery:

June 28–1945

Dear Evelyn

I doubt very much if I ever let you read one of my June's letters. My sister by the way Yes I think the world of both my sisters Perhaps not too well of their husbands. I'd better be quiet about that. Next thing I know your brothers will be saying the same about me. I wouldn't blame them. I would probably deserve it. You will also not where every one tries to keep secreds from me but most of them I already know. I don't believe Pauline keeps any thing from me but June and mom do. I believe the whole family is trying to work against one another. Fight like cats and dogs one day and kiss and make up the next See what kind of family you are getting into. Don't tell me I didn't warn you.

My brother Charles is over here somewhere. I wish I knew what out fit he is in. I'd like to get to see him. Brother Sheldon left home some time last week. He will probably be over here too, soon.

I could use you on a wee bit of math right now. trying to do some sq root. Quite the thing. Never was much good at using my head. If I were I would have never left home. Ha.

Had liberty today didn't do much but make my self a better tent to live in, and than do a little studing. Now I'm trying to write a letter. Not very successful am I.

I'm just about all paint. Was painting some too today. Never did learn to paint Seems to me there is more on me than the table.

Was to the show last night. Was pretty good. Only a few drops of rain. Suprised? I was. The name of it was "Sudan" Pretty woman too. Had nothing on you. You have them all beat. Think I'll sign off for now. Not much news these days. Keep Smilling

Love and Kisses.
Paul.

[Paul inserted this letter from his sister, June]

June 22, 1945

hello, I am adding a little more to this letter of yours, just to make it a little longer.

Boy, did we have a terrible thunder storm yester day & last night. it got so dark around 6: oclock last night you could hardly see, it sure scared a person.

Lightening killed four of Tony's cows and of the best ones at that, you know which tony I mean down at the cement mill. Well it was the worst we had yet this year.

To day we are staying home once, we were down home all week so far. Yester day I washed for Pauline again.

Paul I am going to let you in on a secret, but <u>Please</u> don't mention a thing to any one. The reason I am down home this week every day is. Pauline had a miscarriage four weeks ago & dare not do any thing heavy. She is going to the Doc. three time a week just now she is weak from loosing blood. Please don't mention a thing about it to her, she don't want any body to know it. She had to tell me, because it happened at our house, or may be I wouldn't know it. I am trusting you not to tell any one. Please. Must close now and make dinner. Willard is mowing yard.

Bye now.

Love
June.

Postmarked Jul 1 1945 from Cpl. Paul J. Fogel, H & S. Co 23 Mars. 4 Div., c/o. F.P.O. San Frans. Cal. to Miss. Evelyn Wells., 1101

E. Gadsden, St., Pensacola, Florida. (stamped "PASSED BY NAVAL CENSOR" with initials; with 6 cents air mail stamp)
    On plain, unlined stationery:

June 30–1945

Hello my Honey:—

Two letters from you also today. They were some welome. Val hasn't received mail for about a week now. He is pretty blue. Can't blame him any. I'd be lost without your letters.

Going to have some sort of parade on the fourth. We were all out brushing up on our drilling this after noon. I suppose you have something also planned for that day.

I've got a tiriffic headache. If I were a woman I believe I'd know what was wrong. Being a man it feels some thing like cat fever. If you have ever had it Im sure you know the feeling. I can't think of any thing that caused it. By the way "No HANGOVER"

Yes, theres another thing. I doubt very much if Val would want to take care of me. I'm really very hard to get along with. I have a hard time taking care of him at times. Once in a while he slips off on one of his [illegible].

I don't believe Mamie Lou is as bad as you would have me think. I know Frank doesn't think so. I don't either. Of course those Irish tempers are sort of bad. What type of temper. It must be mighty gentle. I doubt wheather I've ever seen you angry It stands out on me like a sore thumb. Either I talk too much or don't talk at all.

You are becomeing a good girl arn't you. While you become good I do the opposite and go to the dogs I haven't been to church in a month. Awk ful isn't it. We don't have Sundays off. That of course being the main reason.

No I haven't any tan. Just a wee bit brown. Havent been even swimming for better than a month.

That chicken dinner would taste mighty fine about this time. The chow we had tonight. Well I can't think of any thing to compare with it.

The next tent has a radio on ful blast with some cow boys on. If there is any thing that makes me angry is when some party is being held in the next tent when I'm trying to sleep. Your shoulders are broad enough to hold all my worries so there you are. I feell better now. Your wondeful.

All my love for all my life.

Paul.

Postmarked Jul 6 1945 from Cpl. Paul J. Fogel, H & S. Co. 23 Mars., c/o F.P.O. San Frans. Cal to Miss. Evelyn Wells., 1101 E. Gadsden, St., Pensacola, Florida. (stamped "PASSED BY NAVAL CENSOR" with initials; with 6 cents air mail stamp)
On plain, unlined stationery:

April [meant *July*] 4, 1945

Dear Evelyn:—

Yep, received two letters from you today. Now wasn't that just dandy. Had a reall nice 4th of July. Every thing was complete when they arrived. Was thinking of you all day and wondering if those letters would arrive. They did and I was so very glad they did. What a dinner we had. Reminded me of the meal we had when we came aboard ship to come back from Iwo Jima. We didn't have the ice cream but every thing else was there. Wish you could have been here. Every one else had their little native sweethearts in the base here looking around and I would have been the proudest man on island if I would have had you on my arm showing you every thing of interest. Tomorrow one of my best buddies goes to the hospital to get the same operation I had on my tail. I told him all about it. He has lots of nerve. He could refuse it if he wanted to. If I would have known what it was like. I doubt if I would have [illegible] it done. I'm a sucker for any thing once. Any way I was with him all day play ing penacle. We both injoyed resting the whole day. It was good not expecting an inspection any minute.

The mess had had a large cake about two foot square. Was it good Vanilla I think it was. The red cross ladys just finished cutting it up and I brought two peaces over in the tent here for Val and I.

The whole Division fell out this morning to award the men who deserved medals, received on Iwo. It was a beautiful sight. Every one was in full dress with ribbons and decorations. You should have seen it.

We just finished another bull cession. Talking about the experiences we had on the island. Some of them of course are alot of stiff but one person was telling about seeing the pants getting shot off of another fellow. I know that was true because I also saw it. A person would think it imposible, but war dose funny things.

One of our officers put a sign in the QM warehouse some thing like this "Impossible things we do at once" "Mircles take a little longer." He just about lived on that rule till he left. He went to a hospital for some tropical fever he had.

This will have to be all for tonight.

Keep Smilling.
Love and Kisses Awlays.
Paul

Postmarked Jul 9 1945 from Cpl. Paul J. Fogel, H & S. Co. 23 Mars. 4 Div., c/o. F.P.O. San Franscisco, Cal. to Miss. Evelyn Wells, 1101 E. Gadsden, St., Pensacola, Florida (stamped "PASSED BY NAVAL CENSOR" with initials; with 6 cents air mail stamp)
On plain, unlined stationery:

July 8, 1945

Dearest Evelyn,

If I had you hear now I'd make no promises of what would happen. I'm so happy. I'd propably hug and kiss you till you thought I should be in the same room as that man you were describing to me. That mental case you have. I received that picture to day. I think its wonderful. It doesn't flatter you a bit. You are as beautiful now, and more so, as when I left. It makes me feel as if I were floating on air. It makes me also feel certain that when I see you again. I'll never be without you longer then I have to. Now I have every thing I want from you, but you alone. So now if there is any thing you might want from over here. Heaven only knows they just about have every thing. I guess I proved that by the ring. Don't be afraid to ask me about anything and every thing. I keep nothing from you I expect the same in return. I was up in the mountains not too long ago and they had a little store up there. Seemed to me to be miles from nowhere. Any way they had the most beautiful flowered meterial I ever saw. I was thinking of getting you some but than again I thought you wouldn't like it. It was sort of loud if you know what I mean. More red and yellow than any thing else. I don't know what sort of collor you would like so don't blame me if you think you might have liked.

The reason I haven't written for these past few days was because I began to go to school again. Can you imagine that! You cant. By the way what kind of school do you think this is? Wrong. They are teaching me to swim. Can't believe it huh? I couldn't either until they told me I had to attend. It was more fun then any thing else. The Marine Corps has given me five or six swimming tests and never recorded them in my record book. This time I'm making sure it goes in. What a time we had. Camped out on the deck for two days. Some experience.

Had two letters from you today along with the picture. Benett sure has had her time trying to pick a suitable mate. Perhaps some days the right one will stick his neck out. Poor fellow!! He'll have nothing to say. I'm so very glad my neck was in your way.

My boy Val is haveing the time of his life. It so happened he needs twenty five dollars to go on a five day leave so he up and wites his one and only for the money. He spends more money than any two men in the tent. To get back to the story She won't answer his letter and its been over close for a week or so now. Right now he's telling her off. I can't make him under stand a thing. Quite a few fellows do that and get results but I doubt if I could stoop that low. Especially to borrow it for my personal enjoyment. Thats just my opinion. I don't know how you feel about it.

You want to get used to fishing for if I get to do what I want to do. We may be making a living out of it. I've done quite a bit of net fishing. Haulsinging they call it and the more I think about it the more I like the idea. Of course you also have some thing to say about it. If you don't like it or if you if you do, we might not get the chance to do it. Every thing is so uncertain. It seems useless to make plans as long as I'm over here with still a lot of time to do in the Corps. I can't see where there is any harm in dreaming. Do you? Supose you tell me what you would want me to do. It has to be some thing where I'm with you most of the time Some thing we both injoy. That's a pretty hard job to find isn't it?

Hey! tell Sister she would better start snapping too, and put you on day shift. Tell her I said so. I got to protect my security somehow. What does she want to do, make you sick. I'm liable to give her a peice of my mind after I return.

Give Father Dolan my regards. He's a great man to model after. Wish I could be half as he is. You made some chils run up my spin in that letter you wrote July 3. It was a wonder ful feeling. I'll have to hit the sack now. I'll always love you. Keep Smilling

Loads of Love
Paul

Postmarked Jul 14 1945 from Cpl. Paul J. Fogel, H & S. Co. 23 Mars., c/o. F.P.O. San Frans. Cal. to Miss. Evelyn Wells., 1101 E.

Gadsden, St., Pensacola, Florida. (stamped "PASSED BY NAVAL CENSOR" with initials; with 6 cents air mail stamp)
On plain, unlined stationery:

July 12–1945

Dear Honey Bun Bun:—,

Cute little name isn't it. I was just thinking of that play we saw in on the base that night. You remember it don't you. Was mostly musicial. Some sort of Bond drive. A few of the boys from the baracks was in it. I believe you remember the one person that was quite popular around there for his singing. Bird Bardan by name. Getting back to the subject. He's in the 23rd Marines here with me and we see quite a bit of each other now. Its good to have some one around you knew back in the states. I guess you are wondering where the letters have been lately. Its all my fault. Between inspections and doing my washing I guess there has been very little time. I usually go to the show as soon as it gets dark. We have been haveing very nice wheather later so I didn't have to sit in the rain for awhile now.

I just finished a game of penockle. Wow four games and lost two. Don't see how we lost them. I've become quite a good player. Do you hear that. I'm patting my self on the shoulder. Haven't got much of any thing else that is interesting to me.

By the way I received that letter of the fifth. I'll have to wite my mom to tonight. She just send me some very good news also some very bad news. I'll let you read the letter. You'll know what I mean. I feel very bad about it.

I sleep very good nights now that the picture arrived It must be the watchful eye of yours. You seem to locking at me all the time. I want it that way. Makes me feel as though I were talking with you and you all ways agree. Thats what makes the conversation so interesting You look very natural. You haven't changed a bit and I'm so very happy. I can imagine at times the hair become pretty hot. May be I'm breaking down but if you feel as though you must cut them. Do it but not too much. Save a curl for me huh. Gosh I'd like to be back there moving a comb through them. I know it sounds like stuff but I'd rather be with you combing your hair then any where else. Remember I was always anoying you while I was there. Its just a wonder you didn't get tired of me. I'm hoping and praying you will never have to get tired of me. I'm hopeing now I were there in August to have you by my self. I'm very selfish.

I supose I'd better close for now and write to mom I guess I've neglected her as much as I have you lately and more so and thats some thing I shouldn't do. Good night now. I'll always love you.

Love and Kisses.

Paul

P.S. Mom said never to mention it, but Pauline will never be able to have any children. Can't find her letter. Had letter from Iris the other day. Good to hear from her.

Postmarked Jul 16 1945 from Cpl. Paul J. Fogel, H & S. Co. 23 Mar. 4 Div., c/o. F.P.O. San, Frans, Cal. to Miss. Evelyn Wells, 1101

E. Gadsden, St., Pensacola, Florida. (stamped "PASSED BY NAVAL CENSOR" with initials; with 6 cents air mail stamp)
    On plain, unlined stationery:

July–15–1945

Dearest Evelyn:—

You can take my word for it. You don't snore. At least you didn't the few times I had the opportunity to listen to you. I guess you were just trying to be polite eh? I'll never forget that first night in Mobile I must have layed awake half the night, just looking at you. And what a sight you were when you woke in the morning. No make up on and just as white a snow. We had fun while it lasted. I'm just praying we can pick up where we left off. I was just wondering last night. You have a profession that would be of more value to you and could make more money in a month then I'm able to save in six here in the service. I don't know how to put it. But if you feel at any time that I wouldn't be able to support you as you want to be supported. Let me know. Don't just stop writting like lots of other women. Now your wondering why I brought that up. We have a lot of time to do thinking around this place and alot of maybe's and prehap's come up. Most of them you just wonder about and than some day courousity gets the best of you and you start asking questions.
Val went on a five day leave yesterday. The tent seems empty with out him. He's usually the first one in the tent nights. I come in expecting to see him and feel disapointed when I don't

Iris wrote an interesting. She doesn't seem to like the base. You two ought to get together to form one opinion. I wouldn't mind being back at my old job. I'd probably see you every night instead of every other night. I'm sure I would.

Had a letter from Pauline yesterday she seems to be on her way to recovery. If she only listens to mom. Of course all we Fogels are so darn stuborn. I'm warning you you're going to have a hard time making me mind. Well the Marine Corp did soften me up a little.

I'll send Paulines letter along and you can see for your self what she says. And by the way you can explain what she was talking about to me. It has me snowed.

This is all for now Snuggs.

Lots of Love
Paul.

On very small paper (marked "V-Mail"; Paul Fogel inserted this letter from his twin sister, Pauline):

To Cpl. Paul J. Fogel 435156, H & S. Co. 23rd Mars. 4th Div., c/o F.P.O. San Francisco, California from Mrs. E. N. Acker, Nazareth, Pa, Route #1.

July 9, 1945

Dear Paul.

Here I am again almost fit as a fittle. Yes I am home and am getting better day by day. It is 9:00 A.M. and I haven't as yet had my breakfast so I asked mother if I could sit out and write you boys letters. The doctors say I can be out of bed a while each day till I get stronger but must stay down stairs for thirty more days. Walking goes slow but I still havent forgotten altogether how yet you are probuly wondering what the operation is about Well yesterday Dr. Beck told me for the first time until then no one knew exactly what was wrong I had a (bleeding obtomic) which almost took my life It was held in a matter of a few hours the doc said He at the time they operated had no hopes but then finished to see the results. This thing was as round as a well sized ink bottle with a hole in the center the hole came in after the doc examined me and then it bursted that why they rushed me to the hospital and now I am on a good road of recovery

Love & kisses

Sis

Postmarked Jul 19 1945 from Cpl. Paul J. Fogel, H & S. Co. 23 Mars. 4 Div., c/o. F.P.O. San Frans. Cal. to Miss. Evelyn Wells., 1101 E. Gadsden, St., Pensacola, Florida. (stamped "PASSED BY NAVAL CENSOR" with initials; with 6 cents air mail stamp)
On plain, unlined stationery:

July 16–1945

Dearest Evelyn:—

Don't remember the last letter I received from Elizabeth. I remember I answered her last letter. I guess they are both pretty well occupied with one another when they find time to be together.

Had a letter from your mom yesterday. She can sure think up some of the nices ideas Did she tell you how she wants us to spend our honey moon. She and Mr. Myers want to go on a vacation and let us stay at your home for the time they are gone. I think that would be grand don't you. I doubt if you would approve of it though. I guess you want to get away from home eh? We will see how things turn out after I get back. Perhaps by that time we will have thought of some thing else.

I see where Doris doesn't have too long to wait. I wish I were around to see Jimmy when the blessed event occurs. Not that I smoke cigars or any thing.

O yes I found that letter I was going to send you. I got to write my mom yet tonight Haven't written her for a week now. I bet she is worried.

I received a few more lessons on my course and I'm trying to complete them. I thought I'd better write you first or I would get to involved in the subject I never get time. I was just about pulling my hair out last night on a few questions. I'm telling you I was never so discusted in all my life. It takes a lot to get me discusted. The deaper I get into it the more complicated it becomes. I guess it happens that way all the time.

How is Frank. Is he getting any better. I hope he does get that discharge. It was probably help get well quicker. As well as he possibly could, that is. Haven't heard from any of my brothers for quite some time now. Bet it will be the same excuse. "Lost your address.

A dog wondered by about two weeks ago and deposited two newly born pups under our tent floor. One isn't quite as large the other. Probably the runt. The other is nice and big. They don't have their eyes open yet. Seems to me they should, have had them open long aready. The mother truely takes good care of them. Can hardly touch them.

I'm on duty again so you see I can find plenty of time to write an occosanial letter. By the way. Dont look in Webster for any word you don't understand. Its not in his dictionary. You'll have to look in Fogel's.

I'll always Love you.
Paul.

On very small paper (marked "V-Mail"; Paul Fogel inserted this letter from his mother, Mrs. Fogel):

To Cpl. Paul J. Fogel 435156, H. & S. Co. 23 Mars. 4th Div, c/o Fleet Post Office, San Francisco, Calif. from Mrs. Leidy C. Fogel., Nazareth, Route 1 Pa.

July 5. 1945.

Dear Paul: How many fire crackers did you use up over the 4th July? Did they all go true to the target? I hope so. Well the weather was nice & cool, but very hot for your twinie. She was taken to the hospital for a very serious operation of a rupture and gland trouble. It's over a week now and yesterday when dad visited her he said I could go and bring her home. So Aunt Hester & I went and brought her home late tonite, we put her to bed down stairs and there she must stay 30 more days. If its nice and dry she can be put in a chair an hour each day. You know she told you she was becoming a mother, well Paul don't let her ever know I told you, but she can never have children, the old Doc. told me. Perhaps she will write and tell you. Please dont worry about her as I will surely see and pray she will get well and normal again. She stood the trip very nicely but went to sleep soon after we had her in bed. Everybody else seems to be well and happy. hope you are in the best of health, and that you will soon meet up with Charles or Roy, as we still have not heard of both for a long time. Evelyn wrote a week or 10 days ago and I owe her a letter.

Love
Mother & Dad

(*Author's note:* As an aside, Pauline went on to have 3 biological children)

Postmarked Jul 20 1945 from Cpl Paul J. Fogel, HS Co. 23 Mars. 4 Div., c/o. F.P.O. San Frans, Cal to Miss. Evelyn Wells., 1101 E. Gadsden, St., Pensacola, Florida. (stamped "PASSED BY NAVAL CENSOR" with initials; with 6 cents air mail stamp)

On plain, unlined stationery:

[No date]

It must have rained pretty hard last night for there are puddles all over the place. This tent hee has a few holes in it and it doesn't do me any good for my cloth were practically soaked. I'm sure they weren't as bad as yours, that night we were caught in the rain with you and your <u>shrinkproof</u> dress I'll never forget that as long as I live.

I'm sorry this letter isnt any longer. by the boys are yelling to use this pen. I lost my other one and had to borrow the pen here in the office.

I'll always Love you. Keep Smilling

Love and Kisses.
Paul.

Postmarked Jul 23 1945 from Cpl. Paul J. Fogel, H & S Co. 23 Mars., c/o. F.P.O. San Frans Cal. to Miss. Evelyn Wells., 1101 E. Gadsden, St., Pensacola, Florida. (stamped "PASSED BY NAVAL CENSOR" with initials; with 6 cents air mail stamp)

On plain, unlined stationery:

July 22–1945

To My Evelyn:—

I don't know who I have been devoting most of my time to. You are these blasted lessons of mine. All the spare time I can get. I'm trying to read and answer questions. I promised my self last night that I'd write but I found my self still going strong at ten oclock. Than the mosquotoes began to feast on me, so I hit the sack. Right now I feel as though I could use some sleep. Haven't heard from you for quite some time now. Hope you're not sick or anything. That would never do. Its enough to worry about my sister. That kind of news isn't exactly the kind to make me happy you know.

How is Frank injoying his thirty days. I wouldn't mind haveing a few days off my self. It must be fun doing the things you like for a month. I'll see if I can't arrange it One thing I'd like is being with you. I suppose all the rest of the things would be minor. Do you think that could be arranged.

The boys around here are cussing each other out so much I can hardly think of any thing to write. If my tough slipps after I get back I hope you'll turn your head. It really isn't my fault. It's probably the company I keep. No matter what company I keep. They all speak the same language.

To day is Sunday and we are all working as if it were any other day. I can't remember the last time I was to church. Really should be ashamed of my self. You should go for the both of us ha.

It certainly is warm to day for a changed One of the boys just remarked that we get off at two thirty this after noon. Thats goods. I'll sleep part of the after noon any way.

I was working with my shirt off yesterday and got a little brown. I hope to go swimming tomorrow for a while. I'll really be black. I'll have to go visit my buddy in the hospital first. I usually take some doenuts in to him. He's a swell fellow. I have get another watch out of a jeweler also. I don't believe I mentioned. I bought another watch. Its a beauty. Don't know what I bought it for have enough so as it is.

I'll have to get to work now. Its one o clock and the fellows are yelling because I'm taking a little of the Corps time to write you. I don't really mind.

I'll always love you.

Heres a hug and a kiss for you.

Got it? Good.

Love and Kisses.
Paul.

Postmarked Jul 23 1945 from Mrs. Leidy C. Fogel., Nazareth. Pa., Route 1. to Miss. Evelyn Wells., 1101 E. Gadsen St., Pensacola. Florida. (with 8 cents air mail stamp)

On plain, unlined stationery:

Nazareth. Pa. Route 1.
July. 23. 1945

Dear Evelyn:

It has been such a long time I have written you, and also that I have received a letter from you, but I know it is my time to write first. I guess Paul has written you and told you about Polly his twin if not I will tell you now the best way I know how. Paul was plenty worried about her but he as well as we at home here had faith enough to tell us the Good Lord would help her get strong and well again. You see Polly was not well for a long time and then she had cramps all the time when her periods came around. So about 3 months ago she started menstrating period and it never stopped.

This scared us at first then some one told us some people start that way when becoming pregrent, but I had 7 children and never experienced just such a ordeal. We both went to see the doctor and he was puzzled because I know she wanted a child so bad, well it just seemed the doctor could not help her so he send her to a lady specialist and he ordered her to the hospital to undergo an operation right away. When they were ready to operate she went into a shock, but they operated just the same to find out the trouble.

They found out she was pregrent and had carried the baby in the wrong tube. now I dont know what that is, but she was a very sick girl for 4 days she did not know me nor her husband. Nobody was allowed in but Earl & myself. I just did not know what to do because I was always thinking of the boys over there and then to think my two girls at home were not well either. You see Paul's brother Charles is on his way accross and have not heard from him for over 7 weeks. Roy his other brother has not written for always three months either, so Evelyn please forgive me for not writeing much these past few weeks. Well to make a long story short, we brought Polly home today 2 weeks ago she was in bed till 3 days ago now we have her on the porch and she makes up for lost time she has written her brothers a few times especially her twin, she writes him more often. Now all that is almost over. then we had an awful cloud bust and had an awful hail storm which elecruted Mr. Fogel's cousin who left a widow and 4 daughters and the flood drowned a little boy 4½ years old and they just found him yesterday caught in a wire fence about a half block from our home. this flood was on the 9th. The wheat & oats crop is a total loss and we do not know how the potato crops will be. But still we can be thank ful we have our home & barn yet. And believe me we are. It has rained everyday this month so far its raining now. I guess thats why I am writeing. Paul has written Polly a very beautiful letter Saturday and said he received your photo and is very happy to have it. I will surely be very happy when my family can & will be back again. Sheldon hated to leave after 65 days home and is now back in Bryan Field Texas. he writes and tells us how hot it is down there and misses us all. and believe me we all miss him. How is your brother getting along? I hope he can stay home. How are you? I hope in the best of health.

Mr. Fogel and I and Paul's grandparents are all just fine. Write when you find time. I remain

Sincerely
Mrs. Fogel.

Postmarked Jul 24 1945 from Cpl. Paul J. Fogel, H & S. Co 23 Mars. 4 Div., c/o F.P.O. San Frans, Cal. to Miss. Evely Wells., 1101 E. Gadsden St., Pensacola, Florida. (stamped "PASSED BY NAVAL CENSOR" with initials; with 6 cents air mail stamp)
On plain, unlined stationery:

July 23–1945

Dear Evelyn

I have so many things to say I don't know how to begin and by the time I'm finished I will have forgotten what I was going to say. In the first place tell Smitty not to hold too much against us male creachers. There is allways some bad in good. I'm sure it turned out for the best. Rather find out ahead of time than before its too late, rather after its too late. I'm so happy that you trust me because I do want you too. I'm ashamed to admit I was sort of fearful about you. Mainly because you once made a statement, that you didn't like long ingagements. It sort of held me wondering. I've ceased wondering along time ago. Because I know now I couldn't love any one else. Theres only one thing that could change my mind, and I'm not afraid of it. It will be you to do the backing out not me.

I havent heard from Bennett for quite some-time now. Seems to me she will have to be hurt once or twice in order to find herself a mate. Its none of my business so I not discus it. If I do write you need not worry about me mentioning any about Smitty's love affair.

Elizabeth does write a happy letter. I did get quite a kick out of her discribtion of Danny's embarrassing moments. If Doris ever found out I know I'm sure she would feel in the killing mood. Just as Mamie Lou felt when she found out I had her pictures of the grass skirt affair. I still have to laugh to my self about it. It was no laughing matter to her. At least her letter didn't sound the least bit freindly. I promised her she would get them back as soon as I reached the states.

So [illegible—2 words], How in the world do you spell her name. Any way I think about that couple quite a bit. They were swell people to know. I enjoyed listening to them planning there marrage. I remember when ever I talked to Lou he would tell me all about it and then it would go on the same way when I was a lone with Mac. Give them both my regards and I wish them all the hap pyness in the world.

I don't believe I remember this Margaret you mentioned a few times in your letters. You must like her alot from what I gather.

Had a letter from Mom today she hasn't written anyone for over two weeks including me. She was telling me all about the cloud burst they had and about Pauline. She's getting well quickly she says. I'm so glad. Takes a lot off of my mind.

Had liberty today went to see my buddy in the hospital. He's comming alone OK too. Seems to me he is getting well faster than I did. Remember the day you came to see me and I couldn't sit down. All I did was stand with one foot on a chair. Well he's in the same shape now too. and I was telling him all about you and Mamie Lou that day. He said he was glad no one was around to come to see him. I doubt if I'll ever forget those days.

And the day Elizabeth came with you to see me. I believe you imbarrassed her more that day than I've ever seen her. The time one of her curls was hanging down over her fore head. It did look funny didn't it. I hope this letter makes up for that short one I wrote the other day. You are the most wonderful woman in the world

Love and Kisses,
Paul

Postmarked Jul 27 1945 from Cpl. Paul J. Fogel, H & S. Co. 23 Mars., c/o F.P.O. San Frans, Cal. to Miss. Evelyn Wells., 1101 E. Gadsden, St., Pensacola, Florida. (stamped "PASSED BY NAVAL CENSOR" with initials; with 6 cents air mail stamp)
On plain, unlined stationery:

July 26–1945

Dear Snoogs.—

I see where this patient also knows quality when he sees it. If he didn't he would never have choosen you as his nurse. Lucky fellow he is. Yep, wish I were in his shoes. Not feeling quite as bad though.

I'm glad you finally found some one you liked to work for. At least you are different than most people. You don't have to take any job All you do is wait for the job you like to find you. What will sister think now. Refusing her to work for him. There may be some thing in the air.

Iris answered my letter today. I told you red heads were fast workers Nothing slow about her. She claims she is also off of men. What have we done to deserve such treatment from these women. This is becomming a serious problem. I'd think Iris was different from the rest of the girls. I was under the impression she would have to swat them off like flies. All I can say there must be a might big man power shortage. That puzzels me too. The biggest Naval base in the States and cant corral a man. What will become of these red-heads. I'm sort of glad now you weren't a red head.

I haven't seen a red head yet. That if you did some thing wrong. She'd get right and tell you about it. Now you are different. All you have to do is look at me and I feel lower than shoe nails. Solution???

My buddy came back from the hospital. He was discharged quicker than I was. I believe it was the climate. He was only in twenty days and already his incision is healed close. It took me thirdteen day to get the stictches removed. It could be that there is a war going on too, you know.? Ha.

Val was on the range firing his rifle last week He also came back today I asked him if he missed me and he came up and kissed me on the cheek. He's as crazy as I, only I am a little more so.

I'll stop now and go to the show Keep Smilling Sis. You look better that way.

Love always
Paul

Postmarked Jul 29 1945 from Cpl. Paul J. Fogel, H & S. Co. 23 Mars. 4 Div., c/o F.P.O. San Frans. Cal. to Miss. Evelyn Wells., 1101 E. Gadsden, St., Pensacola, Florida. (stamped "PASSED BY NAVAL CENSOR" with initials; with 6 cents air mail stamp)
On plain, unlined stationery:

[No date]

Dearest Evelyn.

I received two letters from you today. The two you wrote in one day remember. I was glad in one respect, that about nursing, and was feeling as low as I knew I would, the moment. It wasn't that I didn't trust or that I had any doubts about you. I just had to know. Thats all. Call me nosey if you want, but now I am content in the answer I received. No matter how many times you tell me you love me, it sounds like chimes in my ears.

I'm sure Dr. McLane picked a wise assistant. Give him my congradulations for he certainly knows his nurses. I'm glad you like him for if you didn't you'd probably have rings around your eyes from frowning. That would never do for I always want to remember you with a great big smill on your face. Thats the best was. I'll admid I was far from smilling when I shoved off on the train, and if I did smile. It was forced from me.

You would better stay out of sisters way till the twenty fifth of August. Than when you the the deplomina in your hand, you can walk up and tell her exactly whats on your mind. I'd like to be around to see that. That ought to be lots of fun. Especailly for me.

I had liberty today. Didn't go out. Stayed on the base washing clothes. What a laundry I had. Can see where you would come in handy. Got a hair cut. Got those beautiful curls of mine cut. I bet you can picture me with curls can't you. Well don't look so sober. It isn't as bad as althat.

Did work all the time played cugzio most of the time. Till I got sick of it. Partner is three games up on me. That wasn't too good

Sort of hate to see tomorrow come. Holidays are much to scarse and so far in between around. Just have to stick at it I suppose. This war won't end to soon for me. I can't wait to get back to you and the good old U.S.

I'm just about half way through that Welding course. I've learned quite a bit from it. I only hope I have brains enough to hole what I learned. Thats my greatest lack of. Wish I had what that other pen Lost it and had to dig this one out of my sea bag. Doesn't write as good.

Started a letter to you on the twenteth When I get enough [illegible] I'll finish it. This is all for now.

Your wondeful. Thats why I love you.

By for now

Love and Kisses.
Paul

Postmarked Jul 31 1945 from Cpl. Paul J. Fogel, H & S. Co. 23 Mars., c/o. F.P.O. San Frans, Cal. to Miss. Evelyn Wells., 1101 E. Gadsden, St., Pensacola, Florida. (stamped "PASSED BY NAVAL CENSOR" with initials; with 6 cents air mail stamp)

On plain, unlined stationery:

July 20–1945 [Paul explains the date in the letter content.]

Dearest Evelyn:—

So rationing is about to get you down eh? Don't take it too hard. This war can't last forever you. Besides, you won't need a uniform when I get back.

It's hard to believe its hot in Florida while I'm down here. We certainly can't complain about the heat. It's been nice and cool.

I finished a letter to your mother yesterday Was practically ashamed to send it. You know what I ought to do is hire my self a secretary, to write my letters. Perhaps you could read the writting than. It's really my fault I write this badly. My mother had me practicing night after night. I wish I could write as beautiful as she can. She has a wondeful hand writting.

The Sisters are as cruel as we think the Sgts are at times eh? That was a dirty trick wasn't it. Why don't you draw up a petition to throw the sisters out and than set up your own system. I had the idea, you do the work.

By the way how did Smitty turn out Did she ever get married to Smitty. Thats just like you. Get me all anxious to find out the outcome of some thing. Than you forget to tell me about the end of it.

I know this letter is a wee bit underdated but it contains as much as I had on my mind than is it does now. The only thing different is that Im a little more home sick now than I was than.

Your letters sure mean alot to me. I doubt if I'd ever get tired of reading them. Its a good pass time. They are beginning to pile up on me now. They date back to the very first letter you wrote to me It will be an interesting book to read when I get back. They are as valuable to me as any-thing I own. I had lost my little address book and was nearly going out of my head trying to find it. I must have lost it a hundred times already but that doesn't keep it from losing it self again. I'd like to get me a big thick one. One I can't carry around with me. I haven't been able to find any around here. One will pop up one of these days I supose. I'll have to write David and give him my congradulations. I doubt if he would remember me. It won't harm to refresh his memory. Keep Smilling.

All ways Loving you
Paul.

Postmarked Aug 2 1945 from Cpl. Paul J. Fogel, H & S. Co. 23 Mars. 4 Div., c/o. F.P.O. San Frans, Cal. to Miss. Evelyn Wells, 1101 E. Gadsden, St., Pensacola, Florida. (stamped "PASSED BY NAVAL CENSOR" with initials; with 6 cents air mail stamp)
On plain, unlined stationery:

July 31

Hello My Darling,

How are you? Me, I have the evening to my self. I think I think I'll write you this letter than go stand in the rain to see some craze moving picture. It strikes me as funny these past few month, the pictures that have been playing are all new to me. Haven't seen any of them. Now isn't that pecular? It's drizzling out side just enough to keep me well annoyed. Bet that.

I'm going on a five day leave starting the fifth of August. It will be good to get out of this old routine. All the sleep I need and every thing. Wish I could take you with me. We would have lots of fun. We always do, don't we? It won't interefer with my thirty days for my honey moon. So they say. I hope not. Those days are going to be some thing to remember. I'll wite you ever day and tell you what I'll be doing. I won't be able to mail them till the week is up though so don't be looking for a letter.

I was to church Suday. The first time for about four month. I guess I should be ashamed. I did feel sort of funny sitting in the chapel listening to the sermon. It was on, the meaning of songs you sing. One time he was bawling us out for not knowing what we were singing and the next time he was praising us.

Had a letter from Pauline yesterday. She is able to be up and around. I'm so glad. I don't know what is wrong with my family. We are the fightiest people in the world. Seems to me. She was telling me about how she and my brother fell out again. They kiss one day and pull hair the next. Figure that one out. Imposible. Dont mention it to her she would problby never wite me if she knew every thing I told you.

I'll have to get up pretty early to morrow morning to go and relieve the fellow that took my place so I'll have to get to bed sort of early. I'll stop now and go to show. Nighty Nighty.

All ways loving you
Paul.

Postmarked Aug 4 1945 from Cpl. Paul J. Fogel, H & S. Co. 23 Mars. 4 Div., c/o F.P.O. San Frans. Cal. to Miss Evelyn Wells, 1101 E. Gadsden, St., Pensacola, Florida. (stamped "PASSED BY NAVAL CENSOR" with initials; with 6 cents air mail stamp)

On plain, unlined stationery:

Aug–3

Dearest Evelyn:—

I awoke this morning at five thirty to relieve the man on watch and here he is still in bed. I'm not sorry though. I've neglected to write to you for two days. This seems the best chance as any. Had wanted to write last night but went to a stage show instead. It wasn't worth my time. In fact I caught a cold just sitting there listening to them. The least they could have done was make me laugh myself warm. There was a moving picture after the show That was really good. "Nob Hill" in technical color. That, I can say, I enjoyed.

I've accumulated three watches, broken watchs by some sort of trade or other any way they were good at one time. None of them are less than fifteen jewel. I have two in a jeweler shop now. I was told at one place they couldn't be fixed or either they didn't have the parts. If they can't be fixed this time I'm going to put them all in a box and send them to J. C. Elizabeth told me he needed spare parts and couldn't get them. Maybe they will come in handy by him. I see what this jeweler thinks first.

Iris send me the Gosport from the station the other day. I was certainly glad to receive it. I wish I knew how I could subscribe for it. It would be interesting to me. I would ask Iris, but it would put her to too much trouble. Don't you mention it too her now. She'd probably do it just for meanness.

Heard from Sgt Maceluch again today. He is some where in the Amphious Tractor out fit. I though he was around me some where, went to look for him yesterday but could find his out fit on this island. Wish I could do duty with him again. I sure would go for that.

The papers are all full about that fire out in the western states. It must be doing quite a bit of damage. Some one must have had it well planned.

I had liberty yesterday again. That was the reason I had time to look for Joe. Me and my [illegible] as I call him. Went out looking up some old buddies. He is on 36 but he is still rather old for a companion. He is such a lot of fun though. He'll make you laugh when you feel the deapest gloom hovering over you. He can also play cards rather well. In fact beat me the majority of the time. Thats very unsual. Miss Wells meet a nother friend of my Cpl Maddox. This is all for now honey. See you later.

All my Love and Kisses.
Paul.

Postmarked Aug 11 1945 from Cpl. Paul J. Fogel, H & S. Co. 23 Mars. 4 Div., c/o. F.P.O. San Frans. Cal. to Miss. Evelyn Wells,

1101 E. Gadsden, St., Pensacola, Florida. (stamped "PASSED BY NAVAL CENSOR" with initials; with 6 cents air mail stamp)
On plain, unlined stationery:

Aug 6–1945

Dearest Evelyn:—

Yesterday started my five days leave. I went down to my Japnesse friends home hoping to go fishing with him in the morning. He had left before I got there. This morning I was to go with him again. Seems to me I stayed in bed to long. Any way I was supposed to be at his home at six the morning and here I am writting you a letter at nine.

It rained all day yesterday. Had to change kakis twice. Wasn't very happy over it either. It was a very poor day to start off my leave. The people I am with are rather old but a lot of fun to be with. The work on a plantation here and the company rents this house to them. It really is beautifuly furnished. Every thing is kept neat and clean. They every have a maid.

You may have noticed by this time. I'm writting with a staff and pen. It is hard to get used to. I had to come down town this morning to buy writting paper and a few other articles so I stoped in at the U. S. O. to write this letter. There is one thing wrong with the old woman. If you stand and listen to her she will talk you deaf, blind and dum. I doubt if I could write you if I stayed at the house all day. The old fellow doesn't have much to say He is very quiet although he keeps an eye on you all the time. He like to hunt quite a bit. He has some very good guns. We have some of the same kind at home.

I went to the show last night. It was a double feature. Both were cow boy picture. I though they were pretty good. Was the first picture I payed to see since I left the states Pensacola as far as that goes. The trouble was I had to walk home in the rain. I'm telling you it sure came down, there for a while. I'll have to go into the base tomorrow to see if I had a letter from you. You'll never know how much I look forward to them.

Some person is playing on the piano right over from me I can hardly concentrate on what I'm writting He doesn't play any jitterbug Its all cly cal. If you know what I mean. It sounds like some chicken kackling.

It seems all so very quite. Although I can hear the birds juping out side. I think I'll close now and go for chow. It is about ten oclock Bye now write you tomorrow again.

Allways Loving you—
Paul.

Aug. 7–1945

Dearest Evelyn

Today, the seventh of August is one of my birthdays I'll always regret. I've ended my third year in the Corps. Don't know how I did it without going crazy. I must have some strong will power I never knew of before.

I went to the show again last night. Was the best picture I've seen in quite some time. "In this Man's Navy," with Wallace Beary. It was really good. Hes good in practically any picture he makes I guess.

The Lady of the house talked me into playing cards all yesterday after noon. Bet her every game we played. Don't know where she gets all her ambition. She must be nearly seventy and she hops around like a girl of sixteen. Can you picture that. There are a few airfields on this island and the planes are buzzing around like a bunch of flies this morning. This house is located on the top of a large hill and a person can look for miles around. I'm looking out the kitchen window and the pacific Ocean rolls out like a desert. I wish you were here. I learned quite a bit from this island. Wish I could tell you about it. I injoyed my self in Pensacola going from City to city. There is some thing lacking here and I know its you.

The Lady of the house already has my morning planned. One of her sons died six years ago today, and she wants me to drive her to the cemetory to put flowers on his grave. She certainly thinks of every thing. Her husband has already gone to work and won't be back till tonight.

I had planned on going to a town on the opposite side of the island this morning about fifty miles away. I guess I'll have to leave this after noon. I'll tell you about the place tomorrow. If it is like the rest of these small towns I won't have much to tell. I also intend to go into the base later this after noon to see if you wrote yesterday. I hope so. I'm pretty sick for letters. Especially from you.

I think I'll close now and write my mom. I doubt. if I'll finish it. When the lady makes up her mind to do a think she usually does it in a hurry and she's picking the flowers now.

Bye now

Love always.
Paul.

Aug. 8–1945

Dearest Evelyn.

What a day this was.! I started this letter last night and before I even finished the first sentence, the pen was dry. I'll tell you what I did yesterday. I did as I planned I went to see that small town on the other side of the mountain. It wasn't much to see reminded me alot like Warrington, only it had a few nice sized stores in it. Not much of any thing in them. The bakery did have good stoft, warm, doenuts. I know I ate two or three of them. This place is very warm and right on the front of the ocean. It's a beautiful sight to look out over the ocean. Fisher men are always busy doing one thing and another. I was fortunate enough to catch a jeep on the way back and there were three other boys beside my self. One was a sailor and the other two were Marines and a civilian The civilian was nine-teen and was drafted into the Army. So he was on his way to be sworn in. We were all trying to give this fellow scoop about Military life. It made me laugh to my self. Every one else had either broke off engagements or there wives were being unloyal or one thing or another, and they were only in the service a year and a half or two years. There I sat as happy as lark, thinking of you. (which isn't uncom-mon) It made me feel sorry so the rest of the fellows for they really loved there sweet hearts. But there was one who was allways talking about going out with some slant eye. Cant blame his wife much. Thoes are the people that don't deserve women. Seems to me life will never satify them.

Well I came back sort of early. About one oclock in the after noon and bought a few things and headed back home The lady [he previously capitalized] of the house had cooked a nice meal for us. If you can cook as well as she can. I'll be well satified. She certainly can run a home, especially for her age. Me and Zarach (the buddy that's with me here) asked her if we could have the pleasure of escorting her to the show. She refused, but when her husband heard us ask her, he began to laugh so much that to spite him she went along. So I got her car and we drove down to the show. We helped her out of the car and we went arm in arm down the pavement. You should have seen the people look. They just stood and stired at us. We were laughing and having fun at the while. You should have seen us. In the show I put my arm around her and the people in the back of us were giggling. Than the lady of the house turned around and siad, "Remember this when you get as old as I." I thought that was pretty cute.

We drove home than and all had some lemon pie. There wasn't a crum left or I'd sent it to you.

This morning they are painting the inside of the house again so I'm sitting on the lawn under a large tree. It's nice and cool here. If there were not so many buggs I'd probably fall asleep

This is all for now

Love always
Paul

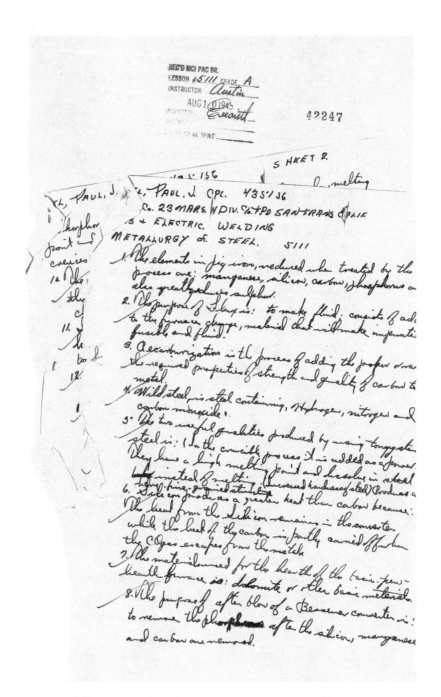

One of Paul's written tests, August 1945

Telegram:

> BY DIRECT WIRE FROM WESTERN
> UNION
> RL15-15 HERRINGTON KANSAS AUGUST
> 7 1:45PM
> MISS EVELYN WELLS
> PENSACOLA HOSPITAL PENSACOLA FLO
> SEND ME A WIRE IMMEDIATELY IF
> JAMES IS HOME OR WHEN HE WILL BE
> HOME.
> SARGENT W. D. WELLS
> SQUADRON C H. A. F.
> HERRINGTON, KANSAS

Postmarked Aug 13 1945 from Cpl. Paul J. Fogel, H & S. Co 23 Mars. 4 Div., c/o. F.P.O. San Frans, Cal. to Miss. Evelyn Wells., 1101 E. Gadsden, St., Pensacola, Florida. (stamped "PASSED BY NAVAL CENSOR" with initials; with 6 cents air mail stamp)

On plain, unlined stationery:

Aug. 12. 1945

Dearest Evelyn:—

Wanted to write you all day yesterday. Never got the chance. Did we have a large wash yesterday. It was so big my buddy said to me. "I hope we haven't got to do this again. Its enough to make a person marry just for a laundry woman." It was sort of large. We have sort of a cow fence about fifty feet up in a field. We hang our cloth on it today and it must have reached a half a mile or more after we finished hanging up clothes. We dont do any scrubbing, all we do is boil them a half hour and than rinse them twice. They don't turn out bad.

Havent heard from you for a week now. I know it isn't your fault. Mail hasn't been comming in too well lately. I'll probably get a few today. Your writting to me, just proves my thoughts. Your are every bit as wonderful as I knew you would be. I love you more than I can write in a letter. Some day I hope I'll be able to prove to to you by making you a good husband. If there is such a thing. If there isn't, I'll make an exception and be one any way.

Had a letter from Mom yesterday. She says Pauline is well now, just about and had a letter from you. I'm sure she was glad to hear from you. She likes you alot. In fact the whole family does.

My brother Sheldon is in Texas where my sister-in law June is. The way mom puts it they have met already. You know I'll bet I have the most beautiful wife of all my brothers. They will all be comeing to see us if we ever get the chance to settle down. They will be comming to see you mostly.

The day befor yesterday I was in the most beautiful house you ever saw. Some day I may be wealthy enough to built one like it. I can't describe it to you. You should see it. I'm sure you would fall in love with it too. Its a one storry building and has five rooms. It has glass doors and every thing. I can't describe it to you. You would have to see it your self. I'll have to stop now and get back to work. Bye for now.

Always Loving You.
Paul.

Postmarked Aug 14 1945 from Cpl. Paul J. Fogel, H & S. Co. 23 Mars., c/o F.P.O. San Frans, Cal. to Miss. Evelyn Wells., 1101 E. Gadsden, St., Pensacola, Florida. (stamped "PASSED BY NAVAL CENSOR" with initials; with 6 cents air mail stamp)

On plain, unlined stationery:

Aug. 14

Dearest Evelyn:—

I'm on liberty again today. Just laying around. Listening to the radio to see if I can get back to the states before I think I will. I do so much hope this war will end soon. I miss you more than I can say, and I do want to return soon to you.

The five days I had were spend enjoyable, as you have probably received the letters I wrote while I was on it. I met another fellow in town that comes from [illegible] a few miles of our home. Never knew him well. He knew me the moment he saw me. I have a hard time remembering peoples names. They just seem to slip my mind. I remembered him after I talked to him for a short time. A very nice fellow.

I've had quite a few compliments on the picture you send me. There was also a fellow who claimed he could read faces. He also complimented me on my good taste. They don't really know you though. You are much more wonderful than you look.

I went to the show last night I was a double feature. Some silly song picture, The other was a shoot 'em up cowboy picture. That was alright. I go for some pictures like that. I like music too but I cant stand this high classed singing.

Especially some one who thinks they can sing. I don't know it just begins to eat some thing, inside of me That one last night I could have spit on her and thought nothing of it. Very impolite arn't I.

Say what ever happened to Shewer, Remember her. I'm pretty sure you do. She went to Panama City. That was the last I heard from her. I knew she was writting to Sinclair too. She still working down there.

So you and Smitty are thinking of boarding to gether eh? You have chosen a good partner. A red head. You ought to get along fine. How is Red's sister. When you get the chance ask her. She used to have a very cute little baby. Still does in fact. Its a funny thing she didn't have red hair too. I have nothen to fear all our children will take after your mother. Ha. They better would.

AFTERNOON

I just returned from a laundry run. Me and the old fellow I travel around with were sitting here peacefully playing cuszino and in comes some one with a telegram for him. I'm still trying to get the lump out of my throat. It wasn't as bad as I expected it was. He is terriably in love with his wife and if any thing were to happen to her. He would never be the fellow I knew. He thinks of her as much as I do of you. Thats plenty. It just happened his brother is in a hospital near us and the Red cross send him a notice to come to see him. That was sort of nice. If it wouldn't have scared us so much. I'll have to sign off for now so keep Smilling and know that I'll always Love you.

Love and Kisses,
Paul

Postmarked Aug 17 1945 from Cpl. Paul J. Fogel, H & S. Co. 23 Mars. 4 Div., c/o F.P.O. San Frans, Cal. to Miss. Evelyn Wells., 1101 E. Gadsden, St., Pensacola, Florida (stamped "PASSED BY NAVAL CENSOR" with initials; with 6 cents air mail stamp)

On plain, unlined stationery:

Aug 15–1945

Dearest Evelyn:—

To day is a holiday. I need not tell you for what. The whole world is in an up roar about it. Its a happy day for the men around here. There isn't too much excitement in Camp here but the news is the the town's are really putting the dog on. How is Pensacola behaving itself. Is there must excitement around there. No one knows quite what will happen to the fourth Division. We all are hoping to go to the states but I'm afraid that [illegible] it won't be as good as all that. I've only been over here ten month and haven't had as much time over here as the majority of the other men in the Corps. So they will probably leave me behind with the Corps if the fourth does go bad to the states. Its only fair. I can see where there folks would want to get them back home too. I've added a few more ribbons to the one's I've already received. It doesn't mean much to me. I guess it is sort of an honor to wear them. I'd rather be dressed in civilian cloths walking about town than be dressed up looking like some foreigner. I'm certainly glad its over now. It does mean I'll be able to get home a wee bit sooner. That is some thing to look forward to.

I was expecting to have a letter from you today. That would have made the day complete.

335

Haven't heard from Elizabeth for quit some time now. Guess she is kept pretty busy pressing J. C.'s pants. Ha. I wonder if Smitty knew what she was in for when she got married. As long as she is happy. I guess thats all that counts. Tell her, she hasn't got any reason now to go out and get stewed. I'm glad she got what she wanted. Some day I'll get what I want, mainly you. I'll probably celebrate then, by going out and getting drunk for the first time. That ought to be quite an experience. You going to help. Thats good. I'll be counting on it.?

I've been thinking if you wouldn't be able to meet me on the west coast when I return. I'd call you on the phone if I could possibly do it or sent a telegram and you could meet me on the way to my home and we could be married before we arrived there. Philadelphia is a nice place. We could stay there a few days by our self and tell no one about it. I want to be alone with you a few days at least. I don't want any one to bother us, not even my family. Its a big city and lots of things to see. My mother will take up alot of your time. You'll like her I know. But she won't if I can help. My pa will probably want to give me some man to man talk. I'm exepting that, I'm telling you so if you sit in on it. I'll be able to give you a wink and you'll know whats happening. You will probably be kidded a lot by my brothers. Just watch Pauline she knows how to handle them. I'm preparing you of what to expect when I take you to my home. Thats more than you did when I first met your parents. Sleeves rolled up color open, and if I were to tell you the rest it would take the rest of the page. I'm glad they liked me. If my parents talk Penna German all the time which won't happen. Don't think they will be talking a bout you. If I'm around I'll tell you what they are saying. Its sort of a habit like smoking. They get into it and can't get out. I used to be the same way. There is one of my aunts that would probably talk your head off if she got the chance but I'll be with you when you met her. Lets see have I missed any thing??? I don't really know my sisterinlaws very well. All except my brother Charles wife. Shes and nice Mamie Lou. Would want to find a nicer person. The rest will be as much a suprise to me as it will be to you. All this is pretty well into the future yet but I did want to for get to mention it to you.

This will have to be all for now. Your wondeful in everyway

Love and Kisses.
Paul.

Paul's letter, August 15, 1945, day following V-J Day

338

Postmarked Aug 19 1945 from Cpl. Paul J. Fogel, H & S. Co. 23 Mars., c/o F.P.O. San Frans, Cal. to Miss. Evelyn Wells., 1101 E. Gadsden, St., Pensacola, Florida. (stamped "PASSED BY NAVAL CENSOR" with initials; with 6 cents air mail stamp)
On plain, unlined stationery:

Aug. 17–1945

Dearest Evelyn

Another rainy day and I am soaked to the gills again. This is getting pretty monotus if you ask me. We had two and a half days to celebrate in and I did nothing but sleep and eat. It was a nice rest. It seems to me this was one of my lucky months! First came the fourlough than came the peace. Just about to good to be true. I hope the next good fortune will be that I'll be seeing the states. It doesn't seem very probable though.

Haven't had a letter from any one for over a week. Don't know whats wrong with the mail mail. Perhaps he doesn't like me any more. I can't seem to get in the letter writting mood. when I don't receive any. Here I am complaining to you again, when you have plenty to think about your self. Ten more days till you get out of the hospital eh? You don't know how much I'm hoping I were back there waiting for you. It's turned around now before I was waiting for you know you are waiting for me. I wish we were able to settle down and both wait on each other.

Saw a very good show last night. Bing Crosby was in it. Some thing about the Wave's I don't know which I'd rather see in a picture. Bing or (blank space) They are both pretty good.

My boy Val is getting harder to get along with every day. He's always giving me a hard time. He's giveing me the devil for some thing. I can here him yelling for some thing. He's always teasing me for some thing. I guess I deserve it because I do the same to him when I get the chance.

I think I told you about the dogs we adopted. You should see them. As playfull as the devil You can just about see them grow.

We had liberty yesterday and I of course had to do my weekly washing. Wasn't quite as large as the last weeks wash.

There are a lot of romors going around none worth mentioning. One day one thing is heard and the next day something happens just the oposite. I don't hope we stay here much longer I'm getting sort of restless. Want to get on the move again.

Still haven't heard from Mamie Lou she owes me a letter. She must really be occupied more than I expected. I can't blame her. I'll sign off for now.

Here's a kiss for you. Got it, Good.

All my Love,
Paul

Postmarked Aug 21 1945 from Corp. Paul J. Fogel, H.&S Co. 23rd. Marines, 4th. Mar. Div. F. M. F, c/o FPO San Fran. Cal. to Miss Evelyn Wells, 1101 E. Gadsden St., Pensacola, Fla. (stamped "PASSED BY NAVAL CENSOR" with initials; with 6 cents air mail stamp; envelope is not in Paul's handwriting)

On plain, unlined stationery:

Aug. 19–1945

Hello Darling:—

You could have blown me over with a feather yesday. Why? Three letters at once from you. Now that was enough to make any one over joy and I was dancing on the clouds. Beside that I could have smothered you with kisses if you were around. Never was I so happy to hear from any one in all my life. If I ever complain again to you. Remind me of this day. If all the fellows had a person like you waiting for them. This would be, with out a doubt the happiest out fit in the world.

I bet your mom will be glad to see you. You make your self too scarce around there to suit her. "Hint" Get it? Ha. These pups of ours are getting more playful every day. We have alot of fun with them. You should hear them when they get into the growling mood. They just about play with anyone. You can have your cats I still like my dogs. I don't mean feet.

I don't believe I mentioned it in my last letter but day before yesterday I went swimming with a groupe of fellows. We had a happy time. We just about missed chow. You should have seen I ever hurried. Its hard to believe the fellows had that much ambition. Ocean was pretty rough and we couldn't wonder very far off shore.

I guess you are wondering about that picture that was in that last letter. It was all a mistake. I happened to hide it in that letter till evening. Evening came and I looked for the letter and it had disapeared

I'm laughing my head off at Val, he's trying to rub flee power into the fur of the pups and its a good two man job but he is westling with them and giveing me the devil for laughing at him and not helping. That was a commical sight.

I'm on duty again this week and I received another series of booklets on my Welding course. So I've been kept busy all day today, and probably the rest of the week.

Went to church today and took communion. First time I've taken it since I left ship on the way to Iwo. I should be ashamed I know. I'll have to see if I cant arrange to do it more often.

I'm glad you don't have very much longer to go. At least when you work for that doctor you will be able to get sleep every night. At least I hope you wont work nights.

You should have seen it rain today. It must have come down in buckets. I'm sure it would have drowned me if I would have steped in it. I was sorry to hear about J. C. I hope you are wrong for I wouldn't want to See Elizabeth the way she was when I left.

Aug 19–1945

Lets see where was I last night. Yes, yes, yes, we were talking about Elizabeth eh? I'll have to write her a letter perhaps it will cheer her up a wee bit.

To day was a happy day pay day. (at least for a while. I bought another watch and its costing me five bucks to get a stem put on it. Man alive, are the prices high around here. You have to just about give your life to get some thing done. There was only one jeweler in town that would do it. If I didn't know J. C. was so busy I would have send it to him.

The mail is just about all censored now so I'll get this one in along with the rest Bye for now. I'll always Love you.

Paul

Postmarked Aug 23 1945 from Cpl. Paul J. Fogel, H & S. Co. 23 Mars. 4 Div., c/o. F.P.O. San Frans. Cal. to Miss. Evelyn Wells., 1101 E. Gadsden, St., Pensacola, Fla. (stamped "PASSED BY NAVAL CENSOR" with initials; with 6 cents air mail stamp)
On plain, unlined stationery:

Aug. 22–1945

Dearest Evelyn,

I just got out of bed so if this letter sounds sleepy don't blame me because that is exactly they way I feel I'm still on duty so there was no great need of getting up real early this morning so I woke up around six thirty. I guess I wouldn't have awoken than if the dog around here would not have started harmonizing. Went to the show in the rain last night. Don't know where I get all that embition from but I seem to enjoy it. "Here come the girls" was the name of the picture. I think it was worth sitting in the rain to see. To day is liberty day for all but me and a few of the other fellows. We get it tomorrow. I sure could do with a day off. There is a buddy of mine who lives with in a few miles of my place. We intent to go to town together. You should see him. He is about six foot five and buit something like me and when we walk together it looks like Mut and Jef. What a sight.

Mamie Lou finally broke down and wrote me. Not a lengthy letter but concideing the circumstances I can reddily see the reason why. She says Frank has received another thirty days. That was nice wasn't it? She seems so very happy. She has all the reasons in the world to be. They also intend to build a new house. As if you don't know by now. I wish we were able to plan things in the future as they are doing. That would be asking fort far too much. Right now all I'm interested in, is getting home. We will start from there.

Perhaps later on this censor ships regulations will be lifted. I hope so. I have a few things you may be interested in. I'd like to tell you more about this place. It has quite a few interesting sights we are not able to speak about. Maybe if I become wealthy and we have nothing to do but eat and sleep, I'll be able to show you what I mean. I'm afraid that will be in heaven when we may assend as ghosts. Know what I mean.

This is just about all the news for today. So I'll sign off for now. The old fellow in that last picture I send went on a five day leave and it seems sort of lonesome around here with out him. We use to play card in the spare time. He used to beat me most of the time. He will be back Sunday.

Tell Smitty she has all my best wishes for a happy marriage. Also tell her to lay off the "drinks. Ha.

All my Love,
Paul.

Postmarked Aug 25 1945 from Cpl. Paul J. Fogel, H & S. Co. 23 Mars., c/o. F.P.O. San Frans Cal. to Miss. Evelyn Wells., 1101 E. Gadsden, St., Pensacola, Florida. (stamped "PASSED BY NAVAL CENSOR" with initials; with 6 cents air mail stamp)

On plain, unlined stationery:

Aug. 24–'45

Dear Honey Chil:—

After receiving that letter with Elizabeth's inclosed, I decided to write to her so last night I broke down and wrote her. I was under the impression that I had written her last, but that was sort of a flimsy excuse. I should be more like you. I can't seem to make my self though. I must be the luckiest person in the world. I wrote to my mom too. I ought to be ashamed of my self for putting off writting to her this long.

You asked if I were on guard duty. I see where you have been listening to alot of loose talk also. No I'm not on guard duty, never was. I'm still a mechanic and will probably be one when I get my discharge. You know about as much as I do of my chances of getting home in the future. I am also hoping I may get home sooner than I expect.

To morrow "my boy" comes back from off leave. I need to wash clothe. There is where he comes in. We usually do our washing together. "He does most the washing" It seems the place isn't lively with out him. Perhaps thats just my opinion.

Three more days till you say bye bye to that hospital eh? By the time you receive this letter you will probably have left it for that new home you were talking about. I know the exact house you were talking about. I knew some folks who lived in it my self. Won't have to go far for the city now. All you will have to do is put your foot on the pavement.

There is another fellow in this tent I don't think I ever told you about. A short fellow about five foot off the deck. Some one just swiped some stamps and is he raising the roof. You would think some one cut his leg off. He sure makes alot of noise for his height. He comes from Allentown, Pa. about ten miles from my home. You would never believe it. He goes with some Jap in town. Spends most of his time with her.

I was rereading one of your letters and you made a remark "It ought to rain <u>directly</u>" or something like that. Thats more the my brother talks. I had to look at it twice to see if I read it right. Where did you ever pick that up. Not from me I hope.

Val is haveing some more trouble with his women. He gets in to some of the worst problems I've ever seen. He has a good time though. Seems to be getting out of them as fast as he gets in to them. You probably noticed his hand-writting on one of my letters. I was called upon, at the time to do some messey joy so I asked him to put your address on it to make sure it got out in the mail that day.

There was a very good stage show the other night sort of lengthy. Very good acting. I usually watch for some faults but I wasn't able to detect any in their act. Right on the ball. I'll have to sign off for now. No more news.

Keep Smilling

Love and Kisses,
Paul

Postmarked Aug 30 1945 from Cpl. Paul J. Fogel, H & S. Co. 23 Mars., c/o. F.P.O. San Frans, Cal to Miss Evelyn Wells., 1101 E. Gadsden, St., Pensacola, Florida. (stamped "PASSED BY NAVAL CENSOR" with initials; with 6 cents air mail stamp)

On plain, unlined stationery:

Aug. 28–1945

Dearest Evelyn:—

A free woman, eh? I'm hoping you didn't celebrate too much last night. It might have had an affect on you this morning. Of course that is your buisness.

I went to church Sunday, we have a new Chaplin to preach the sermon. The original Chaplin went on some sort of church party at a visiting church. It was some thing like that any way. To get back to the Subject. This chaplin based his sermon on "Quiters" He had a lot of good points. I'll probably always remember them. It made me think of you. I mean in the respect that you had the ambition to complete training. That in itself is some thing to be proud of. I am proud of you. I know that sounds childish. But its takes alot of patience and courage to do it. I doubt if I could ever be like you. I'm not afraid to admit it to you. I quit high school to join some thing like this and I'd quit this if it wasn't that I was bound to it. I'm afraid that sermon did me more good than going to church a year, would do.

I was very proud yesterday too. Two letters from you in one day They have been comming that way for the past few weeks. It doesn't make any difference to me how they, come, as long as they come.

Yesterday day was Monday again with me. What a wash we had. Seems to me we wash all the clothes in the Division when we get started. Me and the old man started at eight and ended up around four in the after noon.

I have liberty today and I intend to go in town for a few minutes The old lady I stayed at wants me to drive her into another town to go shopping and get her dog vaccinated. I told her I would since I didn't have any thing else to do but wrote you.

I hear from my mother every other week only last week she must have forgotten this son but today she apologized for it. When she doesnt write Pauline writes and some times they both write

So you have found some one from Bethlehem eh? Yes I can readily see why he would know some Fogels. Is a common name around there. I guess I already told you. There are six Fogels in a row. Starting with our family up to my grandfather. My father was a butcher at one time and used to cover nearly that whole city and my uncle is in the potatoe business and he also has alot of business there. That was probably why he knew of the Fogel name.

How did Sister find out about Smitty or did she tell her. I'm so glad she didn't get thrown out. That would have been awkful.

I'll never come back here so you need not worry. After I get back to the states I intend to stay there. You would know what I meant if you were ever here. Than of course if you were ever here, you would probably like it. I guess I've been here to long under these circumstances. If I were a civilian I'd probably like it too. This will have to be all for now. Keep Smilling and know that I love you

Love and Kisses.
Paul.

Postmarked Sep 3 1945 from Cpl. Paul J. Fogel, H & S. Co. 23 Mars., c/o F.P.O. San Frans, Cal. to Miss. Evelyn Wells., 1101 E. Gadsden, St., Pensacola, Florida. (stamped "PASSED BY NAVAL CENSOR" with initials; with 6 cents air mail stamp)

On plain, unlined stationery:

Aug. 31–1945

Dear Snuggs:——

How is my honey today? Me, its raining out side and this place is as damp as a well. I'm just about shivering. Lend me your coat eh? Had a letter from you yesterday you wonderful person you. You had the last day in the hospital to complete. Seems to me you should go on a vacation now. I know you deserve one.

O yes Iris send me another Gosport yesterday. I certainly did apreciate it. She also blamed me for not answering her letter. I know darn well I answered it. It hasn't come back so she must not have received it yet. You will probably hear about it when she receives it for she said she would let you read it. Don't ask me why.

I guess Margaret is to you as Val is to me. I'd just about feel lost with out having him around. He does quite a few things I disaprove of and I do many he disaproves of but we to stick together.

Gosh you make me hungry with your describtion of a meal. Wish I were able to tell you what we eat. I grumble about our chow now as you did when you were in the hospital and went down to the drug store to a sandwitch. only thing the matter with that idea. There isn't any drug store. Tough isnt it?

NOON.

I just now came back from chow. To morrow is the official V-J. day. So the papers say. It's about time they get around to it. I was wondering if they were ever going to really end this war. I don't know why it should worry me It couldn't help me out one way or the other. Every thing seems to be running along as though there was never a war. I thought things would change alittle but I've got the first thing to see change.

Had a letter yesterday from a girl I knew in Pensacola she is now in New York City and is waiting for transportation to go back to Finland. She originally came from Finland. I wish you could have heard her speak. She had the most pecular accent. I've never heard any thing like it before. He hair weren't red. Thats why I gave her up. She nearly had white hair. Very pretty. One of the boys here is writting to her. He needed some one to write to so I decided to let him have a few addresses. I won't need them any more now since I have yours.

I still hear from that History teacher of mine she still thinks I'm her best pupil. I must have been an angle while in her class. I wish I could have gotten along with all teachers as I did with her. She was a real swell person. I must have had a trusting eye.

Haven't heard from your mom for some time now, think she may have got lost in the garden. She must love to work out side. Can say I blame her. I do too.

I'll have to go back to work now.

Keep Smilling
Love and Kisses.
Always.
Paul.

Postmarked Sep 4 1945 from Cpl. Paul. J. Fogel, H & S. Co 23 Mars. 4 Div., c/o F.P.O. San Frans, Cal. to Miss. Evelyn Wells., 1201 E. Jackson, St., Pensacola, Florida. (stamped "PASSED BY NAVAL CENSOR" with initials; with 6 cents air mail stamp)

On plain, unlined stationery:

Sept–2 1945

Dearest Evelyn:—

Before I forget. I see you have changed your address so don't stop looking for my letters down on Gadsden St because I've formed a habit and untill I get used to this one, I may slip up on a few. I'll try not to. Received that letter of yours today along with one from Pauline. She has been visiting some friends for a vacation. Claims she injoyed her self. I certainly hope she did. She deserved a rest. I'm so glad she is feeling fit again.

Mother wrote me a few days ago that they expect my grandfather to die at most any time. That was bad news to me for he has taught me alot of things I shall never for get. I guess I learned to love nature as much as he did while I was with him. To me he is the most wonderful

man I have ever met. I guess I mentioned him
a hundred times while I was with you He knew
the names of all the trees and birds in America.
I always looked on him as sort of a professor. A
great man. I guess every one has some one they
envy most of all. Well he was my ideal of a real
man. If I had any sort of problem. He was sure to
have the answer When I mentioned to him that
I had fallen in love with you he wanted to know
all about you. He was very interested in you. I
know you would have liked him he always had
nice things to say. I'll never forget him. He was
very tall and Grammy, his wife, was only five foot
and maybe not that. My father took after her,
he is only five six. He is built very husky as you
know from his picture.

I'm so glad you have found your place. I
mean the one you really injoy living in. At least
you wont be too restricted in the house hold. If
she is as nice as you claim she must be a wonder
ful person. I hope she doesn't talk as much as the
person I've described to you for she talks a wee
bit too much. In that case you will never be able
to say what you want. Woo I'll never forget her
she could start a conversation from Nothing and
could top any thing you had to say with some
thing better. Have you ever met a woman like
that? All in all she is one swell person.

Just received word that another inspection
is about to come up. That means that I will have
to get the men in my tent informed of the pro-
cedure and have them ready for it. I know you
know what inspections are so I need not explain
what we have to go through to stand one of those
gruesome jobs. I have no reason to grumble, for

we haven't had one for over a month now that has ammounted to any thing.

Today is J-V day and also liberty day so you see how I am occuping my time. I first wrote to my mom for I have been neglecting her this week a wee bit. I went to church this morning. Not very many there. They must not have though it necessary to give thanks that the war is over. I'm certainly glad its over. All I want to do now is get back to you.

So Phiel finially found some one with money and doesn't care who he marries. Thats the way I feel. I don't like that person for some reason"'s" and I don't care if she knows it.

This letter is going way over my original ones so I'd better not shock you any more by alot more of my foolishness. Heres a kiss for you. Right on that cute little nose of yours. Alway thinking of you so keep Smilling

Always Loving you
Paul.

Postmarked Sep 6 1945 from Cpl. Paul J. Fogel, H & S. Co 23 Mars., c/o F.P.O. San Frans. Cal. to Miss. Evelyn Wells., 1201 E. Jackson, St., Pensacola, Florida. (with 6 cents air mail stamp) On plain, unlined stationery:

Sept–5–1945

Dearest Evelyn.

I'm not in the writting mood today so if This letter is sort of shot don't blame me too much. The censor ship has been lifted and now I'm able to tell you where I am. I think you know already but just in case I'll tell you. I'm on Maui Island in Hawaii Groupe. I've been here all the time I've spend over sea's and it's been a beautiful place to spend over sea's duty. Most islands haven't got too many places of interest but here it has quite a few if you care to look around. I doubt very much if I would injoy comming back to this place during peace time. It's just no place to settle down. The population of the island either work in the Sugar mills or the Pinapple fields so you can readily see what I mean. In later letters perhaps I can think of different things to tell of about this place that I was unable to tell before. If I am permitted to I'll be sending you different odds and ends from here We were unable to send any thing pretaining to this place before. I havent found out as yet wether we are able to send packages un censored or not so when I find out I'll let you know.

O yes, there has been quite a bit of talk going around that we may get to come home soon If the roomers are correct I'll be in the states the later part of next month. Don't raise your hopes too high for they may fall as fast as you have raisen them. Don't believe my self but there is hope. Thought we may be going east after Iwo but you know how that turned out. Came back here and stayed.

I received that letter in answer to the one I wrote suggesting that we stay at some point on my way home. I said that because if I cross the states again it will have to be with a troop train so I couldn't be with you any way. Troop trains only go to the largest city near your home so Phila was the largest and most probable. That was the reason I suggested it. Listen honey I can't write any more for now. I'll make up for it tomorrow I promish.

Night for now. I'll always love you. Keep this letter till I get back and I'll read it to you.

Always loving you.
Paul

Postmarked Sep 8 1945 from Cpl. Paul J. Fogel, H & S. Co. 23 Mars. 4 Div., c/o. F.P.O. San Frans, Cal. to Miss. Evelyn Wells, 1101 E. Gadsden, St., Pensacola, Florida. (with 6 cents air mail stamp) On plain, unlined stationery:

Sept. 7–1945

Dearest Evelyn:—

Had liberty today did a few of my lessons and than decided to sleep the remainder of the day. I slept right up until chow time. Hopped out of my sack and was first in the chow line. What a chow hound I am. I certainly love my food. Its a good thing I picked a good cook for my partner.

Had a letter from Kupsky the other day. He is on Guam. That is a beautiful island. We stoped there on the way back from Iwo Jima. Would have liked to see more of the place but was unable too because we only stayed there a day. I guess I was expecting to much. He was telling me all about the boys that were with him, that I did duty with in Pensacola. Sgt Maceluch is on Okinawa where my brother Charles is also. I had hoped they might meet one another. I haven't heard from either of them lately.

Last Sunday I was up to the creator (means crater). I haven't told you about that as yet. The creator is the main spot of interest. It is a volcanic creator at the very top of a mountain. To get there you have to wind in and out up along the mountain. Some places the road is only about five foot wide Imagine passing a car where the mountain is on one side and a sheer drop of about five hundred feet on the other of course not all the road is in this shape. But we had some trying experiences by the time we reached the top. I was worth while The thing about it that I still can't under stand. The war had just ended and liquor was plentiful around town as some of the boys were under the wheather. You can imagine the rest. I must have been the only sober one among them. I got them home safe. We had a large truck and was it filthy by the time we reached the base again. It was one place we were restricted in mentioning before censorship was lifted because it would have given our location away. The flower silver [illegible] was another. I believe I mentioned it in the last letter. Its a very beautiful flower. The only one of its kind in the world. It only grows up there. Yesteday I went for my laundry into Poella. How do you like that name. As I continue these letters you will wonder how to pronounce some of these towns. I'll spell them the way they sound perhaps it will help you. I never saw so many u's and i's in names in all my life.

All ways Loving you.
Paul.

Postmarked Sep 10 1945 from Cpl. Paul J. Fogel, H & S. Co. 23 Mars., c/o F.P.O. San Frans. Cal. to Miss. Evelyn Wells., 1201 E. Jackson, St., Pensacola, Florida. (with 6 cents air mail stamp)

On plain, unlined stationery:

Sept. 9–1945

Dear Evelyn:—

  We didn't get mail today. We usually get mail on Sunday. Since the war has been declared over they give us Sunday after noons off. We can be thank ful for that. They had a rather large ball game this after noon. It lasted till five oclock. I didn't go to see it but I did attend a cermony in which they decorated some Marines for their heroic doings on Iwo. It was a beautiful thing to watch. The band was playing and they had the whole Bn. that was decorated march before the grand stands. It was more or less a parade.

  We still have the pups and they are as lively as ever. I had a picture taken with one the other day. It came out fairly well. At least the dog took a good picture even though I didn't. They certainly grew these past few month. I'm afraid they are going to grow up to quickly. We will probably have to leave them here when we leave. I can see where I'm going to miss them.

  They say that chow will go in five minutes and I'm never one left behind for that purpose. We can't brag about the chow we eat but it does fill up a space in the pit of one's stomach.

  That landlady of yours must be quite an interesting person. Someday I hope to return to Pensacola To me it will be like a reunion. I certainly met nice people there. I know I'm not sorry I was sent there to do duty. If it were only to meet you. I think fait has served its purpose well.

Its a strange feeling writting what I want knowing that no one is going to read it. It seems as if I'm always on the alert for something I shouldn't be saying. I guess it will be that way for a while yet.

Haven't heard from Elizabeth yet. Im anxious to hear her respond to the last letter I wrote to her. I certainly hope J. C. is fortunate enough to stay in the states. I'm afraid if he comes over now he is liable to be here for a while.

Roomers are certainly flying around this good old Camp Marine. Every one expects to good home. Especially the older men. As for my self I doubt very much if we will be comming home for quite some time. That doesn't keep me from wishing the rest are right and I am wrong. I can hardly wait to see you again. It really hasn't been too long since I left the states but it seems as if it were years since I saw you.

I have eleven more months to do in the Marine Corp to complete one "hitch." I'm beginning to believe I'll be in that long.

Always Loving You.
Paul

Postmarked Sep 13 1945 from Cpl. Paul J. Fogel, H & S. Co. 23 Mars. 4 Div., c/o F.P.O. San Frans, Cal. to Miss. Evelyn Wells., 1201 E. Jackson, St., Pensacola, Florida (with 6 cents air mail stamp) On plain, unlined stationery:

Sept. 11–1945

Dear Evelyn:—

Received two letters from you today. One was dated the 26th of last month. It must have got lost and went around the world a few times before it finally settled down and decided to reach me.

I was suprised with a letter from an old friend of mine yesterday. I might have mentioned him to you once or twice. We used to travel around together while I was still a civilian. That is something you don't know about. I bet you can't imagine the sight I look when dressed in civilian cloth. You see there is a circus! Getting back to him. He finished high school and imediately joined the Navy. I tried to talk him out of it but he didnt seem to want my advise. He is now learning for himself. He is a very good looking fellow. We could depend upon lots of fun when we went with each other. He is now on an ambulance ship as a H A 1/c. I'm happy in knowing he is preserving life instead of demolishing it the way I was there for a while. He is another charcter you will have to meet if you ever get the opportunity. His parents are as wonderful as he is. His mother is as thin as my leg but she is as kind a person as I have ever met. Now the father of the family is just the opposite.

He has a very rough voice and one that would rather be obeyed then disobeyed. He isn't difficult to get alone with but his character seems to freighten every one.

I just now was talking to Berdan. Don't know if you remember him or not. He was the actor and the singer that I often talked about while down in Pensacola. He remembers you quite well, that isn't a suprise for every one knew you, that is, from me talking about you so often. He asked about you. He made quite a few friends there him self, and wants to go there visiting after the war.

There is been a little talk going around that we may come home by way of the Panama Canal. That would be quite a trip. I don't know as yet how true it is. In That case we would be landing at Camp Davis for reorganization. Don't get too excited because its just some more loose talk. It can really spread fast around here.

Don't tell my mom, not that I want to suprise her or any thing. I'd rather tell her when I'm comming home so she can do her crying while I'm not there. I'd rather have her know the exact day I can be expected. We will be confined to the base we are at for a week or longer. That ought to give you time to catch up with me.

I'll let you in on another subject I had planned to keep to my self untill I saw you. You know that friend of mine you saw on that last picture I send you. He has asked me to go in partner ship with him in a machanic buisness. I haven't said I would yet. I'd first like to know a little more about it. I have a feeling I might though. I know this work fairly well and it is a good way to make a living. The place we have in mind is Waterberry Conn. He lives there and has already developed a reputation there. I'm going to wait for your opinion if we are going to have a fifty fifty proposition. I'll have to have your opinion first. Its pretty far from your home I know. Don't keep from giving me the devil because I probably need it.

Again I am writting on Marine Corps time so I'll sign off now and give your eyes a rest. I'll always love you. Keep Smilling

All ways Loving You.
Paul.

Postmarked Sep 14 1945 from Cpl. Paul J. Fogel, H & S. Co. 23 Mars. 4 Div., c/o. F.P.O. San Frans. Cal. to Miss. Evelyn Wells., 1201 E. Jackson, St., Pensacola, Florida. (with three 8 cents stamps and one 6 cents air mail stamp; 12 picture postcards included with letter)

On stationery imprinted with Marine logo—Semper Fidelis, * Roi-Namur, * Saipan, * Tinian, * Iwo Jima:

[No date]

Hello Evelyn:

Yesterday was another liberty and the day before that we had a parade. You should have seen it. We had to review before the General of the 4ᵗʰ Division. I came back with two lovely blisters right on the bottom of my foot. I wondering now if it was worth all that time and trouble. The parade was partly put on because our commanding officer, a col. is being transfered to Guam. So we had to show our respects to him also. I guess there will be quite a bit of parading from here on out.

I was into town yesterday when I say town I really mean a series of towns of about six First we went to Waliaku thats about thirty miles from here. There I bought you "some things" Than we came back to Hahulau. There was nothing there so we ate a ham burger stake and took a buss to Piaia where we stoped just long enough to look around On the outskirts of Makakuna we had a banana split and than went to a U S. O there and played peonacle the rest of the after noon. Beat him every game too. I'll try to send you those few articles today some time. I saw some very flashy material I thought you may like so I bought some of it also. Perhaps you can make a skirt or blouse out of it. These grass skirts around here are sort of out of fashion at home. Besides if you want to be a hula girl you can borrow Mamie Lou's. I'm sure she would lend it to you. I dont think you look your best in one. Know what I mean.

We are still not sure if we are going home or not. In a week or so we should be certain. Some of us are but I don't know if I'll be the lucky one. I sure hope so. Has Frank received his dis charge yet. It shouldn't be very hard for him now. I hope he is out of the hospital by now. I have to go back to work now.

Keep that cute little nose of yours powered and I'll be home as soon as I can. I'll always love you.

Love and Kisses.
Paul.

Postmarked Sep 19 1945 from Cpl. Paul J. Fogel, H & S. Co. 23 Mars., c/o. F.P.O. San Frans. Cal. to Miss. Evelyn Wells., 1201 E. Jackson, St., Pensacola, Florida. (with 6 cents air mail stamp)

On stationery imprinted with Marine logo—Semper Fidelis, * Roi-Namur, * Saipan, * Tinian * Iwo Jima:

Sept. 17–1945

Dear Evelyn:—

It's nine thirty and I just finished playing pinocle with the boys. I have to write you now because I've lost two days some place not writting to you. Yesterday was another liberty day. We have liberty every five days now. Thats a relief because it does get sort of monotus around here

I usually go in town and get a de cent meal and than take in a show "in a soft seat." As far as I know we had our last liberty yesterday so I went and said good-bye to that lady that housed me for five days. She was sorry to see me leave and wants me to write her when I get back to the states. We are still unsure as to where it we'll be the states or another island. When I reached her home there was another fellow from my section there who also spend five days there. He had his sister with him. "Navy nurse" by the way. She was spending an over night visiting him. That was nice don't you think that a brother and sister should meet over here. They came from New York. She will be over here six more month and he is going home with us. She is stationed on the island Honlolulu is. That reminds me I was in Pearl Harbor and Honlolulu on our way to Iwo. Its not much of a city to see, alot of jip joints for the service men. They sure rake in the doe.

If every thing goes well I'll be home in your arms in a few week. I can hardly way. I'll probably be so glad to see you I hug you to death. That wouldn't do me any good be cause I want to keep you, always.

These past few days the boys have really been drinking hard. Seems to me every night some one be comes out of controle. It just to bad if they get caught, for it will me the worst for them. They will either get transfered to a section not leaving with the forth division or they will get court marshaled. That will mean the same thing. I've manged to keep out of trouble this long and I hope nothing will happen these few days here.

We have been having inspections by the hundreds it seems to me. Every time I turn around there seems to be one staring me in the face. I'm in charge of this tent and we had a "field day" to night. You should have heard every one grumble. I guess I'm lucky every one in the tent stoped drinking and that was for the best. I had to give Val a motherly talk. I think it sank in some what.

That school teach of yours has an interesting life. I hope you will convince her that the male creachers are not all as bad as she thinks. I can hardly see to write so I'll sign off now and get to bed. Good night for now.

Allways Loving you.
Paul.

Postmarked Sep 21 1945 from Cpl. Paul J. Fogel, H & S. Co. 23 Mars., c/o. F.P.O. San Frans. Cal. to Miss Evelyn Wells.,—1201 E. Jackson. St., Pensacola, Florida. (with 6 cents air mail stamp)

On stationery imprinted with Marine logo—Semper Fidelis, * Roi-Namur, * Saipan, * Tinian * Iwo Jima:

Sept. 20–1945

Dear Evelyn:—

I'll have to say one thing the chow is beginning to improve since the war has reached an end. Thats nothing to grumble about, its something to be thankful for. Roast beef was on the menu this noon and it was really made to order. I hope your moth is watering, mine was be fore I ate. I doubt if I was ever so hungry in my life. I hardly did any work this morning and I had an appetite like a horse.

I had a letter from your mother the other day. A very nice letter.

—I'll have to finish this letter this after noon. Have to go to work now.

I'm glad I waited to end this letter this after noon because I had a suprise in store for me when I received mail a few minutes ago. You would never guess what it was so I'll tell you. I had a letter from Elizabeth and inclosed in it was a cigar, Doris had put in for me. She also send me a small card announcing to arrival of the baby boy. Wasn't that nice of them. I can't get over it. I wrote to Elizabeth and as a joke told her to remind Jimmy I wanted a cigar to the great event and now the joke has been played on me. She also said that Frank had been discharged on the point system. That also should be a happy event for Mamie Lou. Mamie Lou told me she was planning on teaching school this year. I didn't know Elizabeth had taugh school. Perhaps I wasn't nosy enough while I was going with you. The next time I'll be going with you will be per-minent. I won't want to know any more about you. I guess I knew enough about you the first few nights with you. I'll never for get that first night I took you home from the USO. I have a reason for remembering that day.

I guess I told you about the ring I made on the way home from Iwo. I made it from a half dollar peace. I pounded it in the shape of a ring and to day some thing happend anyway It cut into the flesh and dog gone near took my finger along. It looks much like a wedding ring so I had it ingraved.

A groupe of the boys are playing penocle again. They asked me to play but I said I had things to tell you first. They seem to be having quite a bit of fun from the way it sounds. There is one fellow by the name of Cohlmeyer. He argues the most of any person I've ever known. He usually wins out on his debates too.

I guess I told you that, that buddy of mine likes to drink a wee bit. I think I broke him of it last night. He was so drunk he was put on report to day for not answering roll call besides that he felt terriable all day. I wanted him to get as drunk as he could. I took care of him and this morning he was so ashamed of him self he wouldn't talk to me but a few words.

Had a letter from My mother today and she said she had a lovely letter from you today. I'm praying you will like them when you meet them. I'm sure you will though.

I'll have to work tonight yet so I'll sign off for now, we are still making ready to leave here, but don't know to where as yet. I hope it will be toward the states.

Allways Loving you.

Paul.

Postmarked Sep 25 1945 from Cpl. Paul J. Fogel, H & S. Co. 23 Mars. 4 Div., c/o F.P.O. San Frans, Cal. to Miss. Evelyn Wells, 1101 E. Gadsden, St., Pensacola, Florida. (with 6 cents air mail stamp) On decorated (very faint), unlined stationery:

Sept. 24–1945

Dearest Evelyn.

One of my best buddies is comming home. He lives in Ala. and his girl works out at the

Naval Air base. You can guess what I'm leading up to. He will be stopping down there for a week or so. I told him to look you up. His name is Roy Lester. I may have mentioned him before. He and I were in the same fox hole on Iwo Jima and by the time the operation was over. He knew all my social affairs and I knew his. There is one place a person can get well aquainted. We stayed awake half the night talking about things we did and things were were going to do if I ever got back. I'm not ashamed to admit for a while there, there were some doubts about that small fact. She is liable to drop into see you also. I couldn't say. Don't know a thing about her other than he likes her quite a bit. He is a swell person him self

I know for certain now I will be staying out here for quite a while yet. Ought to be home for Christmas though That seems to be the talk about camp these days. It would be nice spending Christmas home with you. It wouldn't make any difference where we were just as long as it was with you.

I hit the jack pot yesterday. Six letters. Had a letter from Kupsky, he is still on Guam. Says the mosquotous are plenty bad. I know what he meant by that remark because they can't be any worse than they are here. Have to cover my sack every night with a net. Also heard from my old Sgt., Maceluch He is on the same island my brother is on. They haven't met as yet. He is sort of anxious to find out why I put in for transfere to over sea's duty. I doubt if I could explain it to my self much less him. He thought it was because of him. He thought, as he put it, that he talk to much advantage of my good nature. I like that man alot. and was glad to do all and any thing I could for him. What do you think. Do I have a good nature? Than I heard from my Aunt Hester. She has your looks. Very beautiful for her age. She must be in the forties but she certainly believes in keeping her self nice. Very blond hair just like yours. She is living with my grandparents and helping them all she can. I told you about her son's being in the Navy. I also had a letter from my old school teacher. She has begun to teach school again. Going on her 28th year. What a record. She was visiting again in Canada and was telling me all about her trip.

I had a letter from my sister today she says my mother is going on a nother confinement case. Some one else is having a baby. Seems to me she likes that kind of work. It keeps her occupied thats the main thing. I know she worries alot. I don't remember if I mentioned that I received a letter from your mother. I wish I could have seen her more often. If She is half as wonderful as her letters she must be a gem. She told me some thing I didn't realize before and am going to try and correct when I return. I should have thought of it. Than again I am selfish and wouldn't have the brains to think of it.

I'll have to sign off for now. Received some more of my lessons and they are taking up most of my time at present.

If you love me as I love you. Well?

There wouldn't be any more love left in the whole world…

Lots of Love,
Paul

Postmarked Sep 27 1945 from Cpl. Paul J. Fogel, H & S. Co.
23 Mars. 4 Div., c/o F.P.O. San Frans. Cal. to Miss. Evelyn Wells.,
1201 E. Jackson, St., Pensacola, Florida. (with 6 cents air mail stamp)
On decorated (very faint), unlined stationery:

Sept. 26–1945

Dear Evelyn:—

Last week, I thought by this time my friends
would have already left for the state. As it is they are
still here and they still dont know when they will
leave. They were to leave today. But the Navy seems
to have its shipping fouled up a wee bit Since I'm
not going I don't care if they never go. See how selfish I am. They certainly have the right to go home
alright but I also want to get back in the worse way.
My plea doesn't seem to have an effect.

I just came from chow. Its now six in the
morning. Since I had nothing else to do after roll
call but lay around I thought I might as well go to
early chow. Had pan cakes—That was all nothing to go with them but serip We also have liberty
so Val and I plan to go to La Hiwa that is on the
other side of the island. Its a fairly nice place. We
bought a small radio and a few tubes are missing so we have to go way over there to get them.
When I was on my five day pass I was there. I
wanted to tell you about it but was unable to.
Its a small town right on the water front. It was
used for a harbor for a while but since that side of
the island is to rought for loading and unloading
they have put a harbor in Kahalui on this side.

Tokayo Rose came from this island, at least
one of the girls, came from this island. I heard
her speak of it a few times. There were poles put

369

along side of the road to keep Jap planes from landing there and all the city busses were camofloged. She mentioned quite a few small things like that.

They claim she came from a small place by the name of Paia. About ten miles from her. By the way that is the place I spend my five days. You can walk in and out of the place in five minutes. The majority of the towns are small.

Im looking forward to that day of a home of our own. I doubt if it is going to be much fun starting one. At least we will be living in peace with a chance to make a living.

I read about that hurricane that was to have gone up the coast. It must have been big one. The radio sure made a fuss about it.

Wait till Iris hears you called her a "screw ball" Your name while be "mud" than. You two remind me of my two sisters. They are always saying silly things about one another.

So the carnival was into the city again this year eh? Never missed a year yet has it. I remember last year while I was there the Shipping Agent gave me a whole pack of tickets good for any thing. He knew the manager of the show. I was only there long enough to give the tickets to my friends Than shoved off for the hospital. I'll have to sign off for now. Keep Smilling. I'll be seeing you.

Love and Kisses.
Paul.

Postmarked Sep 29 1945 from Cpl. Paul J. Fogel, H & S. Co. 23 Mars. 4 Div., c/o. F.P.O. San Francisco, Cal. to Miss. Evelyn Wells., 1201 E. Jackson, St., Pensacola, Florida. (with 6 cents air mail stamp)

On plain, unlined stationery:

Sept. 29–1945

Dear Evelyn:——

Again I'll have to disapoint you for on Monday the first day of Oct. I'll be shoving off for Ooknawko. By the time I get there I'll probably be able to spell the name of the place. I'm so angry I can hardly write. I had hoped so much in getting to come home with the rest of my buddies. I'd rather be send there than to China. I'll probably get to see my oldest brother I hope so. That will be some thing to look forward to. It would be just my luck to get there just as he is leaving. If that happens you will be able to hear me all the way down there.

I wrote your mother a return letter. I hope she is as anxious to hear from me as I am to hear from her. Mamie Lou must have received her letter writting technie from her. It is hard to decide which are more interesting. They both wite thing a person would like to read about.

I had a letter from Pauline she says my brother Sheldon has at last been discharged. I'm so glad for he has nearly 130 points. He also plans in getting married. It will probably be as soon as he reaches the states. That will leave me the youngest and the only one in the family not married. If I could only reach the states again I wouldn't be single long either. Neither would you.

Ive started to pack my sea bag. I've accumalated more junk than I know what to do with. The other two buddies of mine are going alone with me Val and Maddux (the old fellow.) None of them seem so happy over the idea either.

Went into Lahaina the last liberty day and didn't do any thing but get radio tubes. Went in and came back with the same buss. There are only three busses a day to that deserted place and all of them is to early and the last is to late.

I'm sending you a map of the place, it is sixty miles long and twenty miles wide at the widest spot. Its nearly sixty miles to this place alone. I can give you an idea where we are located

I believe I mentioned that I was up to the big creator its on the map her. Don't try to pronounce the name of it for when I get back I'll do that for you. I'll you wish to learn the language you can find that on the back of it.

This is all for now.

Lots of Love.
Paul

[Paul inserted a U.S.O.-generated map of Maui]

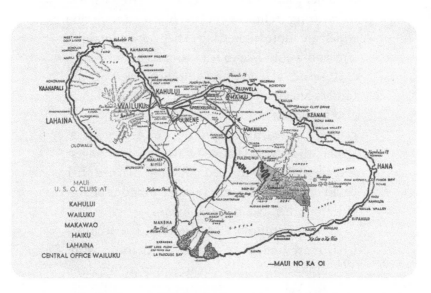

Paul put a small "x" to indicate his camp location

Postmarked Oct 3 1945 from Cpl. Paul J. Fogel, HDQ8 Co. 8th M.P.Bn, (PROV.), c/o. F.P.O. San Francisco, Cal. to Miss. Evelyn Wells., 1201 E. Jackson, St., Pensacola, Florida. (with 6 cents air mail stamp)
On plain, unlined stationery:

Sept. 30–1945

Dear Evelyn:—

This is another one of those letters you dislike to read. If you you know the male creature, you will know that it's not inhuman. I don't know if you have been going out with on fellow or with all fellows. I know if you don't go out I can't say I dont care because I do. I've never told you, you should not go out with any one. This is a long way to get around it. I've been transfered to a new out fit. An M.P. out fit. We will probably be on our way, and aboard ship by the time you receive this letter. We are going to Okwaniane to be trained there, and than send to China. Evelyn I don't know how long I'll be there. The only one who knows that is the Good God. I do know it will be over a year. I trust you with all my heart. And I know you will wait on me. Right now I am ready to burry my self in a hole and never come out. Seems to me there is where I plans have landed I'm giving you your freedom Evelyn, (if you want it) I'll love you till my dieing day. Thats why I'd rather not have you waste your time me. I've been very true to you over here. It was mostly because I had to. I think of you most all of the time. These people here arn't like those in the US. and I don't treat them as such. I love your family as much as I do mine and I love you even more. I've tried my best to express my opinion. I'd like very much to have yours Don't leave out any thing. If you want to wait longer for me. I'll never mention it again but I'll worship for it as long as I live.

I caught a cold the other night and its really a diller Coughing and sneezing all of the time. My throat is so sore I can hardly talk. My eyes seem to be watering all the time. Had my throat sprayed two times yesterday. What a relief that was. I haven't had a letter in two days. It really seems lonesome not getting letters.

We have our first inspection in a few hours so I'll would be get busy and start peeparing, to stand it. Our new C.O wants to see what sort of men he has in his out fit. This is all for now.

Always Loving You,
Paul.

Postmarked Oct 5 1945 from Cpl. Paul J. Fogel 435156, HQ Co. 8 M. P. BN. F.MF. PAC. (PROV), c/o. F.P.O. San Francisco, Calif. to Miss. Evelyn Wells., 1201 E. Jackson, St., Pensacola, Florida. (with 6 cents air mail stamp)
On plain, unlined stationery:

Oct. 4–1945

Dear Evelyn:—

We are still here at Maui, gathering gear together. We have to get all our gear together over here after we leave here we won't be able to draw any thing else. We are sure having our up's and downs trying to get enough tools and equepment to furnish our maintaince section. We were issued some jeeps and a few other havier trucks. It seems as if there isn't a new one in the groupe. All of them are second hand. None of them run worth a darn.

The mail has stoped comming in, at least there hasnt been any for the past three or four days. I can't express in words how much I apreciate your writting me so regularilly. I'm hoping you won't ever stop. I do depend on them alot.

We were living out of locker boxes before were transfered. Now we are living out of sea bags what a job. Most all of the time a person is looking for some thing on the bottom of it. Then is when you see clothe flying from one part of the tent to the other. Val had that trouble yesterday. Lucky you weren't here for he used some words, not even I heard before. We were sitting beside him and the more we laughed the madder he became.

We took some pictures, I guess I told you about them. When we were up to the creator. I have some of them. I'll send you one of them the best one When you see that one you can imagine what the rest are like.

When were with the twenty third we used to boil our clothe in a large G.I. can. Yesterday I was out there with a brush and a bar of soap wearing my knuckles to the bone. What a day that was.

We have quite a few good officers, especially the one in charge of us. We haven't got a Sgt. in charge of us. There are only five of us Cpls and we have twenty eight vehicles to take care of. I've just come in and cleaned up for chow. What a job we had this morning.

I'd just about give any thing in this world to be home with you. By the time I get back I'll probably be fit for Chattahoochee. This waiting around to be transfered further away is sickening. I'll have to go to chow now I'll write again soon.

Always Loving You.
Paul.

Postmarked Oct 8 1945 from Cpl. Paul J. Fogel 435156, HQ Co. 8th M.P. Bn. F.M.F. PAC. (PROV), c/o. F.P.O. San Francisco, Calif. to Miss. Evelyn Wells., 1201 E. Jackson, St., Pensacola, Florida. (with 6 cents air mail stamp)
On plain, unlined stationery:

Oct–7–1945

Dear Evelyn:—

Today we were schuled to leave Maui. We haven't drawn all our gear yet so we will have to stay here another week. It isn't suprising. Thats the way the Marine Corps works. You will never know what they might do next.

Its six oclock in the morning and the whole tent is still asleep. After six oclock rolls around I can't fall asleep any more so here I am writting you. If any one woke me up at half past five I'd probably yell my head off. Don't ask me why a half hour makes that much difference. It just does.

I received two letters from you yesterday, you were still under the impression that I may be on my way home. I should have never hinted it to you. I was in such hopes of thought of comming home that I didn't think they could send me out futher. One let down leads to the next.

I was interupted there for a while for roll call. I certainly hope David does get the chance to be discharged. He already has more than I ever hope to have. A nice family ready to settle down to peace time. To me its only a beautiful dream.

I was on duty yesterday. What a day that was From one jeep to the other. What wasn't wong with one vehicle was wrong with the other

Today they opened their hearts and gave me liberty I think I end this letter this evening I may have someing to tell you than.

We had a little going away party. It didn't mean any thing to me because every time they have a party. There is never less than five or six bottles floating around. What a blow out. Every one was fighting everyone else etc. etc. I went to town this after noon to get away from it all. The way I felt they could have killed each other and I would have been happy. When I returned this evening they were all brused and [illegible—2 words]. Some one must have put them to bed, for they all passed out.

I had a good chow when I reached town. A large stake with all its trimmings. Yum was it nice and tender. I droped into see my old lady friend and bought a few post cards, to send out my change of address on and than headed back for the base.

It is still indefinate as to when we are going to leave here. The orders read on or after the 7th of Oct. That could mean next year too.

The old forth Division is still here. They hope to be in the states by the twenty fifth. Some of those boys have been over here thirty month.

I'll stop this gab for now. I'll always Love you,

Love and Kisses.
Paul.

Postmarked Oct 10 1945 from Cpl. Paul J. Fogel 435156, HQ Co. 8ᵗʰ M. P.Bn. F.M.F. PAC. (PROV.), c/o. F.P.O. San Francisco, Calif. to Miss. Evelyn Wells., 1201 E. Jackson, St., Pensacola, Florida. (with 6 cents air mail stamp)

On plain, unlined stationery:

Oct.–8–1945

Dear Evelyn:——

I just came from the show. That reminds me. I don't believe I told you about the new Theater that was built. It was just finished about two weeks. Its a beauty. It cost some thing like 37 thousand dollars. It will be converted into a pinapple store house when we leave here. It's completely made of wood. Its larger that the Theaters there in Pensacola. You can imagine the size of it. Getting back to the picture. It was very good. Gary Coopper played in it and I forgot the girl's name. She was also very good. In the picture she was as wonderful as you are. I had a letter from you today. It wasn't the one I was waiting for. I know what the answer will be at least Im praying for the right reply. You can't imagine how much I've missed you these month's. It's painful. I love you so much some thing tells me I will be seeing you soon. I'm still praying that they may have made a mis take. Right now doesn't look that way. I can picture you standing by the railroad track as well as if it were yesterday. I can remember my self pinching my self to see if I was really leaving. I watched you till I couldn't see you any more. Its funny but I remember those small things as if they were yesterday. Your letter also remarked where you remembered the private water fountain we had and our special seat on the fountain in the park. They are wonderful things to remember. I'll never forget them I know.

I bet you can't imagine the position I'm writting this letter. I'm sitting on my sack with the mosquotoe net over me. Can you picture that. I can't see how but a few of those pests got in here with me and there are really feasting on me. Having one darn good time. They are like the cockroaches you mentioned, pretty thick and big.

We are kept pretty busy these days trying to repair the worn out equiepment we we issued. It was to new gear. They made a slip up someplace. We were painting jeeps all day, today. You should have seen me. I believe there was more paint on me than on the vehicles.

My boys didn't go to the show. Instead they went to the "slop shute" Three guesses as to what that is. any way they just came stumbling in. Alittle under the wheather. What a sight. Had a letter from my mother yesterday. She tells me my grandparents are still pretty sick. I hope they both hold out till I return.

I'll have to hit the sack now. Keep smilling. I love you so very much.

Always Loving You
Paul

Postmarked Oct 12 1945 from Cpl. Paul J. Fogel 435156, HQ Co. 8th M. P. Bn. (PROV), F.M.F. PAC., c/o. F.P.O. San Francisco, Cal. to Miss. Evelyn Wells., 1201 E. Jackson, St., Pensacola, Florida. (with 6 cents air mail stamp)

On plain, unlined stationery:

Oct. 11–1945

Dear Evelyn:—

I just came from liberty. It's only three oclock in the after noon. I came in because I didn't want to be caught like last week. I went to a show and didn't get out till almost four thirty and than stood around till six oclock trying to get a ride into the base. I finally reached the base three minutes before seven and I was due in at seven. The top Sgt was sure I was going to be A.O.L. While I think of it what do you want for Christmas. You name it and I'll my darnest to get it. As for me. All I want is to be with you. Thats all I'd want in this whole wide world. You can't imagine how wide it is untill you travel all the way around it. I'm doing a good job of being half way around it. It's too far for me. I stoped in to see Mrs Hebert, (the lady I stayed with for five days.) She wasn't home. I took a few pictures of her home. If they come out I'll send them to you. I also took a few of the base here. I doubt if they will come out very good though. Talking about pictures. I had one taken today. Maybe you would like to see the cookie duster I grew. You can't see it so well but it's there all right. By the time I see you. I should be able to twist the ends. I bet you can picture me that way eh?

Remember that other Fogel I was telling you about. Well he is comming home. I just saw him this after noon. He has three children and has over 60 points He shure is a happy fellow can't say I blame him. He has a just cause. He is all packed and ready to go. You don't know how much I wish I were going with him. He is going to live there in Tampa Fla and wants me to visit him. when I get down that way.

Still haven't had word as to when we are to leave. I hope that if we have to go it will be soon.

It is certainly hot this after noon. Last night I nearly froze and this after noon I'm roasting. Pecular weather isn't it? We had an inspection of the tents yesterday and had to have our extra blanket placed on top of the bunk in a roll so I didn't bother putting it on last night. I woke up about three oclock and was to cold I could hardly move. It took me nearly an hour to get warm again. I should have had you to snuggle close to. The coolness didn't effect the mosquotoes though. They were as active as ever. Blood thirsty creatures.

There is going to be a big inspection on Saturday so I'll have to do some more washing. It's common around here. When you arn't writting letters you are washing and visa vesa.

We were paid today and I was looking for something you may like. Didn't see any thing that I didn't already give you that was sensable. I enjoy buying things for you. I wish they could be more expensive things but my promotion hasn't come though yet. Ha. This will have to be all for now so keep Smilling. I'll always Love you very much.

Love and Kisses.
Paul.

Postmarked Oct 14 1945 from Sgt. Paul J. Fogel 435156, HQ Co. 8th M. P. Bn. (PROV.), F. M. F. PAC., c/o. F.P.O. San Francisco,

Cal. to Miss. Evelyn Wells., 1201 E. Jackson, St., Pensacola, Florida.
(with 6 cents air mail stamp)
    On plain, unlined stationery:

    Oct. 13–1945

    Dear Evelyn:—

        Its nearly nine thirty and the lights go out
    at ten. So I'll quickly scribble you a few lines.
    I've quite a suprise for you. It was more a suprise
    to me than it will be to you. I've made another
    stripe. Yes I'm now a Sgt. I don't know how long
    I'll keep it but it does come in handy being a Sgt.
    once in a while. I was told about it night before
    last. I was penocile again and in pops the first
    Sgt and asked me if I knew if I was now a Sgt. I
    was so nervous I could hardly talk. I was recom-
    manded for it a year ago in Pensacola. I might
    have told you about it. It just reached me now.
    Of all places. I had it all planed out to be Cpl. for
    the duration. It does mean a wee bit more money.
    Twenty percent over sea's pay and five percent
    long divity. Thats on my three years service. Add
    that on to the base pay of seventy six and you
    get some thing like ninty five dollors. I'm going
    to increase my allotment home. So we will have
    a little money to begin our home. I still haven't
    heard your reply to my letter but I'm certain it
    will be what I'm waiting for. There is one thing
    I dislike most about this job. That is I have all
    my friends under me. The old fellow I've men-
    tioned so often has been Cpl for three years and
    still hasn't made Sgt. Val has been waiting over a
    year now and still no word. There was five Cpl's.
    to choose from and they selected me. You know

what I have to put up with. A person can't give those fellows orders without making enemies and they are all a bunch of swell fellows. They like to kid me alot about it, but still they fell alittle jilted because they didn't make it also. Can't blame them. Most of them know more about mechanics than I'll ever know. Thoses are my troubles at present. I haven't had a letter from anyone for over three days now. I'm beginning to wander if ever one has forgotten me. I know your letters are in the mail some place.

I bought a box of cigars and began to pass them out tonight they sure went fast. If I had a extra one, I'd send it to you. I can just picture you smoking a cigar. Val sends his regards. He just came from the show. Saw "Week end at the Waldorf." Says it was pretty good. Wish I would have gone with him. I usually do. We were moved futher away from the show so we have to walk a mile to get to it. I was painting jeeps all day so I felt to tired to up up hill that far.

The lights are going out in a few minutes so I'll have to sign off for now. I'll always love you very much. I'm allways thinking of you.

Lots of Love.
Paul.

1990
JJD-fec

EIGHTH MILITARY POLICE BATTALION (PROVISIONAL),
FLEET MARINE FORCE, PACIFIC, c/o FLEET POST OFFICE,
SAN FRANCISCO, CALIFORNIA.

11 October 1945.

BATTALION PROMOTION ORDER)
                          :
NUMBER. . . . . . .1-1945)

Reference: (a) MC - 546746, dated 27 September 1945.

1.   In accordance with the authority contained in
reference (a), the below named man is hereby promoted to the
rank indicated effective this date, to rank from 27 September
1945:

          SERGEANT (MECHANICAL) "ON DUTY ONLY", TEMPORARY:

          FOGEL, 435155, Paul J., Corp, USMCR, 014, HQCo.

          BY ORDER OF LIEUTENANT COLONEL LAUN M. REIS,

                          H. L. HINER,
                  Major, U. S. Marine Corps,
                      Executive Officer.

O F F I C I A L:

John J. Diehl
JOHN J. DIEHL,
1stLt., USMCR,
  Adjutant.
- -
Copy to: CMC.   PRO.
          CG, FMF, Pac.   Sgt. FOGEL.
          PM.   F I L E.
- -

19

Paul's promotion to Sergeant, October 1945

384

Postmarked Oct 17 1945 from Sgt. Paul J. Fogel 435156, HQ. Co 8th M. P. Bn. (PROV.), F. M. F. PAC., c/o. F.P.O. San Francisco, Cal. to Miss. Evelyn Wells., 1201 E. Jackson, St., Pensacola, Florida. (with 6 cents air mail stamp)
On plain, unlined stationery:

Oct. 16–1945

Dear Evelyn.

While I'm still yawning I think I'll drop you a line. It is now six oclock and I made made a remark to one of these fellows that "Ants are flying all over my sack." He said who ever heard of flying ants. Well I did and I told him so. By the time the arguement was over I was proven wrong and also learned a wee bit about insects. I don't know where the pests come from but they are all over my sack this morning. It rained last night so I guess they came in to sleep with me for the night. Thought ful of them wasn't it. We have liberty to day I doubt if I'll go. They haven't got any thing in there that interests me anymore anyway.

There are some more roomers going around that we may be here another month. I don't hope so. I'll never be the same if I stay here any longer. Seems to me that tornado had some thing to do with it. They are using all the ships over there for transporting wounded off that rock.

The radio is on and Val is getting a kick out of the hillbillies that are on. He likes anything that even sounds like it. He turns it on full blast and puts his ear nearly in it.

I went on liberty after all. Here I am soped to the gills. Yep it's raining cats and dogs outside and I was caught in the midst of it. I should have come in sooner to wash a set of gungarees and take those off the line I have on. Before I forget. I send you some thing again. From town this time. It's a baby blanket. It has Hawaian print on it. I bought it for Doris and Jimmy but if you like it you may keep it for your self. You see I lost there address and didn't know where to send it Next time I'll learn to keep my address book up to date. I thought it would make a nice return gift for that cigar they gave me. They probably have more then they know what to do with, but it is different you will have to admit that.

I ordered a good chow for dinner also. Fried chicken Its the first I had for some time. We usually get it every Sunday but they fry to many at one time so most of it is raw. This is exceptionally good. Maddox, the old fellow went with me.

The boys are still giving me a bad time as far is being Sgt is concerned. I don't know but I think I deserved it. Most of the fellows have only been in the corp a year or two and were made Cpl's right out of boot camp. I had to work for my stripes.

We are all ready to pull out at any time. All we are waiting for is the word to start loading. The Twenty Third Marines are again schecheled to leave on Monday I hope they succeed this time They are pretty well discouraged and I can't blame them. This is all for now. I'll always love you very much.

All my Love.
Paul.

Postmarked Oct 19 1945 from Sgt. Paul J. Fogel 435156, HQ. Co. 8th M. P. Bn. (PROV.), F. M. F. PAC., c/o. F.P.O. San Francisco, Cal. to Miss. Evelyn Wells., 1201 E. Jackson, St., Pensacola, Florida. (with 6 cents air mail stamp)

On plain, unlined stationery:

Oct. 18–1945

Dear Evelyn:—

Havent had a letter from anyone for nearly a week now. The fourth Division is leaving tomorrow and I suppose they are holding up all their mail and mine is included in it. All the post offices except the main division post office are shut up. Now I'll have to wait till your letters catch up with me again. I hope that will be very soon. I do miss hearing from you so very much.

I just came from the shower. What a place. No warm water It is as bad as standing out in the rain on the water is a wee bit cooler. It takes quite a bit of nerve to enter a shower around here. I just about have to take one every night. I havent got the cleanest job in the Corp you know. They are certainly becomming regulation here of late. Inspections are coming up one after another. We still haven't heard when we are to leave or where we are to go. That Storm on Okinawa seemed to spoil our plans alittle. I hope they decide to send us home. Talking about storms. There is one stirring up out side at this very moment. The wind is just about to blow the tent down. Sort of like the ones we have in Pennsylvania once in a while. They are lu lu's.

Last night was the first time I attended a show for nearly a week. Sam E. Robinson in some

picture. For got the name of it now. He was playing the part of a farmer. Very good I thought. I've
been staying in playing penocile with the boys
most of the nights.

Oct. 19–1945—

I just woke up so I'll complete this letter
while Im waiting for chow call to blow.
I was up to the creator again yesterday. Man
was it raining I was soaked to the skin. I have the
hardest time keeping cloth dry. I have to change
nearly every day. Any way we went up there to
test radio jeeps. We were talking to a jeep some
thirty miles away. That was quite a distance. We
didn't think we could do.
There goes roll call, be back in a second.
That was quick enough.
The boys pulled out this morning at four
thirty for the good old states. You should have
seen the tent Every one came in to say good bye.
Of course we were sorry to see them good. When
we told them that they nearly tore the tent down.
One of my buddies a heavy truck driver was
caught speeding yesterday and was giveing ten
day bread and water. The Col. caught him. They
sure threw the book at him.
I pulled Val out of the sack this morning
you should have heard him threatening me. He
is the hardest man to get up I every saw Well
enough of this jabber for today Keep Smilling

Always Loveing you
Paul.

Postmarked Oct 22 1945 from Sgt. Paul J. Fogel 435156, HQ Co. 8ᵗʰ M. P. Bn. c/o(PROV), F. M. F. PAC., c/o. F.P.O. San Francisco, Cal. to Miss. Evelyn Wells., 1201 E. Jackson, St., Pensacola, Florida. (with 6 cents air mail stamp)

On plain, unlined stationery:

Oct. 22–1945

Dear Evelyn:—

I havent heard from you for ten days now and it feels more like a year. We are still here on Maui. All ready to go to where we are headed. Where that is no one knows. If we stay here till Nov. 1 I might still have a chance to come home and also a chance to be discharged. Talk is now going around that the points may be lowered to fifty points or two years of service. I hope one of them will hit me. I have fifty two points and over three years so I stand a pretty good chance. All I have to do is wait now and pray that, that roomer is correct.

The other day I has handed two letters and I felt certain that at least one was from you but I was disapointed again. Today is another day so I'm still hoping that at least one of your letters will reach me.

Yesterday was Sunday and we five mechanics went on a beach party by our self. We were swimming practically all after noon and than played a little ball in the surf. The waves were a wee bit rough. Some must have been ten feet hight. One took a beating if he didn't get off the shore. There was a terrible undertoe. I got a cramp in my leg and today my leg is still sore. I was about ten feet off shore when it hit me so I left a big wave carry me in on the beach, by that time my leg muscle was a solid as a rock and hurt as much as if I had an arm cut out. I can't swim very far any more because of that arm of mine. I could feel it giving a few times yesterday. It also hasn't got a pleasant feeling when it flys out of joint. It was sort of funny to me at first when it went out. You get the same effect when you start opening a rusty door. There is a creaking and cracking and than a sharp pain and the next thing you know you are looking for your arm and you will find it in the back of you some place

We had quite a laundry yesterday we did in the morning. We pooled all our clothe in one big laundry and put them in a big G. I. can and boiled them. It took all morning but we finally finished the job and when we came in from the beach they were dry so we brought them in. It was better than scrubbing them by hand.

I hope your radio isn't giving you as much trouble as the one Val hasn't. If it isnt the tubes its some thing else. He is sure having a hard time keeping the thing playing.

Its time to go to work now. So I would better sign off for now. The reason for the mail delay is because of this transfering and every one being transfered to the states. They have to put new addresses on each envelope. There are quite a few men so it takes a wee bit later I supose. Keep Smilling. I love you very very much.

Love always.
Paul.

Postmarked Oct 26 1945 from Sgt. Paul J. Fogel 435156, HQ. Co. 8th M. P. Bn. (PROV.), c/o F. M F. PAC., c/o. F.PO. San Francisco,

Cal. to Miss. Evelyn Wells., 1201 E. Jackson, St., Pensacola, Florida. (with 6 cents air mail stamp; Paul's promotion to Sergeant document included)
On plain, unlined stationery:

Oct. 25–1945

Dear Evelyn:—

I'm waiting for chow call to go so while I have the time I may as well write you as I know of no one I'd rather write. I haven't heard from you for a good two weeks now but I'm not easily discouraged as you know. I had a very nice letter from your mother yesterday. She wrote three pages and had plenty to tell me. I like long letters but I can't seem to get my self in the mood to write them. Of course nothing ever happens to me to write about any way. Your mother told me you tried to get her to tell you what she wrote Now is that nice. Trying to pry into her correspondence. She really wites a wonderful letter. It contains every thing in general. Thats not my way. I skip from one thing to another. I doubt if you can understand the things I write. She also said your step father wasn't in good health. He reminds me alot of a neighbor of ours at home. Remember the time we walked past the gas station on that street the Palafox U.S.O. is on. I for gott the name of it. You had your arm in mine and we were talking alway like a bunch of kids when he called us over. I was plenty nervous so some reason, and that time at Elizabeth's trailer. I'll never forgive you for that. That was a mean thing to do. I doubt if I was ever so embarrassed in my life. I could have jumped into the ocean and thought nothing of it. The next time some thing like that happens give me a wee bit of a warning. That could have given me heart failure you know.

I just came from the chow hall. We had ham. and sweet potatoes. Thats another thing sweet spuds is another dish I dislike. Don't mis understand me. I eat them but I dont love them. We have had them so often I'm beginning to feel like a potato. Have you ever eaten dehidrated carrots. I can't describe to you how they taste but the person that invented that formula must have been a mad man.

Say is Kelly still working in the hospital. I often think of her. Remember the day we went on a weener roast and Johnie Collins and Kelly went with us. She certainly was alot of fun. Give her my regards if you see.

The boys are all getting ready for this big inspection on Saterday. We have to get our gear cleaned and polished and every thing has to be in top condition.

Say I'm going to let you in on another roomer. The men with fifty points may get the chance to come home and I'm one of them. I'm going to have to wait till the 1st of Nov to find out but as soon as I do I'll let you know. I'm so happy that I even have a chance. I have fifty two points. I'll have to wait and see how things turn out now.

This is all for now. I'll always Love You. Keep Smilling

Love and Kisses.
Paul.

Postmarked Oct 28 1945 from Sgt. Paul J. Fogel 435156, HQ.
Co. 8th M. P. Bn. (PROV.), c/o. F. M F. PAC., c/o. F.P.O. San Francisco,
Cal. to Miss. Evelyn Wells., 1201 E. Jackson, St., Pensacola, Florida.
(with 6 cents air mail stamp)
On plain, unlined stationery:

Oct. 27–1945
MAUI

Dear Evelyn:—

If you decided to wait on me this letter
should be the one you have been waiting for. By
the time you receive this letter I will be aboard
ship on my way home. I have fifty two points
and they lowered the points to accomodate me.
Wasn't that nice of them. I'm so happy at the
thought I may be seeing you soon I don't know
what I'm doing. I wish I knew your phone no. I'd
call you up as soon as I reach the states. I wish I
would have asked you for it before. I drop you
a telegram or some thing as soon as I get there.
In the mean time don't write me because the
Government itself isn't sure where I'm located.
Most of my back mail is addressed to the 23rd
Marines and that addressed to the 8th M. P. will
also have to be transfered because again I'm being
transfered to the 4th Division. That is the part that
hasn't been send to the states yet. I've had two or
three letters with in the past two and a half weeks
and none were from you. You must know how
I feel from your experience while I was on Iwo.
Yes very anxious to hear from you. If there idea
which was to send us to Okinawa would have
gone through we would have left and I would
probably would have had to go with them and

spend quite a few month over here yet. Val has 48 points and he is going with the 8th M. P. over there. The points will probably be lowerer when he gets there and then all he can do is wait and that may be a long time. They are going to pull out in two or three days also I do wish he could join me in going back. We have been through alot together. It doesn't seem to be right. There are quite a few fellows that have 49 points that won't be going back. Maddox the person I told you I wanted to go in bussiness with has not quite four years is lacking two or three months. He is also going with them. He has nearly a hundred points but being a regular in the Corp instead of a reserve they make him stay over here.

I've stated a very bad habit on Iwo. Smoking cigarettes. It is bad because after you start its hard stop. I've tried many times but couldn't. I believe I'll be able to when I get back though. They have been very easy to get over here. They just about give them to you. Perhaps when they are harder to get I won't care for them.

Its raining like the devil out side at the moment I'm sort of glad Im leaveing the Hawaian Islands. The rainy season is just setting in and when that happens, It rains for days at a time with out stoping. Last year I was in Pearl Harbor when it hit it wasn't quite as bad is this be because we were nearer the ocean. We are sitting on the side of a Volcanio here and all the cholds seem to accumalate here. Its like a real cloud burst.

Well I was give the after noon off to pack my sea bag so I'd better get to it. I'm laying on my stomach write the letter on the deck and it is

becomming mighty uncomfortable. Bye for now.
I'll always love you very much.

All my Love
Paul.

Postmarked Nov 19 1945 from Sgt. Paul J. Fogel 435156,
Camp Reception Center, Camp Joseph H. Pendleton, Oceanside,
California to Miss. Evelyn Wells., 1201 E. Jackson, St., Pensacola,
Florida. (with two 6 cents air mail stamps)
On Camp Reception Center letterhead, written in pencil:

Nov. 15–1945
7:00 P. M.

Dear Evelyn—

I wasn't going to let you know but I've
decided I'd better tell you. I'm home, at least in
the states and that is much closer to you than I
expected to be at this time I can thank the Lord
Im not on my way to Okainawa. I'll be with you
in a few weeks and it won't be to long before I'll
be on the East Coast. I hope to leave this comming Saterday or Sunday. I'm hoping nothing
will happen between now and than.
Now for the suprise I saw J. C. and Elizabeth
last night and I'm expecting to see Jimmy and
Doris tonight We had about an hour together
last. I was never so glad to see any one since I
returned. I had a hard time locating them. If we
stay here over the week end I will visit them at
there home. I'm looking forward to it. Jimmy
and Doris are to come out tonight to see me I'm
expecting them any minute. I dont know what Ill
say but you can be sure there will be a lump in my

throat as large as a waltnut. I was expecting to see Elizabeth down at the docks when I arrived but than I shouldn't have because I didn't let them know I was comming home. I wrote my mother yesterday and that was the first they knew that I had reached the states. I'm so flat broke now it is really pityful. I would have gone and seen J. C. but I spend it in Maui On different things I'll be going to a seperation center at Bainbridge Md. I will take me about three weeks yet to get cleared out of the Marine Corps. Ill send you a telegram from Bainbridge.

This Marine Corps is still to uncertain. I'm going to try to come down to get as soon as I get discharged They may make me go home first. I'll do my darnest get to you the first thing. That isnt too soon for me. This waiting around is like having led in a persons shoes. That first plan won't work so we will have to do some thing else, to make a living. I have some thing else in mind. I'll tell you about it when I see you. They havent shown up yet. I'm beginning to wonder what is keeping them. J. C. told me last night when he gets dis charged he is going to buy a small trailor and is just going to travel all over this United States. I doubt if I'd like any more traveling. I'm just about fed up with it. I feel sort of ashamed of my self not having you come out to California. I can understand you not wanting to stay in one place all the time. I have had a letter from you for a month now and I told Elizabeth and she said she would let me read the latest one she received. I ought to be interesting at any rate. I'll have to sign off for now so keep smilling. You need not

write any more for I'll not receive they any way.
I'll always love you.

Love and Kisses.
Paul

Postmarked Nov 23 1945 from Sgt. Paul J. Fogel 435156,
HQ. Bn. HQD. Co. F. M F. PAC., 4 Marine Division, San Diego,
California. to Miss. Evelyn Wells., 217½ W. Belmont, St., Pensacola,
Florida. (with two 6 cents air mail stamps)
On plain, unlined stationery:

Nov–18–1945

Dear Evelyn:—

This ought to suprise you. I spend a hole day
with Elizabeth and J. C. Also read the letter you
wrote to them. I had a wonderful time. I guess
it was the happiest day I spend in the past year.
It sure was good to see some white folks. I mean
peope without slant eyes. I also received your new
address. I hope you and Danney didn't fall out
with Mrs [illegible]. I thought you enjoyed her
company. I can under stand your reason. I was in
La Mesa, from Friday noon till Saterday noon. I
had to report in to get ready to ship out of here,
"as they put it. Appearently I was a wee bit slow
because I wasn't on the list to go any way. I was
sort of disapointed till I heard that my chance
will come some time about the middle of the
week. They can't keep me much longer out here
at any rate. The whole fourth Division has to be
broken up by the 27th of this month. I believe I
can hole out that long. The suspense in waiting
to see you again is killing me. I believe they are

going to send me to the Great Lakes now. They seem to be crowed at Bain bridge. As soon as I get out Ill be down there so hang on. Your birthday is creaping up might close and I'm afraid I won't be there to help you celebrate it.

I know what your present is going to be and I'll probable bring it with me when I arrive. I entend to spend some time with your mother when I get there. I'll let you know when to put in the two weeks notice.

Jimmy and Doris has the most lovable baby I have ever seen by the way I guess I may as well tell you now. J. C. told me to tell you that they would like very much if you came out here. I'm sure you would love the senery. I know I did what little I saw. J. C. took me up to the moutains on Sunday morning and the view is the most beautiful I've ever seen. If you want to come telephone or send a wire to my mother be cause I'll call her before I start for Pensacola and if you are on your way I'll not bother. J. C. said either him or Jimmy will be going East with in the next three months and you could come back with them at that time. I don't want my feelings to interfere because I know you wouldn't regret the trip. You would love it I know. It is up to you to decided. We will have a lot to talk about when I return to you. I've had quite a bit of excitement since I've returned and over the weekend.

I've just about decided to go to technical school after I get out. That won't make any difference as far as getting married is concerned. The Government had made quite an offer to the service men and it is hard to pass up. It is too lengthy to describe so I'll not try. I'll tell you about it when I see you, I guess by this time you are beginning to get those letters you wrote to me back again. Its been a month since I've heard from you. You can't imagine how I feel.

J. C. and Elizabeth took some pictures just before I left. In one I was holding the baby. You will get a kick out of that one. I think he is so cute. J C. is getting sort of heavy and Elizabeth doesn't let him forget it one minute. I'll hit the sack now so be careful and God bless you.

All ways Loving you.
Paul.

I'm sort of nervous tonight. Shaking like a leaf for some reason.

Paul Fogel, November 1945, just returned to California and visited Evelyn's brother Jimmy, and wife Doris; and Evelyn's sister Elizabeth, and husband J. C...both families were stationed there at the time.

Paul Fogel received check from Commonwealth of
Pennsylvania for his services during World War II...$11.25

THE END

IDENTITY OF NAMES MENTIONED

- J. F. (Frank) Wells, Mamie (Mammie) Lou Wells—Evelyn Wells's brother, sister-in-law
- Jimmy (Jimmie) Wells, Doris Wells—Evelyn Wells's brother, sister-in-law
- David Wells, Clara Wells—Evelyn Wells's brother, sister-in-law
- Elizabeth Wells Brown, J. C. Brown—Evelyn Wells's sister, brother-in-law
- June Fogel Wambold, Willard Wambold—Paul Fogel's sister, brother-in-law
- Francis Fogel, Charlotte Fogel—Paul Fogel's brother, sister-in-law
- Polly (Pauline) Fogel Acker, Earl Acker—Paul Fogel's twin sister, brother-in-law
- Sheldon Fogel, Electra Barthold Fogel—Paul Fogel's brother, sister-in-law
- Roy Fogel, June Kyle Fogel—Paul Fogel's brother, sister-in-law
- Charles Fogel, Grace Hock Fogel—Paul Fogel's brother, sister-in-law

Mary Evelyn Wells, Nurse Training, 21 years old, 1944
(The locket she is wearing was given to her by
Paul and has their pictures inside)

It was the Daughters of Charity who trained Florence Nightingale at the Institute of St. Vincent de Paul in Alexandria, Egypt. Nightingale was impressed with the sisters' organization, training, and discipline. She wrote: "What training is there compared with that of a Catholic nun? Those ladies who are not Sisters have not the chastened temper, the Christian grace, the accomplished loveliness and energy of the regular nun. I have seen something of different kinds of nuns and am no longer young, and do not speak from enthusiasm but from experience."

—*The Sister Nurses*, Suzy Farren

Florida State Hosp.
Chattahoochee, Fla
March 1, 1944

Dear Paul,

We've now reached our destination at last. We arrived yesterday at 2:30 o'clock with low spirits and black faces from the attraction of dust. You should have seen us waiting at the train station which is situated in a "dust bowl" until a taxi arrived. I can just see how you would have laughed. We feel much better now as it is a nicer place than we had expected. The campus is very beautiful especially this time of the year for the grass is so green and the trees have new leaves.

We don't have as much time off duty as Sister told us we would have. We only have a week-end each month and 11:30 o'clock leave on Wednesdays and Sundays. I don't know what week-end I'll have off yet as they haven't told us, but I'll let you know. If you can get off duty and come up, I'd like to show you about the campus.

We were assigned hall duty the first morning. It's very different from general hospital work. I was assigned to an orthropedic ward which consists of about twenty beds. The patients who are able wander about in the hallways and rooms. Of course the ward door is locked. We also have an eighth month's baby in one of the rooms which belongs to one of the patients. She doesn't even realize she has a baby.

I received a letter from Nellie about two weeks ago and haven't answered it yet. She's probably mad at me, but I don't have much time to write. I'm going to write her tonight or in the morning to let her know my intentions are still good.

Several of the girls invited me to a social meeting last night. We had lots of fun even though I was tired—as the girls were very nice. They wanted me to go out with them tonight, but I had made other plans. There isn't even as many places of entertainment here as there is in Pensacola so use your imagination and feature our one drug store and one movie.

They are planning to have a dance for us next Friday night. They will envite boys from the fields near here.

Every time I try writing a few words some of the girls come in and distrub me. I know I can't be that interesting to them. I could understand the situation better if we were a crowd of boys they were coming to see. I suppose they are just trying to encourage us. I'll make out alright, but Charlene is so depressed. She still talks of packing her things again and going back to Pensacola.

She'll feel better after she gets accustomed to the place and especially the people.

One of the M.P.'s was watching us very closely while you were with me at the train station for he asked me why I wouldn't let the marine "kiss me good-bye." He just didn't see us when you started to leave. I didn't realize anyone was watching us and neither did I care for it wouldn't have been any of his business if we had kissed continuously.

Are you still sleepy from getting up so early yesterday morning? I'll bet you don't make a habit of getting up so early. I still haven't caught up with my rest, but that's all I'm going to do during my three week's vacation.

I hope that you haven't been too bored while trying to translate this awful scribbling. Have lots of fun and think of me just once in awhile any how. I know that you didn't believe me when I said that I'd write, but you know I usually keep my promises. Stay out of the brig and write to me soon—

Sis
P.S. My address is:
Evelyn Wells S.N.
Fla. State Hosp.
Chattahoochee, Fla.
Phone no. if you come: 121 Nurse's Home

Florida State Hosp.
Chattahoochee, Fla.
M–6 *

Dear Paul,

I was so glad to receive your letter. Thanks for being so prompt. I never knew before that letters could mean so much to anyone. I would like this place O. K. if there was any place of intertainment, but there's no place to go. We visit the hamburger stand every night for none of us can eat this food. I won't ever complain of the Pensacola food again.

These patients are very amusing. I stand around and observe them all the time. The work isn't hard at all, but we do have long hours. We work ten hours a day and the night nurses work twelve hours. Maybe I should say that we just sit for that length of time as we really don't work. I will tell you some of my experiences when I see you. I'm writing this letter while on duty.

I'm sorry that the Marine ran over the child, but I'm very glad it wasn't you. Of course, I know you're a better driver than to run over some-one.

How is Paul (Lynwood)? Does he still write to Nellie and has Nellie returned to Pensacola yet? I wrote her a letter, but I don't know whether she has received it yet. Lynwood shouldn't deceive her so. Don't mention the things to Nellie that I've discussed with you. We'll wait and see what happens.

Thanks for the compliment or I suppose it's "just another fact"—since you're always stating facts.

Some of the girls had this week-end off duty so they went home. Pitts went to Pensacola for the week-end. She dates one of the ambulance drivers. They argue all the time, but I've heard that's a sign of love.

If you see Mrs. McLain say "hello" for me. I like her very much as she seems to understand the difficulties of everyone. She trys very much to make the U.S.O. an enjoyable place.

They're having a dance on the campus Thursday night. I surely do wish you could be here. I'm sure we want have much fun as those very much "disliked dog-faces" are going to attend.

I have written this letter with one of the desk pens so please don't notice the many errors.

Try writing me again soon,

Evelyn

Fla. State Hosp.
Chattahoochee, Fla.
March 10, 1944

Dear Paul,

If you could only visualize my surroundings you would wonder how I could even gather my thoughts together enough to write a letter. I'm in a male ward now and we've just admitted four new patients. Everything is in such an uproar, you just can't imagine. I'm the only nurse in this ward among all these "nutty" orderlies and patients. I enjoy working with the men more than the women as they aren't nearly so much trouble.

I went to the dance last night. I knew before I went that I wouldn't enjoy it. Too many people were involved. All the attendants and maids were present.

Paul you know that I wouldn't write you if I didn't appreciate hearing from you. I also would not have told you about my week-ends off if I hadn't preferred being with you instead of some one else. I wish you wouldn't feel the way you do toward me.

I have next week-end (18-19) off so Pheil and I have decided to go to Pensacola. If this is possible we will arrive in Pensacola Saturday night at 9:00 o'clock at the bus station. I would like to see you then if you're about town.

Next month, if you wish, you may come to Chattahoochee and maybe I'll know more about showing you around the campus. It might be possible to get special permission to show you in the different wards. If you haven't been inside a mental institution before I think you would find the patients to be very interesting and amusing. I was rather amused at first, but I seem to be more accustomed to them now.

I suppose I have "spring fever" as the trees are so pretty that I just want to roam through the woods. The hill across from the hospital is in Georgia and there is an old old house situated on the incline of this hill. It looks so homely—

You remember we started to see "Flesh and Fantasy" when it was playing at the Florida theater and there was such a crowd that we couldn't get in to see it. This picture is now playing here and I saw it. I don't think that it's such a grand picture as everyone thought it was. It is a very unusual picture.

I have just received a letter from Nellie Moylin. She said she waved at you and hadn't seen Lynwood at all. She is so glad to be back in Pensacola again.

I also received a letter from my Mother. She told me about the cakes and pies she had just finished baking. Can you imagine her being so cruel as to torture me like that—when she knows how well I like them. She said that Sister Theodore wrote her a very nice letter concerning me. I just wander what she said.

I had better hush and take the four o'clock temps. before the Supervisor visits the ward.

I'll be expecting another prompt answer.

Evelyn

Friday night
M 18–*

Dear Paul,

I have been so confused that I was waiting about answering your letter. The Supervisor had promised to let me off this week-end and at the last minute she tells me that I can't be off as there's no one to relieve me. You can imagine how disappointed I was. We never know when we can really plan to do something. If nothing happens I will see you next week-end as that's the last week-end of this month and I haven't had mine yet. If possible I'll be in Pensacola next Saturday night.

I received the nicest letter from Nellie, and she had made plans for me to spend the night with her. Tell her to keep those plans for next week. She says she is on 3-11 shift in the nursery. I would like to have her as my supervisor. Would we have fun! And just what did you want to ask Nellie? If they (questions) pertain to me—I suppose I could answer them better as I haven't told her much about myself so you couldn't get much information from her.

I was in the general wards Thursday and Wednesday. Those are the mentally ill, but not physically ill patients. You should have seen me in the midst of all those women. I received more unsuspected hugs and kisses than you could imagine and my hair stood straight more than once. One of the patients drew my picture. I'll show it to you when I see you. Of course it looks better than I do.

Evelyn Wells, Chattahoochee, Florida, State
Mental Hospital, March 1944
(one of her patients, an artist, drew this of her; her letters
to Paul began during this part of her required training)

Friday night
M 18 -

Dear Paul,

I have been so confused that I was waiting about answering your letter. The Supervisor had promised to let me off this week-end and at the last minute she tells me that I can't be off as there's no one to relieve me. You can imagine how disappointed I was. We never know when we can really plan to do something. If nothing happens I will see you next week-end as that's the last week-end of this month and I haven't had mine yet. If possible I'll be in Pensacola next Saturday night.

I received the nicest letter from Nellie and she had made plans for me to spend the night with her. Tell her to keep those plans for next week. She says she is on 3-11 shift in the nursery. I would like to have her as my Supervisor. Would we have fun! And just what (questions) did you want to ask Nellie? If they pertain to me - I suppose I could answer them better as I haven't told her much about myself so you couldn't get much information from her.

I was in the general wards Thursday and Wednesday. Those are the mentally ill, but not physically ill patients. You should have seen me in the midst of all those women. I received more unsuspected hugs and kisses than you could imagine and my hair stood straight more than once. One of the

Evelyn's letter describing the picture her patient drew of her

411

patients drew my picture. I'll show it to you when I see you. Of course it looks better than I do.

The Superintendent of the colored male department has been very nice to us. We had better watch our behavior while about him as the Superintendent of nurses is his girl friend. He took my girl friend and me to Bainbridge, Georgia last night. It is about twenty-five miles from here — a very nice little town. I must say that the town is much nicer than Chattahoochee. Will I be glad when I have completed these three months! I don't think I shall care to see this place again.

One of our instructors from Pensacola is on the way to Jacksonville and stopped by for the night. I have just been talking with her. She said we have forty new students. Maybe I shouldn't have told you that for you really will want to be sick now.

You shouldn't let your boy friends make fun of that awful picture of me. You may tell them it's merely a picture of one of the maids at the Pensacola Hospital if you like.

I hope I haven't caused too much confusion about my not going over this week-end. I'm sorry, but it's something that can't be helped. I hope to see you next Saturday —

Evelyn

Evelyn's letter describing the picture her patient drew of her

The Superintendant of the colored male department has been very nice to us. We had better watch our behavior while about him as the Superintendant of nurses is his girl friend. He took my girl friend and me to Bainbridge, Georgia last night. It is about twenty-five miles from here—a very nice little town. I must say that the town is much nicer than Chattahoochee. Will I be glad when I have completed these three months. I don't think I shall care to see this place again.

One of our instructors from Pensacola is on the way to Jacksonville and stopped by for the night. I have just been talking with her. She said we have forty new students. Maybe I shouldn't have told you that for you really will want to be sick now.

You shouldn't let your boy friends make fun of that awful picture of me. You may tell them it's merely a picture of one of the maids at the Pensacola Hospital if you like.

I hope I haven't caused too much confusion about my not going over this week-end. I'm sorry, but it's something that can't be helped. I hope to see you next Saturday—

Evelyn

Wed. P.M.
M–23 *

Dear Paul,

So you have been "stepping out" on me? Just so it's another blonde—don't get too serious though—

I'm almost positive I'll have this week-end off for I ask the Supervisor to tell me for <u>sure</u> and she said she would arrange the schedule so I'd be off. Two disappointments in succession would be a bit too much for me for I think I would pack up and travel anyhow.

I had the P.M. yesterday so several of we girls went along with an attendant to an old old park near by. There were very steep hills and big swamps so you can just picture my appearance upon my return. We had lots of fun as we had a picnic afterwards. I wish you could have been along for I think you would have enjoyed it too.

I'm in a different ward now, but I'm still with men. They're better patients than women, but don't get a stiff neck because I told you that. That's true in a general hospital too.

It is so quiet here—not even a radio playing. I left my radio home and Pheil's radio just won't play so we have to keep each other company in our meek ways.

I went to the movies Sunday night and was hoping that I hadn't seen the picture already, but discovered I had. I just slept while the others enjoyed the picture.

Pheil found a small turtle and brought it in our room to keep. During the night it escaped so we had fun trying to find him. I finally convinced her that the turtle should be freed, so she let him go. I'm not especially fond of that type pet as you never know when you might be minus a portion of a finger as a result of playing with it.

I received a letter from Nellie today. She is planning to move to another apartment soon—maybe this week.

It has been raining again today. I'll have to practice being like a duck in order to get used to this weather. I hope it doesn't rain during the week-end. I'm still planning to see you Saturday night—

Evelyn

Monday night
M 28 *

Dear Paul,

Arrived on time last night even though I did have a difficult time getting a bus in Mariana for there were so many people who were going on the Jacksonville bus that they finally added the third bus. I was at the hospital at eleven-twenty. I was rather amused at the girls and especially Pheil, as they were afraid that I wasn't going to be back on time. They had heard of the detour and also had heard there was a bus strike.

I have been so very sleepy all day that I felt like sleeping in one of the patient's bed—(you know I must have been sleepy to feel like that). Any hang-over would be well worth the nice week-end. You were so very nice to me.

Pheil says tell you that she still likes the Marines even though Sinclair hasn't written her for some time. She sends her regards. She has just had her shower and it's about time I'm having my shower for they'll be calling bed-time soon.

It has been raining here again tonight— "April showers in March." If I had the character-istics of a duck I'd probably like this weather—I believe it rains more here than in Pensacola.

All the girls liked the present you gave me; in fact I was afraid they would become too attracted to it. The girls may wear my dresses, but all those presents just happen to be among my special personal belongings which no-one can borrow.

I didn't realize so many people knew I had the week-end until I returned and so many people were asking if I had fun during my trip to Pensacola. Of course you can imagine what I told them for I dreaded having to return to this awful place. I don't let the people know I dislike the place for it would only cause them to dislike me.

I'm looking forward to the week-end when you & Nellie come to see me and all my mental companions. Let me know what week-end you want to come and I'll try to arrange. After all you're the visitors in this situation.

I know you're tired of reading this boresome letter and it's also time for my shower. I will say "good-night and sweet dreams."

Evelyn

Thursday P.M.
M 31 *

Dear Paul,

I received your letter this morning. This is once that you couldn't have been in suspense about whether you were going to receive a letter from me. Remember what you told me? Don't worry about my not answering your letters for you would know in due time if I didn't intend answering them. Maybe I should be the one to worry.

We have been having a "jam session" in my room tonight. I don't know why so many had the idea of coming down at the same time, but I had about six visitors. Two of them are still in here and one is sitting on my bed beside me—Pheil has gone out some place so I've been entertaining them. You couldn't imagine what we've been doing. We were taking exercises of all types. You should have seen us—or maybe it's best that you didn't. I haven't exercised in so long that I know I'll be sore for days. Maybe I should purchase a "walking cane"—as it may come in handy for support.

Nellie did have things so well planned, but I also think <u>Paul</u> had a great deal to do toward plans for the week-end I spent in Pensacola. I just hope you had as enjoyable time as I did. Nellie is very sweet, but I can't understand why she wants to waste her time on someone like me.

One of the girls came in and saw your picture on my dresser and really gave you a nice compliment (fact). I'll let you in on the secret some day—

The Labratory girls invited me down for chicken the other night. They had prepared it in the Lab. and was it good! The best food I've eaten on the campus.

I was in charge of one of the big wards alone today. I suppose you can visualize me among all those patients. I really enjoyed it for I don't like Supervisors always "snooping" around. They either get in my way or I stay in their path ways.

I wrote Smitty and Bennett today. Maybe Bennett won't be too angry at me for not coming to see her while I was there. I just didn't have time to go see every body as my stay was so limited. You and Nellie were the main ones I wanted to see.

417

I'm getting so sleepy I'm going to sound the "all clear" so everyone can return to her own room and I can sleep.

Don't forget to plan to come one week-end. I'm dreaming already so I think it's time for me to say so-long.

Evelyn

Tuesday
A 4 *

Dear Paul,

If you aren't too angry at me, maybe you'll consider reading this letter. I'm sorry—and if I mention <u>facts</u> again I'll give you special permission to punish me as you wish. The same day I received your letter, I also received a letter from my Sister and she was very angry at me because I didn't see her while I was in Pensacola. We had an examination following the arrival of those two letters so you can imagine how I felt by evening. I'm so disgusted with this place that it isn't even funny. What do you suggest—my joining the "<u>WAAC'S</u>"? One-third of my time here has passed and it's doubtless I'll last the other two-thirds. Down in the "dumps" aren't I? Why worry you with my troubles—

Even though it was raining as though the heavens were pouring down in drops last night, these girls (ducks) went to the movies. They tried to get me to go along, but I decided the dormitory was the best place for me. No movie is worth my walking through those puddles in the rain. When Pheil came in she looked like a "drip."

We went to the Hospital farms Sunday and swiped some onions and carrots. They were so good—and we still have a bag full of them. We eat some every night. The patients told me today they smelled onion—of course I wouldn't know why—wouldn't you enjoy eating a great big onion? They're a prize, you know.

I can't get this week-end off because it's already taken by some of the other girls—Easter Sunday, you know. I'm going to ask for the third week-end if you would like to come up then. I'll let you know for sure as soon as I can find out. They don't usually let us know definitely until about three or four days previous to the week-end. Sure—I want you to come this month if you like and you and Nellie come next month.

Have you seen Mrs. McLain lately? Or do you go to the U S.O. often? I used to enjoy going there so much with Smitty and Bennett.

I haven't heard from Nellie yet. I suppose her time off duty is filled in. I'm just hoping for the time when I'll work in the nursery with her as my supervisor.

Just burn those letters I've written in the past and I'll try not to make you angry again.

Evelyn

Saturday P.M.
A. 9. *

Dear Paul,

Almost Easter—imagine that! Spring once again. It's so nice out, but it seems I'm on duty three-fourths my time so I don't have much sunshine and fresh air.

I'm supposedly on duty with no Supervisor present; in fact I'm the only nurse on the hall. Most of the patients are old men—one was just handing me a line—"too old to know better."

I'm planning to have next week-end off (15th & 16th). I won't be positive of the week-end until Wednesday P.M. I'll let you know as soon as possible so you may make arrangements—I could call you Wednesday night if you haven't planned to go out.

You know I didn't intend your using that small snap-shot for your file folder; in fact I thought you may destroy it with the letter—just my face clipped out. You shouldn't let all your boy friends make comments on my pictures. I don't deserve them.

I haven't yet heard from the exam. I took the other day. I don't care to know what I made and I wouldn't want anyone else to know for I can imagine it's one of the lowest grades I ever made.

I would like to know who told my Sister I was in Pensacola for Smitty didn't tell her and I didn't see anyone else she knew. She doesn't know Nellie.

I went to the patient's dance yesterday afternoon—lots of fun watching them dance, especially the colored.

I must get busy. So-long

Evelyn

Thursday A.M.
A 13. *

Dear Paul,

Did you have a good night's rest? Maybe you could have slept well had I not called you at midnight. I suppose you feel like "kicking" me for waiting so late to call. No excuses available.

I'm almost positive I'll be off next week-end (22-23). The Supervisor has promised that I may be off then as I'll be on this hall for two weeks.

I just finished shampooing one patient's hair—"full of bugs." I'll have all signs and symptoms of everything by the completion of my three months here. I'll also be "buggy" too; then I'll have you wash my hair so you'll be affected. I'd be lonesome scratching by myself.

I went out to the famous little night club last night—the only place near too dance. It's about ten miles out and is such a place as we would be restricted from in Pensacola.

I was writing while on duty and the Supervisor came in so I had an intermission. This is my afternoon off duty—nothing to do. I suppose I should study, but you know I don't enjoy that.

Phiel had a letter from Sincliar the other day. Was she surprised and happy? He's still in Jacksonville. He seems to still be having lots of fun.

Tell Nellie that she had better slow down some with her social life long enough to write me.

Two of the girls who are affiliating from St. Petersburg are going to Pensacola this week-end.

If you see a small blonde and a red-haired girl wandering about town you'll know they're from Chattahoochee.

I have to go to class so I will say so-long

Evelyn

Sunday P.M.
A 17 *

Dear Paul,

I just received your letter a few minutes ago—know that you don't care to hear from me so soon, but I have to do something to occupy my time so I decided to write letters.

So—you're still holding out on me about your age. I don't think you should do that for I told you my age. An "eye for an eye" as the saying goes. Perhaps I'll write your mother. Bet she would know.

I also spent my grammar school years at a country school. I suppose you know that after the number of letters I've written you—something in common. My teachers were grand, but what a "dumb" pupil was I.

I'm on the Receiving Wards now. Every patient is first admitted here before being sent to the general wards. I've taken care of this ward by myself for the past three days as the other nurses had the week-end. You would have had a chance to be referee had you been here this morning. One of the patients almost escaped as the night nurse was leaving the ward. I almost sat on her, but I quieted her a bit. She has been in a camisole all day. Every time we take it off she tries to take our keys or tries to escape when we open the doors. The Supervisor surely trusts me with all these "nutty people" for she seldom comes in.

Did I tell you that Pitts had acute appendicitis and had to have an operation? She had been complaining with her side for sometime. She's getting along fine and as mischievous as ever.

Juanita Atwell, one of my classmates, was up for the week-end and seemed to like this place. Imagine that! You might even like it too. It looks nice for only a day or two, but having to spend three months here.

I'm still planning to have this week-end off. I hope I'm not disappointed this time. What time will you arrive here Saturday? I'll be off at 1:00 o'clock P.M. Saturday.

The Superintendent invites several of us down for lunch every Sunday. He has much better food than they have in the dinning room. He'll probably invite us for lunch next Sunday. He is very friendly and nice.

I received a letter from Nellie at last—you must have told her what I said or did she suddenly awaken from her dream-land? She is a very sweet girl.

I know you'll want to buy this pen staff I'm using—writes so well. You can see what we have to chart with now. I have my pen along with me, but no ink in it.

Tell your Boss's wife "hello." She has a very nice personality.

Poor Boss—if you only did what you would like to do when you get angry. I'll bet you aren't easy to get along with then.

I have thought of several improvements I could make in this chart room so I'll get busy—

Evelyn

Wednesday P.M.
April 20 *

Dear Paul,

Such a rainy day—I hope it doesn't rain during the week-end. It rained last week-end so I was glad I didn't get off.

Yes you may come and look the place over before you see me if you wish, although I would like to show you through. When you call you'll have to ask for the Hospital line and then call Landis Hall Phone No. 121 and if you can't get me there call Phone No. 35, which is the ward where I'm on duty.

You agree to readily to my writing your Mother so I'm not going to write her. She wouldn't know me any way.

Pitts is up walking about in her room. An appendectomy, is a rather minor operation unless there are other complications, but she'll have to repeat the three months here which to me would be worse than the operation.

The nurses here are very nice to us. Most of them have lovely personalities.

I'll make this a short note—Hoping to see you Saturday.

Evelyn

Tuesday Night
April 26 *

Dear Paul,

Received your letter this afternoon and was glad to know that you had a good trip back. You didn't get much sleep though—more than you would have had if you had taken the later bus for I would have kept you awake as long as you remained here.

The Matron has already called bed time, but I'm going to be a bad girl and break the rules by staying up to write to you.

I'm going on night duty tomorrow night and I surely do dread it for I'm so fond of sleep. I just don't see how I'm going to manage to stay awake for I'm such a "sleepy-head." Such long hours—seven o'clock p.m. until seven o'clock a.m.

I'm so glad you were up for the week-end. I enjoyed it, but I know it must have been boresome for you at times.

I haven't seen Mr. Dean or Slim since you left. Of course I don't get about much. I told Phiel to tell Slim what you said. She has a date with him Wednesday night. Unbelievable, but true—neither of them had a drink Sunday night.

You should have seen me yesterday afternoon. I looked like a maid or housewife as I was mopping and rearranged the furniture. I like the new arrangement much better and so does Phiel. She always has difficulty in finding her things after I've cleaned house, but she's so careless with her belongings.

I had another letter from my cousin and she has decided to enter training. I only hope she likes it as it is a very nice profession.

We have one patient who claims she's going to save me. Perhaps I'll be a changed person when you see me again.

All the girls are sound asleep and I'm so sleepy so good-night—

Evelyn

P.S. Don't work too hard. Please burn these letters—

Saturday Night
April 30 *

Dear Paul,

Received your letter today and am very sorry you will have an operation—Just wish I were there to take care of you. Some day I'll become a registered nurse and may take care of whomever I choose.

You didn't tell me your back was bothering you during the week-end. If you had told me we would not have walked so much. You shouldn't mind telling me those things for after all, I'm supposed to be a nurse. I couldn't have helped your condition, but perhaps have made you more comfortable.

I saw your friend this afternoon—"Slim"—and before I could say anything he was asking about you. He fell for you in a big way—I'm getting jealous. I told him what you said about going turkey hunting in Pensacola. I gave him your address so you may be expecting a love note any day. He surely has a grand personality—just wish I had a personality to compare with his. He is supposed to leave Tuesday.

I saw Mr. Dean the other day while having lunch. He says he has something very personal to discuss with me—just wander what it could be. A bit of good advice never hurts any-one. He surely has a good impression of you, but of course you wouldn't care to know his opinion. Said he would liked to have seen you before you left.

I'm on night duty and I suppose you know how I feel—such a sleep-head. The night hours are so long—seven at night until seven morning. I can't afford to sleep any as I'm the only nurse on the hall and if I do sleep I may awaken with a knot on my head, among this environment.

Wish I were with you during your operation. Hope you get along fine, but I know you will.

Love,
Evelyn
P.S. I've almost fallen asleep.

Thursday Night
May 5 *

Dear Paul,

Have served my week's night duty and am on day duty again—what a relief! Now I can enjoy good <u>night</u> sleep again.

Hope you are feeling better and will soon have the operation. I want you to be out of the Hospital by the time I get back in Pensacola.

I plan to have my tonsils out the second day of my vacation. Of course I want have to stay in bed unless other complications should occur. I hope to spend two weeks of my vacation in Kansas, but my Mother wants me home. She says I have never stayed home much, which is right.

Phiel and I are listening to the Famous Major Boles program. We have just had a shampoo, but yet have so much to do before going to bed. I have more work to do off duty than I do all day on the halls.

There is a patient on the hall where I'm on duty at present who recently murdered one of the attendants. Phiel is also on the same hall. She almost got loose from her restraints this afternoon and as Phiel and I were trying to restrain her again she almost kicked me in the face, but hit me on the shoulder instead. She also tried to bite both of us so you see they do get a bit rough at times.

We had planned to go to Pensacola this week-end, but I couldn't get off—as usual. Maybe I'll get to go next week-end. Three of the St. Petersburg girls want to go along.

We were in Marianna yesterday and had lots of fun just playing about. Saw a cute movie, but I don't remember the name of it. Wallace Beery was a main character—so silly, but cute.

Hodges and Phiel were restricted for one night for riding bicycles with shorts on. Can you imagine that? These people are so narrow-minded. They should be very much embarrassed if they visited a summer resort.

Slim has returned to Chattahoochee—(4-F). No turkey hunting in Pensacola. He mentioned getting a job at the Naval Air Station there.

I think Pheil is adding a note.

Love,
Evelyn

Sunday Night
May 8 *

Dear Paul,

Just returned from seeing a movie, "The Thief of Bagdad," which is very good, but I saw it while in Miami some time ago. Had to relieve tonight, but managed to get to the movies by nine o'clock. One of the girls was waiting for me to get off duty.

I'll bet the party was nice and you shouldn't have missed it just because I wasn't there. You know you could have substituted for that night.

Sorry that you have to stay in when it's so nice out—there will be other nice days if not much nicer days.

Yes—Pitts went back to Pensacola. She is staying with her aunt who lives near Warrington and is getting along fine. She will have to return to Chattahoochee soon in order to complete her training. I don't remember her Aunt's name or phone number or I would send them to you.

Was in Marianna last Wednesday and had so much fun. One of the girls from St. Petersburg was along. We were lucky to return to the Hospital on time.

Phiel and Kelly haven't come in yet. They were in Pensacola for the week-end. Phiel's old boy friend came home.

Some of the girls were out taking sun baths in shorts and bathing suits and were almost restricted. These old maids have the most old-fashioned ideas—just because two soldiers came by and began talking to the girls. The boys were very much embarrassed and surprised at the Director's actions.

Since we'll only have two weeks longer here after next week-end, I don't think I shall come to Pensacola during the week-end. I'll let you know if I change my "feeble-mind" again. I have so much work to complete before leaving that I could be busy for the remainder of time here.

When did you hear from Nellie? I haven't heard from her in some-time. Suppose she has forgot me again? Can't say I would blame her if she did.

I saw Slim today and he has written you a letter. He's just the same "Happy Kid."

Sorry the other letter was late. Perhaps I was a bit confused about my days after coming off night duty. It took several days to get used to night sleep again. I would usually lie awake until about two o'clock, but I slept so well last night.

Maybe this letter won't be so late arriving. Good night and sweet dreams.

Evelyn

Friday Night
May 13 *

Dear Paul,

One of the St. Petersburg girls and I had the afternoon off duty since I couldn't have the week-end—hadn't planned anything this time. Mr.

Dean took us for a pleasure drive and then we had a stroll through the town of Chattahoochee. Later we went out to see the patients dance which was rather amusing. Now I'm exhausted and sleepy, but you see I'm staying up to write you.

Remind me some time and I'll tell you of a surprising experience with Mr. Dean. He states, "there is no fool like an old fool," and I'm beginning to believe that. He seems to have changed quite a bit lately.

Slim's address is: Herbert Kennedy, Chattahoochee, Florida. He is leaving tomorrow, but he said to mail the letter to that address and it will be forwarded. He and Pheil are on the "outs" with each other and he was trying to make a date with me for tonight, but I refused although I like him—just as a friend. I think he was rather peeved at me for not accepting.

I didn't know that you ever disliked anyone (other than me), as you were telling me about the Sgt. who was at the party. I'm glad you attended—would liked to have been there too.

Just have two and one-half weeks here—then my three week's vacation and what a relief! I'll dream about these insane patients for months after I leave this place.

I thought you were going to have an operation. Was it cancelled?

Hodges is on night duty now, but I don't think she likes it so much. Can't flirt or expose her physical technique quite so much with only a few hours out during the day.

Have four of ten book reports written up. Would appreciate some help if you wish to come to Chattahoochee. I know you just love it here. I don't care for Pensacola either, but it's a bit better.

Imagine my eating potato salad with my fingers! One of the girls just brought in some and we don't have any utensils about this room. Really tastes better this way—try it some time.

Pheil wants me to get in bed so I'll hush and get some sleep—

Love,
Evelyn

Tuesday P.M.
May 17 *

Dear Paul,

Received the package you sent and was so glad to receive it. Thanks very much. I appreciate your thinking of me. The other girls were also glad that you sent the gum.

I'm on duty and it's almost time to take the eight o'clock temperatures, but why worry about such minor details. I suppose I shall be transferred again tomorrow—just wonder where my final destination will be.

So you were best man at a wedding and who was the lucky man?!! Bet your knees were beating together—wish I could have peeked in on it.

Several of the girls were in Pensacola last week-end and they were telling me of the progress of the nurse's home. Bet it's going to be nice. At least it will be much better than living in the present crowded quarters.

Have been working on all those book reports and surprised myself by getting them in on time. Beginning next Monday, we'll have an examination every day until we leave. Of course, you know we were glad to hear that.

I made a phone call for one of the Doctors as he wanted me to call up one of the student nurses and have her come to the Grill. I refused to make the call at first, but he insisted so I did. The Superintendent of nurses called me down last night and had a short chat. I wasn't campused, but she didn't like the idea of my making the call. She said she was going to have a talk with the Doctor. I know he will really tell her off, as he has a mind of his own and that happened to be none of her business. I saw one of the other Doctors down town this morning and he was so mad because she called me down. You should have heard what he said about her—nothing good.

Does Nellie seemed to have forgotten about Lynwood? She was so much in love with that boy. He is nice and is good company, but seems to be the type person who has lots of fun and never especially cares for anyone. Does Nellie still live in the same apartment? Haven't heard from her in some time.

So many of the nurses have quit training to be married that I'm afraid we're going to be short of nurses. Two of my classmates were married— Davis and Krauss. We'll miss them very much.

I had better get busy.

Love,
Evelyn

Saturday A.M.
May 22 *

Dear Paul,

The Supervisor just brought your letter in to me. Was so glad to get it. Such a nice day and all we're doing is "sitting" playing cards, checkers, etc. with the patients. You can see I'm on a new ward for I had to work a bit on the ward I just left. This is the electric shock therapy ward on which the patients receive one-hundred twenty volts for fourteen seconds—that throws them into hard convulsions. We gave treatments yesterday so they won't be treated again until Monday. I think I shall suggest their giving me a treatment.

I'm sorry you must have the operation, but you know seven months in a hospital wouldn't even compare with suffering for a lifetime. Although, I don't believe you'll have to stay in bed so long.

Mr. Dean took several of us girls out to see a suspended bridge which is about twenty-five miles from here. He surprised us by having coca-colas and cookies along so we had a picnic after we arrived. Had such a good time, I just wish you could have been along.

One of the St. Petersburg girls and I have the week-end. We're just staying in Chattahoochee over-night and we're going to see the mid-night movie. Maybe we'll go to Tallahassee tomorrow. Only have eleven more days here.

Some of the girls made some pictures of the hospital and campus and they are so good. This is a grand place for making pictures. They had them developed in Pensacola.

I suppose I can come to the hospital to see you when I get back to Pensacola, can't I? Hope to see you soon.

Love,
Evelyn

Tuesday P.M.
Oct. 27* [Paul mistakenly marked this as being in October, but by context, it was May]

Dear Paul,

Hope you're feeling better now—wish I were there to help take care of you. Although my patients don't always progress so readily, so maybe it's best I'm not there as my presence may cause more pain?

Is Raining out and can't go any place tonight. We'll probably go to see the State Cavern Friday afternoon. We were out to one of the parks Sunday and had a very nice trip, except for my being caught in a barbed wire.

The Instructor has planned a picnic for the affiliates for Thursday night. We aren't so enthused over the idea for we think it's going to be a rather boring occasion with her along. Of course, we can't refuse to go along as you remember what "Emily Post" says about such things.

You know, Pheil says that the last she heard of Herbert, he was in California. Gets around, doesn't he? Wander if he has been turkey-hunting there.

It was compulsory that we perform a part in the Florence Nightingale Program at the church last Sunday night. Would have rather been on the side lines as an on-looker. I never like to serve as the center of attention. If I had stage talent, it would be quite different.

Had our first examination yesterday and will have one each day for the remainder of our stay here. They're all such simple "catchy" questions, but hard to answer correctly, as they seem to only have one answer.

Won't you have to request that I come to see you? And how will I manage to get a pass into the hospital? Some-one else will probably be along with me if you're still in the hospital when I get back.

No exciting news and I know you must be tired of hearing of my experiences.

Love,
Evelyn.

P.S. You'll probably need some-one to translate this as I'm writing with that pen-staff again.

Friday A.M.
June 9 *

Dear Paul,

Would like to go out to the base to see you, but don't suppose I'll have time. Dr. Heinberg wanted me to come in see him this morning. Haven't been down yet, but just waiting for Elizabeth to get dressed as she is going along.

Did anyone talk "out of terms" to you for coming out to the hospital Tuesday afternoon? Hope not. Bet you didn't feel any to well after having made the trip. I was very glad to have you come out, but don't think you should have made the trip for your own good.

Do you miss your watch? Bet you're wishing you hadn't left it with me. Really keeps good time, doesn't it?

Nellie is really on the "outs" with her boy friend (Sailor). I don't believe she really knows the type boy she likes.

You should read the letter Eva Nell Smith wrote Bennett. If she doesn't have a lovely opinion of Chattahoochee! I agree with her about the place.

Have been on a liquid diet since I had my tonsils out. My throat isn't quite so sore this morning.

Elizabeth is about dressed so we had better run along.

Love,
Evelyn

Saturday A.M.
June 17 *

Dear Paul,

Just wandering what happened when you returned to base. I've worried about what they might do since you told me you didn't have a liberty pass. Do hope they didn't find out. I'm sorry I couldn't stay over yesterday.

Mother isn't home; in fact, I'm the only one here at present. Of course I can find enough to do to stay busy. I'm listening to radio programs as some of them are very interesting. I enjoy the music too. I tried a new cake recipe and Mom liked it. I didn't especially care for that type cake.

Mammie and I made our pictures in the grass skirt that my brother sent her. Of course we had other garments on too. We couldn't feature ourselves with just the skirt on as the natives wear them. If they aren't too shocking, I may let you see them when they are developed.

I will be in town Wednesday, but I don't want you to try coming out unless you have a liberty pass. I don't want you to be restricted whether you mind or not. You know you must think of yourself sometimes.

You need not answer this letter as I probably wouldn't receive it before I go back to Pensacola. Hope to see you soon if you aren't restricted and I do hope you aren't.

Evelyn

Saturday P.M.
June 17 *

Dear Paul,

Just finished packing most of my clothes and back on duty again. I usually do my "letter-writing" while on duty as I like to have something to occupy my time other than entertaining the patients.

I know it must be fun writing while lying on your stomach. Since I haven't ever experienced that situation, I wouldn't know. I'm glad you're feeling better and enjoy having company.

These patients keep hanging around; in fact one patient is sitting by me now. Of course, since they don't know any better, we receive numerous compliments from them. They all comment on my writing, but I think they have a reason for that—maybe just to see what I write.

Was out to the Florida State Cavern yesterday and enjoyed going through so much. We just didn't have time to stay as long as I would have liked as we had to be back for class.

Had another letter from my sister-in-law and she still wants me to go to Kansas during my vacation; in fact, she is having my brother make arrangements for me to go.

One of the Doctors has a nice big baby boy. He is so excited and so is everyone else as you know there aren't many babies delivered here.

The Magnolia trees are beautiful as they're in full bloom and have such a nice odor.

I must review for final examination Monday. Hope to see you soon,

Love,
Evelyn

*Paul wrote these dates in after he received the letters. He used the postmark date (date actually mailed).

Evelyn Wells, 3 years old, 1926

Evelyn, 1934, 11 years old, holding pet fox

Postmarked Jul 18 1944 from Mrs. Leidy C. Fogel. (Paul Fogel's mother), Nazareth Pa., R#1 to Cpl. Paul J. Fogel., M.B.N.ASC., Pensacola Florida; with 8 cents air mail stamp

Nazareth Pa. Route 1
July 26. 1944.

Hi there my Pauly Wally:

Yes I really had a surprise when I read Mike joined the service also, but I knew as soon as he was through school he would enlist. Although it will shorten his mother's life because he was the onely one that stuck to her. Those two sisters of his just made life miserable for her. But I wish him all the luck in the world and if you write him tell him so and also to write me once. I have now twelve boys to write to no wonder my fingers hurt.

Well how is my love sick son. Getting better and tell me what did the doc say when you went to see him. I hope you wont have to take the second operation like Wayne had. Wayne and his bride were to see us Saturday afternoon. Grandma & pa were up to see me yesterday afternoon. Grandma is not well she seems to be getting smaller all the time. Aunt Hester is moving home. Well Paul I am happy this morning because we finished combining our wheat and oats, all the grain is in the bins. "isn't that something to be happy about."

Your sister June is better again she went huckleberry picking last Sunday and came back with a bad head ache. Delores stayed with me. Yes Grace feels lost being her mother is gone now. She stays with her dad just now. I have not heard of Charles since he is back again but I hope his back is better. His back does not want to get better. Dad is very busy acting as Supertendent, he does not like inside work. Got your card yesterday and am glad you are having a fine time. Give my congradulations to Virginia and hope she makes a better life the second time. Also give my congradulations to Jake. The Heller twins passed for the service too, but do not know when they must leave. Will close and hope you can get a few weeks furlough home soon. You may bring Evelyn along if you think we should meet her. Polly is very anxious to meet her. Lots of Love.

Mother

P. S. Little Andy is getting very tricky on Sunday nite he turned the hose on Polly and sprayed her.

Postmarked Sep 14 1944 from Mrs W. W. Wambold. (June; Paul's older sister), Easton, Pa., R #2. to Cpl. Paul J. Fogel., Marine Barracks, Naval Air Station, Pensacola, Fla.; letter written in pencil; with 3 cents stamp

Write Sooner
Sept 14, 1944

Hello Paul

I received your letter yester day so that I would better answer it right away. You must excuse me for using a pencil instead of a pen but my ink is all, I must borrow Elsie's pen to put your address on the envolope.

Paul I do want to get some thing strait, I didn't tell mom that you didn't write to me for so long, this is how it went. We were down home a few weeks ago & she received a letter from you, then she asked me when you wrote to me last, & I said "not for a long time," but I did tell Pauline not for about 3 or 4 months, but lets drop every thing now & for get the matter I did receive one yester day & was very happy.

Paul, Willard & I are very happy to think that you too have picked your self a partner, we saw her picture on Sun. down home & she sure is pretty, and we do hope you will get along in life very nice. Congratulations to you & Evelyn. Snugs thinks it is wonderful to be getting an Aunt Evelyn, She says tell Uncle Paul when he comes home to bring his girl along.

Well, we have been having rain up here for 3 days now, just about every body was out of water, but now all cisterns are running over, it sure rained.

Well I guess I should close & get at my work, I have so many odd jobs to do, & I do want chicken for supper, so I guess I may as well go and perform the operation.

Willard is still working at the Steel but is plenty disgusted about it. He is working days this week the first time for about 10 weeks and as for my self, well I guess I am OK. I mean for to day. Thats the way I am one day I am good the next day I can be in bed. & Snugs she is OK, she got a great kick out of you letter when you said she should stop making noise you could hear her, at the time she was looking at a book, when I read it to her.

Love
June

Postmarked Sep 25 1944 from Polly M. Fogel, Nazareth. Pa, R. #1. to Cpl Paul J Fogel, N.A.T.C. Naval Air Station, Marine Barrack, Pensacola, Fla; written in pencil; with 3 cents stamp

Sept 24, 1944

Dear Paul.

I hope I can fine enough words to write a nice letter now since I have more time. This is the first Sunday that I am home with nothing to do but sleep and eat and what ever else I would like to do with out being hurried or disturbed. For the last two month we had company every sunday and with that went a big dinner and that usually meant loads of dishes which usually kept me busy washing them until late in the afternoon.

Yesterday I told mother I was going to sleep all day to day But Andy is here and he wants to be entertained a little too, so I played with him until he fell asleep on grammys lapp a few minutes ago. He is a fine young fellow and full of fun and trickery. He is becoming a very big boy.

Did Evelyn receive mothers letter yet? I am going to write her a letter today while I have the time. And am sorry I haven't written any sooner, but I tried very hard to find something to write about and now I think I will just write to her as I do to you. I hope she will like me.

Did mother tell you that your cousin John Fogel was married on Sept 4th to a girl from Mass. Aunt Jennie and Dorthy & Rachel were down to attend the wedding. Aunt Jennie got a permiment for the occation.

Norman Werkieser left for the army last Wed. The scouters held a farwell party for him

I had wanted to see him before he left but didn't get a change to. You know he had asked me to go out with him a few time. and I thought the least I coud do was see him before he left

Also the Heller boys are leaving for Wilkberrow this coming Wed. The one wants to go in the Army Air Cour. and the other in the Navy.

Daddy is here in the kitchen with me and he is snoaring so loud that I think if I go out to look the roof will be boncing up and down. Mother took Andy upstairs and both of them are sleeping. In fact every on is sleeping except me. I guess they all put the joke on me for I was the one who said I was going to sleep all day.

Earls brother Danny is almost home. As his letters state he will be home before Dec. We all are very excided about him.

I don't hope I will shock you to much, but Earl and I are going to be married on Nov 19th. We are going to have a church wedding. Deloris will be my flower girl and little Johnie Faust my ring barrier. I had wanted Andy but Francis and Charlotte think he is to small yet for such a part. I am only having a maid of honor and best man. Arlene K. will be the maid of honor and Earls brother if he is home by then best man. I was wishing all my brother were home to be my attendents also. It would make me feel so proud to have you fellows stand behind me. And since you all arn't I hope you will be with me in mind if not in body. We will be living at home after the wedding and I will keep on working for that is how mother wants it and me too.

If you and Evelyn can come home by then I wish you can. Do you think you can try? Please do. If you will I will have you in the wedding after all. Let me know.

To day we had Harvest Home at church and it seemed to me that the congration didn't open their hearts to much for their contributions for the Harvest pile was a very small one.

This Sat Aunt Hester and Gammy Fogel will have their sale. I intend to gou and try for their vacum cleaner. for I will need one. and am getting tired using the broom.

Well so much for that and I think I shall close and write Evelyn letter.

Love and kisses
Sis.

Monday P.M.
October 23–

Dear Paul,

It seems so very odd that I'm writing you instead of talking with you. I still can hardly make myself know that you were transferred, yet I realize it more each day. I received two letters from you today and you'll never know how happy I was when I received them for they were the first I've had.

Elizabeth has been asking each day if I had received a letter from you and wants me to give her your address. I'll give her your address tomorrow for she is going to write you a letter. She was rather amused at your telling her to be sure she writes a "newsy letter" and not just a note.

Your boy friend (the one who lives near your home) was asking about you Saturday night. I would write his name, but I don't know how to spell it. He's the one who drove us to the train station. He's hoping to hear from you, but knows that you must be very busy at the present.

You remember the two nights we were by to see Nellie Moylan and all the lights were out? She was sleeping both nights and was so disappointed because she didn't see you before you left. It's rather difficult to convince her that we're engaged. She wants to still believe that we're only friends, but I can assure her it amounts to much more than that.

You remember my telling you about Ernestine Plant who was my first room-mate, don't you? She is now the mother of a baby boy and I'm so glad for her as she wanted a boy so very much.

I'm getting to be a very good girl recently. I was to church twice since you left and really enjoyed the services, but neither was so impressive as the service at the Main Station.

The girls have been gathered in my room and as always—talking, laughing, and making lots of noise in general. Some are even borrowing clothes again. Maybe this will explain why I've made so many mistakes. At least that's a fair excuse.

Do you suppose I can still send you the pictures if you are sent elsewhere? I don't think I will be allowed to mail them as we couldn't send Jimmie and Frank enlargements. Let me know what I should do about them for you know I can't get them until the last of the month.

I'll send Frank's address in the next letter as I must have misplaced the one I had and will have to get his address from Elizabeth. He would be so very glad to meet you I know if you ever have an occasion to see him. He looks almost like Jimmie other than he is much more mature.

I'm still "chief cook" and "formula maker" in the diet kitchen. I should be able to prepare a complete meal by the time I have completed training, don't you think?

The girls are going out roller skating. Of course, Pitts is the circle leader. I don't think I care to get bruises tonight. I'm getting to be a regular "old maid" about staying in.

I'll excuse you for not writing daily since you are kept so busy, but I want you to write as often as you can.

Don't worry about my not waiting for you, for I will as I love you very much.

The girls say "hello."

Evelyn

Senior Nurses Home, 11ᵗʰ & Gadsden, Pensacola, Florida, 1945; Evelyn shared a room here while attending the Pensacola Hospital School of Nursing

Tuesday Night
Oct 24–

Dear Paul,

Since I'm at the present in the company
of my Sister, I'll take time out to write a certain
Marine whom, I think, is a very nice guy. I wrote
you a letter last night, but you'll probably receive
this letter just as soon.

I gave Elizabeth your address and she is also
writing you at the present. I'm so proud of my
Sister as she's always so sweet and understanding.
She was almost as thrilled as I (if that could be
possible) that I received the two letters from you.

Did I tell you that Iris has quite nurse's training? She decided the training was a bit too tough
for her to tackle. Maybe I should have decided the
same thing when I met a certain Marine by the
name of Paul Fogel. He surely carried me for a spin.

I wander if you'll have time to write Mamie
and send those pictures. I can just feature Mamie
when she receives those pictures—the expression
on her face. Mom would never quite laughing.

Listen Paul, maybe I should keep my big
mouth shut and I'm not going to tell your Mother
about your being transferred, but I think you
should. After all, she's your Mother and she's very
interested and proud of you. It will be such a shock
to her if you wait until the last moment to let her
in on your transfer. It's only right that she should
know. Now, since I've expressed my opinion in a
short speech, I hope you aren't too angry at me.

I suppose your Sister is quite busy preparing
for the big occasion that is in store soon. I know
she must be very happy.

I'm sending J. C's, Jimmie's, and Frank's address. Since Jimmie and J. C. are in Calif. maybe you will have time to look them up. I hope you aren't sent far enough from the States to see Frank, but in case you do, he'll be happy to meet you. He's the "happy go lucky" type unless he's changed since I last saw him.

These are the addresses:

John C. Brown M M l/C
831-31-09 13 I Division
San Diego 36 Calif.
James T. Wells PR M l/C
1812 Hancock St.
San Diego, Calif.
John Franklin Wells C M l/C D-2
18th U.S.N. Const. Batt.
Fleet Post Office
San Francisco, Calif.

Jimmie is now at Camp Elliot and this (the above) is his apartment address. He would be so glad to see you.

I wish I could hear from you every day.

Love always
Evelyn

Wed. Night
Oct 25–

Dear Paul,

I've just had a nice warm bath and am all dressed for bed, but before going to sleep I shall write you. It seems so quiet in tonight. I don't think I've ever known of the girls being so quiet before.

I received two more letters from you today. I'm always so happy to receive them. I hardly receive your letters before I'm looking forward to the arrival of the next.

Glad you sent that negative to me for I wouldn't want anyone to see that picture. Neither did I want you to see it, but you didn't mind my objections.

Just to think I only have two more weeks to cook for all those patients. You know I had much rather cook for just one person and with just one guess you could tell me who that person is.

We're listening to one of the "nuttest" programs. Maybe this letter sounds just as "nutty." No one is in our room except Atwell and me and she is playing solitary—one of those Chattahoochee games. You know most of the patients there played that game. That's where I learned to play.

Now, I'll add a few more pounds to these many pounds of mine. One of my room mates had a birthday and received a couple boxes of candy as presents. She just insists on my eating some every time she is home and you know me I can't refuse as candy is a main dish especially when it's chocolate covered cherries.

I hope they keep you in North Carolina for a few months. Of course, I know you object very readily. Did you write your Mother yet? Hope I didn't make you angry at me about what I said in my last letter. I just thought that if you tell her a bit early she can "kinda" get used to the idea of your going overseas. If you wait until the last to tell her it will be a great shock. I know for I was home with my Mother when my brothers were shipped out.

I completed my course in Urology today, but haven't taken the examination yet and don't know when he may give it. None of us have reviewed for the exam. So he had better not give us a "pop quiz." I really enjoyed that course as it was very interesting. Our Instructor was a Doctor and a Specialist in that field. He also gave a few points on Venereal Diseases. Of course, we've already had that course, but it's something you can never be warned too much against.

My room mate has now been tucked into bed so I think I'll do the same. I'm always thinking of you.

Love always,
Evelyn

P.S. Maybe I'm just "dumb," but what do you mean by the <u>W.F.M</u>. that you write at the closure of every letter?

Thursday P.M.
Oct. 26–

Dear Paul,

I was of duty early today if you can feature that. I can hardly believe it's true. Received another letter from you today and just wander if you have received any of my letters yet.

Do you remember the afternoon that one of the girls made our picture in front of the house? She had the roll of film developed and the picture is very good even if I did have to make use of my muscle power to have you pose for the picture. Of course, if I had not appeared on the scene, it would have been much better. I would send it to you if I had some other pictures of you, but since I only have one other, I think I shall keep this one. I want my Mother to see it.

Some of the graduate Nurses and I decided that we didn't care to eat Hospital food tonight so we prepared our supper at home and believe it or not, it was fairly good. Maybe I was very hungry for I suppose if some one else had eaten it they would have suffered from indigestion.

I received a very nice compliment today. Miss Bell, the Supervisor of the Operating room, was introducing one of the new Sisters and following the introduction told her that I was the best nurse she ever had in the Operating room. She too, doesn't know me very well or she would probably form an opposite opinion.

I don't like to even think of the scene at the train station. I too, shall never forget that Sunday. I was very depressed all day. I'm glad that such incidences don't happen so very often.

I have to study for two examinations and make out some diets for the patients so I had better get busy.

Love,
Evelyn

Saturday P.M.
November 25–

Dear Paul,

I received the card with your address along with two letters from you today. I was a very happy person when I received them as I have been looking forward to getting them for several days. I'm sorry that you became so sea-sick and hope it wasn't too severe. You see, I should have been along to have cared for you.

Received a very nice letter from your Mother. She seems to have such a great understanding of various situations and expresses her feelings so thoroughly. She sent along an announcement of Pauline's wedding and I know Pauline must be very happy. I almost envy her. I do hope she has much future happiness.

I awakened this morning at five minutes until seven and was supposed to have reported on duty at seven o'clock. My room-mate and I were about fifteen minutes late getting over. I didn't mind too much not having my breakfast as the Supervisor was thoughtful enough to give me a half-day. You should have seen me upon my return home for it's been raining practically all day and I was soaked. Thank goodness—I didn't have that non-resistant rain dress on.

I'm not in the diet department any more, but instead I'm doing general nursing on the halls. I have some very nice patients. Those various diets were about to drive me "nuts." The formula room wasn't much better.

The girls went to Jacksonville for State Board exams this week. Bennett was among the group and she said it was plenty "tough." I suppose I'll be among the next group to go since we'll be out in September. I think we'll graduate some time during June. I dread even thinking of having to go.

Elizabeth is planning to go to California within the next two weeks. J. C. seems to think he will be there indefinitely. He wanted to see you on your way through, but you weren't there long enough for him to even receive your address. I sent Jimmie's, Frank's, & J. C.'s address in one of the letters I mailed to you while you were in N. Carolina, but I'll put the addresses in this letter just in case you don't receive that letter.

All the girls except the seniors have moved into the new home. I'm glad we aren't going to live there even though it's really beautiful and very modern. I could live most any place for another eight months, but I've had my share of moving from one place to another since I entered training.

Did I tell you that Iris has quit training? Just a wee bit too much for her. I received a letter from her a few days ago and she was asking about you. That should make you feel much better.

Elizabeth wrote you a letter that you should receive along with the first letters I wrote you. She wrote a rather long letter as she said you informed her "not to write just a postal card, but a long letter."

I'm sending the address of each of the boys so you may write any or all of them if you wish. Jimmie has a home address and so does David. You may see that Jimmie has made chief again and is still stationed in California. Here are the following addresses:

James T. Wells, C. Ph., U.S.N.
7664 El Cajon Blvd.
La Mesa, Calif.
Sgt. W. D. Wells
301 West Walnut St.
Herington, Kansas
John C. Brown, M. M. 1/C
13 I Division, 831-31-09
U.S.N. Repair Base

San Diego 36, Calif.
John F. Wells, C. M. 1/C, D-2
18th U.S.N. Const. Bn.
Fleet Post Office
San Francisco, Calif.

Any of the boys would be glad to receive a letter from you. It would be grand if there would be any chance of your seeing Frank. I had better come to a conclusion for this letter will never go through if I keep writing. I love you very much.

Love,
Evelyn

November 28–

Dear Paul,

I have just returned home from duty and even though it's midnight I think I shall complete my duty by writing you. My room-mate seems to be enjoying her sleep very much, but she will go on duty at seven in the morning and I don't have to report on until three. You know, I "kinda" like the three-to-eleven shift since you aren't here as that's one way of occupying my night hours.

I will mail the pictures soon. My room-mate took one of them and won't return it so I suppose you'll just be minus a picture. I also have a Christmas present for you, but of course there would be no chance of it's reaching you by Christmas. I will mail it so you may expect it to arrive sometime in the future. It isn't much, but as you may know Service men's presents are very limited.

I had thought of going to California with Elizabeth if there is a possible chance of my getting a three weeks vacation at that time. She wants me to go along and it would really be a wonderful trip. Jimmie & Doris live there and they also have a house trailer. J. C. is going to reserve the vacant trailer space by Jimmie's trailer. That will be grand if they can arrange to be next-door neighbors.

I hope you haven't been sea-sick anymore. That must be a very uncomfortable feeling. Since never having experienced it I really wouldn't know the severity of the sickness.

So you are growing long hair. You may continue to let it grow and I will practice the "french braid" style so I can arrange your hair in pig tails when you return. Above all things don't eat half-cooked eggs every morning after you've grown a mustache.

I have a patient who is a biologist and is paid by the Government to carry on experimental lab. work. His office is near the city beach so he promised to show some of us girls through the lab. and then go deep-sea fishing. That should be lots of fun, but I wish he had been my patient before you left as we could have gone together.

I doubt if you can interpret half I've written as I'm getting so sleepy. We will have a final exam. in Urology tomorrow and I have to give a report in Public Health so I will say "Good-night."

Love Always,
Evelyn

P.S. I sent the addresses in the other letter. Let me know if you receive them.

December 1–

Dear Paul,

I suppose I was just being very lazy this morning as it's now ten o'clock and I just climbed out of bed. Since this is the first day of a Winter month, it's rather cold out.

Elizabeth and I were over home yesterday and the family sends their regards. Mamie is going to write you so you may be expecting a letter from her as I gave her your address.

Pitts was just in and said she wants you to "take the slant out of the Japs eyes." Wouldn't that be something! She also wants you to reserve an Island for her when she goes on her "honeymoon." She is a big "nut."

We have had our final exam. in Urology, but we are yet to take our final exam. in Public Health. We will have completed all our subjects soon and in eight more months we will have completed the Nursing course. I'm so glad it's only a short while to remain here.

Sister Theodora has made me Supervisor of one of the halls. I wouldn't mind if I had all of my required survices completed, but I don't have all of them in yet and we will go to State Board in June.

I have decided not to go along with Elizabeth to California. J. C. may have a leave in March and if he does they're coming home during that time so maybe I'll go back with them then.

I received lots of nice birthday presents yesterday. Even my patients gave me some nice presents. You see, they must not have known me very well. It's fun to care for patients who really appreciate what you do for them.

I haven't heard from your Mother recently, but I look forward to getting a letter each day and most of all a letter from you. I certainly hope that you're still in good health.

Love Always,
Evelyn

Dec. 3–
Sunday A.M.

Dear Paul,

I have several letters to write, but first of all, I shall write you. Maybe I should have gone to Church this morning, but working late nights seems to take away all energy for the following morning. Elizabeth went to Church which will probably be her last time visiting this Church for some time as she is leaving for California the latter part of this week. I will miss her very much, but I'm so glad that she can be with J. C. I surely wanted to accompany her, but couldn't possibly leave at this time. The greatest prevention being that Sister Theodora has restricted all vacations for this month and a portion of next month. If they come home in March, I shall try to go along with them at that time.

I had two letters from you the first of this month which is four I've received since you left. You see, you aren't the only one who hasn't been receiving letters. I've written you several letters, but it's just that you haven't received them yet. The last letter I received from you was dated the twenty-third of November.

I received a very nice letter from your Mother and she seems so happy that Pauline is married. I just wander if she's going to like me as you know I have many faults. I've tried to tell you, but wan't believe me.

Sister Theodora made me Supervisor on one of the halls a few days previous and since I know that I'm not capable of such a responsibility, I asked that I be transferred to the nursery. I will begin duty there tomorrow.

I mailed two packages to you yesterday, but I know you wan't receive them by Christmas. One package contained the pictures and you're minus one for my room-mate took it and would not return it. The other package is just a small present I'm sending you. I hope that you receive them O.K. I had to send them separately as eight ounces is the maximum weight of an overseas package.

I received a letter from Iris (red-head). Since she gave up her training, she isn't doing anything special. I'm sorry that she didn't remain in training, but why should I tell her what to do?

I must write some other letters as it is near time for me to go on duty. The family sends their regards.

Love,
Evelyn

December 4
Monday Evening

Dear Paul,

I received a letter from you today dated the 25th of November in which you had enclosed a letter from Sheldon that you wanted me to read. Perhaps you were a bit depressed after having read his letter, but what I'm going to tell you may relieve your feelings. You seemed to think maybe I would learn to care for someone else and I just hope you don't continue to feel that way. I do love you so very much that no-one could possibly take your place as you are the main subject about which my future is centered. Please try to disregard all the upleasant thoughts and think of the pleasant things the future may hold—I know that is difficult, but you may depend upon my promise to you—Remember? I'll be waiting for your return.

Pitts and I were out to visit one of my ex-patients tonight. She is the wife of the owner of Waters & Hibbert Funeral home. We have known her husband since we entered training. They are very nice and by the way, she was one of my patients who gave me a very nice birthday present. Very thoughtful of them, don't you think? They have envited us out again for dinner.

I shall write Sheldon as soon as I have time. I appreciate his wanting to hear from me. I've been rather busy taking examinations, doing the few necessary things here, and helping Elizabeth get ready for her trip, besides hall duty. I have lots of fun taking care of the babies in the nursery. All of them must have well developed lungs as they exercise them enough by crying. Of course, I haven't spoiled any of them for we don't have time for that.

I sent the pictures and a separate small package the 2nd of December which I hope you receive in the near future. I wanted to make some candy to send you, but it would weigh too much to send overseas and would probably be so long reaching you as you don't remain in one location long enough even to receive my letters. I've written you often and just hope you receive all of them.

Here's Jimmie's and Frank's addresses again just in case you didn't receive the other letter in which I enclosed them. Hope you can see Frank—

James T. Wells C. Ph., U.S.N.
7664 El Cajon Blvd.
La Mesa, Calif.
John F. Wells, C. M. 1/C, D-2
18th U.S.N. Const. Bn.
Fleet Post Office
San Francisco, Calif.
I love you very much—

Evelyn

December 7–
2 P.M.

Dear Paul,

I have a few minutes before going on duty so I shall make use of the time by writing. I wrote you a letter last night and left it in the box for the mail-carrier to pick up this morning, but he dropped it while on his route and I found the envelope on the side-walk. The letter was missing and the envelope was wet from the rain and torn apart. From now on, I shall mail my own letters at the Post Office so I'll know they'll be mailed.

I should be an efficient nurse-maid soon if I continue working in the nursery. We have on an average of twenty-five to thirty babies and they all cry for Mother at once. Smitty's sister has a baby girl, but it doesn't have red hair like Smitty; In fact, we don't have a single red-haired baby.

I received a letter from Pauline today and she seems to be so very happy since the wedding. She said they had just received the first letter from you and were so glad to know you're O. K.

Elizabeth is going to stop by in the morning as she begins her trip to California. She plans to leave at eight o'clock in the morning and you know how much I dislike saying the word "Good-bye." I know I will miss her very much, but I couldn't miss her nearly so much as a certain Marine I know.

Nellie Moylan called last night, but we were both on duty and I couldn't see her. I haven't seen her in ages—Kelly left Saturday before you left on Sunday and we haven't even heard from her and don't know when she may come back—

That Sister-in-law of mine (Mamie) wrote you a letter and Sister has written you three. I hope you receive them soon. I don't know the dates they mailed them, but you may be expecting them—

I'm glad my room-mate swiped one of your pictures for since I mailed the other pictures, she has placed that one on the table in our room. The only thing disagreeable is that I have to look at my picture every time I look at you—

I have to run to class now.

Love always,
Evelyn

December 9—

Dear Paul,

I received two letters from you yesterday which were dated November twenty-eighth and twenty-ninth. I was so very glad to get them. You mentioned one of my airmail letters having nine cents postage. Air mail within the States is only eight cents, but I only had three of the three cent stamps so I used them. You have probably received an airmail letter recently with twelve cents postage on it. Beyond me why it took so much postage as overseas airmail is supposedly six cents. I put two regular three cent stamps on and mailed it. The letter was returned for six cents postage due. The total twelve cents and I haven't figured it out yet unless it's just that I didn't have the regular six cents airmail stamp.

I was still sleeping yesterday morning when Elizabeth stopped in to say "Goodbye." She had a nice service boy and wife going along with her to California. I'm so happy for her as she can remain with J. C. unless he is sent overseas. I wanted to go so very much. Maybe I can make the trip some time in the future.

One of my patients who gave me such a nice birthday present also sent me one dozen roses today. They're very beautiful so I placed them in the sitting room so everyone could enjoy their beauty and fragrance.

Bennett asked me to go along with her to the U.S.O. tonight. I hope that I see Kupsky and ask if he has received your letter yet. He called one night and wanted to know your address, but at the time I hadn't received a letter from you and didn't know your address—

Another group of girls left for Chattahoochee this month and I didn't envy them at all as three months in that "dump" isn't so much fun. I hope they find the place to be of more interest than I did. I prefer nursing sane people although I'm proud of my experience with mental cases.

If that telephone would only stop ringing so often. I'm the only one on first floor at present so I am disturbed every few minutes.

My room mate doesn't stay home half the time. She is on duty in the Operating room and has this week-end off duty. She works the same hours that I worked during the summer months.

You have a crude way of receiving ice cream don't you? I suppose it was good just the same. I seldom eat any since you aren't here any longer.

Bennett is here now so we'll run along to the U.S.O.

Love,
Evelyn

December 11–

Dear Paul,

I'm sitting in the class room waiting for the remainder of the students to complete an examination in Surgical Nursing. You should see us at the present as we're such an energetic and ambitious-looking group—

I'm so happy as I received four letters from you today. I was beginning to believe that Christmas was a wee bit early this year.

We have added another dog to our collection of animals. We now have a cat, a parrot, and a dog. We did have a duck, but he disappeared. The "doggie" likes my room, but I don't like him for he hasn't learned good manners yet, but we'll teach him soon—

It rained all day yesterday and is very cold today. Even though it doesn't snow in Florida, it gets very cold as you should know. It's such a moist cold and seems to penetrate any amount of clothing.

You were speaking of seeing the movies. It seems that you must have seen them all even to the latest production. I don't believe I ever saw a movie with you that you hadn't seen already.

I was to the U.S.O. Saturday night. There were several Marines present, but I didn't see Kupsky. I wanted to ask him if he had received your letter yet. I've only seen him once since you left.

So you finally received Elizabeth's letter. You've probably received some more by now. I hope that you've received a number of my letters by now just to prove that I really care much more about you than you think I do.

I suppose you know that I shouldn't be writing letters in class, but it's getting to be a habit with me. I will say so-long as class is about over—

Love always,
Evelyn

December 13, 1944
7:10 P.M.

Dear Paul,

I'm on duty at the present and expecting the
Sister in at any moment. She is supervisor of the
hall and nursery and she checks the nursery once
every night. All the babies are quiet except one
that keeps reminding us he has a good voice. We
don't have so many babies in now, but we admitted two this afternoon and expecting another one
most any time.

I was down town most of the morning
shopping and thought perhaps we may have time
to see a movie "Together Again," but we were late
so we didn't get to see the picture. Some of the
girls said it was very good—a good title anyway.
I haven't seen a movie in ages.

You were asking about where I would like
to be married. It doesn't especially make any difference as to the place we're married. I would
rather just have a very simple wedding wherever
it would be most convenient when you return.
There would be no point of planning a definite
time or place—do you think? This is my opinion
so now you may give me your opinion. You know
this isn't to be a one-sided affair.

I do hope that I'll pass State board exams,
but I hear they're rather tough. I've never liked
examinations, especially final examinations.

I suppose you've noticed that I can hardly
write with this pen and staff. The ink gave out
in my pen so I had to use this regardless of the
terrible results.

It's still very cold out, but for a change it hasn't rained today. I can't feature your sitting in the rain to see a movie. I would probably do the same under the same circumstances. Just don't expose yourself enough to renew that cold you had or maybe you never got rid of it.

Here the nurse comes with another new baby and for some more fun. I wander how many more will come before we get off duty. I do hope this will be the last one for a few minutes.

I haven't heard from Elizabeth since she left but I suppose she has reached California O. K. She should at least have written me a card while on her way.

It's nice to have a boy friend from your own State. Maybe you have some things in common. Boys usually do—you know. You should get along swell together.

I must get busy—so Goodnight.

Love,
Evelyn

December 15–

Dear Paul,

Do you remember what happened two months ago today? I was reminded of that date when I looked at the calender. Nor shall I ever forget how I felt at that time.

I was writing Pauline a letter yesterday when the mail arrived. I received two letters from you. I look forward to getting your letters so very much and they seem to be the only source of keeping me in training. It seems that seven more months will never pass and yet that's only a very short while.

My room mate has acquired another animal—a small turtle. I had one once, but was glad to get rid of him. It was sent to me from New Orleans so the person who gave it to me didn't know that I soon gave it to someone else who would be more interested in it's welfare.

I've been busy all morning mending my clothes. Can you feature that? The night-duty nurses came in this morning and made so much noise that I awakened early. I decided I had enough sleep so I began mending—may as well get in practice you know.

I don't think I would like the climate you're having there. I enjoy the rain once in a while, but not continuously.

I think I shall have to read the letter you wrote Elizabeth. Maybe I could learn a few things—think so?

All of my Christmas packages are wrapped and I've mailed my Christmas cards. I don't expect to have a big Christmas as I will work that day—you aren't here and most of my family isn't here.

Can you imagine who just called—Jake. He said he has received your letter and is planning to answer it right away. He is leaving tomorrow on a fourteen day leave and seemed to be so happy about it.

I'll have to get a bath and get dressed for class. I love you very much.

Love,
Evelyn

December 17–

Dear Paul,

Received a letter and also a package from you yesterday that was mailed on the ninth of this month. I like the ring very much, but I suppose I'll have to put it aside for a period of time which I hope isn't long. That is a nice fountain pen. Is it the one that you thought you had lost? The gum is also very good as I'm chewing some now. It's the first I've had since you left.

I've just returned from the movies. I was along with one of the girls to see "Greenwich Village" which was fairly good. Of course, I'll admit that I've seen much better pictures. I suppose you've already seen it as there doesn't seem to be many that you haven't seen.

Kupsky has gone on his leave you know. I think that he must be planning to stop by to see your family as he asked me for your home address. You had given it to him the day you left, but he lost it. He seems to be a very nice boy. Of course, he must be since he's a friend of yours—

Some of the girls made some divinity— getting into the Christmas spirit if there's such a thing. One girl's mother is giving a Christmas party for the Senior class next Friday night. We drew names as we did when I was in Grammar school. At least, it's rather nice to be reminded of a few incidents that have happened in the past.

I'm looking forward to receiving that picture of you that you are supposed to have mailed already. I'll have one made and send it to you since you don't like the one you have at the present. You know that I don't make good pictures, but you can understand why I don't after the first glance at me.

It's so nice to know that I will be out of training next year at this time—such a wonderful thought. I did hope that you would be present at my graduation, but that would be too good to be true.

This has been a wonderful day. The sun was shining and was rather warm out. I just wonder if it's still raining where you are now. You'll soon have to begin swimming about if it continues to rain so much.

Don't be afraid that I wan't keep my promise to you for I love you so much—

Love,
Evelyn

December 19–
11:00 P.M.

Dear Paul,

You know I couldn't sleep well tonight without first writing you. I was just out to another movie—taking them all in at one time aren't I? We were to the <u>Strand</u> Theater tonight to see Lucille Ball in "Meet The People." I just can't stay home when I have such long hours off duty as I become so darn lonesome so I amuse myself by seeing some movie.

I hope that you have received those packages by now. They will probably travel to the end of the rainbow and back again before they finally reach you.

So you have already received Mamie's letter and she sent you a picture of me. You just wait until I see her again!! I don't have the least idea of which one she might have sent, but all the pictures I've ever made are simply awful. They shouldn't look so much like me.

I'll be off duty at ten o'clock Christmas Day. Mr. Myers is coming over for me so I'll have Christmas lunch with them. I also have off the day after Christmas. Some vacation, don't you think?

The family will be so glad to receive your letters. I'm glad you were energetic enough to write all those letters. I only write them once in a while—just according to the mood I'm in at the time I'm off duty.

One of the girls happened to see the ring you sent me and I told her that you just wanted me to keep it until you returned, but she wouldn't believe me. I can't convince her that we aren't married. Of course, I don't mind what she may think for it would be wonderful if that were true.

I enjoy working in the nursery so very much. The time seems to pass so quickly while there. It seems that so many people are having these two-legged Christmas presents this year. One baby weighed two pounds and three-fourths ounces which was the smallest one in the nursery. You should have seen it for I could hold it's body in one hand. We have a number of large babies as they aren't unusual at all.

I'm slowly becoming so very, very sleepy so may I say "Good-night."

Love always,
Evelyn

P.S. I received the picture and like it very much. I'll see if I can have one made soon.

December 21–
12: Noon

Dear Paul,

If I can get my eyes open and keep them open long enough to write you a letter—I'll be doing good. I did my regular shift in the nursery and then did special duty with a patient from eleven last night until seven this morning. I only had about three hours sleep and have to go on duty again this afternoon at three. I think perhaps I'll survive though.

You should see the nice present your Mother sent me—two of the prettiest handkerchiefs I've ever seen. They're so very odd that I suppose that's why I like them so very much. I appreciate her thoughtfulness.

You know I've only had one card from Elizabeth since she left and it was mailed from Mississippi. I'm just wandering if she has arrived in California O. K.—I surely hope so.

I know that I wouldn't enjoy having so much rain although there's little one can do about the type of weather we have. I suppose you like the mountains or do they compare to the mountains of Pennsylvania?

It seems that you should receive the packages I mailed soon. They wouldn't insure them since they were to go Overseas so I hope they don't get lost on the way.

Remember you left two rolls of film with your camera. I've already used one roll and as soon as I finish taking the other roll, I'll have them developed. I might even send you some—that is if they come out O. K.

I received another letter from you today. I enjoy reading them very much and always feel much better after having received a letter from you.

This writing is terrible, but I don't seem to have control over the direction of my hands while writing. Maybe I'm a bit sleepy yet.

So you are enjoying Western pictures now in exchange for the various productions. Remember the kid who used to go to the Strand and would become so much excited during a picture? He probably would have become especially excited over a Western picture.

We have the most beautiful Christmas tree and have it well decorated. It kinda reminds me of the ones Elizabeth and I used to have at home each Christmas.

Have you been to Church lately or do they have services very often?

I will begin getting dressed for duty. If you'll keep this letter until I see you again I'll try to translate it for you.

Love always,
Evelyn

December 23–

(Nursery) on duty

Dear Paul,

Received your letter of the fifteenth and appreciate your writing such a long letter. I only wish we could be together at Christmas, but since that is impossible, I hope that you have the very best time possible. I sincerely hope that we may be together next Christmas and each succeeding Christmas that follows. My thoughts remain with you constantly. Perhaps I've never prayed much during my lifetime, but there comes a time in everyone's life when the answer to a prayer means everything. Not only shall I pray for you Christmas Day, but every day and have been praying for you often since you were transferred. I only pray that God may protect and soon return you safely to your family and me.

The girls seemed to have had a very nice time at the Senior Christmas party last night. I did not attend as I was on duty from three yesterday afternoon until eleven last night. I could have changed shifts with one of the girls in order to have been present at the party, but I was a bit too tired as I have done private duty extra of my regular shift. They haven't been able to get registered nurses to go on with the patients who need them so I suppose I'll remain on duty tonight with a baby in Children's ward. It seems that I just can't refuse a case.

We only have twelve babies in the Nursery at the present. Of course, we would have another premature just to set off the Christmas Holidays! This is the least number of babies we've had since I've been on duty in here. It's so very quiet at the present as they're all sleeping. You should be in when they're all crying at once. Some times I think they'll rupture my ear drum.

It's been such a wonderful day—almost like a summer day except it's not quite so warm. I would even enjoy going swimming on a day like this. It would have been a grand day to have made pictures, but I didn't awaken until one o'clock this afternoon. I didn't have time to make pictures as I had to dress for duty.

I received a lovely Christmas card from your Mother and Pauline. I know I'm going to like them very much; in fact it seems that I know them very well already.

Mother sent you a Christmas card a few days ago. You've probably received it by now. She wanted to buy you a present, but it was too late to mail a Christmas package; in fact, the present I mailed will probably be a New Year's present. I hope you'll receive it before then but I'm afraid you wan't.

We were bringing the babies back to the Nursery and suddenly heard some people singing the Christmas carols. I thought the patients had begun singing, but discovered that Sister Theodora and a group of Nurses—also some Cadets were parading the halls serenading the patients.

My Co-worker is wondering when I'm going to complete this letter. She's beginning to think that I'm writing a novel.

Sister was just in and it's just a good thing that I had the letter in such a place that she didn't see it for she would probably have torn it up so quickly I would hardly have realized what she had done. They very highly disapprove of our writing letters while on duty.

I will say "Goodnight." I wish you a very Merry Christmas.

Love always,
Evelyn

Christmas Night

Dear Paul,

Mamie is writing Frank a letter so I decided to write you at the same time. You know, I can't let her get anything on me. She has been telling me about the letter from you and seemed to be pleased to have received it.

I was at midnight Mass last night. You see, I am being a good girl. My third Christmas in training and the first time I have attended Midnight Mass. It was really beautiful. The Chapel was lit with candles and all decorated in the regular Christmas fashion. Of course, to complete the Spirit of Christmas the Sisters sang the Christmas carols. Father Dolan, the one you liked so well, led Mass. Sister seemed so happy that we attended since we weren't Catholics.

I was on duty this morning from seven till eleven. There are only a very few babies in the Nursery at the present so I didn't have much to do other than spoil a few of the babies by playing with them. I know the Mothers will appreciate that.

Mr. Myers came down for me at twelve today and now I am home. Mother, Mr. Myers, and Mamie—besides me. It seems so odd that none of the others of the family are home. Regardless of that, my thoughts remained with you throughout the day.

I received a number of presents—some very nice ones and appreciate the thoughtfulness of the various individuals.

Elizabeth had a bit of trouble with her car (tires) and had to stop over at Boloxi, Mississippi.

I had a card from her mailed from there and hope that by now she has reached her final destination in California. I was afraid of that when she left, but she was so excited about having the chance to go and be with J. C. that I just couldn't mention any of the bad points. I want her to be with him so very much as they are much happier together.

My little neices are over to spend the night and Mother is in reading Bible Stories to them. They seem to enjoy the stories and have been commenting on the pictures of Jesus. I remember when she used to read to us and don't think I shall ever forget those moments.

Today was another wonderful day. I intended to bring the camera along with me and make pictures, but I dressed in such a hurry that I forgot the camera. I suppose I should have one roll developed now so I can send you a picture. I'm sorry I've waited so long.

And now Mamie's singing Christmas carols with the girls. You know, Mamie used to instruct music classes and can sing very well; in fact, she was once my instructor while in Grammar School. That was before she and Frank were married.

I'm getting a bit sleepy so may I say "Good-night."

Lots of Love,
Evelyn.

P.S. Mother & Mr. Myers said give you their regards. Mamie Too—She has written you another letter.

December 27–

Dear Paul,

Mother and Mamie brought me into Pensacola yesterday about three. I didn't have to go on duty as I had the day off and don't have to report on duty until three today. One of the girls and I went to see "Casanova Brown" which was playing at the Saenger Theater. It was really a grand picture. If you haven't seen it already, I hope you have a chance to see it soon for I think you would enjoy it too.

When I returned yesterday I found out that I had received a letter from you and a card from Elizabeth. Nothing would have had a more welcome greeting unless you two should have walked in. Elizabeth had more tire trouble and is in Junction, Texas. Maybe she can make it in to California by New Year's Day. I surely hope so. She said she has a nice couple with her so I hope they remain with her the rest of the journey.

So you've been washing clothes. I hope you get well in practice for you can also wash mine someday. I know you'll agree to that!! I'll bet the Natives don't wash their clothes very often since they take such a long time to dry.

I was just over for lunch, but we had nothing special. I suppose we should be very thankful for what we do have. I enjoyed the cream puffs, but didn't care much about the remainder of the lunch.

I sympathize with you if all the boys in your tent was "high" during Christmas. Perhaps they aren't so hard to control as the girls. You remember the night at Chattahoochee, don't you? I'll never forget it. Those girls used to embarass me so very much.

The New Year is drawing near with the many things it holds dear in the future. The past year shall remain in memory forever as it has been one of the happiest years of my life time. So many things have happened that mean so much to me. It all began in February and you know my experiences from there. The close of the year isn't so bright, but there lies happiness in the future.

I want to write your Mother a letter before going on duty so I'll begin writing her.

Love always,
Evelyn

P.S. Have you received the packages yet? Hope you have a Happy New Year!

December 28–

Dear Paul,

I've just finished writing your Mother. I'll bet she'll have a great time trying to translate it. You know what difficulty you have trying to read my letters so you can well sympathize with her.

So you did receive the card from my Mother. She told me that she had mailed you one. And I was home when she received the letter from you. She seemed very pleased to get it.

I don't have to report on duty again until tomorrow at three. I just don't know what to do during the many long hours off duty. I suppose I'll have to do some special duty to occupy my time.

I don't work in the Nursery now, but I am on duty with the undelivered obstetrical patients. I'll probably enjoy this work after having become a bit more familiar with this type patients. Some excitement!

Nellie Moylan joined the Army Air Corps (Nurse). I don't know if she was accepted but she did have a physical examination. She seems just the type for that and I believe she'll really enjoy it. That's what I wanted to do until a certain Marine changed my mind for me and I'm so very glad he did.

This room mate of mine has returned home and is kidding me again. I can hardly write a letter when she's home as she disturbs me so often. She always tells me of her experiences with the opposite sex. She never hears any bed time stories of mine. I don't fancy telling my personal secrets to every one.

My former room mate, Ernestine Plant was in town today and called me while I was on duty. I wanted to see her and her young offspring so very much, but didn't get to as they had to leave right away after she called. She wants me to spend my vacation with her which would be lots of fun. I probably wan't take a vacation in order to get out of training three weeks earlier.

I will say "good-night" and get some sleep. I love you so very much—

Evelyn

January 1–45
1:15 A.M.

Dear Paul,

I'm on duty with two patients tonight. I had to do something to occupy my extra hours off duty so I do special service with the patients who need attention. As I have told you, we don't have enough registered nurses to care for the seriously ill patients so the Seniors are asked to care for them.

I haven't received a letter from you for the past four days. Of course, I know you aren't to be blamed for that for I know you have been writing frequently.

I believe it will begin raining within the next few minutes. It has been such very nice weather all during the Christmas season and Christmas Day was wonderful. We'll probably have cold weather again following this rain. Is it still cold weather where you are at the present?

I took the roll of film down to be developed. I hope they are good for I will send them to you as soon as I can get them. You might hide them away some place for I wouldn't want the other boys to see them. The pictures would probably frighten the room-mates.

It has begun raining and I'm getting so very sleepy. Both of my patients are sleeping. I hope they continue to sleep for a few hours anyway for I could very well endure a bit of rest.

Don't let those room-mates of yours kid you too much. Just ask them to argue with me. I'll bet I would win any of their arguments.

The other Nurses seem as sleepy as I—wander why we don't go on a sit-down strike. Perhaps that would be a good idea—don't you think?

Sister had a New Year's dance in the Nurse's home tonight. They must have had lots of fun. I wouldn't know for I wasn't present.

What are your New Year's resolutions? I'll let you in on mine some day—I hope they come true.

I love you very much—

Love always,
Evelyn

January 2–

Dear Paul,

I thought I was dreaming for a few minutes after the mail arrived for I received four letters from you and also the package you mailed. You know, I was always so happy to receive the various surprise gifts you've given me. You are very thoughtful and I appreciate that very much.

I was on duty from three yesterday afternoon until seven this morning, but I had the day off so I had a very good rest. I slept from eight this morning until about five-thirty this afternoon. When I awakened, I realized I was very hungry so Bennett and I went down town and had supper. It was too late to eat at the hospital and I can't say that I thoroughly enjoy the food there. After having eaten, we went to a movie—"Frenchman's Creek," which was fairly good. I remember when we saw "Going My Way" which was playing some time ago. That was a grand picture.

Have you heard from Mammie recently? She told me about your apologizing about the pictures of the grass skirt. She really called me down about that, but I don't think she was really angry. She was also kidding me about her telling you of my <u>many</u> faults. You may believe anything she may tell you, for I have no doubts, but that it's true.

I wrote your Mother a letter a few days ago. I didn't intentionally neglect writing her; in fact, I thought that I had written her last and was waiting for an answer. I hope she wasn't offended at my not writing during that period of time.

It will be wonderful if it is possible for me to meet you in California when you return.

Thanks for the gifts and I like them very much.

Love always,
Evelyn

January 4–

Dear Paul,

I was just down town and got the pictures, but none of them were good. That's just what I expected though. I'm sending two of them, but if I were you I would keep them locked up so no-one can see the awful looking girl you're engaged to. I'll make some more later and I hope they'll be good.

I just had a call from my cousin. She reminded one of the girls and me of the dinner date we had planned for tonight. I honestly had forgotten about it for she planned to have us out about a week ago. We'll have to go now in order to prevent her being angry at us and I couldn't blame her. I'll finish this letter when I return.

Just returned and I'm so uncomfortable. Why did I eat so much? She had the most delicious dinner prepared and we were so unappreciative as to forget the dinner date. She understood for she was also a nurse once. She is going to have a baby soon and is so very happy. Her husband wants me to care for her during the time she is in the hospital.

I haven't heard from Elizabeth recently. I'm just wandering if she finally reached California O. K. I sincerely hope that she has for she deserves a bit of happiness; in fact, she deserves all the happiness she could possibly have during the remainder of her life-time.

Kelly just returned today so you see she must not have been so anxious to complete her training. She stayed home for two and one-half months other than the month and one-half she was ill and remained in bed at the hospital. She'll have about six months to make-up and I doubt if she'll be able to graduate with the rest of the class. We've already chosen our graduation uniforms for as you know, we shall graduate this June. Several of us wanted to get a class pin, but I don't suppose we'll get one for the majority of the class doesn't care for the class pins.

Why should you mind if I discover a few things by reading the letter you wrote to Elizabeth? I think that would be fun. She probably hasn't received it yet unless she has reached California.

I doubt if you've been able to read this terrible writing. When I was in school I could write fairly well, but since I entered training I only scribble.

I must go to bed in order to report on duty in the morning at seven.

Love always,
Evelyn

January 5–

Dear Paul,

Before going to bed, I shall write you. It is almost mid-night, but I don't feel sleepy at all. Perhaps it's because I've been used to working nights.

I was off duty at three o'clock this afternoon and don't have to report on again until tomorrow afternoon at three. I change shifts every fourth day which is nice as I work four mornings in succession and then four nights. I didn't care for the night shift when you were here, but now I don't mind at all.

Bennett and I were to a movie tonight which was such a very silly picture, but we enjoyed it. She is spending the night with me as we're on the same shift and don't have to get up so early in the morning. I do enjoy sleeping late which is a bad practice.

I hope you have received the last letter (Jan 4) I mailed. You wanted a picture of me so I sent a couple—Of course, I know that the pictures resemble me very much, but I don't consider that a compliment to the picture by any means.

I haven't yet heard if Elizabeth arrived in California or not. I can't keep from wandering just where she might be. I had a card about a week ago from her and it was mailed from Texas.

Just which one of my family did you receive the letter from. You know, the one you merely mentioned in your last letter that I received. You're going to learn quite a bit about me if you continue writing my family and I don't think you should know so much about me—do you? And what was this relative of mine telling you about me? You should wait until after we're married and then find out what I'm like for yourself—I've tried to tell you of my bad points and you wouldn't listen to me.

Bennett says that she would advise you to buy a double bed instead of the three-quarter size we have for they don't very easily accomodate two. She & Kelly send their regards. I will say good-night—

Love always,
Evelyn

Jan 6—[*Spoiler alert:* exactly one year later... January 6, 1946... Evelyn and Paul were married]

Dear Paul,

It's now twelve-thirty and I've just returned from duty, but I'm not too sleepy to write you a letter.

Received the letter from you today saying that you have received the pictures. I'm sorry that you're angry at me for not sending the one picture you wanted and I deserve it, although I don't have the picture. When I went down to get the pictures, they told me that <u>one</u> exposure didn't make well so they sent it back for a reprint. I didn't tell you for I thought it would only be a few days and I would mail it as soon as possible. I've tried very hard to get it for I knew that you especially wanted that one picture, but every time I've been down they hadn't yet received it and would tell me to call again. They'll probably have it misplaced with some one's pictures. If I finally get my hands on it, I'll mail it to you right away.

Kelly is in the room at the present and she says for you not to flirt with too many red-heads. She also says that she's keeping close tab on me although that would be hard to do for we work opposite shifts. Don't worry about that for I love you too much to care for anyone else.

I thought that perhaps Kupsky would call me when he returned, but he hasn't as yet. I'll bet he had a wonderful time and he was going by to see your Mother too.

Pheil was engaged for two days to an Ensign, but broke the engagement the second day. She seems to like him very much, but doesn't care to wear a ring yet.

It's been raining all day and I was beginning to believe we would have to swim home, but some nice couple drove us home. We were thankful for that ride. It will probably be very cold following this rain, but we haven't had much cold weather all winter.

I wander why you didn't receive the other package that I sent you for I mailed it the same day that I mailed the pictures. I wanted to send them air-mail special, but that "nutty" post master wouldn't let me.

I need to write some other letters so I'll say "Good-night—

Love always,
Evelyn

January 8–

Dear Paul,

It's past midnight and it's so very quiet. I was on duty from three this afternoon until eleven tonight and I'm now on with a special duty case until seven in the morning. She is rather old and such a very nice patient; in fact, she reminds me very much of one of my grandmothers. She had an operation about a week ago, but is getting along grand.

I was just down for hot coffee and was it a "life-saver"? I'm becoming a regular old "coffee-drinker." I know, I shouldn't begin such bad habits. After all, we need something in order to have a cheerful attitude during such long hours.

Class study has begun again. My class only has two more courses to complete before we graduate. It just doesn't seem possible that we'll ever complete this course. Sometime it seems as though I've been in training the greater portion of my lifetime and again, it seems that I've been in only for a short period of time.

Bennett and I went for a stroll down by the bay shore and it reminded me of the night we were there and it began to rain. Remember the dress I was wearing that night? It happened not to be water-proof and I shall never forget it.

My patient is sleeping soundly so I went along with my roommate to the post office. I thought that perhaps the fresh air would assist in keeping me awake for the remainder of the night. I almost fall asleep at intervals.

It's getting rather cool out and the wind keeps the windows banging against the wall. I believe we're really going to have a bit of cold weather before the season's over.

I've just finished writing a letter to J. C. He's been quite worried about the trouble she's (Elizabeth) had and I hope that she has reached California safely by now.

I'm getting so very sleepy that I can hardly keep my eyes open.

I love you very much—

Love,
Evelyn

January 10–

Dear Paul,

I haven't received a letter from you during the past few days. The days seem to merely "drag" by when I don't hear from you as I look forward to receiving your letters so very much. I wish it were possible for you to receive my letters so quickly as I have been receiving the letters from you. I shall be the happiest person in the world when you return.

I had a card from Elizabeth that was dated the thirty-first of December and she had arrived in California at last. When she makes a decision, she usually accomplishes her goal, for she is so determined. I wasn't worried about her other than for her health. I just know she almost feels like a different person now that she and J. C. are together again. She said that they have received letters from you and intend to write you as soon as they get comfortably arranged.

It was about one o'clock last night when I reported off duty and had to report on duty again this morning at six o'clock. I asked for my half-day and as soon as I reached the house, I went to bed. I awakened at three o'clock and should have been in class at that time. My room mate also over slept, but the Instructor didn't call us down for being a few minutes late. She is very considerate at times, but at other times she even for gets that she too, was a student once.

After class I went in to see Bennett and stayed the remainder of the afternoon with her. She only has about twenty-one more days of training and she is sending in an application for the Army Nurse's Corps. She is so thrilled about completing the course.

I haven't heard from your Mother and Pauline recently, but I know they'll write as soon as they have time. I enjoy receiving their letters so much.

I will write you again tomorrow and hope that you'll receive these letters soon—I'll keep praying for you. I just know you'll come through safely.

Love always,
Evelyn

January 12–

Dear Paul,

I am waiting for Bennett to come over as she, Margaret, and I are going to a movie. Some excitement, don't you think? I do enjoy a good movie more than any other type of amusement in Pensacola. I did see a picture Wednesday night that I wish I had never seen; in fact, I hope I never see another one like it.

So you had two nice days without any rain. That must be wonderful. I was beginning to think that you should imitate "ducks." Of course, that would never do so I wouldn't want you to try it.

I was down to the U.S.O. club last night and enjoyed dancing. You know, I haven't been dancing for ages, it seems. As you know, I'm not a good dancer so I only like to try dancing. Kelly said that she was going to write you all about it in order to live up to her promise to you.

I surely would like to see Mother and Mammie as I haven't seen them since Christmas— I'll see that Mammie doesn't send you any more of those old pictures of me. She does have some of the most awful looking pictures which were made during my "teen" age. You wouldn't want them, I'm sure. I sent you a couple of pictures recently.

It's very nice out as it's just cool enough to be comfortable. It won't be so long until Spring again and it doesn't seem that we've had the Winter season yet.

Bennett is here so we'll run along to a movie. Always loving you—

Love always.
Evelyn

January 14–

Dear Paul,

Sunday again and such a beautiful day. I would like to just walk for hours on days as this. It reminds me very much of the Sunday we went to church on the base. Remember what a wonderful day that was too. Yesterday morning I was beginning to think we needed our swim suits in order to report on duty. The streets were flooded and it was still raining so we called a taxi. You know how difficult it is to get a taxi, but he finally came in time for us to report on duty on time.

I do miss your letters very much, but I know that you write as often as you can. I do hope and pray that you are in a fairly safe place for I know that no place is absolutely safe.

Bennett's boy friend has just returned from overseas and they were by last night to see me. I met him sometime ago and he seems to be a very nice boy, but she doesn't seem to care for him. Smitty, Jancsik, and I went to the U.S.O. last night, but I didn't enjoy it. After we left there we went to the mid-night movie—such an exciting picture was playing—Edward G. Robinson was playing in another murderous production.

I told you that I'm on the maternity floor. I have assisted with fifteen deliveries, but we are required to have twenty so I have five more yet to go. I will be glad to be transferred to another service.

I haven't yet heard from Nellie and I just wander if she passed the physical for the army. She might even be in the Army by now. Some of the girls were asking about her, but I haven't seen her in ages.

I just got out of bed and was over to the Hospital for lunch. The usual Sunday menu— fried chicken, mashed potatoes, string beans, and ice cream. I can almost tell you what we'll have each day in advance.

I do love you so very much.

Love always,
Evelyn

January 15–

Dear Paul,

I was just in class and have an hour yet before I have to report on duty. I'll make good use of this hour by writing you.

I'm getting to be a regular sleepy-head as I didn't awaken until ten o'clock this morning. Of course, it was rather late when I reported off duty last night.

I received two letters from you today and was so very happy to get them. They were dated the third and the other the fourth of January. You were speaking of pictures of me. I mailed you a couple which I supposed you have received by now. You wouldn't want too many of me for you would become tired of looking at the same face so often. I enjoy looking at the pictures I have of you, but as you know I only have a very few of you.

I haven't heard from Elizabeth again since I received the card. I don't blame her for not bothering to write. I know that she is very happy.

Pitts just came in and is waiting for me to finish writing this letter. She says to tell you she'll be in the Army soon and will see you overseas. Could happen, but I hope that it doesn't for many reasons. If this happens it may involve the entire class and I wish to remain a civilian, but don't you worry about that.

For some unknown reason I have an awful cold. I think that probably Bennett handed it down to me as she had a cold when she spent the night with me. As you know, it's very easily contracted.

That November letter was a long time arriving wasn't it? It had time to travel over the globe twice. I wish you could receive the letters a bit sooner than you do, but I suppose we're fortunate we can even exchange mail from overseas.

I'll run along for Pitts is getting impatient. I'll always love you very much.

Love,
Evelyn

January 16–

Dear Paul,

Just received two letters from you dated the eighth of January. I also received the bracelet and

I think it is beautiful. That too, shall be placed among my prize possessions.

I also received a letter from J. C. and Elizabeth. Maybe I should say just a note for she wrote it while J. C. was getting dressed for duty. She was telling me of the letter you wrote her so you see you can't have any secrets—or can you? She said California is beautiful and she had a wonderful sight seeing trip except for the numerous "blow-outs."

I enjoyed reading your Mother's letter that you mailed along with one of yours. She does write very cheerful, pleasant letters. Please don't mail her any of the letters that I write you, for I'm afraid she would find them very boresome.

You mentioned the time that we were in Panama City together. Perhaps I felt too much as though I belonged to you and the first time there as you remember, we weren't even engaged—I've always felt differently toward you than any other person I ever dated, but I don't regret it.

Some time during the mid-portion of next month is our anniversary, but it seems that I've known you much longer. It also doesn't seem possible that it's been almost a year since I was at Chattahoochee, but yet it seems ages since you left Pensacola just three months ago. Such a riddle—that is if you understand the way I put it.

I want to write Elizabeth and J. C. before going on duty so I'll say "so-long." Thanks very much for the bracelet.

Love always,
Evelyn

January 18–

Dear Paul,

Have just returned from class again. It seems that all I do recently is sleep, duty, and class and is becoming more boresome by the day. What's your remedy for that?

Do you remember the Hobbs' girl? You know the one who was with Nellie the night I came from Chattahoochee and you met me at the bus station. She was married to Bryan Nobles and they now have a baby. I admitted her last night and Nellie was up to see her. She was supposed to report to Eglin Field the following morning for a physical examination. I was so surprised and happy to see her.

It's rather cool out and looks as though it will rain—some more of your lovely weather. I thought you were getting all the rain, but it seems that we'll have our share of it too. We aren't having any snow, but I think I'll enjoy living where it does snow. Just hope I don't get frozen feet as you said you did.

My room mate is on night duty and she never stays home when she's off duty. She must sleep while she's visiting. Her boy friend left for overseas' duty recently and do I know how to sympathize with her?!!

Have you heard from any of my family recently? Just wandered if you had found out any more of my faults or could that be possible? I think probably you know everything about me— even more than my Mother knows.

I'll be so happy to hear from your Mother and Pauline again as it seems ages since I've heard from them.

I wrote this letter in a hurry as I only had a very few minutes so I hope you'll excuse the many mistakes. I love you very much—

As Ever,
Evelyn

January 20–

Dear Paul,

Just received a letter from you, but it surely took a long time traveling as you wrote it the seventh of this month. I was very glad to get it anyway.

I also received a letter from my brother, David and his wife. They want me to visit them after having completed my training if I have nothing else definitely planned. They live in Kansas, you know. Beyond me as to what I will do until you return, but I do hope that I can meet you in California.

I've completed the service I'm on at the present—maternity and I'm just wandering what they'll have me doing next. There isn't much left that I haven't had some experience in except mopping floors, so I suppose I'll be doing that soon. That wouldn't be a bad idea for a bit of practice in that line might help.

My room mate is home today and is asleep at the present as she's on night duty. I'm afraid to make the least bit of noise for she is so easily awakened. Quite different from me for I sleep so soundly.

You were speaking of your thinking about me so often. If your ears would burn every time I think about you they would probably be burning continuously. At least, they would be burning too often to please you.

Do you still have your same tent mates? You used to tell me quite a bit about them, but you never mention them anymore. You must have agreed on a happy medium.

I must get dressed for duty so I'll say "so long" until I write again.

Love always,
Evelyn

January 22–

Dear Paul,

A night off duty with nothing to do, but since I can't talk to you personally, I do have the pleasure of writing you. You should have seen me when I discovered that I had received four letters from you yesterday. I suppose I was the happiest person in the house hold. It seems that it takes your letters much longer to arrive recently.

I was to a movie last night—"Belle of the Yukon" was playing and was very good. Of course, I didn't have to sit in the rain to see it as you do. You won't know how to enjoy a picture soon unless it is raining during the time it is playing.

Just who do you suppose came into the Hospital as a patient today? Iris Wells had her tonsils removed so I'm going over in a few minutes to see her. I seem to understand quite a bit how her throat must feel since the operation.

Doctor McLane calls me "Cookie" since I worked in the diet department. Today he said that he was going to bring some flour and Crisco over so I would make him some dough nuts— the "nut" he's never eaten any of my cooking and will probably live a healthier life if he never does.

So your friends are writing a letter to me which concerns your behavior. Tell them that I'll believe everything they say providing it's all nice. I couldn't believe anything other than the good points.

I have my day off tomorrow so I'm planning to spend the afternoon with my cousin in Ensley. One of the girls is also going along and I know we'll have lots of fun. We'll have a lot in common as she is a nurse too.

I'm enjoying listening to the radio as the grandest music is on at the present. Wish you were here to enjoy it too. I'm afraid I wouldn't pay much attention to the music if you were near.

We do have the most unusual weather. One day we wear summer dresses and perhaps the next day a rain coat and the following day an overcoat. That's the nice Florida "sunshine" State. Always nice the year round—some joke.

Did you ever hear from Jimmie or J. C. and Elizabeth? "Good-night" and sweet dreams—

Love Always,
Evelyn

January 24–

Dear Paul,

I was just re-reading the letter that I received from your Mother yesterday. I'm always very glad to hear from her and I could read her letters over numerous times and enjoy them each time. She says that it's very cold in Pennsylvania at the present and I can understand why it would be. She also said that Pauline and Earl were out sleighriding which must be so much fun. Just wish we could have joined them.

I was over to see Iris and she was rather weak from not having eaten for a number of hours. Otherwise she was feeling O. K. although she'll have a sore throat for a few days. She said she's very happy that she's going to have you as a cousin and wanted me to give you her regards.

This old pen just scratches so you see I should write with the one you sent, but I don't have the energy to get it out and fill it. I'd probably ruin it if I did write with it as I haven't yet learned the proper position in which I should hold the pen while writing.

I'm at last being transferred to another service. I suppose that I'll be caring for Medical patients now. Oh, just anything is alright if it helps to occupy the time until I'll complete the course. And I hope that they don't begin drafting nurses into the Army as they've been debating on that for some time. The President seems to be much in favor of the idea.

I just had a final examination in E.N.T. today. These are just the final grades on the subjects as we complete each course at the Hospital.

We still have to take State Board exams. on all the subjects in June.

Has been raining most of the afternoon and it makes me feel so drowsy especially since I'm a bit tired from having worked all day.

I'll always love you very much.

As ever,
Evelyn

January 26–

Dear Paul,

It is so very quiet at the present which is rather unusual at this place. Maybe I spoke a bit too soon for here comes the gang—you know what I mean. It seems as though a cyclone hit on the North side of the house. I was just in class again, but I really don't know why because I'm not interested in Professional Adjustments. I'll have to report on duty at three and it's about two-thirty now. Every time I begin writing you the girls comment on my writing you so often. Just so you don't mind as I enjoy writing you.

My room mate wanted me to go along to the bakery with her so I have a bag of cookies near me. I write a few lines and then eat a cookie—some system, don't you think? Now my room mate insists on my hearing her read aloud the incidents of the newspaper. We don't have the pleasure of reading one very often.

It's such a wonderful day and we've had so much warm weather. It doesn't compare to the previous Winters in Pensacola.

I'll be in charge of men's medical wards and I don't enjoy taking care of old men. They always make a bigger "mess" than I can keep cleaned up. At least I like to make the surroundings as pleasant as possible.

I must hush and go on duty.

Love always,
Evelyn

January 28–

Dear Paul,

Some party we're having. Bennett spent last night with me and we didn't awaken until ten-thirty this morning. Of course, there is a reason for our having slept so late for I worked from three yesterday afternoon until eleven last night. Bennett was out on a date and didn't return until after I had already gone to bed. She lives in the new nurse's home, but they lock the doors and check the girls in at ten o'clock at night. She is a graduate nurse and doesn't have to check in so she just spends the night with me when she feels like staying out late hours. She is a terrible bed-companion for she does have such cold feet. She knows I'm saying this about her for she is reading from over my shoulder. She thinks the double-decker idea is grand. (me too)!!!?

We were just over for lunch—the same Sunday menu, but the fried chicken is always good. At the present we are both sitting on the side of my bed writing letters. The best way I know to occupy my time.

I received two letters from you yesterday. You're really rating to have received so many letters in one day. I'm very happy that they do write you and I hope they continue to do so and I think they will. You have me curious as to what my Mother wrote you. Don't you think you should let me in on what she said? You'll probably receive a letter from Elizabeth and J. C. soon for they said they were going to answer your letter right away.

Each Sunday always reminds me of one special Sunday we spent together. You know, I seem to miss you more and more each day and I just live in hopes of the day when you shall return—what a happy day that will be.

I'll hush now as we've planned to go to a movie before I go on duty. I'll always love you very much—

Love,
Evelyn

January 30–

Dear Paul,

What a day—it's been so wonderful, but you know what I've been doing for the past two or three hours? Just answering letters which keeps me busy if I stay up to date with them. I've just finished answering your Mother's letter and of course, my many brother's and sister's letters. I've enjoyed the afternoon so very much for most of the time I was all alone and it was so very quiet and nice. My thoughts were with you the greater portion of the time; in fact, I can't do my work efficiently for thinking of you—you "thief" to swipe my thoughts so often.

I was so surprised when I returned home from duty last night as I discovered a package on my table. I found it's contents to be such very delicious fudge. My former room mate, Ernestine Plant, made it and was so very generous as to give me a big box full. I was a bit tired and very hungry at that hour of the night so the fudge really hit the spot. I believe it was about the best I had ever eaten. Of course, I didn't eat all of it by myself for I shared it with the girls—what a picnic. I wish you could have been around as you would have enjoyed it too.

J. C. finally found time enough to type me a nice long letter. He said that he had neglected writing you too, but had been so busy for he repairs watches during his extra hours. Elizabeth managed to write four or five lines at the very latter part of the letter. And don't you say anything about her sending me the letter you wrote her because I enjoyed reading it and maybe she'll send me another one some time.

I bought some meat this afternoon and the girls are in the kitchen preparing it. I told them they would have to prepare it if they were hungry for I had to write you.

This gas heater of ours makes such a noise sounds as though an engine running. But then, we could do with a good many repair jobs around this house. Sister isn't much interested in this place as she will sell it as soon as we complete training. Of course, we aren't interested either, but why should we be?

My room mate had the nerve to ask me to clean out her turtle dish—some job. I couldn't say "no" so here I go with the turtle dish.

Love always,
Evelyn

February 2–

Dear Paul,

Just off duty and feel a bit tired, but all I need is a nice warm bath and I'll feel refreshed again.

One of the tubes went out on the radio and I've had it in shop about three weeks. I'm going for it this afternoon and hope that it's ready for I miss it so much. Once you get used to a radio, it's hard to do without one. I'll bet you would enjoy having it with you—and I wish it were possible that you could.

So you are reading quite a number of books lately? That is a wonderful way to occupy off-duty hours especially if there are very few means of entertainment. Maybe I should try reading more often. Do you have a library? If so, you should have a nice variety from which to choose. We have a nice library, but most of the books only pertain to nursing alone.

We're having a Senior party tonight at this house. The large room near the kitchen has been arranged for dancing. Some one even did a very good job at polishing the floor. I suppose we'll have a nice time, but as you know I would have a much nicer time if you could be present.

I have to go down town within the next few minutes and get some paper plates, cups, napkins etc.—you know the usual accessories of a party. I suppose I had better get dressed so I'll write you again tomorrow.

Love always,
Evelyn

Feb. 3–

Dear Paul,

I just awakened at ten o'clock and feel as though I have been put through the mill. I was just in the kitchen and the maid was so angry and I can understand why she would be. Beer bottles were all over the place and the paper cups, plates etc. covered the table.

At the present Pitts and I are in the sitting room and it's so nice and warm by the fire, but it's rather cold out. Pitts had her eyes dilated and can hardly distinguish one thing from another. I shall never forget when Kelly dilated her pupils at Chattahoochee, of course accidentally, but she couldn't see well for days. We had an examination during that time.

We had a very nice time last night until everyone got to feeling a bit too good. That's when I returned to my room for I didn't quite "fit in" with the company.

I got the radio yesterday and it plays very good again. It's wonderful having it back again as I did miss it so very much.

I hope that you don't continue thinking about what the "fortune teller" told me, for I grant you that it doesn't amount to anything. Don't ever be afraid of losing me for you would have such a difficult time getting rid of me if you tried. I love you very, very much so don't ever doubt that.

I'm glad that you like the pictures I sent you although I never make good pictures. Maybe I can make some more and send you in the future just to let you see that I still haven't had my hair cut.

Pitts wants me to go along to lunch with her so I'll say "so-long"—I'll love you always—

Love,
Evelyn

February 5–

Dear Paul,

I received a letter from you which was written the 26th of January and you hadn't received a letter from me during the past four days. I sincerely hope that you have received the letters I have written by now. I seem to just live for the letters that I receive from you and the hope I have for our future together so I understand how you must feel when you too, don't receive letters.

It has been such a rainy day and looks as though it may continue raining for some time. Of course, we may as well get used to it for that is typical of Springtime and next month is the beginning of Spring. It just doesn't seem possible for it seems that the past year has gone by in such a hurry. It especially doesn't seem that long since I left for Chattahoochee for you know I went there the last day of February in '44. This is an outstanding month which marks our first aniversary—one I shall never forget. I do wish you were here so we could celebrate in a big way. We will when you return and what a happy day that shall be.

I received a letter from Elizabeth today. I don't know why she and J. C. wrote separate letters, but I'm glad they did for I enjoy getting letters and they were both long and interesting. I will let you in on a nice secret, but don't write the family anything about my telling you. Jimmie and Doris and also David and Clara are going to have a baby—some increase in the Wells family. They are so very happy about their future family. You see, I'm beginning to feel my age quite a bit knowing that I shall have more neices & nephews.

I was supposed to have had class during this time, but it was cancelled and I'm glad that it was. I would probably have written this letter during class if it hadn't been cancelled. It was such a great help that I didn't meet you until I had completed the most of my subjects for I haven't been able to accomplish a thing in my studies since—you shouldn't stay in my thoughts so often.

I would enjoy hearing from your brother so tell him to write me. I'll answer his letters if he will write. You know, that I want to know all of your family and I can't meet them otherwise at the present.

Bennett spent last night with me and is still sleeping—such a "sleepy-head" and who's talking? She has completed her training and is working for the Hospital until she is called to take her physical examination. She said if she was in <u>love</u> with some boy she would never enter for she wants to be married.

My room-mate is also sleeping so you see I have to stay awake because I want to write some one I love so very much. I would lose lots of sleep for that certain person if it were necessary. I'm sure that I'll enjoy being his special nurse.

I suppose that it does make you home sick to hear so much about the snow. You know it's going to seem quite different to have me along when you return home, don't you think?

Love Always,
Evelyn

February 7–

Dear Paul,

It is almost time for me to get dressed for duty again. I don't think that I've told you but the entire Senior class, except the ones on night duty have been assigned to (3-11) shift indefinitely. Some life to sleep all day and on duty again. I don't mind for you aren't here and I'm grateful that I wasn't on that shift continuously while you were here; in fact, I had fairly good hours then, but didn't realize it at that time.

It's such a wonderful day—a bit chilly, but nice and the sunshine is grand. My roommate and I were just down to the morning movie "To Have and to Have not." It was a very unusual and cute picture. She doesn't have to report on duty until eleven tonight so I left her down town with a friend.

I'll be so happy to hear from your Mother again. She's such a grand person that it isn't difficult to understand why she has such a nice son. I'm very proud of him too.

You couldn't guess what I'm doing at the present other than writing you. Did you ever hear of any one doing two things at once and making a success at either? I was just mixing some soup so watch that I don't add the letter too as one of the main ingredients. I wish you were here to help me for I found out that you're a good cook the night you roasted those weinners. That's a great memory and perhaps we can live that over again some time, but not in Pensacola.

I met the Post man while on my return home and was hoping that I would have a letter. I wasn't too much disappointed for there's always a tomorrow so maybe I'll receive one then. I always feel much happier after having received a letter from you.

Nothing exciting or unusual ever seems to happen and I suppose Pensacola is about the same as you left it. You see there are no news of interest and it's getting rather late so I'll hush and get dressed.

Love Always,
Evelyn

February 9–

Dear Paul,

No letter today and I've waited so long— Really, I haven't had a letter for the past four days. Of course, you know how I feel as you've experienced the same situation. I don't feel alone for none of the girls received a letter and were almost as disappointed as I.

There was a large party of us girls in the sitting room, but most of them have gone upstairs to dress for duty. I have the day off and nothing planned so I suppose I'll go see a movie. I've enjoyed listening to the radio programs.

I just called Mr. Myers a few minutes ago to find out how Mother and Mamie are as I haven't seen them for quite a while. Have you heard from them recently? Mr. Myers said that Mother had a letter from Frank and he's very anxious to meet his future brother-in-law. Maybe you will have a chance to meet soon. I hope so and he couldn't help but like you very much—just as the remainder of the family does.

Your Mother wrote me that they were snowed in for two or three days and couldn't receive any mail during that time. I suppose you can remember such days in the past. I'm going to enjoy that especially with you. Have you heard from your Mother recently? She always writes some thing nice about you.

Bennett hasn't yet gone for a physical examination, but she is expecting to be called at any time. Personally, I wish she wouldn't join, but why should I advise her. Of course, she has asked my opinion a number of times, but I think she should decide that herself. She will be a great help as the services are in need of more nurses. Don't be afraid of my joining for I plan to wait for you if it takes a number of years. Of course, I hope that it doesn't take that long.

Take good care of yourself until you return to the States and then I shall take care of you.

Love always,
Evelyn

February 11–
(Sunday)

Dear Paul,

I just wander what you are doing today! I suppose you did go to church for one thing as you usually do and I'm proud of that fact. I realize that I should have gone, but I was on duty from three yesterday afternoon until seven this morning. I had to sleep a bit for I have to report on duty again this afternoon at three. I'll make up for lost time in the future as I hope to join you in going then.

It has been such wonderful weather—so nice and warm, but this morning reminds me of the time at Panama City as it has begun raining. I hope that it doesn't continue to rain until I have to report on duty for I don't care to walk so far in the rain.

I hear an ambulance going in—some emergency I suppose from the noise it's making. I'm glad that I don't work in the Emergency department for I had my share of that when I was in the Operating room—Remember!?

My room mate is sleeping so soundly that I almost envy her. I couldn't sleep very well during the day. I've always preferred night sleep.

Here comes Hodges and a friend and I'll have to give up the sitting room so here goes. My room mate is sleeping so I can't stay in the room with her as I may awaken her and she's still on night duty. I'm upstairs with another friend until I finish this letter. And of course, Pitts is around doing some of her original stunts. She's such a big "nut."

I hear an alarm clock ringing and the vibrations seem to shake the house. Some one probably thinks that it's six o'clock in the morning, but it's really four o'clock in the afternoon.

I'm rather hungry so I'll get dressed and go over for supper—(chow) Maybe it sounds more familar when I write it that way. I'm sending the conclusion of one of Elizabeth's letters. I would have sent the letter, but there is too much writing. You see that she does think of you more than you suspected.

Lots of Love,
Evelyn

February 14–

Dear Paul,

Valentine's Day—I just remembered. During school days I never forgot, but since I've been in training, I seldom remember those days. I'm still waiting to receive another letter from you as I haven't received one in several days. I know that you write me as often as you can, but I do miss your letters so very much.

The wind has been blowing as though it were March and the birds have come to life again with their singing. It's seeming more like Spring time every day.

Smitty was telling me the other night that Kupsky has been transferred. She said that he's in Little River now and probably be shipped on to the West Coast soon. I hadn't seen him since before his last leave. He's been transferred about two weeks.

I only have one night out during a week so I was out last night. I went along with Smitty to a formal at the U. S. O. We had a fairly nice time. Every time I go to that U.S.O. I think of the first time I ever spoke to you—at the Spring Street U.S.O. I suppose I remember most everything that happened since that night.

I haven't been home for a number of weeks, but I don't have enough time off-duty to go—It seems a shame and I live so near although I may as well be miles away—

You seem to be a rather popular person of this household for seldom a day passes that the girls don't ask about you. They think you're a swell person and so do I.

I must hush and get dressed for duty as it's almost that time. I sincerely hope and pray that you are well.

Love always,
Evelyn

February 15–
10:30 P.M.

Dear Paul,

I've just finished signing off my charts and decided to write you while the other girls complete their work. This is the first time in ages that

I've had time during duty hours to write a letter. It's just my good luck that Sister isn't around as I would probably lose my day off-duty for the week as punish ment.

Iris Wells' Sister is in for an operation and Iris was down over-night. She says "hello" and as you know she's always "handing out" nice comments about you. Of course, you may accept them as <u>facts</u> if you wish. I'm sure she meant every word she said as she is very serious-minded.

It's such a beautiful night with all the stars and moon light. All we have the privilege to do is look out the window at the many people who can enjoy it. It was so comfortable out this afternoon and is really like Spring time. I wander if they're still having lots of snow at your home and surrounding States.

I haven't yet received a letter from you, but I know I'll hear from you as soon as you have a chance to write. I'll feel like framing the next letter that I receive from you.

2-16-45–

I remained on duty from (11-7) with one of my patients who is rather seriously ill. It's now three-thirty in the morning and I suppose you're in dreamland; at least I hope so anyway. I'm so very sleepy, but this isn't the appropriate place for that.

Here's hoping that I receive a letter from you today.

Love Always,
Evelyn

February 18–

Dear Paul,

I only have a few minutes before going on duty and I shall make good use of that time. I just awakened a few minutes ago as I have been doing "double shifts" again. It's fun to keep my time so well occupied and especially if I can help some one who really needs help. I have been on duty with private room patients, but I will be transferred to the Operating room tomorrow as they need a Senior nurse there. You remember I was in surgery all last Summer.

I miss hearing from you more and more each day and I look forward to receiving your next letter so very much. I can hardly exist from one mail to the next hoping to hear from you. I haven't had a letter for so long although I know you'll write as soon as you can.

I haven't seen or heard from Nellie Moylan since she had her physical so I don't know if she has been called to service or not. A number of the graduate nurses have joined. Bennett hasn't had her physical yet, but she probably will have soon.

Have you heard from your Mother or Pauline recently? I hope to have a letter from them soon. And have you heard from Mamie, Mother or Elizabeth. I haven't been home in four or six weeks, but I will probably go over some time during next week as I'll have more time off duty.

The other girls have already gone to report on duty so I had better run along. I love you very much—

Love always,
Evelyn

February 20–

Dear Paul,

I was so very happy to receive your letter today. You just don't know or realize how much it meant to me. I hope that you received my letters during that time and also your letters from home. Just to know that you're alright means so very much to me.

At the present I'm listening to a radio program and my room mate is getting dressed for night duty. I'm so glad I'm not on the night shift. I like surgery so very much and so happy that the Instructor sent me back again. It seems just a continuation of my past experience. I do miss the social part very much—you know the nights you came out while I was on (3–11) shift and I was always late coming down to see you. I shall never forget those nights and also the week-ends off-duty. I never realized just how happy I was at the time.

I was just down town with some of the girls who wanted chili. I surely won't forget that dish of chili for I still feel as though I had swallowed flames. The cooks surely knew the "hottest" type pepper to use. My Mother probably would have enjoyed it very much and I can see that I didn't inherit that sense of taste from her.

Paul, I had an idea that you were on one of the Islands of the Philippines, but I have no proof for as you know your letters were very well censored. Anything that pertained to your location whatsoever was clipped out. Just so I know that you're well and fairly safe I'll be well pleased.

Don't try getting such a sun burn as you did last Summer—Remember? Your nose stayed pink for days. Of course, I liked you that way, but you won't be near so I can see you this time. We will have so much fun when do return—

Love always,
Evelyn

February 22–

Dear Paul,

I'm home for the first time since Christmas Holidays. I think that Mom was beginning to wander what had happened to me and Mamie thought I had passed out. Well, anyway It's very nice being home for the night and not having to worry about going on duty again tomorrow morning. What a relief! Although I do enjoy my work in Surgery again.

Mamie is sitting opposite me at the table and is writing a letter to Frank. She's very faithful to him and a very nice Sister-in-law; in fact, I like all of my "in-laws." I think Mamie is becoming a bit tired of teaching school—do you suggest that she retire?

Beyond me how Mother found out that I was coming home tonight, but she knows how much I like chicken breast so she had one cooked.

Did I enjoy that chicken?!! "Yum, Yum." We never did keep that chicken dinner date with the people across the street from the Nurse's Home. We'll have to make a dinner date with them and keep it when you return. Won't that be fun?

Maybe you'll be surprised at what I'm going to tell you as I was. Mom had a present for me when I returned from Mamie's home tonight, but she said that I would have to answer a question for her before she gave me the present. She wanted to know if we weren't already married. Of course, I would have liked to have said "yes" truthfully, but you know what my answer had to be.

I think Mom has every species of the animal kingdom around. You should see the various "pets." I'm glad she enjoys having the many dogs and cats and other animals for company. She surely didn't have time for such when the family was home.

Mamie has finished writing Frank and is now writing you so you should receive our letters the same day. You can bet on a novel when you receive one of her letters for she surely knows the technique of writing them.

Have you heard from your family recently? It seems that I haven't had a letter from them in ages. Of course, I never give up hopes for I expect a letter most any time. I also haven't heard from Elizabeth & J. C. recently. I believe they've forgotton about my being in Pensacola. They'll come to life again some day. I can understand why they are neglecting writing letters at the present. They must be very happy.

Mr. Myers said that Iris is going to work at the Navy Yard soon. I hope she soon finds something that she really likes to do.

It's about bed time and I'm very sleepy so I think I shall retire—Hope to receive a letter from you tomorrow.

Love Always,
Evelyn

February 24–

Dear Paul,

I was just reading some of the letters that I've received from you in the past. I can enjoy them more each time I re-read them. Some of the things you mention bring back pleasant memories. I also re-read the last letter I received from your Mother in which she was telling me about their being bound in by the snow for a few days. A wonderful way of occupying my Sunday afternoon time.

I'm working (3-11) shift in surgery this week so I was on call all night. I was sleeping so very soundly at mid-night when I was awakened to help perform an emergency operation. I practically slept during the operation but I don't suppose I made any mistakes as the Doctor didn't say any thing.

You should see me now for I'm on duty and felt a bit chilly so I put one of the Operating room gowns over my uniform. You bet I could almost be confused with a Nun.

I'm all alone at the present, but it's nice to be alone when I'm talking with you even though it is by means of writing. As you know, there isn't much doing up here when there are no Operations scheduled. We do general house cleaning every day, dusting, scrubbing and clean-ing instruments, tables, etc. That can be a big job if there is much surgery during the day.

I will have next week-end off duty. You know, the same as I did last summer. I really dread having so much time and too, the same schedule keeps reminding me too much of past experiences. I'll be so happy when you return.

I was just reading the war news in today's paper. Did you happen to be in the battle at Suribachi? I saw that the third, fourth, and fifth Marine divisions were a part of that battle. I pray that you're in good health and as safe as possible. I'll love you always—

Evelyn

February 26–

Dear Paul,

I really hit the "Jack-pot" today as I received four letters from you. They received a great wel-come as usual for I'm always so happy to hear from you. I don't suppose you could guess what I was doing today when the Postman came. While waiting for your letters, I began practicing a bit of what I learned while in High school. Remodeling a coat and don't you think that isn't a job. I'm sure the Tailors could have done much better, but I may as well know how to do a few things any-way. I haven't yet heard of anyone who knew too much. You know that I also had three semesters of cooking instructions besides the training I've had here and I don't know as I've learned much about cooking yet. I just don't have enough practice for a long enough period each time. I'll just wait and have you teach me. I think you would make a grand Instructor, but do you think you'll like your student?

I do hope that we aren't called out at midnight for an operation. I would enjoy a night's rest so much since we were called the past two nights and were on duty most of the night.

You were wise not to get a sunburn when the other boys did.

Feb. 27–

Just as I completed the last sentence I was called to assist with an operation so I was up until two o'clock last night. When I returned to my room I was a bit too tired and sleepy to complete the letter at that time.

I didn't awaken until ten o'clock this morning and besides writing you I'm listening to a radio program. Kelly was just in and sends her regards. She's just as "nutty" as ever. We're going over for lunch in the next few minutes. I feel as though I might take a bite of the furniture if I don't get food soon.

I'm so proud of the picture you sent as it's one of the best pictures I've seen of you. I don't understand why you don't want to send me another sometime.

Don't worry about my being a part of the service unless I'm drafted. Perhaps I won't be—at least here's hoping for I want very much to wait for you as a civilian.

Love always,
Evelyn

March 1–

Dear Paul,

I was just listening to the President speaking over the radio. You should see the party of girls who have been listening to his speech. The most of the girls are now playing "rummie," but I would much rather write you. I told them that I didn't know much about the game which is true, but I did learn the game from the patients at Chattahoochee.

I have listened to the news broadcast every day of the battle of Iwo Jima for I believe that you are a part of that. No one knows just how much I hope and pray that you're alright, but then, Paul I know you'll come through O. K. I'm very proud of you and just live in hopes of the day the war shall be over.

I won't tell your Mother anything that I think will worry her. I'll leave it to you to tell her when you think best. I realize how easily a Mother will worry about members of the family for Mother worried so much about my brothers.

I plan to spend the week-end with Mom and Mamie wants to make some pictures then. I'll send you some of the latest productions when I have them developed. I don't know why you want so many "funny" pictures of me. It's a wander I don't haunt you already with the many pictures you have of me.

Spring begins this month you know and the weather is really wonderful. Some of the girls have been going to the beach already.

I'll get dressed for duty again so the best of Luck.

I love you very much—

Evelyn

March 3–

Dear Paul,

I just reported off duty a few minutes ago and don't have to report on again until Monday morning. I am going over home with Mr. Myers this afternoon. I'm taking along your camera with the other roll of film you gave me so I can make some pictures while there.

Do you remember the day that you left I made a couple of pictures of you? Elizabeth had them developed and I received them today along with her letter. They're very good even though you didn't want to pose for me. I'll show them to you some time when we're a bit nearer each other and don't have so much water in-between us.

We're having the most wonderful weather and the most beautiful moonlight nights you ever saw. Usually we notice the sun-set and moon light most during an operation. Some people! I miss you most at that time for I seldom saw you during the day. I'll never forget the day you stopped for me as I was walking home after duty hours. I really didn't intend to be so rude, but of course, I was thinking of my personal appearance at the time. I suppose there are a number of incidences that I'll never forget.

The telephone rings every five minutes it seems and disturbs me for I have to answer it. There's no one else on first floor.

No complaints of the brightness of the light in our room. If Sister Theodora only knew that my room mate and I put in a three-hundred watt bulb, she would then understand why the bill is so high each month. We shouldn't affect our eyes with a poor lighting system—do you think?

Don't get too much of a sun tan for I might think that you are one of the natives from the Islands when you return. Of course, I'll love you just the same and I do think a sun tan is very nice. Some of the girls went out to the beach today. I can't take much of the sun light for I practically burn to a crisp.

You're really doing a wonderful job on the Island so here's hoping the worst is over by now. I know you're the best Marine any where and I love you very much.

Lots of Love,
Evelyn

March 6–

Dear Paul,

Wander what you're doing now. I have only a general idea, but I'll be so happy when I can hear from you again. At present I'm in my room alone and it's so very quiet and nice except for the various noises of the outside world. I have the windows open and the Spring (March) breeze is wonderful. It looks as if it may rain during the afternoon, but we've had our share of sunshine too, I suppose. I was just over for lunch and I wan't tell you what we had on the menu for the day as you may become a bit nauseated.

I was at the train station last night for the first time since you left. You can't imagine how much I remembered of the night we were there and it even made chills down my spine—a night I'll long remember. Jancsik was going to her home in Pennsylvania for a three week's vacation and she wanted me to go along to the station with her. She was so thrilled over going home and I can understand why she would be.

Oh! but the number of girls who have just been in my room and I'm tired of talking with them. I would never get tired of your company though.

Frank wrote and asked me not to join any of the services after having completed my training. I think Mother is a bit worried too, but really I don't know why she should be as I haven't said a word about joining and don't care to.

We made some pictures while I was home over the week-end; in fact, we took four rolls of film and I think Mom is going to send you some pictures of home. I'll send you a few more pictures of myself to add to your collection. You could start a zoo on my pictures alone.

I have the day off-duty for we get a day each week. It's just wonderful to have the time off since I've begun sewing a bit during my off-duty hours. Would you believe me if I tell you that I baked some cookies while over home during the week-end? I enjoyed it so much as it's quite different from performing an operation, but I enjoy both very much.

I'll hush for I want to go down town.

Love always,
Evelyn

March 8–

Dear Paul,

I'm honestly so very <u>full</u> from the supper I ate tonight that I can hardly move about—I know it's a sin to eat so much. Such parties only occur a few times during a lifetime. Bennett is going away soon so we had a special supper for her and I think she enjoyed it very much. They wouldn't even miss me if I should leave; in fact, they would probably say "good riddance".

This is the most noisy place tonight and I think every radio in the house is going "full blast." The girls seem to be very happy about something—beyond me for I don't feel that way. If you were here I would feel quite different; in fact, I'd be the happiest girl around.

Since I can't receive letters from you, I have to get out the old ones and re-read them. Although I enjoy them, I would much rather have an up-to-date letter from just to know that you're still alright. The news sound rather good from the Pacific area, but I suppose you know much more about the situation than I.

I don't know how I'll manage to awaken on time tomorrow morning since the girl who has been awakening me doesn't have to get up for duty. I over-slept this morning and was over just in time to report on duty. I didn't have any breakfast so of course, I was practically starved by lunch hour.

It's a bit chilly out tonight, but is very nice. I would enjoy walking miles on a beautiful night as this. Suppose it's still very warm where you are and I suppose it must be very hot there during Summer. We'll probably have very warm weather soon for you know Summer usually begins early here. Every time you mention so much rain I think of Panama City. I believe it rains there continuously.

Pitts was in a few minutes ago and said for me to remind you that she still "Loves You." The boy to whom she was engaged came home recently from overseas duty, but he hasn't been over to see her yet. She wrote her Mother that she's going to be married so soon as she sees him so I don't know how the story will end. I do know that I wont to see you as soon as you reach the States again if possible. That will be the greatest moment of my life when I see you and talk with you again personally.

I'm becoming very, very sleepy so I'll say "Good-night" and remember I still love you very much.

Love Always,
Evelyn

March 10–

Dear Paul,

When I returned home from duty this afternoon who should I find waiting for me but

Mamie. She told me last week that she would probably be down today so I kinda expected her. I went along with her to town for a few minutes and I also had some clothes at the cleaners so we came by there. She has already left for home so here I sit with some of the girls. They're making coffee and we have some of a wedding cake which is left-overs from last night. It surely looks good but I haven't eaten any of it yet.

I received the most precious letter from your Mother today. She's just wonderful, but of course, I suppose you found that out years ago. I have also come to the conclusion that two Mothers are better than one.

I told you about the wedding cake, but I didn't tell you who was married. You don't know her, but she is my roommate's best girl friend and she was married to a Marine Officer. My roommate said that the wedding was beautiful.

I was invited, but didn't go although I would have liked to have gone. I have only attended very few weddings, but there's one that I'm looking forward to in the future of which I hope to be a part. You too, shall be a main part.

I can get the pictures out next Wednesday so I'll send you some whether they're good or not. Of course, I don't expect too much of my pictures for I'm afraid I'd be in for a big let-down as I never make good pictures.

I always think perhaps I may get a letter from you each day even though I know you have been unable to write. I still look forward to receiving your next letter so very much. I want to really know that you're still alright.

The girls want me to go along with them to the U.S.O. tonight so I suppose I'd better get dressed. Hope to hear from you soon.

Love Always,
Evelyn

To Cpl. Paul J. Fogel 435156, H & S. Co. 23 Mars 4th Divi, c/o Fleet Post Office, San Francisco, Cal. from Mrs. Leidy C. Fogel, Nazareth, Route 1, Pa., Mar 12 1945
[Paul's Mother; sent via V-Mail.]

Good morning <u>Baby</u>. Twenty years ago at half past 12 midnite a pair of twins arrived at my house and it was quiet noisey for a while. now on this day every thing was so quiet but for the guenas that were chattering to the moon, but listen. honey I was not asleep I was awake and thinking & wishing you and your twin could still be in my room where I could watch over you. Francis & I had our supper together because Polly & Earl are still up home. We had a dinner for Polly Sunday Francis & family and June & family were home. How I wished you and Evelyn could have been here too. I gave Polly a pair of gray slacks and a blouse while I put $10. to your account for a birthday gift. Hope you are well and not to lonesome. I hope and pray it will soon be over. I had a letter from Sheldon and he is well and says his hands hurt so much from never having time to rest. I also had a letter from Roy's June. she had a letter from Roy and he is well. Grandpa walked up this morning to see if we had news from you and the rest. He really looked fine. Well spring is here and the neighbors are branding their [illegible] while Francis went after his grass seed which he wants to sow one morning. We still have a few snow banks around. Emma Miller was out hunting dandelion but I was not yet. I am afraid my knee would start giveing me pain again. so I will wait awhile longer to [illegible]. I wrote Evelyn last week so I will receive a letter from here soon. Dad is busy having county meetings just now Dad & I are both fine and hope and pray you are the same With all our love to you

Mother & Dad

P.S. Happy Birthday to you

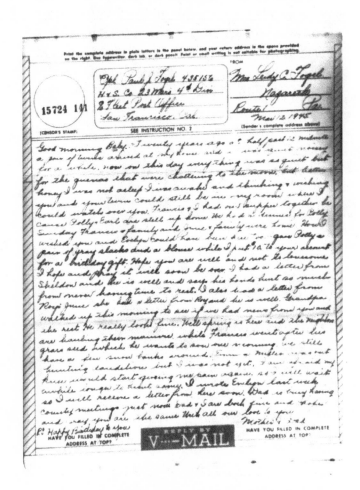

Mrs. Fogel, Paul's Mother, V-Mail dated March
12, 1945 (to Paul for his 20th birthday)

[From Evelyn's brother Jimmy.]

3/12/45

Hello Paul:

Plenty has happened and you've seen so much too I'm sure since you wrote to me. I've really intended to answer your letter ever since receiving it, but I've been so busy and time does pass so fast.

Well, Paul quite a lot has happened with us too since we last saw you in Pensacola. We made it out here in three days from home without any trouble with the car. We were quite proud of that record for it is more than twenty-three hundred miles between the two points. I surely do like the Ford and couldn't have found a better car for the price—thanks to you.

As you probably know, we own a trailer which we've had since October. It surely is a nice one and we had much rather live in it than an apartment. We save so much on rent too.

Now for the latest—Doris and I are going to be "Pop" & "Mom" within the next five months. It just doesn't seem possible that we are really going to have a baby. You should see all the clothes that we have for "him," it's got to be a boy, already. The lady friends have given Doris a baby shower already too.

It's too bad, Paul, that you didn't get around to see us before you went across. Suppose that was quite an experience for you going over. Were you sea sick? It surely was my first trip across. J. C. is still here and hopes that he won't have to go over, but he never knows from day to day just when he might go.

Of course, I know where you are from the papers and radio. You surely have had a tough time of it for the past couple weeks. The island should be secured by the time you receive this letter.

Paul take care of yourself and be sure to dodge all those bullets. J. C., Elizabeth & Doris sent their best regards.

Good luck Paul and write when you can.

Sincerely
J. T. Wells
7624 EL CAJON BLVD.
LA MESA, CALIF.

March 13–

Dear Paul,

Happy birthday! Although you say this isn't your birthday, I still believe it's the date you told me once. I'm so very happy today for I just received a very nice long letter from you. You kept me in suspense so long that it was such a great relief when I received your letter and to know that you're alright and fairly safe again. You don't know just how much I hoped and prayed that you would come through safely. I saw a news-reel of Iwo Jima which was only a very slight phase of the real battle. I know that you experience plenty even more than you'll care to remember.

I've just finished writing a letter to your Mother. I would like so very much to be able to talk to her personally for I know she's wonderful.

I'm glad that you had a letter from J. C. for he does write very interesting letters. I do hope that he isn't sent overseas. He and Elizabeth like California and are very happy there. She would feel so very much alone if he should have to be transferred.

Nellie is already in service but I don't know where she is stationed. It seems that she would write, although she was rather angry at me for I didn't visit her very often while she was here. Bennett is leaving Saturday and I know that I'll miss her, but I could never miss anyone so much as I do you. Believe me, I never loved anyone so much as I love you either.

We've had such wonderful weather, but it looks as though it may rain today. Some of the girls have been going to the beach and have a very nice sun tan already.

One of the graduate Nurses is to be married tomorrow night. She's so thrilled over the occasion and who wouldn't be? I don't think you know her although you may have seen her a number of times. Her name is Juanita Wilkerson and she was transferred here from another hospital.

I saw a very cute picture yesterday "Practically Yours." Fred McMurray and Claudette Colbert were the leading characters and they're very good.

I'll send you some pictures in my next letter for I'll get them tomorrow.

Love always,
Evelyn

March 16–

Dear Paul,

I should have written you last night, but honestly I was so very tired when I came off duty so I hope you'll forgive me. Soon after I went to bed, I fell sound asleep so maybe a bit of work is good for me only I should try it more often.

I have the pictures now and they are terrible. I wouldn't send you these two if I hadn't already promised you some. Don't you think that it's a very good picture of Mom, but I look as old as she? She thinks there's nothing half so precious as that doggie in the picture—It is cute, don't you think? I believe you said that you like dogs and I prefer cats so we'll have to compromise. You can at least see from the pictures that I haven't trimmed my hair yet, but if it were only red!!!

You should see the effect that Spring has on the flowers, trees, etc. for they're just beautiful. I admire their beauty every time I go for a walk. The Wisteria vines are also very pretty as they cover the tree tops and we can see them very well from the windows of the Operating rooms. I know that the Azalea Gardens in Mobile must be beautiful now for the few we have here are in full bloom.

Bennett hasn't gone yet, but is planning to leave tomorrow. I'm going along with her to the train station. I'm so tired of saying "Goodbye" and if it continues I'll soon be left "holding the bag" (in Pensacola). Some day I shall leave too.

I was hoping to receive a letter from you today, but was disappointed again. Oh! Well there shall be another day so I can look forward to the day I shall hear from you again. Sometimes they seem like years apart, but no complaints for I know you can't help that. You were lucky to get my letters while you were in action on the Island.

Patterson wants me to go along with her to a movie tonight and neither of us know what is playing. I really don't care to go any place, but she is a nice girl so I couldn't refuse.

I have been invited to another formal and haven't yet decided to go. It's too much trouble to have to get dressed and I would much rather wear street clothes. I would enjoy dancing so I'll probably go.

I'm expecting another long letter soon—I love you very much—

Love,
Evelyn

March 18–

Dear Paul,

When I returned home from duty yesterday afternoon Mamie was waiting for me so I was down town with her the greater part of the afternoon. It's very nice having her around. Three rolls of the film that I had developed belonged to her so she was as disappointed with the pictures as I am. I'm sending two more pictures of myself that are about the same as the others I sent you. You're going to become very tired of looking at those awful pictures of me.

Bennett came over last night and was along with Smitty and me to to the formal. After the dance, Smitty and I saw her off at the bus station.

We're going to miss her very much. She asked for your address so maybe you'll hear from her soon. I hope so. Mamie said she would probably write you today so you see, you're rather popular. You're much more popular with me; in fact, I think you're wonderful.

The Supervisor of the operating room came to the conclusion that I had been working rather hard so she just gave me the day off. Don't you think that's very thoughtful of her? She's a grand Supervisor. I have slept most of the day. At the present Smitty and I are sitting in the kitchen and have just had some soup. Really hit the right spot too.

I haven't heard from you for a number of days, but you know I never give up hopes. I know you'll write me as soon as you can again. It's just wonderful to receive a letter from you as they're so few and far between recently.

I'm glad that you heard from Kupsky. And about the <u>Little</u> River, that's very original, I suppose. Hope that you will see Kupsky if he is sent overseas. So far, you've be unsuccessful while trying to locate the relatives.

Just had a brief intermission as one of the younger students came in to see me. She only stayed a very few minutes for she was just asking about some clothes she had left here.

Hope to hear from you tomorrow. Good night and pleasant dreams.

Love always,
Evelyn

March 20–

Dear Paul,

I just received a letter from you and was so very glad to get it. I have been looking forward to receiving it for days, but I know you can't write very often. I'm grateful that I can even hear from you and know that you're still alright. No, I wouldn't say that you're living in luxury exactly. It must be a terrible experience; in fact, an experience that I hoped you would never witness. Since you are a part of this war, I do hope and pray that you'll come through safely and I know you will. The boys who are a part of the numerous battles deserve the greatest reward possible.

It has been cloudy for a number of days and has been raining practically all day. I was beginning to wish that I had the facilities of a duck and perhaps I wouldn't have been quite so damp when I returned home from duty.

I was down to the Spring Street U.S.O. the other night which was the first time I've been there in ages. I never enter that place that I don't remember the first time you ever talked with me. I shall never forget that night. At the time I merely thought that you seemed to be a nice boy. I wasn't wrong about that and soon found that I cared so very much about you even though I didn't admit it to you or anyone else until a while before you left. Everyone knew that I loved you just from my actions while with you and several told me that I would marry you even before I knew it myself. The saying is true that "actions speak louder than words."

My room mate seems to be so comfortable. She is lying on her bed and practically asleep. She too, has just finished writing the boy to whom she is engaged. He has been overseas about two months and she says it seems like ages. Of course, the five months you've been gone has seemed like years.

We have had hamburgers nearly every afternoon for all of us like them and we don't have to walk over to the Hospital just for what they call supper. They don't usually prepare anything which is very appetising. Why should I complain for I know that the food you have isn't nearly so wholesome.

We've just been in the kitchen having some tomato soup and listening to some of Hodge's wild west stories. Don't you think that girl doesn't know her way around and quite well. You should hear her talk about some of her experiences. No, I wouldn't wont you to hear them.

I'd better run get my bath before all the bath tubs are taken.

Love always,
Evelyn

March 22–

Dear Paul,

It's slowly becoming dark and is so very quiet which is rather unusual at this place. My room mate and I have confidential talks often, but then, the other girls wouldn't be interested in our conversations. She serves more or less, as a Sister for we know many things in common and have known each other so long. During one of our conversations a few minutes ago, her father came by for her. He drives to his home in Milton every night so Margaret has gone along to spend the night. I miss her when she isn't around. That's why I miss Elizabeth so very much because we could always trust each other with personal affairs. I believe you have the wrong impression of her since she sent me that letter, but she can really be trusted and so can Jimmie. I would confide in them much more than the remainder of the family. So much for my affairs.

I received two letters from you today and as always I was very happy to get them. You don't realize just how much I appreciate hearing from you; in fact, I nearly went "nuts" during the time I couldn't hear from you. After all, you are of great importance so far as I'm concerned.

I can't understand why you haven't yet received the package I mailed you months ago. I realize it takes quite a long while for packages to reach the Islands, but I didn't think it would take so many months. It's best that I didn't try sending along some food too, for I'm afraid that it would be a wee bit on the spoiled side by the time you received it.

Golly, it seems almost like Autumn even though the outside world has the appearance of Spring. Since the recent rain, we have had cool weather; in fact, I only have one blanket on my bed and I nearly freeze at night. My feet stay cold most of the time, but I don't practice Margaret's stunts. She practically runs me out of this joint at times by placing her cold feet against me. Some time she gives me such a surprise attack that I almost kiss the ceiling. Well, I don't jump quite that high for I'm afraid I might regret the results.

I'm still in surgery and hope they will leave me there for a long while. Miss Bell has promised me next Saturday, Sunday, and Monday off duty (Easter week-end). I don't know why she believes in such favors. She just gave me an extra day off for this week. She really shows partiality and I don't think that she should for the girls may dislike me for it. The only service I haven't had is Public Health and I'm not anxious to have that right away. It will be good experience, but I don't believe I would especially care for that field of nursing.

Bennett's orders were awaiting her when she arrived at her home. She is to report to Camp Rucker the first of April. I do hope that she likes the service and the Army is much in need of Nurses. An Army Nurse who had served overseas lectured to us the other day. She seemed to have changed the view-point of many of the girls so far as joining the services is concerned. Many have filled in applications to be sent to a Government Hospital for the last six months of training.

Some of the girls wanted me to go along with them to a movie last night. We had seen every movie in town except one which was a Western picture. I was never quite so bored as I was during that picture. I can't understand why anyone would care for such productions.

I hope that you have received a few more of my letters by now. I'll love you always and very much.

Love,
Evelyn

March 24

Dear Paul,

I have just awakened so I suppose you know who I thought about first of all for I find myself writing to you. I'm still yawning, but I think that I've had enough sleep and too much helps to make one lazy. I've found that out too. The girls in the next room are making so much noise that I think they would make good pals for the children in kindergarden school. That must be a great relief from the strain of hall duty.

This is such a nice morning and I haven't even been out yet, but I can enjoy the sunlight by looking out the window. It is a wee bit cool yet and I suppose will be until after Easter. I just dread the very hot weather we have in store for the Summer.

Received a letter from Bennett yesterday and she wanted me to answer it right away, but she forgot to give me a return address. All I can do is wait for another letter from her and during that time, she'll probably think that I've just neglected writing. It won't be long before she'll be wearing a uniform. I would enjoy watching her return her first salute.

I've written all over these two pages so maybe I'm still in dream land. I can't seem to guide my pen in the direction it should go in order to have a straight line.

Margaret and I will be working opposite shifts this week for she'll work (7-3) and I'll work (3-11) shifts. Of course, I'll be on call each night which includes two shifts. I enjoy it when we don't have too many emergency Operations at once. I would rather they come one at a time.

I'll probably spend next week end at home. I haven't told Mother that I'm coming over yet so she won't be expecting me. If I don't go home when I have time off, I don't know what to do with myself since you aren't around anymore. You're here all the time, but just in thoughts and dreams. I'll love you always,

Evelyn

March 26–

Dear Paul,

Sunday morning and I can hear the church bells. The March wind is terrific so I suppose that's why I can hear the bells so clearly. It is now nine o'clock and I have just returned home. You know when we're on call for surgery, we have to sleep in the Hospital annex. Of course, it's much more convenient there.

It is so very quiet for all of the girls both day and night nurses are sleeping. The day nurses will have to report on duty at three this after-noon so they probably stayed out late last night. The usual bed time around this joint seems to be either two or three o'clock in the morning and some time even later (maybe I should say earlier). I have known of boys staying around until four-thirty which isn't a very good reputation for this place as a whole. Just wander what the neighbors think. Sister Theodora doesn't know about it, but I know definitely she would not approve of the situation.

I told Pitts what you said about the Island so she says for you to reserve it until after the war. She is "nuts," isn't she?

One of the Doctors discovered that we're engaged. You should have heard the lecture he gave me for he was afraid that I wouldn't complete my training. After he had finished lecturing, I explained the situation as it is at present so he felt better about the idea. He then gave me a bit of good advise. This conversation was during a minor operation so I'm glad the Supervisor wasn't around at the time. We aren't supposed to carry on a conversation even during a minor operation. I'm sure we didn't endanger that patient's life.

I have been studying a bit for State Board examinations in May. I do dread them so very much for the girls who have already taken them say that they're asked some of the silliest questions about things they would never think of studying for.

Just wander what you're doing today. Wish I could be with you wherever you are for I would never be afraid with you. Most of all, I hope that you're still alright and well. I'm expecting a letter from you tomorrow so you had better not disappoint me.

Love always,
Evelyn

P.S. Did you say that you had to borrow paper?

March 27–

Dear Paul,

It is now twelve o'clock (day) and I just awakened a few minutes ago. We were called out last night about midnight to perform an emergency operation. After having finished with the operation, we had to clean all the instruments and put them away to be sterilized. You can bet we were rather sleepy by the time we reached our beds again. I will be on call four more nights and I'm always glad to go on day shift again. I'm very glad that I will have the week-end off for I can be home during that time.

I received a letter from you yesterday and I'm always glad to hear from you. I can't understand why you haven't been receiving my letters for I write as often as ever before. Maybe you'll get them all at once.

I received the most beautiful Easter card from your Mother yesterday. She's such a wonderful person. I can understand why you care so much about her. I wanted to send her an Easter card too, but I suppose I went down town too late for I couldn't find any Easter cards at all.

Did you receive those awful pictures yet? You know Rox wouldn't make "blow-ups" of the 616 film anymore. Their reason is that it takes too much negative material and they're trying to conserve. I suppose there is something to that too.

Just had company—Smitty and Kelly were in for a short while. They send their regards. Now I'm all alone again for my room mate is probably on duty.

I haven't heard from Elizabeth and J. C. for some time. They've probably forgotton about me. I hope you aren't sent out on another operation ever and I do hope the war ends soon. I love you very much—

Evelyn

[From Evelyn's friend, Lt. Bennett.]
28 March

Dear Paul:—

Hello and how are you? Let's don't talk about Iwo Jima—let's forget all about it. I know it was horrible—Thank God you are safe.

What day is or was your birthday mine is next month—I feel older than I really am.

The kid brother is in Germany—hope that God keeps him safe, however if it is his will that he must go in that manner—then we will just be one more of the hundreds of families that have to go thru it—he is so young, so sweet and so—well I love him more than anything on earth. I can remember the first day he started to school and the day he graduated—I shouldn't start on that subject because I could go on for hours.

We go into Summer uniforms next week—we will sure appreciate them too—hot as heck here.

Got a wire from my best girl friend last nite—her twin brother is in the Marine Corps. Been over for 22 months—arrived home Monday nite Reports to Cherry Point the 27 of April.

To nite is G. I. nite so that means a certain gal is going to wax, wash and scrub to get ready for Inspection tomorrow.

Fred Waring and Band were here last nite—couldn't go as I had the duty—they said he was swell. I saw him yesterday at noon at lunch—

Please be patient for that photo. I had some taken while home—mom and dad got them that is the last I ever saw of them—never even got one myself—nice, huh!—

Just showed some captain his room—real nice but old.

Looks like we might have some rain and soon—having a lot of forest fires—rather dry now—need some rain—

I feel like going out and trying to get a tan but guess I would look like a ripe tomato if I did and oh the freckles—horrible things.

Things in Europe sound pretty good now—let's hope they continue—

Getting Mess Duty in May—another furlough either in June or July—life gets so boring here—

Guess better try working for a change—might help pass the time.

Got that hug and a kiss—here's one in return—

Lots of Love
Eleanor

March 29–

Dear Paul,

Another quiet morning for most of the girls are on duty. The ones who aren't have gone to the beach for a sun tan. I can just feature my appearance if I should go on the beach for only a few minutes for I would return as red as a beet, I know. You would take a nice sun tan for your complexion seems the type that would tan easily. I like you with a real pink nose as you had a few times during last Summer when you came out—Remember? You didn't care to be touched on some spots.

I was called out again last night for a couple of operations. It didn't take long for either operation so we were to bed again by two-thirty this morning. I would much rather help with an operation during the day, but as you know, the night work is emergencies only.

Sister Theodora is having me relieve Saturday and Sunday three to eleven shift in the Emergency room. I was supposed to have had this week-end off-duty, but they will make-up the time due me during next week. Since I've been in training I've lost all faith in planning any thing. I suppose you've noticed that I don't like to plan for the future too much. I know I shouldn't be that way, but I like for things just to happen without making plans. Maybe my attitude toward that will be quite different after having completed training.

The maid is in at the present cleaning the floors and dust is covering everything. Don't be surprised if you find some on this letter when you receive it. I could go into the other room, but I'm more comfortable here and I don't think I'm distrubing the maid too much.

The telephone seems to ring every five minutes and of course, I have to answer it. Some one usually has the wrong number.

It is almost time for the Postman so maybe I'll receive a letter. I can think of nothing except you in person that would be more welcome. I love you and think of you always—

Love,
Evelyn

March 31–

Dear Paul,

I was over rather early this morning for I have several things I want to do before going on duty this afternoon. I've just had a shampoo to start the day off right and also improved my feelings quite a bit.

Here's Patsy again with that mop and duster outfit to clean the room. I seem to always be present when she comes around. I enjoy kidding her for she's rather comical anyway.

Pitts was just in too and said she is starving. We could live off the fat we have stored away. She was talking about steaks, chicken, ice cream and everything in general just to make me hungry and she did succeed.

I have planned nothing especially for Easter for as you know I'll be on duty in the Emergency room. If you were around, I'd refuse to work (3-11) shift during that time. Since that isn't possible now, we'll hope to be together next Easter which is a great future to look forward too.

I have your picture on the table by me. You seem to be looking at me and if that picture could only talk.

Have you heard from any of the family recently? You hadn't even been receiving my letters when I heard from you last. I know how much of a "let down" it is to expect a letter and then not receive one. I have experienced that myself. Here's hoping that I receive a letter from you today. I love you so very much.

Love Always,
Evelyn

April 1ˢᵗ

Dear Paul,

I have just reported on duty in the Emergency room. I do hope that it isn't so rugged tonight as it was last night. It's very quiet other than for the news on the radio as there are no emergencies in at the present.

Some Easter! It seems as though it were the first of March instead of April for the wind is blowing almost the same as a hurricane. Maybe I exagerated quite a bit, but it is rather rough out.

Just had a kid in with a slight laceration of his forehead so it only took a few minutes to treat him. He was such a cute little fellow so I cared for him while his Mother went over to the drug store. I also had other company as one of the Sisters and a Lieutenant (Nurse) from the Station were in for a short while. Now, I'm all alone again. The radio is behind me and at present classical music is playing.

We usually have a very good Easter lunch, but today the steak was a bit too tough. I won't complain about the food too much anymore after what you told me about your having only cheese for a whole week. I'm very glad that your food situation has improved. Listen Paul, if there is anything that you want and don't have, I'll be glad to send it if you'll only let me know.

I have searched through all the letters I've ever received from you and I remember now that I never received the letter that you wrote on the nineteenth of November. In a letter written on the twenty-third of November you told me there was a very valuable stamp in the letter of the nineteenth and to be sure to save it. I never received the letter with the stamp and what kind was it? I wish you could recall the things you wrote about in that letter for you said it was something that would interest me very much. You have me in suspense now trying to figure out what it might have been about.

I think of you so very much. I don't believe that there is a moment ever that I'm not aware of you in my thoughts. I love it that way so I don't try to forget you for one moment.

Mamie was down yesterday afternoon and stayed with me until my duty hours. She's grand company and I really enjoy having her around. She asked me to apology for her neglecting to write you recently. She said she really hasn't been in the mood for writing letters, but will write you again soon.

Happy Easter! and thanks for listening. Hoping that you are receiving mail by now.

Love Always,
Evelyn

April 3–

Dear Paul,

It's so very warm tonight and I don't believe there is any breeze at all. I suppose we'll really have some hot weather soon. The wind was blowing so very hard and it began raining Sunday night while on my way home. The wind practically blew me in the opposite direction. I was rather tired after having survived the task of the Emergency room over the week-end. The suspense is what gets me as you never know how many or what type patients are going to come in next. They always assign me to that department during the times that no Doctors are available.

I will have Thursday off if nothing happens so I may go over home tomorrow night. I haven't seen my Mother for quite a while and I'm always glad to see her. You'll probably receive another letter from her soon.

Ernestine sent me some pictures of her baby. He's such a precious little fellow and I would like so much to see him. I haven't seen her but twice since she married and that was before the birth of her baby. She lives in New Smyrna Beach, Florida so she wants me to spend a couple days with her when I go for State Board Examinations. I don't think I'll have any time for visiting, but I would certainly enjoy going there for a few days.

All the girls stayed home tonight. Even Hodges didn't go out and that's quite unusual. She brought about four Officers here the other night and they had four quarts of whisky and some beer along. Some party as you can imagine—a very cheerful crowd.

I haven't received a letter from you since Saturday, but I'm hoping to get another one soon.

This is such terrible writing, but maybe I can do better next time. I'm very sleepy and I couldn't sleep well without writing you first.

All my love,
Evelyn

April 5–

Dear Paul,

I haven't heard from you for such a long time. I look forward to each day in hopes that I will receive a letter from you. I know that you write as often as you can so I really appreciate the letters when I do receive them.

Well, I didn't get to go over home last night, but I wasn't too much disappointed for I'm getting used to such treatment. I'm beginning to wander what they would do without me and don't think I'm bragging at all. I'm due three days so I asked Sister if I could have Sunday off duty, but she said she just couldn't do without me on the halls that day. I don't know how she came to that conclusion but I don't appreciate it at all. I'm not in surgery anymore for I'm on Public Health now. Today was my first day and I really enjoyed it. We visited one of the local schools and gave Typhoid shots. Poor kids—reminds me of my school days. Some of the kids came in crying and the remainder were pale from being afraid. They were so cute, especially the beginners.

Jancsik was just in and wants me to go along with her for a hamburger. These hungry girls! I've never seen a nurse who wasn't hungry and I'm included. Of course, you know that already.

Hodges is in the sitting room with a crowd of boys. She wouldn't feel at home otherwise.

I just received another letter from Bennett and she is now stationed at Camp Rucker, Alabama. Several of the Pensacola graduates are stationed there unless they have already been transferred to other places.

They're having open house for the new Nurse's home Monday afternoon beginning at four o'clock and if we aren't present we shall be punished for Sister wants us over to intertain, I suppose. Following that, we're having a formal, but I don't think I'm going to be present.

Hope to receive a letter from you soon. I love you very much—

Evelyn

April 8–

Dear Paul,

Sunday again and what an afternoon! At the present Smitty and Margaret are in the room and as "nutty" as ever. I dread Sunday afternoons more and more each week. The remainder of the week passes alright. I might go to Church tonight if I can find some one who would like to go along for I don't fancy walking the streets alone at night.

It's been very cool for the past few nights; in fact, we had to wear our coats again after having packed them away for the Summer. It's beginning to warm up a bit now and seems more like

Spring. Some of the girls just left for the beach, but I still think it's too cool to go swimming.

Everything is too quiet so I wish something exciting would happen. I'm not hoping to have any emergency cases come in, but of course, that isn't really excitement.

I had another letter from Bennett and she said that she has cleaned more floors since she's been in the Army than she ever cleaned at home. Maybe that isn't saying much for she probably didn't do much work at home. She thinks Army life is quite exciting, but I can't understand why it would be.

And now Pheil is trying on one of my evening gowns which will make the second gown I have loaned out this week. I don't mind but it takes so much time and money to have them cleaned after having some one else soil them. Of course, they would never think of having them cleaned before returning them. So much for my troubles, but I just haven't learned to make use of the word "no."

Mamie thinks Frank may come home soon. Isn't that wonderful? Just wish I could say that about you and looking forward to that time is a pleasure. It will seem more or less as a dream for such happiness would seem as a wonderful dreamland.

We've just had some coffee rolls and coffee and I feel so "stuffed." Kelly is now upstairs getting dressed for we're going to a movie as no one wants to attend Church tonight. Kelly surely makes nice comments about you and sends her regards.

Love always,
Evelyn

April 11–

Dear Paul,

I received three letters from you yesterday and you can't realize how they brought me out of the "dumps." I'm much happier now that I've heard from you again.

I was over home last night for a short while. You know I don't have much time off duty since I've begun working at the Public Health Center. That's the reason I could only stay home for a few hours. Really enjoyed the time I was there. Of course, Mom had to show me her flowers and introduce me to a few new members of the cat and dog families. She thinks there's nothing that compares to her various animals. I don't agree with her for even though the dog is cute, I still don't care for dogs. I do think that small kittens are precious. Don't you think that we should have a house full of cats? ha/. I can just hear your answer.

Smitty just came in and is resting on Margaret's bed as Margaret isn't home at the present. She is so much in love with a Sailor and doesn't want to marry him just yet as she still has about ten month's training to complete. I can understand just how she feels for something tells me that I am experiencing the same situation.

Received a letter from Elizabeth today and thought perhaps you might like to read it. I'm just wandering if you have received their letters yet. And just what did my Mother say to you in that letter that changed your opinion of a few things? Did you change your impression of me?

I was along with one of the Public Health Nurses to Malino today which is about twenty miles out from town. You've probably been there a number of times when you drove the Marine truck. We visited the school and then took care of the patients who were at the clinic there. While on our way home, we made a couple of home calls which were very interesting. We really find out the private life of various people which is very confidential.

Have you received those pictures yet? Hope to hear from you again soon.

Love Always,
Evelyn

[From Mamie, Evelyn's sister-in-law.]
At School
Apr. 12, 1945

Dear Paul,

First of all I'll ask your forgiveness for having not answered your last letter but at first my morale was so low I couldn't write. Then I just got out of the habit I guess and kept neglecting to write. I'm truly sorry that I haven't written because I know how much the fellows over there enjoy letters from the folks back home.

I've seen that Evelyn three or four times I think since I wrote to you last. She came home for a little while last Tuesday night and then I have been to town two or three times. I always go out to see her when I am there.

She is the same sweet girl that she always was and thinks as much of you as ever. She would probably feel like breaking my neck if she knew I told you all that I do but I know that it helps your feelings to know this and I'm sure that you will understand. She is just living for the day when you can come home and making all kinds of plans for a happy future with you. I'm sure hoping that those plans and dreams will soon come true. You sure must have a bit of magic about you some how because it works like a strong magnet. I can start talking about any thing in the world and the first thing I know she is right back on her main topic—"Paul." I sure hope that you two will be as happy as I'm hoping you will.

Now—Heres my main topic. I'm thrilled to death over the fact that Frank has made it as far back this way as Hiwaii. He is in the hospital there but I'm living on the hope that he will get to come on home from there and that it won't be long before I can have him here at home. I'm living for the day when he can come home. If Evelyn hasn't told you I guess that you'll be wondering why he is in the hospital. He hurt his back in February and has been in the hospital ever since. At first I nearly went crazy but then I decided to try not to worry so much. If anything happens to him I just don't believe I could ever live.

I'm mighty happy to know that you came through Iwo Jima safely. I thank God for taking care of you and I feel like it was just answered prayer. I for one was praying for you. I'm still praying that where ever you are God will take care of you and send you back home safely and—soon.

I had a lovely day Easter Sunday. I was determined to attend church some where. We were not having an Easter service here so I went to Milton. I sure did enjoy the service there too. That afternoon I went to a singing in Pensacola. I have always attended and enjoyed those singings. I don't suppose that you have them around your home. I had a flat tire but I had enjoyed myself so much until even that couldn't mar the day. I was all alone but I was perfectly happy. The tire went flat in Pensacola, so it wasn't too much trouble to get it fixed.

I went home last week-end. That isn't but about fifty miles from here but the people are so much different and they are interested in such a different kind of things until it seems like a different world to me. I guess that the main difference is that it is "home" and this is not. I couldn't explain it well enough for you to understand the main difference in the two communities so I won't try.

Friday night I went to hear the John Daniel Quartet put on a variety show at the school auditorium. They sing over W.M.S. on the Grand Old Opery program. However, I had never heard them because I can't endure the "Grand old opera". They sure were good. In fact it was the best program of the kind that I have ever attended. They sang Gospel songs, spirituals, gave musical readings, instrumental numbers and had some jokes. Usually the jokes are a bit on the vulgar side but these were not and I just enjoyed the program thoroughly.

Sunday, we had our regular singing convention. That is the next best thing to Heaven to me. Singers come from every where and we sing all day and have dinner on the grounds. I enjoy myself so much until the hours seem like seconds to me. I've been going all over South Alabama and all of this section of Florida for years to these affairs. The best people in the world are there (along with some of the worst) and I sure like to be with them. Maybe some day you can attend one and you'll know what I am talking about.

I've really been working for the last few days. I've planted our garden and done a lot of work around the place besides this job of teaching. I hope to have some peas, beans, tomatoes, corn etc. to eat this summer. I really like to make a garden.

I have some tiny biddies that I hope to convert into fried chicken before too long. I sure like fried chicken. In fact I just like all kinds of good things to eat too well as you can see by my size. I also like to cook too. If I ever do get Frank back home I am really going to feed him and doctor him up and get him well.

I got a letter from a fellow that has been with Frank all the way until last February. He was sent back to the States for Hospitalization. I have gotten letters from about a dozen fellows like that. When they get back to the States they always write. I'm always glad to get their letters even though they don't tell me any thing of any importance. This fellow said that if there is any thing that I want to know to write and ask so he is really going to get some questions as soon as I can get them ready.

I'm always glad to hear from you and I'll try not to wait so long to answer your next letter. I'll try to write often if I can possibly find time.

By the way this fellow that I got this letter from called Frank "Jeff" of all the names. I can easily figure out how that came about. You see his initials are J. F. and they shortened it to "Jeff." I think it is sort of cute.

Sincerely your Sis,
Mamie Lou

April 13–

Dear Paul,

Friday the thirteenth—good thing I'm not superstious. I have no complaints for it's been a wonderful day. I can say that my arm is becoming a wee bit sore for one of my brutal classmates gave me a typhoid vaccination today. Of course, I had to repay her and did we make each other suffer! The needles seemed a bit too dull.

I was out to Fort Barrancas yesterday to give Typhoid shots to the school pupils there. One of the schools out of town burned so they're using five of the empty barracks on that field for schooling purposes. We made two home visits on Mainside. I'm really learning what Public Health work includes in it's program.

I recalled many pleasant memories when we drove passed the Hospital on Mainside. It seems that those things happened only yesterday and yet they're an event of the past. It's very nice to remember our many experiences, some of which shall live on forever.

The girls keep coming into my room and are continually disturbing me. I don't mind too much for it's very quiet when I'm alone. My room mate is on the opposite shift so we never see each other except occasionally for only a few minutes.

I saw "Keys Of The Kingdom" Thursday night and it was really a grand picture. It's of a religious type so you would probably enjoy it.

It was certainly a shock to me and everyone else I suppose to hear of the President's death Thursday. He was really a great man and one whom it will be hard to replace. This is the day of the funeral services so all of the places of business are closed.

Are you still reading very much? Very good way of improving your education. Of course, I don't care much about reading unless I have a lot of extra time with nothing else to do.

I'm very sleepy so I'll hush and sleep a bit.

Love always,
Evelyn

April 15,

Dear Paul,

Received two letters from you yesterday which made me very happy. I'm glad to know that you finally received the Christmas packages after so many months. They must have circled the globe several times. Oh yes, I'm glad that you like the bracelet and I wish you could wear it. Aren't you allowed to wear jewelry? I suppose it's more or less in the way for the type of work you do. I would have had something printed on the back of the plate, but I didn't have time to wait for them to engrave it. Maybe I can have that done some time in the future. I'll just bet you really enjoyed the fruit cake and all the trimmings too. Your Mother will be glad to hear that you've received it for she probably knows the kind of food you like best.

Have had quite a time since I began this letter. Smitty's friend was out so they wanted me to go along with them down town. I felt as though I was an intruder, but I joined them. We walked to town and first of all we stopped in at the Dainty and had a steak dinner. It was very good, but I've been so uncomfortable for I must have eaten too much. Our next stop was the movie, "Circumstantial Evidence" which was a mistery so I'll probably have fearful dreams tonight. I don't like unpleasant dreams for they interfere with my dreams of you. After the movie, we went to the Palafox U.S.O. There wasn't much doing for we weren't allowed to dance because of the mourning of the death of our President. He was worth many sacrifices of which that is only a very minor.

I'm glad Jimmie wrote you. He seldom writes me or any of the other family members. Of course, I know he likes you very much, but it's rather surprising that he wrote. He hasn't written me for months. I suppose he's been quite busy making his plans for the future family.

I bought a beautiful evening gown last week. I needed one for the Doctor's dance will be during next month and I don't have an old one that would do for the occasion. We had to pay $16—for a very small class pin, but it is nice. Personally, I don't understand why it should be worth so much. Even so, I'm proud of it.

Frank isn't on the same Island any longer and he's a bit nearer the States. We're hoping to see him soon. Mamie is so thrilled over the idea. I really wouldn't know how I would act if I thought you were on your way home. I do know I would be very happy. The day you arrive in the States again will be the happiest day of my life time.

That was a very sweet letter your Mother wrote you on your birthday. I'll bet that is a day she'll never forget and I can well understand why she will remember it. There could be several reasons. That was probably a very happy day for her and your Father.

So Pauline thinks that married life is a bit difficult for the first year. I've heard a number of people make the same statement and I think they're correct for there's so much adjusting and a very special understanding of each other which takes place during that time. I'm merely judging from the actions of other people for you know no personal experience is involved. It just happens that my type work includes a number of personal problems of others. Maybe I can tell you more about that in the future when we know our own experiences of married life. I know Pauline will discover some means of solving her problems. Then maybe she can give us some advise.

I'm becoming very sleepy for it's rather late now; in fact, it's midnight at the present. Just because you only have cold water, you shouldn't try shaving so often during each day. Good-night and sweet dreams.

Love always,
Evelyn

April 17–

Dear Paul,

Just returned home from a double-feature movie. You know, the Strand Theater's specialty. I enjoyed both pictures, but did feel a bit numb in spots when I left the theater.

I received a letter from you today and as you already know your letters are very welcome. I always re-read them for I don't want to miss any part of them. I'm wondering what I said that made you so angry at me. I've worried about it ever since I received your letter. I'm very sorry and I surely didn't intend to offend you in any-way. Please tell me what this is all about.

It rained practically all day and we had to visit three colored schools this morning. I can't describe my appearance, but I know that I was a sight for "sore" eyes. We'll probably make a visit to a school that's about twenty miles out tomor-row. I enjoy those trips and it's such hard work you know.

Phiel received a letter from Ernest Sinclair today. He is now at Camp Lejeune, North Carolina and is expecting to be sent overseas soon. You may have a chance to see him again.

The girls are getting dressed for duty. I'm certainly glad that I'm not on the night shift for it takes all my energy and leaves me feeling in the "dumps" most of the time.

I had another letter from Bennett and she still enjoys Army life. I haven't heard from Nellie in ages and just wonder what has happened to her. Hope she's enjoying service life too.

I'm glad you like the Island where you are stationed at the present. Hope you're well & happy as possible—

Love always,
Evelyn

April 19–

Dear Paul,

I have just returned from a movie, "Thunderhead," a horse story as you know, but it was rather interesting. Kelly was along with me and did she make a favorable comment of you! I don't really think that I should tell you for you never let me in on anything my Mother writes you. You only say enough to arouse my curiosity. Kelly said that you were the nicest and sweetest boy she has ever known. She also said that you seemed very much like a brother and that she has missed you almost as much as I which is a very, very broad statement. I don't believe she realizes just how much I miss you. This conversation was during dinner after the movie. Oh yes, we had quite a conversation of you and I'll bet your ears were certainly burning at that time. You're always with me for I carry a visual picture of you in my mind constantly. You must feel haunted at times.

My room mate and I are in the kitchen—she at one side of the table and I'm on the other side. She is also writing a letter to the boy to whom she is engaged. We've just made some coffee for it's nice to have something to drink, especially during the time of writing a letter. Margaret makes very good coffee.

I was out to Fort Barrancas and Mainside again today—poor kids! I'm afraid they'll dislike me if I continue visiting their school and giving them Typhoid shots. Of course, they have my sympathy.

I'm so glad that your Uncle is home and your brother is on his way home. It's a coincidence that both are returning to the States about the same time. I know they're so happy to be back and your Mother must be very much excited. I too, shall be very excited and happy when you return.

Sister hasn't yet set a date for our graduation so we only know that it will be during next month. Even though you're many miles away, you shall still be with me on that day. I'd like so very much for you to be present, but I know that would be impossible.

Glad you're receiving my letters more regularly. Good-night & sweet dreams.

Love, Evelyn

April 21–

Dear Paul,

Most of the girls have gone out already and it's only about five o'clock in the afternoon. The remainder of them will probably have dates tonight. They asked me to accompany them, but I prefer staying home. The main reason is that I've had a severe headache all day which is the effects of the Typhoid shot yesterday. I will take my third shot next Friday that will complete the series. I'm glad this doesn't continue indefinitely.

Received two letters from you today and you seem to be quite pleased with your present location. I'm glad you're at a base that you like and it will be so wonderful if your brother is sent there also. Maybe he would enjoy having his youngest brother as nurse-maid! You know, I've always taken care of Elizabeth except for the number of times she took care of me. Don't worry, for she usually won. I can truthfully say that we never had an argument. She is very agreeable most of the time, although she is stubborn occasionally.

I'm sitting on the porch at the present and there seems to be so much traffic. The children are playing base-ball in the park and seem to be having so much fun. Reminds me of my school days when I took an interest in the various sports. As you know, I've never learned to bowl and I think that's such an interesting game.

Haven't I told you not to think of "red-heads" so often? If you continue, your hair may even change to red some day and I would surely have to dye it another color. May even have to bleach it. And don't keep reminding me that we'll have red-haired children for they will be blondes and brunettes. That would be much nicer, don't you think?

You may send me three or four of your watches and let me try dropping them on the floor. My watch doesn't seem to want to "tick" after having been dropped on the floor for the sixth time. I'm a bit too careless, don't you think? It only cost fifteen dollars every time I take it to be repaired. I could have bought a new watch already with the money I've paid for repair of this one.

We've had wonderful weather for the past few days. At the present, it's very cloudy and looks as if it may rain tonight, but I don't mind because

I can enjoy my sleep more when it's raining. You know, your getting soaked in the rain so often when it isn't necessary, isn't too good for you.

Two Lieutenants have just arrived and of course, I seem to be the entertainer until the girls finish dressing. One of them is trying to complete the letter for me, but I don't trust anyone to write my letters, especially yours.

The Public Health Department isn't open on Sundays so we relieve the Supervisors at the Hospital on that day. I will be in charge of the pediatric department tomorrow and those children just drive you "nuts." Maybe I'll survive the day.

Have you heard from your Mother recently? I haven't, but I know that she must be so excited about your brother and Uncle's coming home that she hasn't had time for writing. I hope Pauline is more adjusted to married life and doesn't find it quite so difficult now.

It's really wonderful to receive your letters so regularly again. I know that you're rather bored by now so I'll hush.

All my Love,
Evelyn

April 24–

Dear Paul,

We received our graduation uniforms today and it's a wonderful feeling to know that we shall wear them soon. The graduation exercises will be the sixteenth of May unless Sister changes her mind again. They say that's a woman's privilege and Sister really takes advantage of the opportunity. We will probably graduate at the new nurse's home instead of the Sacred Heart Church. I don't suppose our class rates so highly as the previous classes. As soon as I receive my invitations, I'll send you one that you may keep in your scrap book. The only present I want from you is for you to return to the States as soon as possible. That will be the greatest of all. I shall miss your presence very much that day, but I'll be thinking of you all the time. I would become very lonesome without the nice thoughts of you. I do wish your Mother and Pauline could be here at that time.

We visited all the clinics today—Tuberculosis' Sanitorium, Gulf Coast Medical Center which are the Venereal diseased patients, Crippled Children's Home and the Orphan's Home. Some day! And I enjoyed the trip very much. The Supervisor left us at a movie downtown. Of course, we weren't supposed to be there of all places in uniform. If Sister could only have seen us there, she probably would have sent us home for the duration including the extra six months.

Received a letter from Iris yesterday and I can see where I would have quite some trouble with you two if you were still at Mainside. I'm sending the letter along just in case you would like to read it.

Also received a letter from Bennett and she has mailed you a letter. You've probably received it already. Just don't try to get her to tell you too much when you answer.

I'm very sleepy so I'll say "Good-night until tomorrow—

Love Always,
Evelyn

[This typed, green-colored letter from Evelyn's cousin, Iris, is included with above letter to Paul.]

U. S. NAVAL AIR TRAINING CENTER
PENSACOLA, FLORIDA
April 18, 1945

Dear Evenlyn,

I guess you will be surprised to get a letter from me. Well I have nothing else to do this morning so I'll take it out on you.

How is everything at the Hospital? Are you still in the Operating Room? Have you heard any more about being drafted? Gosh! I hope you won't be.

When did you hear from Paul last? I look at every Marine twice down here trying to make Paul out of one of them but every time I get dissappointed. Tell him he will have to get transfered back down here and then he can go to lunch with me every day and you can't do any thing about it. That's a laugh isn't it. What is his last name which will soon be yours too?

I am working at the Navy Yard now. I am doing Clerk Typist work. I like it fine. I have only worked one-&-one-half weeks. Have'nt even been paid yet. That's what I look forward to and Sunday when I can sleep. I have been up ever since 3:30 this morning. Mama was sick and she came in called me and told me that it was 4:30 and I got up dressed and waited for Jesse for half and hour and looked at the clock and it was only 5:00.

Was there much to the Dediacation of the Nurses' Home? Did they have a dance?

Brit Gainey has been reported missing in action. Mrs. Gainey is about to go crazy. He was in Patton's Army and is probably dead.

Buddy Ira and Buddy Willie were home three weeks ago last Sunday. Buddy Ira looks bad. He has been having trouble with his stomach. Buddy Willie is fine. He is so fat.

How did the girl's face turn out that plastic surgery? I would like to see her now.

When do you think you will get to come home again? Tell Paul hello for me.

Well it (rest of the letter is written) is time for me to go to work. Had a slip up on bottom of this letter. Ha!

Love
Iris

I am sending you a picture. Hope it doesn't scare you to death. I still have the one you don't like of yourself in my album and will leave it there until you send me another. I am a little late mailing this but it is just old "forgetfull" me.

Sign Off.

Pvt. Iris Wells

April 26–

Dear Paul,

Haven't had a letter from you for four days and I miss hearing from you. The first thing I do each afternoon is run into the house to see if I received a letter from you and I'm always so happy when I receive one.

My room mate is dressing for duty; in fact, it's about time she was at the Hospital. Pitts was just in and she also will go on duty at three o'clock. I'm taking a vacation so you see, I'm a privileged character. I did report on duty at the Public Health Department this morning and just because I became a wee bit pale and uncomfortable, my Supervisor escorted me home. She even wanted to put me to bed, but that wasn't necessary. I feel fine this afternoon so you see, there was no need of her bringing me home. The first time that has happened.

I don't know what to do about getting graduation shoes. The girls have searched the stores in town and haven't found any nurse's shoes. You send me a pair of your shoes or maybe I could even wear bed-room slippers. That would be very professional, don't you think?

I'm supposed to have Saturday off so I've planned to go over home that day. I haven't been over for a number of days for I don't have much time off duty. We have long hours, but I like Public Health work very much.

Don't get involved in anymore arguments for I wont you to return in one piece. How are your fingers? Have they healed yet? You must learn to take better care of yourself.

School classes must be finished for the day as a number of kids are passing on the streets. They're such noisy brats. Of course, I didn't realize that when I was in school. Now, I can understand why the teacher scolded us so often.

It's so very hot today and the slight breeze that's coming in the windows is very much appreciated. This time last year I was at Chattahoochee and you came over for the week-end. I shall never forget how much Pheil and Hodges embarraced me that night. I know you felt the same.

I haven't heard from Elizabeth and J. C. for quite a while. They surely don't believe in writing very often. Have you heard from them recently?

The day has seemed so long and I don't know what to do with the extra hours. I'm not in the mood for studying, so I suppose I'll answer some letters that I've neglected.

I promise to have my picture made one day next week. As you know, it will be some time later before I can get the enlargement. It usually takes about four weeks, but I'll send one as soon as possible.

Hope that you're well. I think of you continuously and love you very much.

Love,
Evelyn.

April 28–

Dear Paul,

I'm home for the day and I'm enjoying the quietness of the surroundings. I came over with Mr. Myers last night and will have to return to Pensacola tonight.

Frank was on the Hawaii Islands, but is at a Hospital in San Francisco at the present. He has been having some trouble with his back and having a number of day's rest, I think will help him very much. I'm very glad that he's in the States again and Mamie is just thrilled beyond words. Mother is also very happy.

I believe you must have been near him before he left for the States. That Island must be very beautiful from the many things you have said about it. Wish I were with you, but since you prefer my waiting in the States, that's where I shall wait for you—I hope that you will want to be married as soon as you return.

Mother is busy some where in the house— It's a wonder that she isn't playing with her cats and dogs. They are very cute. You should see them.

I've been making a list of the people to whom I'm sending an invitation. I'm not sending many of my relatives an invitation because I only know very few of them; in fact, I've never seen a great number of my Mother's people. I've just heard her talk of them and there's quite a large family.

Mr. Myers has a nice little boat and it surely looks inviting. I would like to go fishing or even boat riding. Maybe we will do that when you return. I've never been fishing much and when I did go, I always caught very small fish. I hope you're good at catching them, but then, I know you must be.

I will be on Public Health for another week and then I will be assigned to Children's Ward. I don't like to care for children unless they're nice and healthy. Most of the ones in Children's Ward are deformed, undernourished, etc. I do like the nursery very much so I would like to go there again.

It's becoming very cloudy and looks as if it may rain in a few hours. I hope that it doesn't begin raining until after I've reached Pensacola for I don't enjoy going any place in the rain unless I'm with you. Remember how it rained at Panama City that day?

Mother wants me to go visit one of our neighbors who is a nice friend of the family. Hope that I've received a letter from you today.

All my Love,
Evelyn

April 29–
Sunday P.M.

Dear Paul,

I just lay on my bed and tried to go to sleep, but I began thinking about you and of course, I couldn't sleep. It's one-thirty o'clock and I have to report on duty at three o'clock. I'm relieving one of the Supervisors on St. Vincent's Hall— three-to-eleven shift. Smitty is also working the same shift today so in order to keep from walking over to the Hospital for lunch, we just went around the corner to a small store and bought some food. Of course, the cooking wasn't so good as that at the Hospital, but we enjoyed it much more. We're going to become good cooks yet if we continue the practice!

Oh! But did it rain last night! I came to Pensacola on the Bay Line bus and I was beginning to think that we needed a motor boat instead of a bus. The streets resembled lakes so you can imagine how much rain we had.

I wrote you a letter yesterday at home, but it rained so much and so hard that I didn't get anywhere near a post office so I'll mail it along with this letter today.

Today is wonderful—nice for a hike. The sun is shining so very brightly and there is a nice breeze—all the girls must have gone places unless they're on duty for it's very quiet. Smitty and her boy friend, Smitty are next door in the sitting room so I can hear them laugh at times. She says that she's in love with this boy Smitty and they plan to be married in the future. The only thing she doesn't approve of is that his name is Smith too and she doesn't want to have that name the remainder of her lifetime. I'm glad our names aren't the same for I prefer the name "Fogel," don't you?

You know, Mother told me yesterday before I left that she would be the happiest Mother in the world when her other son came from overseas. She calls you her son too, so all the boys are back except you.

I'll let you take a rest now. Remember that I love you very much—

Love,
Evelyn

May 1–

Dear Paul,

Have just returned home from duty to find that I didn't receive a letter from you again today. I can't help but wander why you haven't written. You must be on your way to another Island, but I hope not for I wish your next move would be to the States.

It is almost sun-down and seems as if it were Autumn except for the beautiful Spring flowers. Since the heavy rain Sunday night, we've had rather cool, comfortable weather. Maybe we won't have such hot weather this Summer which would be wonderful.

I took another Typhoid shot today and my arm is becoming very sore and red. This is the last of my series so I don't have to take another until next year. We visited one of the schools today and gave about five-hundred Typhoid shots.

I haven't heard anymore from Frank. He is to be sent to a Hospital near here soon. I would like very much to see him and I know that he wants to come home. Jimmie and Elizabeth have probably been to see him for he is at San Francisco.

I saw Iris during the week-end and she invited me to a "fish-fry" Sunday night, but I had to return to Pensacola so I couldn't attend. A number of boys from Eglin Field were there including her boy friend.

Do you know if your brother has been home yet? I hope so for he has been overseas so long. Wander where he'll be stationed after his furlough.

Had a card from Bennett and she has been transferred to a field in Georgia. I hope that she likes the place for that will make her work more interesting and enjoyable. Did you receive her letter yet?

I do hope that I receive a letter from you tomorrow—

Love always,
Evelyn

May 3–

Dear Paul,

Received two letters from you today and were they more than welcome! I was becoming more anxious by the day to hear from you for I'm always so happy to get a letter.

I haven't had any sleep since night before last as I was on a special duty case last night and worked at Public Health today. We were out to Fort Barrancas and Naval Air Station again which was our last visit there. I enjoyed the trips there for I recalled many pleasant memories each time.

It seems that every time you have liberty, it rains. I thought I was the only one who had such luck. You seem to enjoy your strolls through the town and I can imagine it must be rather interesting.

So you did receive the letter from our Lieutenant friend. I told you that you could expect one for she said when she left that she was going to write you and let you in on every-thing—did she? She doesn't know as much about me as you do.

The entire class is so upset about our grad-uation. Frankly, I believe that it's going to be a "flop," but I hope that I'm mistaken. Nothing has happened the way that we had intended. Sister Theodora is in retreat and will remain the same until time for our graduation if not longer. You see, we have no one to instruct our practice for the graduation exercises. It will cost each of us at least one-hundred dollars just to graduate and pay our State Board fees.

My eyes are beginning to burn and I'm sleepy, but I promised Jancsik that I would go along with her to town so I'll keep my promise.

I'm sorry that your jacket was stolen. It's too bad that there is a great number of people who can't live above the act of swiping other people's possessions.

Who is Wayne? Is he in service and is he stationed near here? You tell me about him.

Well, I'll say "so-long" until later. Hope that you're well and happy—

Love Always,
Evelyn.

P.S. Pheil just came in and she says "hello."

May 5–

Dear Paul,

I'm on special duty with a patient and I'm very sleepy as it is midnight and past my usual bed-time. The patient is sleeping soundly at the present and do I envy her of her privilege! I'll probably join her in dreamland within the next few minutes. There is one woman in this ward that doesn't look as though she'll survive much longer. Some of the other patients are very noisy so I am very thankful that I have a nice patient. The nursery is next door and the babies test their lung power all night. I believe some of them can even cry louder than I so you can imagine the noise. I don't understand how the patients have any rest at all. I've been doing double shifts (16 hrs.) each day for the past four days and slowly becoming a physical "wreck."

Mamie left day before yesterday for Oklahoma as that is where Frank was sent. He called her long distance and was she thrilled to hear his voice again! I'm so glad that she has gone to join him for I know that he'll be so very happy to be with her again. I did think that perhaps he would have been sent nearer home. I surely would like to see him and wish that he were able to attend my graduation. You know, he left the States just before I entered training.

I just wander if your brother has reached home yet? I do hope so. I'll certainly be glad when his youngest brother returns and I had better know the minute he arrives.

My patient has promised me a shoe stamp and I can surely use an extra one. I had to use one of my stamps for some nurse's oxfords which made me short on other shoes. Don't be surprised if I'm walking about in bed-room slippers when you return.

I don't know why I haven't been receiving your letters recently for I seldom hear from you. I do miss your letters very much.

I just bought my invitations today so I'll send you one.

I'm going to say "good-night" before I fall asleep.

Love Always,
Evelyn

P.S. I saw a number of the purple heart boys of the fourth Marine division the other night down town.

[From Paul's friend; on United States Marine Corps stationery, with emblem.]

> Replacement Battalion,
> Transient Center,
> Fleet Marine Force, Pacific,
> c/o Fleet Post Office
> San Francisco, Calif.
> May 6, 1945

Dear Paul;

I know this letter is going to be a surprise to you, but I read your last letter to Jake & told him not to say any thing about seeing me here. I guess from my address you should know where we all are, for no doubt you came through here too. I've been here for almost two months now, and for the past couple of weeks I have been standing by for transfer. I know the name of the outfit I'm going to, & I'm sure you understand censorship regulations well enough to know that I cant tell you.

However I'm not coming to your outfit or Kofferl's. Black went on tentative transfer today but of course we dont know how long he will hang around either. Maybe you have already noticed my initials on Jake's last letter to you. If you haven't take a look at the envelope and you will see that I was the censor that passed his letter to you. I was going to put my letter in with his, but I had already initialed the envelope so I couldnt put my letter in, because we cant censor our own mail. I know you have already received Jake's letter because he sent his airmail and I'm to cheap so I'll send mine free.

Say Paul I was awfully glad to hear that you came through the two campaign OK, that was quite a rugged battle from what I've heard and read about it. I hope you have that kind of luck all the time you're out here. Dont you wish you were back in Pensacola driving and to have a date with Evelyn in the evening. I know you do. From all the dope I've got on Pensacola it is not the same place, they have a new C O and I understand he has made many changes for the worse.

Yes, Margaret & Johnnie are now in New York, both are fine, but like myself, they're lonesome. If you're interested her address is: 25-50 23rd Street, Long Island City "2," N.Y. If you want, drop her a line, I'm sure that she would be very happy to hear from you. Say Paul, I came darned near joining your division, my whole draft joined your outfit but I was left behind. If you get a chance in the next couple of days look up a QM—Sgt. Robert E. Seng in Headquarters Company, 3rd Battalion, 25th Marines, give him my address & tell him I wrote to him on April 23rd but since at that time I didn't know his full address I just addressed it to 4th Division.

He is a darned nice guy so be sure to see him and give him my regards. I hope by now he has received my letter. I dont know how far apart your outfits may be but if it would be to inconvenient just forget it.

Paul that is all I'm going to write for just now, how about a few lines from you. I'm OK and hope you are the same. Take care of yourself and best of Luck to you. Margaret & Johnnie wanted to send best regards to you if I ever saw you, so you can consider it done in this letter since I dont think I'll get to see you. So Long now & write when you get a chance.

Always,

Joe.

QM—Sgt. Joseph Z. Maceluch, (251600) U.S.M.C.

May 7–

Dear Paul,

Just wandering why I haven't heard from you recently. The last letter was dated the twenty-third of last month. I do hope and pray that you're alright.

I have just reported off duty and it seems so good just to sit for awhile. I'm working in Children's Ward now and do those youngsters keep me busy! I'd much rather care for adults.

Have all my invitations addressed and ready to be mailed. My mouth was rather dry after having stamped and sealed all my invitations. I suppose that only Mother and Mr. Myers will represent my family. I do wish the whole family could attend. Most of all, I wish you could be present.

The Sisters of Charity

and the 1945 Graduating Class

of the

Pensacola Hospital School of Nursing

cordially invite you to attend the

Commencement Exercises

Wednesday, May sixteenth

Nineteen hundred and forty-five

Nurses Residence

Five P. M.

Miss Mary Evelyn Wells

Did I tell you that Bennett has been transferred? She was sent to a base near Atlanta, Georgia. I must write her again before she begins to think that I've forgotton her. She is a very nice girl, but she talks too much at times. (so do I) I miss having her around to go places with me.

We've had cool weather most of the Spring so far and I wouldn't mind if it continued so. Today is beautiful for there's a nice breeze which makes it comfortable weather.

I had a letter from Clara & David and they sent along two pictures of Ronnie. He's just precious and has grown so very much. He looks like a perfect specimen of health. David is still stationed in Kansas, but thinks perhaps he'll be sent overseas soon. I do hope that he remains in the States for Clara will have another baby in a short while.

I'll have to run down town and see if I can find some Nurse's oxfords for graduation.

Let me know if you're alright. I love you very much—

Love,
Evelyn

May 9–

Dear Paul,

I received three letters from you yesterday. It's just a good thing that I received them for you were driving me "nutty" as I hadn't heard from you for some time. I can hardly wait 'till I get home each afternoon to see if I have a letter from you.

You must have had lots of fun spear fishing and I believe that I would enjoy that too. I don't know as I would care to make a living at it. Some experience, I suppose. Are the fish very different from ours?

I was off duty a bit early this afternoon for we had intended to have a class meeting. Most of the class was not present so we didn't come to any conclusions about graduation.

Children's Ward is driving me "nutty" and I'm beginning to think that I'd never care to have any children. Maybe I would have a different opinion if I didn't have to care for so many at once. I enjoyed caring for the new-born babies in the nursery, but that's quite different from Children's Ward. I'll be glad when I'm transferred to another service.

I have tomorrow off so I think I'll go over home for the night. I was just over one day last week, but I don't suppose Mother will mind too much if I come over again so soon.

Had another letter from Iris today. She must not have much to do for she writes letters during her duty hours. That's very nice so long as she can continue and not be called down about it. I told her that I was going to dye my hair red and she said that she would "ring my neck" if I did. Of course, I wanted to please you so don't be surprised if I have red hair when you return.

Haven't heard from Mamie since she left, but she has probably written to Mother.

I will have to get dressed in a hurry if I go along with Mr. Myers this afternoon.

All my Love,
Evelyn

May 12–

Dear Paul,

I'm writing this letter with one eye half open and the other one closed. Well, isn't quite that bad, but I'm very sleepy. The girls just wan't give me a chance to rest. I've been doing double shifts, sixteen hours, for the past three days with an eight-hour break. I came in at three this afternoon and had my bath and then tried to sleep. First of all, one of the girls awakened me for a phone call; Then I awakened with one girl patting me on the cheek and wanting me to go along to town with her. Last, and the tops of all, Pat came in and said that I would have to intertain a couple of her friends tonight until she returned from the movies. I'm afraid she's going to be disappointed for even my best friends wouldn't care to be with me at the present.

It's so very warm for there is so little breeze. The cool weather seems to have finally ceased. We had wonderful weather for a long while.

I will not have completed my three-year training course until August even though I do graduate this month. I still don't know what to do until you return. I suppose I'll find something to do.

You're getting in more schooling than I. You can understand why I nearly fell asleep during all our "long-winded" lectures. We aren't having classes any longer, but we are reviewing for State Board Exams, for next month. It seems that I've been to school all my lifetime and really I have except for the first five years. I'm merely complaining, not bragging for I feel as though it's about time I should take a rest from studies.

The girls are having a beach party next Thursday for the Seniors. We'll probably have lots of fun and I haven't been on the beach this year. I'll never forget the weinner roast we had last Summer when you did all the roasting. Had lots of fun.

You seem to be having a nice time and I surely hope so for you deserve it. Just wish I were there with you which would make me very happy. I would also like to go spear fishing if I wouldn't get "banged-up" so against the rocks.

Smitty received her engagement ring today and seems to be as thrilled as I. Well, probably not quite so much as I, but she is very happy to be engaged. She doesn't plan to be married until she's completed her training which will be next February. She will graduate with me, but I came in training six months before she entered. Hope you return to the States before next February, but if not, maybe we can have a double wedding. Smitty and I prepared supper one afternoon and during the time we were eating she began talking about getting married. Then she said that we would have to live in the same house and prepare our meals together. She says she enjoys eating with me so much and I can't understand why.

Received a letter from you today and I'm always happy to hear from you and look forward to each letter.

All my Love,
Evelyn

May 14–

Dear Paul,

Check and I have just returned from Toronto's Drug Store and I'm so full of ice cream that I'm miserable. The first good ice cream I've had in months and did we take advantage of the opportunity of eating it! Wish I could have sent you some but I'm afraid it might become a bit soft by the time it would reach you.

At the present Check is on my roommate's bed, reading some magazines while I amuse myself by writing you which is the best amusement I've had yet. Some of the other girls are preparing supper in the kitchen. Pheil was just in and wants me to go along with her to town, but Check is waiting for me to finish this letter so I'll go along with her. I don't really care to go any place, but try and get out of it.

Hit the "jack-pot" today with four letters. Had a letter from Mamie, Mother, you and Bennett. Of course, yours was the most welcome so I read it first. Bennett said she didn't know what to get me for a graduation present so she sent me $5.00 instead and wants me to tell her what I buy with it. That was very nice of her, don't you think? She also sent Smitty the same for you know, we three have been good friends all during training. Bennett said she was very glad to receive your letter.

I do hope that Charles will be in California long enough to visit Elizabeth & J. C. I'm sure they would be very glad to meet him and so would Jimmie & Doris. Wish I could meet him too for I know he's very nice since he's your brother.

We haven't yet practiced for graduation and aren't going to until noon Wednesday and the graduation is at five o'clock that day—I just know that it's going to be a big "flop." I'm sorry that you want be here and wish very much that you could be, but I'm afraid that you would be disappointed in the graduation exercises if you were here.

I was on special duty with a patient for three nights. His nephew was in during that time and had just returned to the States from Iwo Jima. He was in the fifth Marine division so I told him about you. I enjoyed talking with him.

I'm sending Mamie's letter for I thought that you might like to read it.

All my Love,
Evelyn

[Evelyn included this letter with the one above; from Mamie-Lou, her sister-in-law, married to her brother Frank. Written on USO letterhead.]

Norman, Okla.
May 11, 1945

Dear Susie Q,

I guess you know by now that I'm the happiest gal in the whole world. I arrived here last Saturday noon and I've been in Heaven ever since. Frank got weekend liberty when I got here and then Monday P.M he got 48 hrs. special liberty. It still seems too good to be true.

Clara Lee & David came I think it was Tuesday night and they left this A.M. (Fri.) You can bet that we were really glad to see them. It did Frank a world of good to see David and I could hardly keep from crying I was so happy to see them walking down the street together.

That Ronnie is sure mean but he is so cute and sweet until I just love him to death. He has a mouth full of teeth and can talk real well and run all over the place. I can't realize that he is so large.

Frank is getting along fine. He looks exactly like he did when he left home and his nerves are as calm as mine. He just can't stand or walk very much. He doesn't know how long he will be here but not long. He thinks that he may get transfered next week. He thinks that we will go to Pensacola Naval Hosp. I sure do hope that he can for that will be his only chance of going home. He won't get a leave until he is able to leave the hospital but if he gets to Pensacola he can get special liberty to go home etc. He will be kept in the hospital for about four or six months and then he hopes to get a discharge.

Tell Paul that I am mighty happy but that I think of him often. I would write but I was so excited when I left home I forgot to get his address. There were a group of Iwo Jima causualties brought into this hosp—a few days ago. I don't suppose any one of them could tell me about Paul though.

I can go to see Frank from 2:00 to 4:00 on the days that he can't come out. That is wonderful.

We hope to be there for your grad. Pray that we won't get disappointed.

Love Always,
Mamie

May 16–

Dear Paul,

Well, it's almost four o'clock now and we are to graduate at five. We aren't excited at all because it isn't going to be the type of graduation we have looked forward to since the day we entered training. We haven't practiced at all until today and have spent most of today for that purpose. To top it off, it has just poured rain today and is still very cloudy. We would probably have looked like "drips" anyway. So much for graduation, but we're so disappointed. The main thing that I look forward to, hasn't come to pass yet and that's your arrival to the States again. Then I'll really be happy.

Received a letter from you today along with some cards of congratulations. Received two beautiful cards from your Mother and Pauline— Elizabeth and J. C. wrote a long letter and mailed with their card. They are so precious.

That was very nice of you to send my Mother a "Mother's Day" card. I know that she appreciated it very much for she speaks of you as her son anyway. She was telling me about the last letter you wrote her and she seemed quite thrilled about some of the things you said. I think you two should let me in on what you write to each other.

I really shouldn't have taken the time to write a letter just now, but I wanted you to know that I'm thinking of you even when I'm very busy. I'll hush and get dressed.

Love Always,
Evelyn

Evelyn Wells' Graduate Nursing Class, June 1945
(she is seated 2nd from left)

[Evelyn included this letter from Elizabeth, her sister, with the one above.]

Wednesday–

Dear "Sooky,"

It has been about two weeks since we received your letter, so I suppose I'd better write "at you" again. J. C. said he is going to write to you, but when—I don't know. He stays so busy all the time that he has little time to write or to do any of the things he'd like to do.

I surely got a laugh off him this morning. He said that when he started out to catch a bus to go to the Base last night about eleven-thirty, he suddenly heard a loud flapping of wings and the next instant the big bird squawked about three or four times just above his head. That startled him so that he said he could feel his hair slowly rising. About that time, he was passing a concrete porch to a trailer and someone scraped his feet on the porch and J. C. almost took off. He said that he would have disliked having the trailer people see him running, but if that bird had touched his head which it almost did, that's exactly what he would have done.

We are still having a lot of fun together (we & Jimmie & Doris). We go a lot of places together. We went up in the mountains one Sunday where there was a lot of snow. We took quite a few pictures and some of them are pretty good. I'll have some made and send to you and the others.

Doris is expecting her baby about the last week in July, and Emma wrote that Clara is also—a coincidence, don't you think? They just gave Doris her shower early so she wouldn't buy a lot of unnecessary things. She received quite an assortment and so many pretty little things.

By the way, they played some games at the shower. One thing they did was to tell the most embarrassing experiences of their lives. Of course, I couldn't tell them, but I could see us in Bay Front Park in Miami, in the front room at home, you in your night gown on the front door step, etc.; so when it was my time which was shortly after the beginning of the game, I said that I had had plenty of embarrassing experiences, but none of them would do to tell ha. I just didn't tell one.

One woman told the funniest thing that happened to her. She said that she and her husband went to an Easter program and took a friend's two children—a boy and a girl. They were very interested in the program when suddenly they missed the little boy. They noticed that the people in the seats ahead were turning their legs as if to let something pass. They found the little boy crawling around everyone's feet and pulled him out. Then the little girl wanted to stand so that she could see. Just ahead of her was a lady with a "crazy" little hat perched "just so" on her head. The child suddenly put a hand on each side of the hat, lifted it in the air, and then set it back on the lady's head. Then the little girl looked at her and said, "Goody, you can't whip me here!" out big and loud. By that time she was almost embarrassed to tears, so she got up and started out. She was bent over guiding the child out and didn't notice that her hat pin had caught in the crepe paper decorations. When she got outside, she felt a pull and noticed that she had a long trail of decorations behind her. She said that she had never been back to that place since. Quite an experience, eh? She said she thought her face burned for hours.

Young lady, you didn't tell us what to get for your graduation, and we don't know anything to get. You'd better tell us or <u>we won't get you anything</u>. When's the graduation date?

Do you hear from Paul regularly now? How is he? J. C. and I both wrote to him quite sometime ago, but haven't heard from him. Perhaps he never received our letters.

Poor Frank! He surely is having a time. Are you writing to him, Sooky? If you aren't try to write him a note now and then. I know that letters from home mean a lot to boys overseas, and I imagine he needs something to cheer him up.

Well, I must quit and get in bed. Give my best wishes to the girls and to Bennett when you write to her.

Love
Your Sis

May 19–

Dear Paul,

I'm sorry that I didn't write you yesterday for I really intended to, but I've been going around in circles for the past three days. Maybe I can settle down at last to the great task of studying for the examinations we shall take next month.

The graduation was very simple, but wasn't quite as much a "flop" as I had suspected. It was still raining when we left the house so we had to ride over. You couldn't count the number of extra wrinkles in our uniforms from being so crowded into the cars. The x-ray Technician has a flash-bulb camera, so he made pictures during the graduation. After having received our diplomas, we went into the large dinning room of the Nurse's home and had the most wonderful banquet I've ever attended. That was the best part of the program for it was so well planned and we had such delicious food. No one was invited except the Staff members and the Graduates. Wish you could have been present. After having finished eating, the class will, prophecy, and history was read which everyone commented on and it really was very good. I'll let you read them sometime for you are also concerned.

You mentioned that you wandered if my address has changed. I haven't completed a three-year course yet so I'll be here until August and I'm the first of our class out at that time. After then, well, I still don't know just what I might do, but I'll find something to do until you return.

Can you imagine it's still being cool weather here. Florida, of all places! I had to wear a coat out last night and so did everyone else. Maybe we aren't going to have the Summer season at all this year.

Had another letter from Bennett yesterday and she was afraid that I might be jealous to know that she has written you another letter. Don't you two get too "chummy" and forget about me.

You should see the nice present your Mother sent me. I don't know how she guessed that I was really in need of one. Maybe I should tell you what it is so as not to keep you in suspense the way you do me. It is a very nice compact and I appreciate it very much.

I'm still waiting to see those most awful proofs so you will probably receive the enlargement in time for a birthday present next year at this rate.

They're having a formal at the U. S. O. tonight and Check was just in and wants me to go along with her. I really don't care to go for I have several letters to answer and need to review. Try and make her understand.

I know you must be tired of trying to translate this letter by now—I'll say "so-long" until later.

All my Love,
Evelyn

May 21–

Dear Paul,

I really enjoyed the book-length conversation with you this afternoon. I would enjoy it more if you would try writing those long letters more often. I couldn't keep track of the number of the chapter; in fact, I could hardly believe that you had written such a long letter. It was wonderful so long as it lasted.

I was very much amused when I read of your eating with chop sticks. I suppose I'll have to learn to use them too for you might become a professional at eating with them and forget that you ever ate with a fork, knife, and spoon. How do you eat soup with them? You must have enjoyed such a delicious meal, but I'm glad that I didn't have to help eat such food for I never liked the idea of cooking fish with their eyes still in. I just couldn't bear the thought of eating an eyeball. Those people must either be very lazy or very conservative. By the way, if we learn to use chop sticks, we wouldn't have so many dirty dishes to do after each meal. That's an idea, don't you think? If you continue telling me how well you can cook, you shall have a permanent job after we're married. I think that would be very nice.

It must be lots of fun to go spear fishing so I'll have to try that some time when I have a chance to visit that Island. That must be an interesting place from your various descriptions.

Smitty asked me to go along with her to the Naval Air Base yesterday morning, so I did. Her boy friend Smitty met us at the gate, but we couldn't get passes onto the base as only relatives are allowed in now. I'm glad it wasn't that way when you were there. Of course, I could always play the part as your wife! Since we couldn't get on the base, we went down to the boat house, but all the sail boats were taken. We had hoped to go sailing. We then went to Warrington and had breakfast and spent the remainder of the morning there. I really had an enjoyable time for that brought back precious memories of the times we had breakfast together.

I have just finished writing a letter to your Mother. She's so very nice. I can now understand why you are so thoughtful for you must have inherited that trait from her.

I'm still caring for babies and haven't learned to like that service yet. I'll soon become a professional at "diaper-changing." I much prefer the hall work with adults than the Pediatric department. The Supervisor of the Operating room has asked the Superintendent of the Hospital to send me back to surgery for the remainder of my training, but I don't know if she will or not—surely wish that she would. I have been to surgery twice already and have served twice as much time in that service as is required, but I've completed all the other services too.

I'm getting so sleepy that I'm only making mistakes so 'Good-night.' I'll always love you very much.

Love,
Evelyn

May 23–

Dear Paul,

I received the package from you today and also another letter. The fountain pen is beautiful and I like that type pen very much. The parachute material is very nice so I'll have to think of something that I can make with it. You'll be sorry that you sent me your watch for soon it may be like mine if I continue giving such rough treatment. The staff must be broken again in my watch for it won't "tick."

I've certainly been taken for a "spin" today and kinda feel the results. I was supposedly Supervisor of Children's Ward and also had charge of a ward of my own. If you don't think that I was busy, you should have been around. Those poor kids!

I know just how uncomfortable you must be if you are taking your Typhoid shots. You probably only had a booster which is enough, but I had a series of three. I suppose you also have a few other shots to take, don't you?

My room mate left for Miami last Friday for she has a two week's vacation. You see, I was in training six months before she entered so I'll be out in August and she will not have completed her three-year course until February. That's the reason she is getting a vacation at this time. We don't rate our last vacation; at least Sister Theodora won't let us have any time. Of course, we'll be out two weeks earlier than we would have if we had our vacation. Don't I wish I could have gone along with Margaret to Miami? I wish you could have visited there for you have no idea of how beautiful it is. Pensacola seems more like a part of Alabama for it doesn't even compare to Southern Florida.

I'm so hungry, but I don't want to have to dress just to go out for something to eat. It's almost five o'clock in the afternoon and the usual supper time at the Hospital. Some of the girls are going over and asked me to go along, but I want to write some other letters and study for State Board so I don't have time to go. Maybe it's mostly because I don't care for the food they serve in the afternoons, but I shouldn't complain.

Have you heard from Bennett recently? She said she was going to write you again soon. I hear from her often and she wants me to write her as often as I write you. That's almost asking the impossible for I never wrote to anyone so much as I write you. Of course, I never cared so much for anyone else. It seems odd that we never met sooner since you were stationed here so long. I often think of the time we met at the U.S.O. even though we only had a very short conversation at that time. I believe Smitty was with me that night. She said if you were still here, we would have a double-wedding. Of course, if you had been here all this time, I'm afraid we would have already been married—that is if you had wanted to. I'm almost sure she'll marry soon so you see, there's no chance of our having a double-wedding.

You seem to be receiving a number of letters from old friends. I'll bet you were really surprised when you found that the girl was in Italy after having known her in Pensacola. Wouldn't you be surprised if I wrote you from there? And wouldn't I be more surprised?

Your watch really keeps good time and I'm already wearing it.

I had better hush and write some other letters. You know, I always write you first for I love you most. Now, I shall write to Elizabeth and Doris.

Love always,
Evelyn

[Letter from Paul's Swedish friend.]

402 E. 146 St.
New York 55, N.Y.
May 24, 1945

Hello Handsome!

What a pleasant suprise it was to hear from you. I often wandered what happened to you.

I'm very pleased to hear everything is O.K. with you and I hope with all my heart that it will remain so.

I'm not with the Lees anymore. I left them last year on Oct 1st. They are now in Pensacola. I do miss the children terribly. Jane I raised from 6 months and Ricky I had from birth. They have a new addition Laura. She came last July 19th. A sweet, blonde, blue eyed baby.

Now I work at a perfume shop. My work consists bottling and lableing perfume. I have Saturday and Sunday off. Business is very slow now but it will pick up in a month or so.

Isn't it wonderful that the war in Europe ended. I hope it will be over with Japan soon too so all of you boys could come home.

They have quite a few jokes on the radio about the point system of letting men out of the armed forces. One was: A wife gave birth to a baby and wired her soldier husband, "Just gave birth to 12 points." Husband replied "Want to try for 24?"

There is a joke about cigarettes Miss Cigarette walked down Chesterfield Lane in the town of Raleigh where she met Philip Morris. He gave her a Sensation and if she doesn't look like a Camel in nine months it was a Lucky Strike.

Baseball season is in a full swing. Today Yanks and Chicago White Sox played. Yanks won 3 to 2. Yesterday they played and Yanks won 5 to 2.

Circus is in town. I went to see it. It is much smaller this year than when I last saw it. They had a beautiful display of Alice in Wonderland. The bare back riders were excellent.

My sister, Irene, from Norfolk stayed a week in Brooklyn and then went to Conn. to stay a while with my mother. She has her baby with her. Boy is he cute.

I was up to Conn. to visit my father last week end. I spent a day and night with my mother also. The farm looks so summery even if they haven't been able to plant anything for it has rained too much.

Golly it has been so cold here this spring. Nothing like Pensacola. This time in Pensy I used to be brown as a Indian and swim all day. Here I can't hope to go swimming untill in July and I'm getting whiter by the day.

There just isn't any pictures of me lying around. I haven't had any taken for years. I still look pretty much like I did in Pensy. My hair is a little darker but I still have bags under my eyes and a few new wrinkles. After all I'm a year older. I had my 22nd birthday May 4th. By the way how old are you? You allways kept that under cover. If you should have pictures of yourself I would be very happy to receive a few. Remember you promised me one in Pensy but you never did give it.

I'd love to have you writing to me. You are not budding into any romances of mine. For I haven't anyone to romance with. I knew and went out with a few 4 F's but they wanted too much symphaty because they were rejected from the Army so I got tired of mothering them.

What do you do for recriation there? Have you any U.S.O. shows that way?

I have a friend who belongs to U.S.O. Camp Shows Inc. In June she is going to go over seas. She belives it will be Europe. Her name is Paula Dee. I've known her as long as I've been in U.S.A. for I came to her house. She is a swell kid and an excellent dancer. Her specialty numbers are toe acrobatics and acrobatics. If she should ever come across your way don't hesitate to talk to her for she is not a bit high hat. She has belonged to U.S.O. for three years. Her last trip was to Alaska and Aleutian Islands.

I finally heard from my brother in Europe. After four years of complete silence it was a great joy to hear he was alive and well. My brother is in Sweden and says he will get married to a Swedish girl this X mas.

Paul, I'm terribly sorry I didn't write you sooner. Do be careful.

With Love Aili

[Letter from Paul's sister-in-law, June, married to his brother Roy.]

Beaumont, Texas
May 24, 1945

Dearest Paul,

You will never know how thrilled I was to-day to receive your nice long letter. I have been intending to write you ever since Roy and I married but I find myself very careless at times. I am glad we are now getting acquainted through a letter so we want feel so strange when we get to see each other.

Roy has told me all about you and of course Pauline talked about you a lot when I visited your folks for the first time summer before last.

You asked me how I liked your folks. I think they are just wonderful and I enjoyed being around all of them. Roy tells me they like me also. I feel sure they do because they have been grand to me ever since Roy went over-seas.

Next November Roy and I will have our third wedding anniversary and we have only lived together about ten-months. Those months were great happiness for us and both of us are glad we went ahead and married.

You said in your letter that you knew some boys that lived around Brownwood yet not in the town. I suppose they live somewhere in Brown County. Some of our friends in Brownwood have a son which is a marine and his name is Jack Tipton and he was on Iwo Jima same as you were. I wondered if you happen to know him and his folks live about fifteen miles from Brownwood.

You said Mother Fogel sent you a picture of Roy and I just after we married. I thought that picture was just terrible of me but I am glad you got a good impression of it. I have dark brown hair, blue eyes, and light complexion. Roy thinks I am pretty but that is just his side of the story because I'm not. We are really in love with each other and that is what counts in a happy married life.

Mother Fogel wrote and told me about your Florida girl. One of my best friends last year was from Florida and she was a honey. I would like for you to bring a Florida girl into the Fogel family and then I wouldn't be alone on my southern accent. They don't talked exactly like Texas people but they do have a little southern accent. Maybe after the war Roy and I will be able to see you get married if you are still in love with this girl. I wanted to see your sister Polly get married very much but it was too long a trip for me to make up there alone and my dad passed away only two months before.

I am the only child so mother and I are the only family that is left. I am planning to start a new home just as soon as the war is over and my honey comes home. I am looking forward for you to visit us after we get a home of our own. (Believe it or not but I can cook.)

Will close for this time and hoping this letter finds you safe and well.

Sincerely from your Texas Sister,
June

P. S. I almost forgot to tell you but Mother and I are now visiting my aunt and uncle here in

Beaumont, Texas which is about 320 miles from Brownwood.

I am having my mail forward to me so I just got your letter to-day.

Bye—now,
June

May 25,–

Dear Paul,

I had the day off so I didn't awaken this morning until ten-thirty. It was about eleven when Mamie called and was I happy to hear her say that Frank had just checked in the Hospital at the Naval Air Station! She and Mom came out and of course, we went out to the Hospital. It remined me so much of the times I went out to see you and I told him about the the time you met Mamie and Elizabeth. He was first admitted on "B" ward, but was transferred to "F" ward. I don't believe he has changed at all since he left, except for his back. He has chronic arthritis which is incurable as you may know. I don't know whether he realizes that or not. He told me of the letters he had received from you and showed me one he received just before leaving Oklahoma. I believe he really wants to meet you and I can't say I blame him. He couldn't help but like you.

Pat and I are sitting on the porch and it's getting so dark that I can hardly see how to write. The breeze surely is nice, but I don't care for so much train smoke. Some of the girls have just returned from our park as they have been playing tennis. I get enough exercise on the halls so I don't care for such streneous recreation.

My room mate has just returned from Miami and said she had a wonderful trip. She's going to end her vacation next week by having her tonsils out. Imagine that! I can think of much nicer ways of spending a vacation, although I had my tonsils out during my vacation. Of course, you were still in the Hospital at the time so I didn't mind staying in as I couldn't be with you. You were even angry at me because I went out to see you.

Father Dolan is still around and asks about you all along. He usually says, "how's the Marine now" and "Do you hear from him often." He's so very nice, but I'll never forget the day we saw him at Fort Walton. Remember? I'm sure I didn't have the usual appearance that day.

I'm hoping to receive another full-length novel again soon—

Love Always,
Evelyn

May 27–

Dear Paul,

My finger is so swollen that I can hardly write. You may have guessed that the infection was caused by a safety pin—still taking care of kids as you can see.

It is now mid-night and my room mate is already in bed sleeping. It's quite unusual for her to be in bed before me. I'm becoming very, very sleepy too, but it's time I was writing you again so I mustn't miss a conversation with you.

Oh yes, I received the proofs yesterday and I'm warning you not to expect a beautiful picture for it will be far from that. You shouldn't care to show it to anyone for I wouldn't want them to be so disillusioned about what you've probably told them about me. I'll take the proofs down tomorrow so maybe it won't be very long before I can mail you the picture.

I went along with the Smith couple to Bay View this afternoon and had a very enjoyable afternoon. I would have given anything if you could have been along—The more I go about places with them, the more I seem to miss you. They mention you often, and of course, I enjoy telling them about you—I don't believe you know Smitty very well, do you?

It's so very quiet that I believe I could hear a pin drop across the room from me. Everyone is sleeping soundly.

My room mate is having her tonsils out Tuesday—does that remind you of something? I well remember the sore throat. Of course, I also remember practically everything you said that day—Father Dolan was in just before you came and I could hardly talk.

I must go to bed before I fall asleep—

I always look forward to receiving your letters.

Love Always,
Evelyn

May 29–

Dear Paul,

I was so glad to receive your letters yesterday. Three of them in one day—isn't that wonderful? Along with your letters, I received two packages— one from Elizabeth and J. C. and the other from Jimmie and Doris. They're very nice presents so I'll show them to you some time in the future. That will be the day when I see you again.

Had a short intermission for Sister Theodora called and said for Mahon and me to report to the office. I couldn't think of anything I had done wrong or visa versa. We dressed and went over right away and she only wanted to tell me that I was to go on night shift Friday night— what a relief! Supervisor of Children's Ward—

I don't know what Bennett may have told you, but it must not have been so good—I can only say that I haven't changed at all and don't have any intentions of doing so. You have my promise. I love you very, very much and always will and I hope you have realized that already. The sooner you return—the sooner I shall be very happy. You can't realize how much I look forward to that day.

It has been so very hot today and there isn't much breeze which doesn't help the situation. We're beginning to have real summer weather after the delay.

Frank has a liberty pass for this week-end so we're going over home. He hasn't been over since he reached Pensacola. I haven't been out to see him since Sunday although I would like to go out. He showed us a few things that he made while overseas and they're beautiful.

I took the proofs down yesterday and they said that I can get the pictures the twenty-fourth of next month. I'll mail it to you as soon as I get them so maybe you'll receive it for a Christmas present. Hope that it won't be so long (late) arriving as the other package I sent.

I believe Smitty will be married when she has her vacation which will be soon. I'm so glad she is going to be married even though she has about ten month's training yet.

I thought I had written your Mother last is the reason I hadn't written her for so long. I was waiting for an answer, but I'll try not to make that mistake again. She must have a great opinion of me now after my having neglected writing her. I wrote a letter to her about a week ago so I hope she'll forgive me this time.

Have you been spear fishing again recently? You'll soon become a professional at that and then you wan't care to go fishing in our simple way. It must be very difficult fishing with a spear. And I can imagine it's twice as difficult to try eating it (fish) with chop sticks.

So you're having to desert your buddies— Perhaps you'll be with some who don't enjoy arguing so much. I was beginning to think I'd have to go over and keep peace in the group.

Had a letter from Jimmie and Doris and they are so very happy. We will be too some day and I hope it won't be long.

I'll say "so-long" until later. Always loving you very much—

Love,
Evelyn

May 31—

Dear Paul,

I reported on duty at eleven tonight and was this place a great confusion! At the present the babies are very quiet, but you can never rest assured that they will remain quiet for any length of time. I only wish that babies knew they should sleep at night. We'll be different and teach our children that. I'm Supervisor of this ward you know and the girls I have working with me are swell and very conscientious workers. A couple of very seriously ill babies expired just before I came on duty so we don't have but one who is seriously ill. I do hope that it won't expire while I'm on duty.

I have just performed the great operation of killing a roach (one with wings at that!) for he was making a raid on this room. And now here's his mate and I do hope there are no small ones. They irritate me so much running about over the walls.

The Senior class had a party last night at the Gadsden Street home. We barbecued hamberg-ers in the back yard which was lots of fun and they were very delicious. Wish you could have been present. I would have made you a "dagwood sandwich" with all the extra dressings. You would have enjoyed it too, I'll bet.

We're having the Doctors' dance next Wednesday night at the Country Club. I think I've told you about the previous Doctors' dances. You probably know what I mean for practically everyone drinks but me so you see, I do feel a wee bit "out of place."

I was out to see Frank again yesterday and asked him if he had answered your letter yet. He said that he's going to answer it right away. You should see the number of things he's made since he was overseas. He can take just scraps and make something beautiful. He has liberty over the week-end so he's going over home Saturday afternoon. I'm going over on the Bay Line Sunday morning and Mamie will probably drive us back Sunday afternoon.

Had a letter from Bennett today and she seems to be having quite a time lately. She thinks she has fallen in love with a sergeant in the Army and dates him every night. She isn't supposed to date enlisted men so I hope she doesn't get into trouble by doing so. So far as his rating is concerned—that shouldn't make any difference to her but you know the rules and regulations of service.

Please don't worry about my being drafted for I don't believe Nurse's will ever have to enter service. There is a surplus of nurses in the Navy or at least there seems to be for a few of our nurses have tried to enter the Navy and were rejected because of very minor defects. The Army could probably use a few more Nurses, but I believe that enough Nurses will join to meet their demands.

I've already made my night reports and it's very quiet on the ward. You see, I haven't been very busy. It's now two-thirty in the morning so I suppose you're sleeping soundly unless you're unlucky enough to be on night duty too. Just hope I'm a part of your dream. I'll say "Goodnight" for now.

All my Love,
Evelyn

June 2–

Dear Paul,

It was yesterday—one year ago that I returned home from Chattahoochee. It really doesn't seem as though it's been that long since I was there when I think of the many things that happened during that time. But when I think of the many things that have happened since then and it seems as though it were ages ago. I'll never forget the number of times I visited the Hospital to see you and you were usually playing cards with the boys. And the times you came off base to see me and didn't have permission. I was always so afraid that you wouldn't get back through the gate O.K. After the Hospital days we had so much fun. I spent the happiest moments of my life with you and yet have much happier ones in store for the future. I enjoy looking forward to that day when we shall be married.

This is a "military secret" so don't tell Bennett. Smitty (Nurse) and Smitty (Sailor) are to be married next Saturday night and they're so excited they had to tell some one so they told me. They're going to keep quiet about it for we aren't supposed to be married during our training and Smitty has nine more months yet. She showed me her wedding ring last night and it's beautiful. It makes me happy to watch them for they're so much in love and they tell me everything (all their plans). I'd love to make it a double wedding. This boy she is to marry has been married once and has a child about two year's old that he seems to worship. His former wife has the child and I suppose will keep him. He just recently got his divorce papers. I'm glad you haven't been married although it shouldn't make a lot of difference, do you think? I would love you just the same—I'll be so happy to add the second ring to my left finger.

I was sleeping soundly at two-thirty when my room mate came in and when she turned on the light (although it's daytime), I awakened. It was wonderful to awaken and find that I had received two letters from you—"You wonderful man you." I also enjoyed reading Pauline's letter which was very interesting. Say, we're going to have lots of neices and nephews, aren't we? Bet she would make a wonderful mother.

Practically all of my fingers are sore from having been pricked with the "wartime" safety pins. That's the reward I get for working in Children's Ward.

Pitts just came from downtown and said she saw Mamie while she was there. I wish she would call and stop by for a few minutes anyway. She's going to drive Frank over home this afternoon.

My room mate is busy washing clothes and I have several dresses to do this afternoon. You should be well experienced in that line by the time you return home. That's wonderful!

It's so very warm today and this long hair is driving me "nuts" so don't you think it would be a good idea to have it cut? The girls are just returning from duty which reminds me of the day you stopped me on the street while on my way home from duty. I didn't want anyone to see me so dirty and especially, I didn't want you to see me just then. You seemed to have never forgotton what I said to you and I know that I won't forget my appearance that day.

I suppose I had better get busy washing my clothes. You should be here to help me.

I love you so very much—

Love always,
Evelyn

June 4–

Dear Paul,

It's now almost two o'clock in the morning and I hope that you're enjoying your sleep— Remember the times that I wouldn't let you sleep! I'll never forget that along with many other things that happened. I'm very sleepy now for this night shift really "gets me down." I can't sleep well in the day time for there's too much commotion among the girls. If I stay on this shift long enough, I'll get accustomed to sleeping in the day time, I hope.

We've just admitted a child and he began yelling "Mother" as loud as possible and awakened all the kids. You should have heard the noise! He soon fell asleep and the others have quieted too—what a relief! Wish you could visit this ward and then you could understand why they have so many "freaks" in side shows. They have my sympathy for there's nothing much that we can do for them as they're so deformed. Of course, we have some very cute babies too.

Last night when I was walking over to report on duty the wind began blowing with a terrific force. I was beginning to believe that I would be blown back to Gadsden Street, but managed to reach the Hospital with difficulty. It had been so very warm during the day so even such a strong wind was wonderful. After the wind ceased, it began raining which was also very welcome. It hadn't rained for several days and I do appreciate rain once in a while. It seems that you always have your share of rainy weather wherever you're stationed.

All the Seniors have Wednesday night off in order to attend the Doctors' dance. I would like for you to attend if you were here, but otherwise, I don't care to go. I have a new evening gown for the occasion, but I haven't yet decided to attend.

I hope that you can send those pictures you were telling me about. You know, I would appreciate some recent snapshots of you just as much as you want the enlargement of me. I'll be looking forward to receiving them so don't disappoint me.

I didn't get home until eleven o'clock Sunday morning. You know, I worked until seven o'clock and had to take the ten o'clock bus out. I had lunch with Frank and Mamie and they had such delicious food prepared. I spent the afternoon with Mother and had to take the five o'clock bus into Pensacola. Then, I slept until time for duty again.

Mamie said that she didn't intend to neglect writing you, but she has been so excited and happy since Frank arrived home again. You'll probably receive another letter from her soon.

Hope to receive another letter from you tomorrow as I haven't heard from you for four days. It isn't your fault that I receive them all at once. "Good night" and "pleasant dreams."

All my Love,
Evelyn

June 6–

Dear Paul,

I haven't been able to sleep all morning so I can think of nothing I would rather do than have a conversation with you. I had hoped so much to hear from you today, but the Postman just came and I still find myself wishing for a letter. I'm thankful of the fact that I can write you even though you can't write me at times. I do miss your letters so very much for I always look forward to receiving them.

Someone is practicing music next door—should be a good musician some day, but I can't say he is at the present. I always liked piano music and wish I had taken it when I had the chance.

June 7–

I began this letter yesterday afternoon, but was interrupted so didn't finish it. Mamie came by so I went along with her to the Naval Air Base to see Frank. I don't like to visit the Hospital very often for it brings back so many pleasant memories that are wonderful, but it does help to make me miss you more.

When I returned home the girls were waiting to have me dress for the Doctors' dance. I had already decided not to go, but they insisted so I went along. It was given at the Country Club which is a beautiful place. You probably know if you were ever there.

Paul, I'm afraid that you're gone into combat duty again for I haven't heard from you in a number of days. I just know you'll come through safely in all the combat duty you have if prayers help much and I think a well-meant prayer is everything.

It is only eight o'clock morning and I'm up already so you see who I thought of first—this morning and every morning. My room mate is still sleeping and it's beyond me how she can sleep so much during this hot weather. At the present it's rather cloudy so maybe we'll have rain by this afternoon. Sending us a bit of your rain, are you? I could well appreciate a nice rain.

Maybe I'll have a letter from your Mother soon. You know, I wrote her last this time. I like to receive a letter from her so very much and it seems that she is so sincere in everything she says.

The maid is here again and as usual "fussing." I can't say I blame her, but she always tells me her troubles—

I'll write some other letters and then study for State Board—

Love always,
Evelyn

June 9–
2:30 A.M.

Dear Paul,

It's so very warm tonight in this small chart room even though I have a fan on. Since I came on duty this place has been in an uproar. We have several seriously ill babies and just had an emergency case come in. This child fell out of a car and another car ran over one of her feet. She was brought to the hospital immediately and her foot was amputated. Too bad, for she is a beautiful child and only five years of age.

You made me very happy when I received a letter from you yesterday. You know I'm proud of your being such an expert shooter. You came so near receiving the medal this time so maybe you'll receive it next time. You know, I was once rather accurate at target practice, but I wouldn't even attempt the practice with you. You would make me ashamed of my score.

I haven't yet accustomed myself to sleeping in the daytime. You can understand why I remain sleepy all the time. My eyes are about closed now, but I can't afford to sleep on duty especially since Sister might make a visit at any time.

I had a letter from Clara and David yesterday. They think there has never been a child to compare with Ronnie. He is as sweet and healthy as can be. I just know that he'll be so mischievous for David will teach him such meanness. He's always been such a great lover of children. Since I was the youngest of the family, I always received a great deal of kidding and rough treatment from my brothers.

Jancsik just came in and is spoiling my babies. She has one of them in the chart room now and it is a cute thing! I like to play with them too, but you can't afford to very often because there are too many of them. They would want to be held all the time and that would never do.

I often wander what ever became of Nellie Moylan. I haven't heard from her or anything about her for so long. I would also like to know if she is a flight nurse as she applied for that service. I believe she would do very well at that for she is a good nurse and also a swell conversationist.

Wouldn't you have a wonderful surprise if you should see her overseas some place?

So Roy's wife is glad to welcome another Southerner into the family. She might not feel that way once she really knew me. She is from Texas, isn't she? I'll be happy to join the family.

I must get busy before I fall asleep. Hope to hear from you again today—

All my love,
Evelyn

June 11–

Dear Paul,

Have just reported on duty again and the babies are very quiet at the present. We have a mid-night lunch so I was just down and had a very nice lunch. We have chicken every Sunday, but it taste so very good tonight. Maybe it's because I haven't eaten anything during the day.

One of the babies has begun crying which really breaks the silence. You can imagine how it must be when all of them are crying at once!

Are you still angry at yourself for not making the other two points as expert shooter? I'm sure you'll make it next time. How I would like to be there with you and go spear-fishing! I know that must be lots of fun and such an unusual experience. Don't you need a special nurse for if you do I'll come over?

I have slept practically all day which is the most sleep I've had since I first reported on night shift. I don't usually sleep more than three hours a day so I must be getting used to night duty by now.

I shampooed my hair this afternoon and have it rolled in small curls. If Sister Theodora only had the chance to see me now she would probably restrict me for the next month. She has given us strict orders as to the way we should wear our hair so I'll arrange it differently before morning—

I saw Fitzpatrick a few days ago, but she's been back for some time. Her husband is in Norfolk, Virginia at the time, but she seems to think that he'll be sent overseas soon. I hope he isn't shipped out until after she has the baby. You know her—she is as "nutty" as ever, but has a wonderful personality.

The roaches are about to take the joint again tonight and there seems to be hundreds of them. Maybe I exaggerated a bit, but I do believe there must be a producing factory somewhere near and what a production!

If it weren't for this fan in front of me, I'm afraid I would be a crisp by morning from the heat. It has been so very hot recently, but then, you know of the Summer climate of Florida and it hasn't improved at all.

Had a letter from Ernestine yesterday and she always asks about you. She is very interested in you and is looking forward to meeting you some day. She has asked me so many times to visit her when I have enough time off. She is such a wonderful person so I know you would like her.

Hope you're having pleasant dreams.

Love always, Evelyn

[Following letter written by Paul's Grandfather, Charles A. Fogel, 1864–1945; he was a teacher and self-taught botanist. From Paul's own words: "Perhaps the person that influenced my life most was my grandfather... He taught first through eighth grades in a little red schoolhouse... Placed a verse of scripture in my hand when I left for the military—Proverbs 3:5–6. I never saw him again; he died before I got back."]

Monday Morning, June 11, '45

Dear Paul:

We were certainly surprised the other day when we got your book on Central Pacific Birds. I'm looking it through over and over again. They certainly have peculiar shapes and colors. One outstanding fact about them, I guess, is that they must be all good swimmers as well as flyers since where they are there is more water surface there or land so that they must be in the air a good deal of their time. Many of their nests are remarkable. That bird called The White Tern really makes no nest and lays its single egg on some limb or somewheres where it cannot easily fall off. It's a wonder that those birds are able to hatch out any young at all. I suppose they must sit very still when on the bare egg.

I cannot thank you enough for having gone to the trouble to send me this interesting book. If I live till you come back home I will give it to you again and you can place it among your other books as a memento of the terrible time you spent in the Pacific.

As your folks have been telling you, grandma and I are not very well this Spring. I had, you know, the grippe this winter and it seems I can't quite recover from it. Rheumatic pains and colds make it very bad for grandma.

We have been gathering our news from your mom and dad and it seemed to us that you must have had some most remarkable experiences. I suppose you could write a good-sized book about what you saw and did.

I take it for granted you have nice sunny weather where you are. With us it has been unusually cool and rainy up to the present.

I'm glad for those specimens of flowers enclosed in the book. I shall mount them on a sheet for future reference. Thank you very much.

Affectionately yours
Grandpa and Grandma

[Following letter from Paul's twin sister, Pauline]

June 13, 1945
9:45 A. M.

Dear Paul,

Well I was up bright and early this morning and for a change I am not sleepy. Grandpa came walking up at eight or around there to see how all you boys are. He received your book and is really very tickled with it. I showed him the things you send home and he said, "we should put them in the musuem for an exoiped". He said, "they were wourth while having." Now since the weather changed to sunny days grammy is getting better. All last month it was rainy and she was down more then she was up.

On Sat. Verna Klotz is going to be married to a Sergt. in the Air Corp. It will be a big wedding in the Lutheran Church in Bethlehem. With a reception following at her house.

And on the 23rd Robert Keck and Anetta Kneckt from Nazareth will be united in holy matromony. He is going to have a week end to get married.

Mother is away on a confinement case. In fact it is the case I was to take. It is a boy born to Mrs Charles Shulze. (Mildred Dickensons) You know her don't you? At least you should her mother was our school teacher for five years. The baby weighed twelve lb. and one fourth ounces. And she gave birth to it in fifteen minutes.

The reason I am not taking it I have to stay off my feet as much as possible again I am under the doctors orders. You see on the thirdth June I had a miss carrage. So we won't have our little Paul after all. I can't believe it but I have to just take the facts. Doc. Beck said if I follow his orders I can have other children and with out trouble. Don't ask me how it happened I don't know. There are many thing could have caused it. This time I learned the hard way.

It isn't that I didn't ask mother about child birth because I did only she told me that if you menstrate every month you were not pregnate. But all the while I felt that I was. And so one day I started to menstrate and it wouldn't give up, and that is when my trouble started. I am well now and am taking care of the house while mother is gone. Sheldon and Earl takes care of the yard and garden which I used to do. I am trying to forget about it, but some how it is hard to do because both Earl and I wanted a child a boy like "Andy, or snuckie."

I am raising rabbits and on Mon. 11. I had a nice nest of young ones seven in all. and the are about four inches long. And this morning I had another nest I don't know how many she had but she had two dead ones in the front of the box. And since the mother was very nervous I didn't look. I have two bucks and four ladies besides three bunnies about three weeks old.

Believe this or not but now the Bauers turned to farming. They bought a cow and Mrs Bauer who would never never go near a stinky thing as a cow is milking one now. Nor Mr Bauer didn't loose his job but they can't buy any milk from any of the farmers around here and the milk in town is to expensive so they almost was forced to do just that.

Gee there goes the mail man and I wanted to send this letter with him. Well don't worry I will have to go to Bath to day any way and will drop it there.

I see we had a letter from you to day swell. You must be in a lot of mud because the letter is all muddy. You had a very interesting letter. Do you know what every time you write you have to do some laundry. You will be quit a handy man around the house.

Well I have to stop now so be good.

Love & kisse
Sis.

[Following letter from Evelyn is written on "Hotel Seminole, Jacksonville 1, Fla." stationery]

June 13–

Dear Paul,

As you can see I am now at the Hotel
Seminole in Jacksonville. It's not really because I
want to be here, but State Board of Examiners say
I must come. Have really had a day and do I feel
it now! Five examinations which follow one after
the other. I doubt if I've passed any of them and
if I did, the good Lord was with me. What those
old maids can't think of to ask and most of the
questions aren't even in the book. We have five
more exams. coming up tomorrow so I'm well
prepared for the wrost of them—Wish you were
here with me and I wasn't taking the exams—we
could have so much fun, but we'll look forward
to the day we will be together again.

The buses were so crowded, but the bus
drivers were very nice for they reserved seats for
us. Some of the people were so angry because
we had preference to them. I can't say I blame
them for I wouldn't care to stand for such a distance either. When we arrived, we looked as if
we hadn't had a bath for months so we felt much
better after getting cleaned up a bit.

We have through Saturday off duty so after
exams tomorrow, I'm going by home and stay
until Sunday morning—Mother doesn't even
know that I'm here.

I had a very sweet letter from your Mother
yesterday—I'm always so glad to hear from her
for after all she's practically my Mother too.

I do hope Sister Theodora doesn't have me
on the night shift and especially Children's Ward

when I return—I grow more "nutty" each day I'm on duty with all those kids.

It's so nice and cool in this room that I could remain here indefinitely. Surely slept well last night for I hadn't had any sleep for two days and nights—You couldn't guess who I drew for room mates here? There are four of us to the room for we couldn't make more reservations. Hodges is one of the girls and you don't know the other two. They're very "high-strung" if you know what I mean. Last night I was dressed for bed, but was doing a bit of last minute reviewing when all of a sudden three men appeared on the scene. Was I embarrassed for they didn't even knock! Of course, they were with the three girls and the girls had told them not to enter. I really told them what I thought of them, but they had been drinking and didn't seem to mind. I just hope that doesn't happen again.

I had better review a bit before going to bed so I'll say "Good-night." I love you very much—

Evelyn

[Following letter is from Evelyn's sister-in-law, Mamie Lou; married to her brother Frank.]

At Home
June 14, 1945

Dearest Paul,

Guess that I shouldn't mind but I'm beginning to wonder why you haven't written to us. Maybe you've been waiting for us to get our feet back to earth again and let you know where we are.

I'm sure that you know that Frank is back in the States and that I'm about the happiest person in the world. He came to Frisco first and was sent to Norman, Oklahoma from there. I went to see him there. The three weeks that we spent there were the happiest of my life. He was able to get liberty most of the time that I was there and we really enjoyed those days. When I think of Heaven I'll always associate it with Norman. We were there—just the two of us with no one to interfere with our happiness and it was complete. Of course there were couples that we met with whom we ate our meals and went to shows etc. but what I mean there was none of his family or mine there to claim any attention or get puffed if we didn't do this or that. In other words—I didn't have to share him for three whole weeks with any one. The first week-end that we were at home I'll bet there were fifty people in to see him and I didn't get to say a dozen words to him. I knew that it would be that way. I never get to go to the hospital alone to see him either. I guess that I shouldn't be so selfish but after all it has been three years almost since I saw him. There's a few people that I would like to tell that "marriage is a private affair" if I thought it would do any good. Take my advise and when you come home and you and Evelyn are married—Go some place where neither of you know any one and where you won't have any obligations to any one for a while. There will be changes in both of you for you will have been separated so long until you'll have to become adjusted to each others ways again.

Frank is in the Naval Hospital here at Pensacola—Ward F. He has arthritis in both feet & legs and has a spinal injury. He stepped in a hole on Tinian and hurt his back. Sounds simple doesn't it? He looks well but if he stands or walks very much his feet swell all up and he suffers terribly. He has no idea how long he will have to stay in the hospital or how long he will get to stay in Pensacola but I hope that it will be a long time. When he goes back to duty it will be in California or Rhode Island. I don't know where to from there. If there is any thing that I can do to keep him here he will never go over seas again. He has done his share. Let some of these U.S.O. soldiers etc. get a share of what is going on over there. Of course I know what I might do or say wouldn't do any good.

I was in Pensacola yesterday afternoon and last night. Frank got special liberty and we stayed with my sister. She works so I carried every thing and cooked Frank a real supper at her house. We thought perhaps Evelyn could eat with us but she is in Jacksonville taking State Board Exams. I saw a letter from you to her that had come in since she left. It was postmarked June 6 and I was very glad to know that you were able to write up till that time. I was glad to know that she is hearing from you. The last time I saw her she hadn't heard from you for <u>five</u> days and she was worried nearly sick. I hope that she doesn't have to wait five weeks and longer to hear from you like I did from Frank while he was over there. I guess she would be really worried then and I know how it makes you feel. I know that you have a lot to do and there are days and days when you can't write. You will get so discouraged because you are not getting mail that you won't care whether you write or not but do write to her and your Mother every time you can. They'd be so glad to hear even if it might be just one page saying that you're still well. I know what I'm talking about for there have been lots of days when it seemed I couldn't go on if I didn't hear from Frank. We would like to hear from you too but don't fail to write to them so you will have time to write to us. I hope that Evelyn had heard before she took her exams for I'm quite sure her grades will be higher if she did.

Frank isn't a bed patient. He can get around and they have put him in charge of a craft shop at the hospital. He has always made things from wood etc. He is in his glory there for he has tools and materials to work with. He has made me two pillow tops and one for Evelyn and some desk markers etc. He is going to make some model airplanes.

I'm worried about Frank's condition. Naturally I hate to know that he is ailing in the least but when I look at him and then look at the hundreds of others who are so much worse off I want to get on my knees and thank God for sending him home in such good condition. Really we have a lot to be thankful for.

It sure has been dry here. In fact it hasn't come a good rain since some time in April. Our garden hasn't done well at all because of the dry weather. Mom Myers has a wonderful garden though. She has been canning quite a lot of vegetables and selling some too.

I've been checking the news again trying to keep up with the 4th Marines but I haven't seen much that would give me an idea of your where abouts. I understand that you have been in Hiwaii and judging from the time it took for that letter to come through I think you must still be there. I hope so at least. As long as you are there we don't have to worry about your safety.

Be as careful as you can and try to come home safe and well. Frank and I will be mighty glad to see you along with the others who will be glad too. Remember that we will be thinking of you and wishing you the very best of luck always.

Frank sends his very best regards. He hasn't wrote but one letter since he has been home. I'm his private secretary so I'll be writing our letters to you now. You know I sort of like to be his secretary too.

I've written to Elizabeth for the first time in about six months. I've got to go to her Mothers to get her address. Shouldn't I be ashamed? Well, I just got so blue and down in the dumps before Frank came home until I didn't write to any one.

We got two new tires for our car last Saturday. I'm hoping that we can get two more right away. Maybe we can enjoy riding when we don't have flats. We had one the first Sunday that Frank was home.

I really must be getting at some of this work that I have to do. I stay on my way to Pensacola and back so much until the work all piles up here for me to do.

Write us when you can find time our permanent address is Star Route, Mary Esther, Fla. You can say Mr. & Mrs. either one or both.

Always,
Frank & Mamie Lou

June 15–

Dear Paul,

Just me again! I came over home this afternoon with Mr. Myers and since they're out at
the present, I'll write you—what a trip back
from Jacksonville! Oh, but those buses were so
crowded although I managed to have a seat all
the way—I really needed support of some sort
after those examinations. Maybe I should have
stopped in at Chattahoochee for the duration or
longer. I had a letter from you to welcome me
home along with the pictures of you—I was so
very glad to have such a welcome for it's been
some time since I have seen a recent picture of
you. They're very good and I only wish I could
receive some more often. Of course, I know you
don't have much extra time to make pictures. We
can't get the film to make pictures or I haven't
been able to get the size for your camera.

It's very hot today so a bit of moisture
would be very welcome. It hasn't rained here for
about seven weeks and everything is so dusty. It is
slightly cloudy so maybe we will have rain.

Mamie was down for a short while and said
that she has written you another novel. She really
has a "Gift of Gab." It must be wonderful to have
such a personality.

You should see Mother's dog for he is beautiful. She has just bathed him and of course, that's
the first thing she had to show me. He is all white
and has long hair. She also has several cats and
some of them are so cute! I wouldn't care to have
so many around, but I'm glad she finds pleasure
from them.

June 16–

Saturday morning and I don't have to report on duty until tomorrow morning. Isn't that wonderful? Mamie is going to Pensacola for Frank as he is coming over for the week-end. I'm going along with her and it's about time she was down for me. Of course, she had to press a uniform for Frank so that will take quite a while or at least, I can imagine it would. I don't know much about pressing uniforms so maybe I should practice on Frank's uniforms. I'll just wait and let you teach me for then I would enjoy learning.

Mamie is here now so we'll run along— Mom, Mamie, & Mr. Myers send their regards—

Love always, Evelyn

June 18–

Dear Paul,

On duty again! I'm still on the night shift in Children's Ward and as sleepy as ever. I don't believe I could ever overcome being sleepy at night for even though I rest all day, I could still sleep nights. We only have very few babies so it's very quiet.

I had two letters from you yesterday, but I hope to hear from you again today. Aren't I selfish? But I do enjoy receiving your letters.

So you and my Mother's secrets still continue. Just you wait for I'll hear all about that some day. Hope you keep those letters for it will be fun reading them. You know, I just love to read other people's letters, especially when they interest me.

Maybe I'll have that picture ready to mail you soon—Hope you aren't too disappointed with my appearance. Maybe my appearance will improve some day—at least we'll hope so—I might be a bit too old for such a change.

I had intended writing your Mother tonight, but I'm so very sleepy. I'm afraid that I may make so many mistakes she couldn't interpret the writing. I'll try to write her during the day so maybe I can write a more interesting letter.

Frank made me the most beautiful "tufted" pillow top. He has made several others since he has been stationed at the Naval Air Station. He was put in charge of that little work shop—I suppose you know the one I'm speaking of as it's in back of the Hospital. He has liberty every week end so Mamie comes down and takes him over home. He seems to really enjoy each trip over. I'm so very glad he is near home and has that privilege.

For the first time, my room-mate and I are on the same shift. She is relief nurse on third hall. I believe I prefer caring for babies if I had to choose between the two services. I would appreciate being on day shift again, but Sister can't see it that way.

Frank seems to think that you must be at the same camp where he was stationed before he left for the States. You know, he saw those pictures you sent me. They seemed to interest him quite a lot for he thought he recognized the place.

Let me "hush" before I fall asleep. I'll love you always and very much.

Love,
Evelyn

June 20–

Dear Paul,

I'm sitting in the Supply Room with Kelly at the present as she isn't feeling very well. She is also on the night shift so maybe that has a great deal toward making her feel so depressed. I was busy in Children's Ward and Kelly called and wanted me to come and be with her for a short while until she begins to feel better. She says that she hasn't felt well since her operation. She asks about you frequently and really has a great opinion of you. Margaret, my room mate, also asks about you often and she too, thinks that you are a swell person even though she only saw you once. Of course, she has heard a great deal about you from being my room mate. I always agree with them about you—

One of the girls heard from Nellie Moylan the other day. She is stationed at a base in Memphis, Tennessee and they say she comes in stewed nearly every night and really goes in for the various intoxicating beverages. Can you feature that? You know she would never even take a drink while here and was such a devoted Catholic member. I was sorry to hear that about her for I thought she was such a nice girl.

I wrote your Mother a letter yesterday. I know she must become very bored at my conversation, but I enjoy hearing from her. She's such a wonderful person.

The most wonderful breeze is blowing in the windows and it's very comfortable here. Of course, I could really sleep if I had the chance.

Even this hard floor would make a good bed as I could very easily fall asleep any place.

We had a grand rain yesterday which was very welcome. You don't seem to appreciate rainy weather so much as I do. Of course, it always seems to rain when you have liberty so I can't blame you for your objections.

I had a letter from you today and was so glad to get it. I also received a letter from Elizabeth & J. C. and they always ask about you—"Goodnight."

All my Love,
Evelyn

June 22–

Dear Paul,

What a murderess I am! Just killed nineteen of those huge flying roaches. You can't imagine the fun we've been having for they were about to take the place—us included. Beyond me how they can multiply so rapidly. The girls were so amused at me when one came crawling up my stocking for I began teaching them a new step in dancing lessons. Such "crawly" things just give me a "creepy" feeling.

Received your letter today along with the one you sent from Pauline. I can understand why you were very much amused at her letter for I had to laugh when I read it. I'll bet she is lots of fun.

You asked about Check. She is a Senior nurse who was transferred here from a Hospital in Wisconsin. I become so bored when I go out with her so I always try to have something previously planned when she is around. She is a very nice girl, but I don't care to be a close friend to her.

Margaret and I were to a movie Wednesday night "The Diamond Horse shoe," which was very good. Last night we were to another movie and saw some "nutty" picture in which Wallace Berry played. He's a very good actor.

Smitty and Smitty didn't get married as they had planned. You know it is a Florida law to have the license three days previous to marriage. He came out for her to go along for the license, but she had changed her mind. They have decided to be married when she gets her vacation which will be soon. Smitty (the Sailor) is at his home in Texas at the present as he has a seventeen day leave, Smitty (Nurse) doesn't seem to know what to do with her off duty hours. I thoroughly understand how she feels since I'm having the same experience.

I'm sure glad one of these girls has a good friend around. He just brought her a quart of chocolate ice cream and was it good! I told her to have him come around more often.

We've had so much fun tonight for we only have a few babies and they aren't very sick; in fact, several of them are well enough to be discharged.

I'll hush and let you have a rest. I love you very much—

Love,
Evelyn

June 24–

Dear Paul,

Have just finished with my night reports and will write you before I become so sleepy. I was hoping to have a letter from you today, but since I didn't, maybe I'll have two from you Monday. I awaken about noon each day and wait for the Postman in order to see if I have a letter from you. You know, letters are a wonderful substitute since I can't be with you, although I would much prefer being with you.

Margaret and I have planned to visit one of the Doctor's home tomorrow—Dr. Dodson and his wife as you may know him. They want to make some pictures so maybe I can get some of them to send you.

We plan to go to church tomorrow night— Margaret and I. She was so surprised because I said that I would go along with her. I know that I will enjoy going. I'll never forget the time we went to the chapel on the Station. One main reason is because it was the day you left which wasn't a very happy event. I would never be able to express my feelings of that day. I hope that I never have that same feeling again for I hope that you never have to leave again after you return.

If you should see me now, you wouldn't even claim that you know me. My hair is rolled in curls and I have my belt off. After having made myself as comfortable as possible, one of the Doctors came in. He is a Navy Doctor and doesn't have any patients, but just came by to see how things were going. He laughed when I reached for my belt, but of course, I didn't care if he did see me without it. He should have warned me of his visit at this hour of the night. He should have been out at the Station sleeping. Wish I had such a chance! It would be wonderful to sleep during the night hours again.

Bet you have a nice sun-tan by now. I don't tan, but instead, I just burn to a crisp if I'm exposed to the sunlight for a long period of time.

The owner of one of the Funeral Homes and his wife have invited me out to a chicken dinner so I'll probably visit them one night next week. Wish you could be in on it too. I remember the chicken dinner that we didn't have with the Gadsden Street neighbors.

I'll say "Good-night" for now. Hope you're having wonderful dreams—

All my Love,
Evelyn

June 26–

Dear Paul,

You made me very happy today as I received two letters from you. What a wonderful dream! And to awaken and find it was real. It would be even more wonderful if some of my other dreams were real. Of course, you're always the leading character which makes them so interesting.

I'm becoming so very <u>lazy</u> for I haven't really worked since I've been on night duty. I begin day duty again tomorrow so then I shall return to the midst of work again. I'm really glad that I'm not going to remain on night duty for you know how much I dislike this shift. I have always wanted to sleep at the proper time so day sleep doesn't rest me so very much. I always feel drowsy if I should even sleep all day.

I haven't seen a single large roach in this ward since the great killing the other night. I can well do without those "crawly" things around.

You said that you saw, "The Very Thought of You." It played here some time ago and I don't think I saw it. It must be very good and you can bet I'll see it if it plays here again. I have seen some very interesting movies recently as that's one of my favorite types of amusement.

Tell Val that I want him to take good care of you. Don't let any of them put you too wise to married life. That is reserved for the future.

Mammie was by today and said that it's about time she should have a letter from you. You may suffer the results if you haven't written for you should see her when she gets that Irish temper in an uproar! All jokes aside, but she does want to hear from you.

Margaret and I did go to church Sunday night and had a wonderful time. Rev. Rogers really planned a grand sermon. I know you would have enjoyed it so very much and I thought of you all during the sermon. Afterwards, we had singspiration hour and I sang until I was hoarse. Imagine that!

I have made so many errors while trying to write this letter so I'll let you have a rest now.

All My Love,
Evelyn

June 27–

Dear Paul,

What an evening! Smitty, Patterson, and I just had the grandest hike so I'm quite exhausted at the present. We walked out about mid-way the Pensacola Bay bridge and was it beautiful! Just wish so much that you could have been with me for the moonlight on the water was so wonderful. It reminded me of a number of nights we were out together. Such trips just aren't good for my moral when you aren't along.

Here I now sit in my room and the perspiration is trickling down my back. Just wish I could have spent the night near the water front for it was so cool and nice there. Patterson is on my bed asleep and I'm sorry that I'll have to disturb her within the next few minutes.

You should have seen our front porch last night for it looked as though we were having an "old maid" session. There were eleven of us on the porch at once.

It's a good thing that you weren't in on the discussion for I'm afraid you would have been quite shocked and maybe a bit embarrassed. I believe my face even changed colors a few times.

What a noise in the hallway! Let's find out what's doing. Oh, it's just Hodges and Phiel again with some more of their stunts. They're moving a mattress into the sitting room and are going to sleep there tonight. Imagine that! Those girls are always up to something.

I'm on day duty again and in charge of Maternity floor. It seems they really want me to be well trained in that line of duty. If I'm not caring for the babies, I am in charge of the Mothers and now I have both combined. Sister Theodora asked me today about accepting a permanent job there after I am through training in August. I really don't care to do that for I only want a temporary job until you return. I hope that wan't be long. Of course, I'll still be waiting and hoping regardless of the length of time you're overseas. It will be so wonderful to have you back in the States again. It can't be too long before you return.

You should receive the enlargement some time in the future. I mailed it about a week ago, but couldn't send it airmail so I sent it "first class." Maybe it wan't take too long a journey before you receive it. I hope you aren't too much disappointed at my appearance and don't you go showing it to everyone. They'll wander why you chose such a girl for a future wife. I agree with them and I'm glad you weren't hard to please. If so, I'm afraid I wouldn't have had a chance.

Had a letter from Bennett today and she says that she has decided that she isn't really in love with that Sargeant. She's tired of his company already. If she were really in love, she wouldn't become tired of having him around, for I know from experience. She would want to be with him every time she had a chance; in fact, all the time if that were possible.

I haven't yet heard from my State Board examinations and am rather afraid of what the results may be. All I can do is retake the exams. if I have failed them.

It's passed mid-night so I had better have some sleep so I will be able to report on duty tomorrow morning. I love you very much—

Evelyn

[Letter below is from Iris, Evelyn's cousin.]

June 29, 1945
Saturday A.M.

Hello! Paul,

Now don't fall out of you seat because it is only me. I had a letter from Evenlyn the first part of this week and she said for me to write to you. Heck, I don't know what to write but I'll try. When it gets so boring you can't take it any longer, tear it up and forget you ever received a letter from me.

Do you remember the first time I was ever on the Naval Air Station of Pensacola. Well, I wish this morning I could still say I had never been on the Station. I have been working down here two-half months. It sure is tiresome every day. Every time I see a Marine I try to kid myself by saying "that could be Paul," but no I guess it will be quite a while before you will be back. Heaven knows we hope not.

We are holding a Revival at the Church this week. I can hardly hold my eyes open. I would go to sleep on the Preacher some night but he keeps such a close watch over where we sit that he knows every time my eyes are just a small crack to say I am not asleep.

My main Boss has been on a two weeks leave and is due back tomorrow. I wish he would get lost and not find his way back. He won't tho' he has found his way out to this place for thirteen years.

It is time for me to go to work now. I have been reminded several times all ready so I guess I had better get down to business.

Take care of the dark-haired girls over there. But be sure you forget them when you head back to the United States.

I hope you were not bored too much. Write if you get time and would like to. I'll send them to Evelyn after I read them.

A Friend
Iris

P. S. I saw Evelyn last night. She looked good and was in high spirits. She passed State Board and was asking everyone to give her a pat on the back. She told me I had better be sure and mail this letter today. I wrote it yesterday and had left your address at home.

It is raining this A.M. I nearly froze coming to work. I believe it is winter again.

Be a good little boy and remember us back home.

Again So Long,
Iris

June 31 [sic; there's no June 31!]—

Dear Paul,

Have just returned from home and am sitting on the front porch with Patsy, the maid at the present. I was along with Mr. Myers over home yesterday and came back with Mammie today. I went with her to the station for Frank and to our surprise, he was checking out on a thirty-day pass. Isn't that wonderful? And he seemed so excited over the leave.

When I returned home, I was very happy to find a letter on my bed awaiting my arrival. I expected one for I can always depend upon your letters. I'm very disappointed if I don't receive them on time.

I hope that you receive the picture soon as you can well see that my appearance hasn't changed. You should hope that it would change for you could then endure my presence with more ease. I hope that you don't change, but of course, if you do, I'll love you just the same.

Smitty is in the diet department now and likes it fairly well. I've had some good laughs from her numerous mistakes already. Maybe she'll be a good cook some day. I shouldn't talk so much for my mistakes were too stupid to tell anyone. I'm sure that I wouldn't tell you for you'll understand in the future. Most of the food in the diet department is prepared with no seasoning at all. You see, I'll be trying to feed you non-seasoned food. And wouldn't you enjoy that!

We had the most wonderful breeze last night and did I sleep well! I believe it even rained, but I wasn't awake to enjoy it. I know that you regret our having a share of your rain for you seem to have a monopoly over that phase of the weather.

There are a number of children playing in the park and seem to be having so much fun. "Kinda" reminds me of my childhood days.

I hope that you aren't too shocked that I passed State Board Examinations. I was very much surprised for I was quite sure I had failed some of the subjects. I'm certainly not a brilliant student, but very lucky. When I told Mr. Myers, he wanted to celebrate, but when I told my Mother, she wasn't excited at all. Even though I tried to convince her that I wouldn't pass, she wouldn't believe me. It must have been your confidence in me that made me pass for I surely didn't have confidence in myself. Hodges didn't pass along with a few of the others. She isn't so "high-strung" since she received that report.

I received a letter from Elizabeth and J. C. and both have gained weight recently. I don't know how much J. C. weighs, but Elizabeth weighs one-hundred twenty-seven pounds now. That's the most she has weighed in years. She seems to be in better health and I'm very glad.

Today is my day off duty so I'm going to try answering all my letters. I love you very much—

Love always,
Evelyn

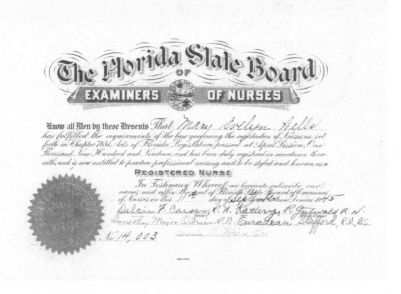

Evelyn's Florida State Board RN License

[Letter below written by Paul's Grandfather Fogel (Charles A).]

Monday Morning, July 2, '45

Dear Paul:

I'm certainly glad that your love of nature, like mine, urges you into the woods, hills and shores after bird and plant life. You must have that same desire as myself to inquire into the world of winged creatures and the almost innumerable kinds of plants. You are the only one among all the Fogels, except myself, who is really interested in these lines of knowledge. When you get back home you and I may be able to explore and build up a large collection of plants of our own country. I know now from what I have experienced in you, that you would take great pleasure to do that. Such a collection would be fresh and would become very dear to you as you could add to this from time to time.

Those specimens you sent me I'm taking care of and when you come home I want you to tell me on which Islands you found them and if possible the names of them, for my botanies include only plants of U. S. Your specimens then will be interesting relics of your activities in this region of the world.

It's a funny thing that you, Charles and Wayne are practically close together in the Pacific and at the same time not capable of seeing one another. In times of peace it would be easy.

At this point of my letter Francis with his big truck came driving along so I went out to see what he wanted. He was wondering whether Harrison could help him bring in baled hay from their field. He didn't know Harrison was working to-day. Francis said if he couldn't get anybody to help him with the hay, he would go to fetch a truck load of cattle at Lancaster, Pa. He certainly is hauling a lot of things with that truck. He is able, he says, to carry stuff to any part of New York City with it. It's a fine thing to be able to do this without having to inquire.

We are having lots of warm weather now and you were righ when you said this would make me feel better Grandma also is feeling pretty good just now. We are very to know you are fine just now. We hope you will have the best of luck during the rest of the struggle out there.

The wheat fields around here are fast coloring yellow and in about a week will be ready to cut.

Well here is sending you our good wishes.

Sincerely yours
Grandpa and Grandma

Paul Fogel's Grandfather, Charles A. Fogel, 30 years old, 1894
(was school teacher; had degree from Butztown Teachers College;
self-taught botanist; died the month Paul came back from war)

July 2—

Dear Paul,

I'm on with a special duty case and it's about two o'clock at the present. The patient has been asleep ever since I came on duty except for the time I awakened him for his temperature and medication. I was on duty on the maternity floor from three until eleven. Did we have some excitement then!

The patient that I'm on duty with now is supposedly a mental case. I guess I will realize that if he awakens. His wife is in the room too, but is sitting near the window asleep. I surely would love to join her.

You're really going to be a "jack of all trades" and I'm very proud of you. I expect you to say that you're studying to become a Doctor, the next time I hear from you. That's when I wouldn't agree with you for I don't care to marry a doctor.

I'm just wandering how I'm going to manage to keep my eyes open for my eye lids feel as heavy as lead.

I was just down stairs for some coffee and also had some good fried chicken. That's almost some thing of the past. You're lucky that you could find steak, even though it was a bit costly.

I searched the town for some bath clothes and couldn't find a single one. Frank bought a dozen nice ones at the base so he is giving me six of them. Isn't that wonderful! Now, I can begin taking bathes again.

I'll hush before I fall asleep so I'll say "Good-night."

Love Always,
Evelyn

July 3—

Dearest Paul,

Well, I'm on special duty again tonight and I've been on since three this afternoon. It's really fun other than it is rather tiresome after several nights in succession. Of course, I don't believe I'll be on tomorrow night so I can have a rest.

What do you know—we had a bit of rain tonight. It was wonderful, although I would liked to have been sleeping during that time. You know me, I enjoy my sleep—

Mamie was down last night and brought one of our neighbors. She (the friend) was admitted to the Hospital on my floor—a maternity case of only a few months. Although I was in charge of the entire floor, I practically specialed her.

Smitty had a letter from Bennett today and she really believes that she is in love with her patient. So long as she changes her love affair so often, I'm quite sure it's not love. She'll find one some day that she will really love. This patient she likes is in the Air Corps T/Sgt., I think. He has one leg off above the knee. Of course, she won't think of that if she really loves him. She is wearing his wings at the present. I wander if she really likes Army life for I don't believe I would. I much prefer being a house wife.

I have next Sunday off duty so I suppose I shall go along with Frank on a fishing trip. He wants to come down for me Saturday and will bring me back to Pensacola Sunday night. I always enjoy going over. How I wish you could be with us.

This patient I'm on duty with is a mental case so in order that he stay here, Sister made his wife have two police guards with him all the time. You can see I'm not the only one caring for the patient. Of course, when I was at Chattahoochee, I was in charge of the whole ward of "nuts" at once. Since this Hospital isn't well enough equipped for the care of such patients, she doesn't like to have them admitted.

Have you received the picture yet? I'll always love you very much—

Love,
Evelyn

July 5–

Dear Paul,

The light is dimmed out so that I can bearly see to write. I'm on special duty again with a very nice patient this time. She was up to surgery this afternoon so of course, she is so very drowsy yet that she doesn't know what the score is. She was in nurse's training for eleven months, but that was before my time, so I didn't know her previously.

Received a nice letter from you today along with the one you sent from June. I'm very sorry about Pauline. I know she must feel very badly as everyone always does with the loss of the first baby especially. That happens in many cases of the first one so we'll hope that she doesn't have the same trouble again.

We've had a great deal of rain recently— what about your part of the country? Is it still as damp there as ever?

How well I remember last Summer this time for we were having so much fun together. We'll have to continue where we left off when you return. We, at least, won't have these awful duty hours to interfere. It's such a great relief to have passed State Board mainly because I didn't want you to really know how "dumb" I am.

Father Dolan asked about you again yesterday so you see, he seems to be rather interested in you. He said that he hopes he isn't present when we two see each other again. Wander what he meant by that "wise crack"? He's always kidding me and seems to get such a great "kick" out of doing so.

I wrote Bennett a letter about three days ago and just mailed it today. I carried it about in my pocket until it was practically crushed. It's a good thing that I don't carry yours around for so long for I'm afraid you might be a bit angry by the time you received them.

It's such a beautiful night to waste away so I'll think of the many beautiful nights we were together which will help make this night pleasant

All My Love,
Evelyn

July 7–

Dear Paul,

I'm all dressed and just waiting for Frank to come by to take me along home with him. I had permission to leave the hall a bit early this afternoon so I could go over home. I also have tomorrow off and Monday until three o'clock in the afternoon. I'll probably come back to Pensacola tomorrow afternoon.

I have a regular floor show when Margaret and Smitty are around. Margaret was busy arranging her pictures in an album when Smitty came in. They can't seem to get along for they're always throwing "dirty cracks" at each other. I only sit around and laugh at them—"just like two old maids."

I have decided to do special duty for awhile anyway. Sister Theodora has asked me to supervise one of the halls, but I don't care to have any dealings with the Sisters at all after I'm through with this course next month. If I do special duty, I don't have someone always telling me what I should do next and the work is much more pleasant. The pay is also much better for I would make twice as much per month. If I'm on duty with one patient for eight hours a day for one month, I would make two-hundred twenty-four dollars and if I care for two patients at a time, I'd make three-hundred thirty-six dollars a month. That is much better pay than any of the other services and I don't care for a permanent position. I just want something to do until you return.

Tomorrow is Sunday and I can't hear from you again until Monday. It's wonderful to wait for the Postman and not be disappointed.

I'll run along now. I love you so much—

Love,
Evelyn

July 9–

Dear Paul,

I'm writing this letter by the light of a heat cradle so you know that I can't see too [illegible; stationery had gotten wet at some point]. I'm on duty with a burned patient and will probably continue to care for him for quite a while. He's a very nice patient; in fact, he complains very little for his condition. At the present, he is sleeping soundly, but when I first came on duty, he was very uncomfortable. He can certainly do with plenty of rest so I hope he continues to sleep well.

Just returned from home yesterday afternoon along with some of Frank's friends who had visited him. Everyone is the same as ever. Mother and Mamie both owe you a letter and said they're going to answer soon. At least, their intentions are good! Every time I see Mom, she tells me of the Mother's Day card you sent her and she never seems to think to thank you for your thoughtfulness when she writes.

I was just down to the dining room and had some coffee. I've formed such a habit of drinking it that I can hardly do without it. Hope you like coffee too for then you can't make any wise cracks at me. I didn't care for coffee or tea before entering training, but soon learned to like both. Coffee was a wonderful stimulant just before a night operation.

The patients are very quiet tonight, but the Nurses are very noisy. They must be having a general session at the other end of the hall.

Smitty and Smitty have again set a date for their marriage. They say that they're going to be married next Saturday, but I'm not going to believe them this time unless I see the certificate. Smitty (Nurse) has such a changeable mind and they have so many arguments. She told me this afternoon that she wished they could get along so well as we do. Do you think that would be an improvement? I'm afraid you would be the one to change your mind for I'm sure I won't change mine. I hope you don't either for you would have a hard time getting rid of me.

Having quite a lot of lightning so maybe we'll have some more rain. We've had frequent rains recently so you must not be having so much as usual.

These people who snore make me so very sleepy. I don't know if I snore during my sleep or not for no one ever told me.

Frank thinks that he'll probably get a medical discharge following his leave. If so, he and Mamie are "kinda" planning to go to California and have asked me to go along. Wouldn't that be wonderful? I'm just hoping that he will go. If I don't go with them, I hope to go some time in the near future.

Margaret wants to be with me wherever I go. She has followed me about ever since high school and seems almost like a sister. She has six more months training so she doesn't like the idea of my going to California at the present for she wants to go too.

Love always,
Evelyn

P. S. Hope you haven't had too much difficulty trying to read this letter. I'll learn how to write some day maybe, without making so many errors.

July 11–

Dear Paul,

Haven't heard from you for the past week which makes me believe that you are probably being transferred. If so, I do hope that it's not into action again. I know that I would have heard from you if you were in a position so that you could have written. If my prayers are answered, you will come through safely no matter what may happen.

Have you heard from your Mother recently? I haven't heard from her in some time, but I know she has plenty to occupy her mind and time. I do enjoy receiving letters from her very much.

We've been having frequent rains which is very nice for the weather is fairly cool then. It was lightning and the wind was blowing so very hard last night, but that lasted only a short while. When I reported off duty at eleven o'clock, it was very nice out.

I've been doing double shifts recently, but last night I decided to come home and sleep after duty instead of going on a special duty case. I slept from about twelve o'clock last night until eleven-thirty today which is almost twelve hours. I feel as though I'm wandering about in a dream now from having too much sleep. It's usually just the opposite. I will go on duty again this afternoon at three o'clock.

My room mate has just returned from duty. She is working down at the Public Health Center and likes it very much. Of course, since school term is out now they don't have to make trips to the schools as we did when I was there. I also enjoyed that service.

Had a letter from Elizabeth and J. C. yesterday. I'll send it along in case you would like to read it.

Just wander if you have received that picture yet.

I hope to have another letter from you soon—I love you so very much—

Love Always,
Evelyn

[Evelyn included this letter from her sister, Elizabeth, with the one above.]

July 3–

Dear "Sooky,"

I suppose that by now you've heard the verdict—whether or not you passed the examination for nursing. What happens when one "flunks"? Isn't she allowed to take again the next time? Well here's hoping that you passed, and I'll

bet you did. How many took with you—I mean
from there?

Yes, Mamie Lou finally wrote and told us
all about Frank's condition. We were all so sorry
to hear about it, but I suppose we should be very
thankful that he is even as well as he is. It's awful
though that he has arthritis in his feet and legs,
for the work which he does keeps him on his feet
so much. Perhaps he can change to something
else. I know there's no known cure for arthritis,
but let's pray that the doctors will find something
that will do him some good. I'm so glad that he's
there so near home. Being able to be at home
with Mamie on weekends will probably help him
a lot. I'm glad for both of them.

Doris is still getting along fine. She doesn't
have much longer, you know—just until the last
of this month. She has so many baby things that
I told her that she'd have to have about two more
in order to use them. She has a lot of cute things.

A funny thing happened to her a few days
ago. If I had been with her, I'm afraid I would
have chuckled right out "big and loud." She was
in a big market and had gone back to get something out of the refrigerator when her panties
fell off in the floor. She was telling me about it
the next day. I asked her what she did. She said,
"Why I just stepped right out of them and high-
tailed it out of that store as fast as I could walk."
She said that she decided that there was nothing in the store that she wanted after all. I said,
"Well, didn't you even get your panties?" She
said, "No, I left them right where I stepped out
of them." She didn't think anyone saw her lose
them. I imagine a lot of people wondered who
lost her pants, don't you? <u>ha</u> There was some-

thing else funny that happened to her which I wanted to tell you, but I've forgotten what it was now. Maybe I'll think of it some other time.

J. C. is still as busy as everything. He almost just works, eats, and sleeps, and he doesn't get enough sleep. He has only one meal a day at home so I don't see much of him except on week-ends. He has Saturday nights off and does no repair work on Sundays. He says tell you a big "hello."

Do you hear from Paul very often? Where do you think he is now? I hope he doesn't have to go back to the fighting area.

J. C. got a kick out of your roach story. He said he would have liked to have seen you dancing about.

We were very much surprised to get letters from Mr. & Mrs. Phrouch and Mr. & Mrs. Davis saying they were going to be near us out here. The Phrouches will live near Los Angeles and they were supposed to get there today. The Davises are living in Tuscon, Arizona which isn't very far from here. Of course it's a few hundred miles.

Well I'll quit for now 'cause I'm sleepy.

Let us hear from you soon

Love
Your "Sis"

P. S. Give the girls our best wishes. How are "Smitty & Smitty" getting along?

July 13–

Dear Paul,

I am dressed to go down down, but it has begun raining so I'll wait a few minutes and see if it slacks a bit. It even rains when the sun is shining so we don't ever know when we should wear a rain coat out. Patterson is going along with me to town and she isn't quite dressed yet.

I had such a nice rest this morning for it's been real cool so I have slept well. I had hoped to awaken and find that I had received a letter from you, but was disappointed. At least, I keep my hopes up for I'll receive a letter so soon as you can write again, I know.

Do you know what those darn Sisters are doing for our class? They've taken our last vacation time and added it to our regular time which will make us three weeks later getting out of training. That's very "dirty" of them, I think, but we have to do as they say or we don't receive our diplomas.

Smitty has just returned from duty. She's "chief-cook" yet and seems to like that service. I didn't enjoy cooking for all those patients because they're too hard to please.

I'll continue where I left off—Have just returned from town and I'm as soaked as can be. It has been pouring rain ever since we left. I had to go to the ration board and apply for a nurse's shoe stamp for my old ones are about played out. I don't know where I'll find any nurse's oxfords as there aren't any in town. Maybe I can order some from a Mail Order house. I also have to get some uniforms which is almost an impossibility.

My room mate has just come in and one of our former students is here. I went to high school with her (Ethel Mathis) and she graduated from Nurse's training two years ago. She was stationed in California (Navy Nurse's Corps) since she first entered service. At the present, she is stationed at the Naval Air Station.

I'll close with all my love.

Evelyn

War ration booklets

[Following letter is to Paul from his twin sister, Pauline.]

July 15, 1945

Dear Paul,

To day is Wit Sunday and it is raining cats and dogs. So people tell me that we shall have forty days and forty nights of rain. The creek is over its banks already. and if it is going to rain so long it will probuly be over the bridge.

To day is the first day I am all dressed up for the first time since I left the hospital two weeks ago. and it sure feels strange to be wearing so many cloth when I was used to so little. I feel fine and have enporved with my walking a lot. I have only a little drainage in my insicion any more. Dr Beck said that he thinks in about two weeks he can remove my bandage. I am glad because every time he dresses it, it pulls like any thing.

Last week we had a terrible storm ending in a flood. It did a lot of damage to a lot of farms. We had quit a lot of slates torn of the barn roof. And all the fenses torn down by the high water. The water was up as far as the yard fense about three more inches and it would have gone in the celar. The wind torn down the two big willow trees in the meadow down from the house. and also the big oak tree back in the field.

Millers had two young heffers electricuted. And just by luck they got them in time and butchered them. Earl helped them till almost three A.M. It had to be done by flash light and landren because the light were gone.

The little town of Bath is all washed out. Some people have no homes at all while others have only the frame work. Some people had to shovel the mud out of the rooms before they could remove any furniture. The store keeper are going out of business alto gether Because the damages are to great to start rebuilding.

The Co-op in Tatamy is no more either the storm smashed the buildings and uprooted their big gas tanks and sailed them down the creek. The safe they found down the creek a half mile and every thing distroyed. They estimated the damage to be fifteen hundred thousand dollars.

Bauers can't go through their lane yet, because their lane is almost all washed out.

We had a letter from Sheldon yesterday. And he asked Mother to send all his things to him, that they are getting ready to make some kind of move. At present he is at Bryn Field Texas.

Charles is as yet not at destination but somewhere in the Pacafic.

June expects Roy home soon I hope so.

Well that is all the news for just now. So I will close.

Love & kisses
Sis.

P.S. Mother says she will write next week. She is kept pretty busy these days.

July 15–

Dear Paul,

I don't know of anything that has ever been quite so welcome as the letter I received from you yesterday. You can't realize how happy I was to receive it. I'm glad that you weren't transferred as I had thought since I hadn't heard from you during the past week.

I'm doing special duty again tonight and really love this work. It seems that all I do recently is stay on duty sixteen hours and sleep and rest the other eight hours each day. In this way I stay well occupied and the time passes so much faster. I don't have any social activities at all, but that can wait until you return for we can have so much happiness together.

I was very much surprised yesterday when I was walking down the hall way and met one of my former high school class mates. He also seemed very much surprised for we hadn't seen each other since our graduation and he didn't know that I had chosen nurse's training. He is a second Lieutenant in the Army Air Corps and is stationed in California. At the present, he is home on leave and will probably be shipped overseas when he reports back to duty. He dated Jancsik last night and they seemed to like each other very much. Oh yes, he is Mary Annie Hobbs' brother.

Who should report on duty tonight but Merle Smith! I was also very surprised and glad to see her for she has been in California for the past three months. She has been doing duty in a Veteran's Hospital there, but didn't like the work so she resigned. She said that she liked California very much and would liked to have remained there, but living conditions are so high at the present. She wants me to rent an apartment with her and do special duty nursing after I finish here. That's not a bad idea for if I don't get to go to California, I would enjoy that very much.

My patient is snoring so loudly and I'm afraid to move about much for I may awaken him. He is very nice and wants me to remain on duty with him for several nights. I get eight dollars per night and all I do mostly is sit here and listen to him snore. I sure hope you don't snore— not so loudly as he anyhow.

You should have seen the crowd at the house last night! I'm really glad you didn't see them for I know you would have been as disgusted as I was. The sitting room was full of drunk people and Hodges and Futral were so "tight" they could bearly walk. Would I have appreciated their having their parties other places than just opposite my room! I had to listen to all their noise so you see, it is a pleasure to be on duty. I'm so glad my Mother doesn't know all of this for I'm afraid she would highly disapprove of such.

I was very much surprised for it wasn't raining when I came on duty tonight. Rainy weather is becoming quite a usual affair.

Pitts is so angry tonight for she had to take charge of an extra hall tonight. She is just about as "lazy" as I so that's why she is so stewed over the idea. I can't say I blame her for she has a great responsibility. It's the same as I had when I was in charge of this floor. Of course, I'm still in charge of the maternity floor at the present. I do become so amused at the young fathers for they're even pathetic at times.

I'll hush and write Elizabeth and J. C. Oh yes, I suppose you thought I was "nutty" since I mailed you Elizabeth's last letter. I'll bet you got

a "kick" out of it. I wouldn't have sent it if I had
thought of what she had written at the time.

All my love,
Evelyn

[Letter to Paul from Miss Dwyer—one of his history teachers]

July 17th

Dear Paul—

Im writing this up in New England near
Boston where I have been spending a little time.
Your letter was sent along to me—the one of July
1st. I dont know just how I put things in that
letter but I <u>do</u> know I wasnt bauling you out.
Guess it must have been advice for you see Paul
Id like you to "get somewhere." I know that the
Marines have "toughened you up" plenty & I
know you're not the <u>boy</u> who left here a couple
of years ago but I do know that you've still got in
you the sound sensible basic things that count &
you'll have them when you leave the Marines &
with them and schooling theres no reason why
you couldnt be independent as youd like to be &
still do things the way you want to do them. You
would have stayed in school if you could but the
war came & called you away & it has changed
many things for you but still you can get in a
lot of schooling and pick up—in part any way—
where you left off. Id like to think of you just
going ahead & getting the education you'd like
to have & then making the most of it & getting
the most out of it for a happy successful life. The
way things go with you from day to day—that

is where you are & what you are doing & life <u>so</u> uncertain—isnt conducive to planning for the future but you can think a little bit ahead any way. So if there is opportunity to go to school where you are now or to take extension or corre- spondence courses—take them—you'll find later that it was worth while. Now this time Im not bauling you out either—do you hear? I want to get to Canada for a bit this summer but Im not sure right now if I can make it. Ill try tho for I haven't missed a summer up there for 'bout 12 yrs So youre not always easy to get along with? Well by gosh you were when I had you—you are the fellow from my classes these last few years that I pick out & think of always as just the fin- est most wholesome real boy I had. You know I could be rough & really "hard on 'em" but that didnt make me callous inside & I could see "with a clear eye" and often felt I was much too rough & tumble for lads like you (this of course was <u>pre</u> marine!!!). Any way Paul Ill remember you always as just about "tops"—I think the job situation for you fellows coming back will be quite a problem but then if they get rid of the women in industry & send them back home (& they belong in the kitchen rather than the machine shop etc) this will provide places for thousands of men in most all fields & there will be place for the indudualist who wants to be his own boss too. That I sup- pose will adjust itself as time goes by. The turn back tho from war to peace (?) will be a terrific problem

Well, enough for now Paul. Write again, when you can and know that there's one ol' gal 'way back here thats thinking of you & hoping for the best for you. Good luck & God take care of you always.

Sincerely
Miss D.

July 17—

Dear Paul,

Received a letter from you yesterday saying that you have received the picture I sent. I was very much surprised to know that you received it so soon and I'm very glad that you like it. You remember, I told you not to expect a good picture for I never make good pictures.

I'm becoming very tired of doing double-shift duty each day, but I just don't know how to go off the case. He is such a nice patient and I also like his wife. She is a registered nurse, but is rather old. They can't seem to understand why I can't remain on with him until he is discharged. If I do that, I'll have gray hairs before my time. At the present, the patient is sleeping soundly.

The roaches are taking over again. Here comes one around the door smoking a cigar so I think I'll have them polish my shoes before going off duty. Of course, these are the smaller roaches!

I was just down and had some coffee with Smitty—the "red-head." She asked about you for she had heard nothing of you for quite a while. She is very much in love with a Sailor who is stationed here. She has known him for some time for she dated him before going to California.

Eva Nell (Smitty) and Smitty have called it "quits" all of a sudden. They were going to be married this week, but he suddenly decided that he is still in love with his former wife, although he has a divorce from her. Smitty (Eva Nell) is very much in love with Smitty, but he has surely handed her a number of dirty deals. He led her to believe that he was very much in love with her and even had bought a wedding and an engagement ring. Eva Nell was very shocked and hurt over the idea so after he left last night, she went out and drank until she could bearly stand alone. She has been sick all day. I felt so sorry for her, but yet there was nothing I could do for heart-sickness. Maybe that's one reason I'm glad you were never married before I met you, although I didn't once think that such would happen to them. There was one great thing missing and that is they didn't trust each other. I seem to appreciate you more and more each day for that's one thing I'm very proud of is the fact, I trust you fully. I've never had any reason for doubting you and don't suppose I ever will. I could never feature your doing any one the way Smitty has treated Eva Nell.

Sister Theodora called me while on duty this afternoon just to comment on my work. She said that the Sister who is in charge of my floor said that I was very efficient, used good judgment and very intelligent. I practically hit the ceiling when she finished telling me all that.

I know I don't live up to all that so I don't believe she really meant it. She just wants me to work for her when I have finished, but I don't fancy doing that. These Sisters are too unfair so I don't care to work for them.

You're certainly taking in a variety of classes recently. You'll have to teach me those things when you return for all I know how to do well is hand out bed-pans.

I know you must be bored by now so I'll hush. Don't mention Smitty's affair to Bennett.

I love you very much—

Love Always,
Evelyn

[Following letter from Paul's mother.]

Wednesday 7/18/45

Hi there my honey:

Last Sunday my old honey was mad at me because I would not let him put the cows in the pasture because all fences were down from the cloud burst we had, and now I wonder how is my young honey because its over 2 weeks since I wrote any body so this morning its raining again and all out side work at a stand still I will start my own letter writeing again.

I presume by this time you know all about Pauline's illness and operation and that she is just doing fine she is able once more to be up and around and walk around outside and enjoy life. Polly was a very sick girl but thank goodness she can smile once more But is scared to think she may never have a child onely dont ever tell her, the doctor said she can have children. And listen dont blame her or Earl because neither could help for what she went through June & Willard blame her for not takeing care. but I know better. Well did you still not get to see Wayne or any body else down there. Last nite Norman W. came home he was in Belgium & France his brother Roland is in a France Hospital with appendicitis. Norman looks grand. Sheldon is in Texas now his address is Sqdn "C" 2511 A.A.F. Base Unit. Bryan Air Field. We still have not heard from Charles & Roy. I hope both are well. The Grand parents are both well. and so is every body else around us. Hope you are in the best of health. We are

> With all my love.
> Mother & Dad.
> Polly & Earl.

P.S. Polly is still sleeping this morning

July 19–

Dear Paul,

I would love to be with you now, but since I can't, I do have the pleasure of writing you again. I had expected a letter from you yesterday and since I didn't receive one, maybe I'll hear from you today.

It's one o'clock in the morning—my usual bed-time and how I could enjoy sleeping! I'm still on duty with the same patient I told you of previously. He's very nice and is sleeping soundly at the present.

You should be quite surprised when I tell you this. Three of the Doctors have asked me to work for them, the Supervisor of the Operating room has asked me to work there and Sister Theodora wants me to continue working for her. I still think that I would rather do special duty nursing, but I may consider working for one of the Doctors. There are so many people wanting me to do numerous things and I don't really know what to say or do. If you were here, I would know very well what I would want to do. You see, you just left me stranded. I do want to meet you in California, when you return from overseas. I want to be the first one to see you.

Do you know who I saw tonight? Fitzpatrick slipped up behind me and tapped me on the shoulder. Her Mother is in for an operation so she's on duty with her. She has a four week's old baby boy; at least, she's beginning the family right. She said that Lou is really anxious to see the baby and will have a leave soon so he can come down. She's just as "nutty" as ever and says for me to say "hello" to you for her.

We had our usual rain last night which was very nice. It was so cool this morning for sleep and did I sleep soundly!

You know, Sister Theodora should have realized by now that I don't know enough about Maternity cases to supervise the students. She gives me credit for knowing much more than I really do and I told her so. She still persists on my remaining there.

Smitty says that she has lost all trust in men and is going to be an old maid. Of course, she'll change her mind so soon as she finds some one else she cares for.

I have all day off tomorrow so I'm going to sleep all day.

I love you very much—

Evelyn

July 21–

Dear Paul,

It surely seems nice to be in a nice quiet room after having been with Maternity cases all afternoon. I'm still doing special duty with the same patient and suppose I'll be with him a few more nights yet. Every time I mention not coming back with him, he asks me to stay a few more nights. He is sleeping soundly so he really isn't much trouble. It's just the continuous long hours that are getting me down. If I ever get a good chance to sleep again, I'm afraid I'll cultivate the sleeping disease.

Mom received a telegram from David saying that Clara has a baby girl. Isn't that wonderful? You know the other one is a boy and what a "rounder" he is! Of course, I knew David would spoil him.

One of the Doctors (Doctor McLane) the one who calls me "cookie," looked me up this afternoon to ask me to work for him. I was just waiting for him to ask so I'm going to accept his offer. He is an eye, ear, nose, and throat specialist and such a jolly old fellow. He is also a very good Doctor and very popular. A number of the girls in my class wanted to work for him so that's why I didn't really think I had a chance.

I don't know when I'll get to go over home again, but I surely would like to go this week. It will probably be about two weeks from now before I can go over again. Mom tries to get me to come over more often and I know she gets very lonesome.

What a wonderful dream came true—I awakened today to find that I had received another letter from you! I always feel so happy when I hear from you.

We are having our share and also your share of the rain too. It rains every night and tonight there's a hard wind blowing in the windows so I had to close them. I could enjoy the breeze very much, but it isn't too good for the patient for he was already feeling rather chilly when he went to sleep.

Smitty (red-head) and I are planning to get an apartment together. She still dates that same sailor she was dating when you left. They plan to be married some time in the future. He's afraid he may have to be shipped out so he doesn't want to be married if he has to go overseas. If it was left for her to decide, they would be married now, but he can't see it that way.

I'm going to fall asleep if I don't hush. I love you very much—

Love Always—
Evelyn

July 21—

Dear Paul,

It's now almost six thirty in the afternoon and I'm on duty, but I'm not busy at the present so I'll bother you with another letter. I suppose you're wondering why I'm writing you twice during the same day. I received a letter from you today along with one you sent from Pauline and was as happy as ever to receive them. You must have been rather down in the "dumps" when you wrote it for it made me feel the same. Some time ago; in fact, about ten months ago I had my choice between you and my profession. You know which I chose and I'm proud of my decision. It's true that I remained in training until I completed the three year course, but I thought at the time that was the best thing to do and then be married. If you only knew how much I hope and pray that you'll soon return so we can be together again, you would well understand that I don't care for further extension of my profession. I am only trying to choose the best paying position in the nursing service for I don't care for anything permanent until you return. I hope this will convince you for you seem to be a bit uncertain about me at times. If I've given you any reason to doubt me, I didn't intend doing so. It's definite that my profession shall not interfere with our marriage.

I'm very glad that Pauline is feeling much better now and hope she soon recovers. She probably had an ectopic pregnancy which is too much in detail to tell you in a letter. I'll tell you all about it some time and will also let you read the interesting parts of my numerous medical books. Of course, you'll miss out on the many lectures we had, but I usually slept during class period. I have a box packed with books which are very good reference.

One of my former class mates was admitted last night and had a baby boy. She was really celebrated for practically the entire class was in to see her.

I suppose I've said enough so I'll hush. I do hope that you believe me for I love you very much and love is something sacred.

Love always,
Evelyn

July 23–

Dear Paul,

I have just reported on duty and since there are no undelivered patients in, I'll begin a letter to you. The girls are busy with the patients and here I sit doing nothing and just in hopes Sister doesn't wander back while I'm writing you.

The most wonderful breeze is blowing in the windows and I hope it continues for it's so nice and cool. You remember it's usually very hot here during July, but we've had wonderful weather this month. How well I remember last year this time; at least, those are grand memories. I can hardly wait till I see you again.

I found out today the exact date that I finish here which is the twenty-fifth of August. I promised Doctor McLane that I would find out the correct date and go down to see through his office tomorrow. He is really a swell person and a very good Doctor. He knows that we're engaged and will be married so soon as you return.

I had a letter from Mom the other day so I suppose she is wandering why I haven't been over home recently. I just haven't had the time since I've been doing double shifts for the past week and a half.

I had better make this letter short for I'm afraid Sister may come in at any time and she would probably punish me by taking my day for this week. I'll always love you very much.

Love,
Evelyn

July 25–

Dear Paul,

It has seemed so long since I received your last letter and I was disappointed again today when the Postman was by. I do look forward to receiving your letters so very much.

I had the most wonderful letter from your Mother today. She knows just how and what to say each time she writes for I always feel better after having read a letter from her.

Jancsik and I were just down to the grocery store trying to find something we would like to eat. We finally ended up with a picnic affair and ice cream for dessert. Some of the other girls came in and ate with us. If I had a great imagination, I would have placed you at the table with us (me); Nevertheless, I was thinking of you.

Now, I'm so uncomfortable that I can bearly write so you see, I shouldn't have eaten so much. Maybe my food should be rationed even more.

Today has been as an autumn day usually is here; in fact, I was even chilly at times. It's very pleasant so I wouldn't mind if it would remain this way.

Margaret's cousin, Anna is here for the week. She is on her way home (Tampa) from college and stopped by. I like her very much, but she is as comical looking as I am so you can readily sympathize with her.

Margaret is leaving the first of August for Tampa and stay until the fifteenth. Then she is to report to Vanderbilt University for her last six month's nurse's training. I hope she likes it there.

Oh yes, has Val returned yet? I love you so much—

Love Always,
Evelyn

[Following letter from Paul's friend, Joe Maceluch.]

July 25, 1945.

Dear Paul;

I received your letter just a few days ago. As you can see I have already received orders and am with my new outfit. I believe I told you in my last letter that I expected a change of address. Jake and all the others were transferred shortly after myself and as far as I know were put in the 1st Division. I suppose by this time you have heard from Jake giving you all the dope.

It is really a shame that you didn't take that 5 days off and relax a little. Of course with the number of men that were there at that time the chances were around a thousand to one that you would have met any one of us.

All of us were very glad to hear that you came through the Iwo campaign alright and all wish you the Best of Luck on any others that you may be in. I was very much surprised to hear that you were no longer in the QM, what's the dope, did you get tired of it or isn't there any room for you in the Motor Transport of your outfit.

That QM-Sgt that you looked up for me wrote me a letter of apoligy for the way he acted towards you, throwing all those questions at you and then he didn't even find out your name. He said when you came to see him he thought I might be somewhere on the island and wanted to know where.

Jake and I talked it over the day he wrote you and since I was a censor I passed his letter to you & told him not to say he saw me. We both wondered if you would recognize my initials on his letter. I wrote you that night or the next in reply to the things you wanted to know in Jake's letter. I'm sure Margaret would be very pleased to hear from you when you can find the time to write.

I don't know where Roberts is now, I suppose he is someplace out here in the Pacific. I've written to him two or three times but still haven't received a reply.

Margaret and Johnnie are both in the best of health and getting along as well as could be expected. With that I think I have covered all I have to say for now so I'll leave it up to you. Until the next time, take care of yourself & the Best of Luck to you.

Always,
Joe.

QM-Sgt. Joseph Z. Maceluch, U.S.M.C.

[On Pensacola Hospital letterhead; on half-sheets of paper]

PENSACOLA HOSPITAL
Pensacola, Florida
July 27–

Dear Paul,

Since my patient is sleeping, I'll write you. It's now two o'clock in the morning and again I'm doing special duty, but this time with a maternity case. I don't know why I continue taking night cases and working double shifts, but she really needed a special and they weren't able to get anyone who's on the registry.

I received one nice long letter from you today along with a another very short note. You must have been in a hurry when you wrote the latter for it consisted of two paragraphs. I was very happy to get them.

What type classes are you having now? You're certainly taking a variety of them which may be very beneficial to you some day. I must say that you have much more energy than I for I never want to attend classes anymore. It seems I've been in school all my life time and have accomplished very little. I hope you wan't be too disappointed in me for I don't know what type housewife I'm going to be. I do hope to be a good one, but you'll find out some day.

It's so very quiet on the halls tonight and seems so nice not to have a lot of noise. Even the babies are quiet at the present. Just wait until feeding time again and we'll hear plenty from them.

I had better run in to see about the patient for she has lost a great deal of blood so I'm afraid to leave her for a long period of time. She had a Ceasarian section and has a baby girl.

I'll say so-long until later.

All my love,
Evelyn

P.S. How do you like my stationery?

July 29–

Dear Paul,

If you could see me now, I'm sure you would laugh for I'm standing in the hallway of the delivery rooms and using a stretcher to write on. I have two patients in who will probably deliver on my shift. I don't like this type duty, but it seems that Sister is going to leave me here for the remainder of my training. Oh well, I'll know the art of having a baby.

I wrote your Mother a letter last night and I know she will be so bored having to read it. I really enjoy hearing from her.

Well, I had a slight interference for we just had a delivery. It was a boy, of course. It seems that she would have had one of the better sex, don't you think?

Father Dolan was just in and was kidding me as usual. You know what a big tease he is. I'll never forget the day we met him at Fort Walton. I was so afraid he might tell Sister and you know what that would have meant.

I'm surely glad that Pauline is feeling well again. She must have suffered a great deal from what your Mother said. We have had patients with the same disorder so I know fairly well what she has endured.

Oh yes, about our honeymoon—I can think of many places I would much rather be than at my home. She was just kidding, I suppose, for she knows that I don't want to do that.

I still haven't found a place to move to after I leave Gadsden Street. I have to move out for I'm not going to work for the Hospital and it's reserved only for that purpose. I know a girl who used to teach school at the same place as Elizabeth and they were very good friends. I might be able to get a room from her so I'll call her soon. It's so difficult to find a place to stay.

Frank will soon have to report back to base again for his leave is up the last of this month. He still thinks that he'll receive a Medical discharge when he returns. If so, he and Mamie are planning to go to California and asked me to go along. I would like to very much, but I would rather wait and meet you there when you return from overseas. I can assure you that the latter would be much more enjoyable.

What did you tell your Mother about that terrible picture I sent you?

Oh yes, Sinclair is overseas some place so you may see him. Phiel had a letter from him and he tells her that he still loves her. Phiel is in charge of the other hall which is on this same floor so she comes back to visit me once in a while.

I love you very much—

Evelyn

July 31–

Dear Paul,

This has really been some day! I've only been down town three times today. I had the day off duty so first of all, I went along with Jancsik to town and stayed only a few minutes. Just as we returned Smitty asked me to go back with her, so I did. Late this afternoon Patterson and I decided to go to a movie so I went down town again. We saw the "cutest" movie. You may have seen it "Can't help Singing" with Dianna Durbin. She's a wonderful actress, don't you agree?

Oh yes, you wondered who Margaret Murphy is. You remember, I introduced you to her one day and told you she was my roommate. I believe I also told you of our being in High School together; then we worked in the same dress shop. Afterwards, we were in Miami at the same time so I left there in order to enter training. A few months later she called me at the Hospital and said that she was also entering training in the next class. We have been roommates since Ernestine was married so you see, we've been together a great while.

8-1-45

Eva Nell Smith has forgiven Smitty for all the things he did and they are to be married tonight. They wanted me and one of Smitty's boy friends from the Station to stand with them. I surely would like to, but I can't arrange to get off duty and will be working from three-to-eleven. I was down town with Smitty and helped her choose a dress for the occasion. She's so very happy, but to express my opinion, I don't believe that he is so much in love with her. I surely wish them all the happiness possible.

Our maid, Patsy has been on a vacation, but returned today. She said she wished she could have stayed on her vacation after having taken one look in the house. I can't say I blame her.

We had the cutest pup here for some time. We named her Amber; don't you like that for a doggie? She was run over by an automobile once and later just disappeared. We miss her very much for she was always biting our toes.

It will soon be time for the Postman so I hope to have a letter from you.

All My Love,
Evelyn

August 3–

Dear Paul,

I'm about roasted for it's so very warm this morning. It's beginning to get a bit cloudy so maybe we'll have some rain which would be very much appreciated.

I'm on special duty with the head Supervisor's sister and will be on with her again tomorrow. You see, I keep my patients sleeping most of the time so then I have time to write you.

I was so happy to get home last night and find I had a letter from you—you wonderful man! If you only knew how much I look forward to those letters.

Well, the great event has at last happened. Smitty and Smitty were married Wednesday night and are very happy. She doesn't want Sister Theodora to know for she wants to remain in training as she only has another six months to complete. Her two week's vacation begins Monday which is very nice. How I wish we could have made it a double wedding! At least, I want have to worry with Hospital hours when you return.

I have at last found a nice place to live when I have to move from Gadsden house. It's location is twelfth and Jackson and a very nice little brick home with all the modern conveniences. I told Smitty about it so I'm going to take her around to see it for we plan to room together. The woman who owns the place is a widow and doesn't have any children. I believe I would like it there very much.

I only have twenty-two more days at the Hospital. It just doesn't seem real that I'm getting out so soon—yet it seems so long ago when I first entered for so much has happened since then.

It's about lunch hour and I'm starved so I'll run along to eat.

Love Always,
Evelyn

August 6–

Dear Paul,

It's so very warm in my room so I'm sitting on the porch for it's a wee bit cooler even though there isn't much breeze—You're very lucky to have such nice weather there. I wouldn't want you to see me as I am at the present for I have my hair pinned tightly on top of my head. You would probably run in the opposite direction if you did see me.

Hodges came by and wanted me to go around to the grocery store with her as she was very hungry. We have just returned and I've eaten until I'm miserable. That's a great sin to eat so much I know, but it was such a great temptation. Hodges is also complaining of the stomach ache. Maybe we'll learn better eating habits some day.

I was down town with Van Allen all afternoon and roamed the streets so much while shopping that my feet don't seem to want to cooperate with my body anymore. I was expecting Smitty (Merle) to be here when I returned, but I suppose she forgot our date for tonight. You see, we were going around to see a room that we're planning to live in when I leave here. I don't know how I could get in touch with her for she doesn't have a telephone. I'll probably see her while on duty tomorrow.

Don't you worry about David and Clara not being able to remember you for they've heard quite a bit about you. Other than that, you were introduced to them one day—Remember? They'll be glad to hear from you. I can tell you that neither is much at writing letters for I seldom hear from them.

Smitty and Smitty were by only a few minutes ago and they are so very happy. It made me happy just to be with them. They have a nice little apartment on Moreno and Davis Street and have envited me over. Maybe I should get a few clues on married life. You think I should?

I'll probably go over home Wednesday night for Mom always seems happy to have me over. I really can't understand why, but I suppose if I stayed home all the time, she would become tired of having me around.

I want to shampoo my hair so I'll get busy.

All My Love,
Evelyn

August 8–

Dear Paul,

This is my day off duty and have I been house-cleaning! I really did away with a lot of <u>rubbish</u> from my trunks and closet. To top it off, Jancsik came down while in the midst of my cleaning and asked me to go along to town with her. Of course, as always, even though I didn't want to go, I couldn't say "no." Now my feet are tired and I feel very dirty, but I'll write you before bathing.

You must be having lots of fun on your leave. 'Just wish I could be there with you for we would surely have lots of fun, I know. To be with you would make me the happiest person in the world. The war news sound very convincing that the war can't last so very much longer. I hope that's true, but time will tell.

It's very cloudy so we'll probably have a bit of rain directly. I don't mind if it does rain for it's been so very warm recently. The breeze is wonderful at the present and I hope it continues the same for a while.

Smitty was over last night to press (Sailor) Smith's uniforms for they don't have an iron. She said that was the only thing she disliked about marriage was the fact that she couldn't just have fun all the time. Although, she didn't like the idea of pressing so many uniforms, she still is very happy.

Margaret will be leaving next Monday and I'll miss her so very much, I'm sure. I believe I've told you that she is going to Vanderbilt Hospital for the remainder of her training which is six months. She wants me to go along and work there, but I can't see that so I'll remain here for a while anyway. When I do leave, I want to go to California for I want to be there when you return.

I had planned to go over home today, but changed my mind for I had so many things I needed to do—Maybe I can go over next week for I would like to have a talk with my Mother.

I'll hush for I have some other letters to write. I love you very much

And Always,
Evelyn

August 10–

Dear Paul,

It's already past midnight and I'm becoming very sleepy. You may know that I'm on a special duty case again, but I don't feel tired from the extra hours. It always makes Mom mad when I tell her of my doing extra duty hours.

I listened to the President's speech at nine o'clock last night which was very interesting. The war news sound very encouraging and especially true with the last great discovery.

I could very easily compare this room to a hot oven for there would be only a slight difference. I'm about roasted and the perspiration is trickling down my back. I wish we would have another nice shower for the rain does help to lower the temperature a wee bit.

I can bearly see how to write for I have the light practically dimmed out. The patient seems to be enjoying her sleep emencely, but she doesn't snore. I wish she would for that may help to keep me awake.

I was talking with Smitty the other night so I'll tell you what she said very unexpectedly. She said that all the girls of my class were very jealous of me for a number of the Superiors at the Hospital had commented among themselves about what excellent work I have done. Also, a number of the Doctors have asked me to work for them and the Hospital Staff has asked me to work here. So far as I know, none of the others have been asked the same, but I don't understand why they should feel that way toward me. I have only done my best while on duty and I'm sure my fellow classmates could do the same if they try. I'm proud of the number of compliments I have received, but I don't go about repeating them to everyone. I tell you, for I know you'll understand. I'm going to continue to do my work so well as possible for that was one of my first intentions when I entered training. Oh well, I'll forget all this when you reach the States again.

Had a nice long letter from Elizabeth and J. C. today. J. C. thinks he may have to go overseas, but don't repeat this to Mom or Mamie for Elizbeth doesn't want them to know just now. You see, she tells me all her troubles for we've always been so close. Now, I tell you for we seem more close even though we aren't married yet. Here's hoping it won't be long before we can be married and how I look forward to that day!

I want to write Bennett a letter so I'll end this boring conversation for I know you must be tired by now.

All My love,
Evelyn

August 12–

Dear Paul,

Merle Smith and I were just down for some coffee as you know, we have to do some thing in order to remain awake. She is on special duty with a patient on second floor and I'm still on with the patient on third whom I've told you of previously. She is a very nice patient and wants me to remain on with her during the rest of her stay here. I can't be with her after tonight for my shift will change so that I will be working day duty.

I've been listening to the new's broadcast every chance I get for the recent news surely sound good. I knew those darn Japs weren't so smart that we couldn't handle them.

It's just so terribly hot tonight—don't even have to take my daily bath any more since I perspire so profusely. I will certainly appreciate the Autumn coolness and even the cold days of Winter.

(Hours later)—Have had quite an intermission since I first began this letter. It has begun to rain and there is a nice breeze. Hope this continues the remainder of the night.

Since I didn't go over home last week, I suppose I shall go over on my day off this week. I would like to have a week's vacation before beginning to work for Doctor McLane, but one of his nurse's is leaving the first of September. He wants me to become familar with his office before she leaves.

Haven't heard from your Mother recently, but I suppose she is kept quite busy. Would like to know how Pauline is feeling now.

Going to church today? Sunday, you know.

All My Love,
Evelyn

August 14

Dear Paul,

Oh happy Day! And what a celebration! I'm just so much excited and happy. This afternoon I was upstairs with Smitty when all of a sudden Mahan ran by the door and yelled out that the war had ended. We sat on the porch and watched the many cars pass and of course, everyone was making so much noise as possible. We then dressed and went down town to watch the parade. It was all wonderful except for so much kissing that was involved. I don't believe I've ever been kissed by such a variety of people before except for the time I was at Chattahoochee. I didn't like the idea, but that didn't seem to help much for everyone laughed at me. The main thing I'm so excited about is that maybe you will return to the States soon. Nothing could make me more happy.

Margaret Murphy, my room mate, left last night for Tennessee for as I've told you, she will complete her last six month's training there. She will also have a post-graduate course and receive a B. S. degree after having completed two year's study following the nurse's course.

Pitts moved down to take Margaret's place as my room mate. When I returned home this afternoon, she had moved everything about in the room and I had to think twice in order not to invade her dressing table by mistake. She is a "screw-ball" if I ever saw one and wants me to be her "Maid-of-honor" if I'm here when her boy friend comes from over-seas.

Oh yes, Phiel is going to be married to an Ensign so soon as she has completed the remainder of her days here. I don't believe she is really in love with him. She has said for some time that if she met a nice boy she would marry him for she just wants to be married. It's quite different with me for I never felt that way. I wouldn't marry anyone if I didn't love him for it's so wonderful to really love someone.

I had a letter from Bennett today and wish I had brought it along so I could send it to you.

I'm sending another letter that I received from Elizabeth. Her letters are few and far between.

I believe I told you that Frank had a back injury other than Arthritis. His back will probably always be weak from that.

I hope so much to hear from you tomorrow.

All My love Always,
Evelyn

August 14

Dear Paul,

Oh happy Day! And what a
celebration! I'm just so much excited
and happy. This afternoon I was upstairs with Smitty when all of a
sudden Mahan ran by the door and
yelled out that the war had ended.
We sat on the porch and watched
the many cars pass and of course,
everyone was making so much noise
as possible. We then dressed and
went down town to watch the parade.
It was all wonderful except for
so much kissing that was involved.
I don't believe I've ever been kissed
by such a variety of people before
except for the time I was at Chattahoochee. I didn't like the idea, but
that didn't seem to help much for
everyone laughed at me. The main
thing I'm so excited about is that
maybe you will return to the States
soon. Nothing could make me more
happy.

Margaret Murphy, my roommate, left

Evelyn's letter, V-J Day, August 14, 1945

last night for Tennessee for as I've
told you, she will complete her last
six month's training there. She will
also have a post-graduate course
and receive a B.S. degree after
having completed two year's study
following the nurse's course.

Pitts moved down to take Margaret's
place as my room-mate. When I
returned home this afternoon, she
had moved everything about in the
room and I had to think twice
in order not to invade her dressing
table by mistake. She is a "screw-ball"
if I ever saw one and wants me
to be her "maid-of-honor" if I'm here
when her boy friend comes from over-seas.

Oh yes, Phel is going to be married
to an Ensign so soon as she has
completed the remainder of her days
here. I don't believe she is really in
love with him. She has said for some
time that if she met a nice boy she
would marry him for she just wants
to be married. It's quite different

Evelyn's letter, V-J Day, August 14, 1945

703

August 16–

Dear Paul,

I received the most wonderful letter from you today. Maybe I should say letters for they were written during your vacation—or leave. I know that you must have had a grand time. Golly, but I wish I could have been with you. I hope to be with you during your next leave which I'm praying won't be long.

I was over home last night and would liked to have stayed over through tonight, but I had to come back in order to find out about a room. You know I only have nine more days in training—isn't that wonderful! Just continue to use the same address until I'm sure of another place. I could still have the room I told you about some time ago, but I would rather live in town for it would be more convenient. The place I have in mind and hope to get soon is directly behind the Post Office. The lady said that I could have the next vacancy which I hope won't be long.

I had today off duty and slept most of the time. About three-thirty this afternoon Check came by my room and wanted me to go along with her to meet the train as she expects her brother to arrive most any time. He didn't come in on that train so we drove out to her home in Warrington. Her Mother and Father are very nice so I've been out several times. After having eaten, we came back to town and saw a movie "Nob Hill" which was rather odd, but fairly good. Just as I returned to the house, I received a call from the Main office. They were unable to get a registered nurse for a patient so they asked me to do special duty with her. Her breast was amputated yesterday and tonight she began hemorrhaging. She also has a rash on her back and complains of severe itching. I made her as comfortable as possible and she is resting well at the present.

Oh yes, Jimmie and Doris have a big boy and are so very happy and excited about the new offspring. I know they must be "thrilled to pieces" that the first one is a boy. I wish I could have cared for her since that is my line of duty at the present.

My jaw is still sore from having so many Sailors kiss me during the celebration Tuesday night. Wish you could have been with me for they wouldn't have bothered me then. I felt a bit nauseated by the time I reached home and was I glad to get there safely!

David thinks that he will have a furlough next month. I surely hope that he will for I would like to see them very much—especially Ronnie for he must be so cute.

I have several other letters to answer so I'll say "Good-night."

All My love,
Evelyn

Ella Wells Myers with her six adult children
From left: Frank Wells, Elizabeth Wells Brown,
David Wells, Emma Wells Broxson, Jimmy Wells,
and Evelyn Wells Fogel, September 1948

Ella McKinney Wells Myers, Evelyn's Mother, and
her second husband, Mr. Phillip Myers, 1950
(Evelyn's father, John Wells, died of advanced
diabetes when Evelyn was two years old)

August 18—

Dear Paul,

It's almost day light and I feel as wide awake as can be. I was on special duty with the same patient last night and she wants me with her again tonight. I tried to get out of coming on with her again for she doesn't really need a special anymore. Of course, she couldn't understand why I should become tired of doing double shifts so I promised I would be back for one more night with her.

I'm sitting at the chart desk which is directly in front of the Nursery so you can imagine the noise. It used to irritate me so very much to hear a baby cry, but I must have become quite accustomed to the sound for now it doesn't bother me at all.

These creeping roaches continue to peek around the corners. Something of any value would never be so plentiful. We also have our share and more too at Gadsden house.

Aren't you on Guard duty? If so, does that mean that you will have to remain overseas longer than you would otherwise? I surely hope not for I want you to return as soon as possible. I do want to see you so very much.

I have just finished answering a letter which I received from Ernestine. I was beginning to believe that she had forgotten me, but she apologised so of course, I couldn't be angry at her. She sent me the most beautiful picture of her small son and he is just precious. I surely would like to see him and also Ernestine and Bill. She still wants me to come see her and I would visit her if I had enough time.

I miss Margaret a great deal, but I'll finally get used to not seeing her around. You know, we just can't be together the remainder of our lives, but she has surely made big plans.

I'll hush for I have to bathe the patient. I love you very much.

Evelyn

August 20–

Dear Paul,

Have just returned home from duty and what a riot! The place is full of drunk sailors and of course a number of the nurses are involved. One sure has to endure a lot of nonsense in order to remain around this joint. You may well understand that for you saw quite a few performances during the time you were here.

The letter I received from you today was written on V-J day—a date I shall always remember. Another date I shall never forget is the day I see you again. What a happy day that will be!

You said that one of the boys who saw my picture could read faces. But you didn't tell me what he said about me and all bad points included. Did you agree with him on everything?

Oh yes, you asked me about Elizabeth Sherrer. I haven't seen or heard from her for ages. She was in Panama City the last time I heard of her. Did you know that she was in charge of the first ward where I worked when I first entered training? I really thought she was a wonderful nurse and she did help me a great deal.

Just four more days now and I shall be free. I'm getting a room down town which is directly behind the Post Office and by the Church. Isn't that wonderful for I'll only be only three blocks from Doctor McLane's office. I'll work for him until you return and then I will go with you wherever you go. If you go back to Hawaii, I'll go there too.

You may address my letters the same until I find out my new address.

I have to work tomorrow morning so I'll get some sleep. Goodnight.

All My Love,
Evelyn

August 22–

Dear Paul,

When I came in from duty this afternoon, Pitts had just awakened and was very hungry. She is on night duty so of course, she hadn't eaten anything since breakfast. We went around to the corner grocery again and bought a few things and came back and prepared our afternoon meal. After having eaten, we decided to sleep for a few hours and then go for a walk. It just happens that we awakened in time for her to get dressed for duty as it is ten-thirty now and she has to report on duty at eleven.

I was hoping so very much to receive a letter from you today, but was disappointed when I returned home. Maybe it just wasn't time for another to arrive yet, but I surely look forward to them.

Do you hear from your Mother often? I haven't heard from her for quite some time. I do hope Pauline is well again by now.

Oh yes, I'll move to 1201 E. Jackson Street next Tuesday. That's the room I first told you about and it's very nice. The woman who owns the home is a so sweet. I believe she would do most anything to help someone.

I suppose I shall begin working for Doctor McLane Monday as one of his nurses is leaving the first of September. He still calls me "Cookie" and it wouldn't seem right if he didn't.

I discharged a patient from the Hospital today whose husband is from Bethlehem, Pennsylvania. His name is P. J. Cicchine and he said that he knew of the Fogels, but didn't know your family.

I see the Smittys quite often and they're still very happy. She is back on hall duty again with Sister Theodora's approval. Isn't that wonderful for she was so afraid Sister would kick her out of training.

I'll say goodnight and sleep some.

All My Love,
Evelyn

August 23–

Dear Paul,

I haven't heard from you for the past five days so you've probably been kept quite busy recently since the end of war in the Pacific. I do hope that you will return to the States soon. That's the way you can make me very happy.

Tomorrow is my last day in training and a day I shall long remember. Everyone has been telling me how much they shall miss me, but I think they're only kidding. I didn't plan to do anymore special duty, but I find myself sitting with a patient for the night. She isn't very ill and really only needs someone near in order to turn her frequently.

I received a letter from Margaret today and she likes Vanderbilt Hospital very much. It must be a very nice place and I knew their training is highly rated. I've been so busy, I haven't had much time to think of missing her. She was seldom home when I was.

Pitts and I slept all afternoon so when we awakened tonight, we were very hungry. We bought some cake and ice cream and as usual, ate too much. I've been miserable ever since.

We've had such beautiful moonlight nights recently. I would just love to be with you so we could really enjoy the beauty. But here I sit with the sick—and you many miles away in the Pacific.

It's very warm tonight so I'm fortunate to have a patient who has a fan. This Summer hasn't been nearly so hot as that of previous years so why should I complain.

My hand just doesn't care to write tonight so I've certainly been scribbling. You're probably used to my writing by now so maybe it hasn't been too difficult for you. I'll try to scribble better next time.

Love Always,
Evelyn

August 25–

Dear Paul,

It seemed rather odd, but a very happy occasion to have all the girls congratulate me and say "Good-bye" yesterday. Since I had done double-duty (sixteen hours) I was rather tired so I came home, had a bath and went to bed. Some way to celebrate, don't you think?

Sister Theodora still hasn't given me the class pin and diploma. It's about time she has those things ready to hand out. We also are supposed to receive our registration papers to be completed before we can legally work for anyone. Of course, since everyone knows the members of our class, we can begin working right away; in fact, I'm supposed to report on duty at Doctor McLane's office Monday morning.

You should have seen the washing I did this morning and I ironed them this afternoon. Since I've been doing special duty so much, I haven't had the time or energy to keep all my clothes clean. I haven't yet learned to wash and press men's clothes. It will be fun having you teach me.

You didn't even mention the picture you sent along in the letter that I received from you today. It's very good of you and who's the friend? Could he be Val—the one whom you speak of so often? I'll bet he is really a character. You know I love surprises of that type so you may try sending pictures more often.

I have most of my things packed to move Tuesday. I will be at (1201 East Jackson Street) so you can use that address now.

Wander why you hadn't received any mail for such a long time. I hope you've received numerous letters by now.

I love you very much now

And always,
Evelyn

[Letter below from Paul's friend, Jake Kupsky.]

Guam
28 August, 1945

Dear Paul:

Say how about answering my last letter I wrote you. Did you ever receive same, if not I apologize.

Do you get to see Austin (scoop), Krensavage? I met Krensavage at P. H., when I was there. Kuhn was here also for about a month and I got to see him almost every night. Met him during the operation. He is not here anymore. You probably have as good an idea as I have as to his whereabouts. Also met Sterner here a few weeks ago. Sunday I went to see him and spent the day there with him. He is working in operations on detached duty with Army. He was with me when I went to see your folks. Think you should remember him. Sterner also met Kuhn here for first time since "boot camp," he still recognized him. Sterner's a T/Sgt. McCoy is nearly working in the P. X. Wallace, Young, and Blass are as far as I know with 3rd [illegible] Corp, further more I can't say as I don't have either's address nor heard from them. Dunbar is with

1st Div., so is Maceluch. Incidentally got letter from Joe yesterday. Says he's doing OK. Surmise you corresponde with him. Is Kopperl anywhere's nearby? Did you get to see him? If you see him give my regards.

How did you celebrate when you heard the war being over? We raised plenty of noise that's about all. What we needed was something to celebrate with (bottle). Get a case and 15 Cokes per month. Thats divided throughout the month.

Ever get to hear from "red." I've heard from her about twice. She's probably married, or in the Navy by now. Who knows we might have a run in out here. When I left Fla., she was rushed by a sailor.

How about it drop me a line when you get the ambition or the latest dope. Until then take care of yourself and I'll see you in Pa., in about a year??????

As Always,
"Jake"
Sgt. Jacob Kupsky, Jr.

August 28–

Dear Paul,

I'm beginning to believe that I shall never get straightened out again, but I still have hopes. I am now at Mrs. Chavers on Jackson Street and suppose I'll be here until I leave in order to meet you. Of course, that time can't be too soon.

Mrs. Chavers is so very nice and I couldn't have chosen a better place to live. She just makes me feel as though I were at home and I believe she would do most anything for me. She has a nice little brick home and my room is just the type I had hoped to find.

Doctor McLane is also a wonderful person. I began working at his office yesterday and he treats me as though I were someone to work with instead of being "bossy." He is always so jolly and happy even after having worked all day. We have long hours, but we have off every Thursday, Saturday afternoon and Sunday. We will also have Monday (Labor Day) off next week. Isn't that wonderful? I was certainly lucky to have such grand opportunities and I'm very grateful. Maybe I don't deserve such.

David and Clara may get to come home soon. I want to see them so very much, but mostly Ronnie. He must really be a character by now.

Oh yes, I had another letter from Margaret today. She still likes Vanderbilt very much and I'm very glad she does. So far as I'm concerned, I don't care to ever study books again for it seems that I've been in school all my lifetime and I have been really.

I'm very tired tonight and sleepy. I love you so very much and do hope you can return home soon.

All My love,
Evelyn

P.S. Phiel was married yesterday afternoon at five-thirty o'clock.

August 30–

Dear Paul,

As I may have told you, I'm off every Thursday so I had a chance to sleep late this morning. I slept until almost nine o'clock and I still feel a bit sleepy. That's just laziness, I suppose.

The first thing I did this morning was treat Mrs. Chaver's cold. She must have slept in a draft during the night for she awakened with a most awful cold. It was so nice and cool in the early morning; just as an Autumn day. There is still a wonderful breeze.

Mrs. Chaver's home is situated on a hill just above the ball park and is a little brick home— you may remember it. I have already learned her life history and more too, although she is very nice. She has me come in every morning to have toast and coffee with her.

Oh yes, I like the idea of meeting you in some State on your way home if I don't have the chance to meet you on the West Coast. If you know in time that you are coming in at San Francisco, I'd like very much to meet you there so we can make the trip together. And I do want to be married to you before going to your home and I hope we don't have to wait three days for our marriage license. It will be so wonderful to be with you again and this time I wan't let you out of my sight again for such a long time anyway. I seem to miss you more all the time.

I had another letter from Margaret yesterday and she was so home sick when she wrote the letter. She said if only I was there with her, but of course, that's quite impossible at the present and I don't want to go either. She says it's a wonderful Hospital and everyone is swell, but even so she is still home sick. I don't suppose she can find a cure for that so long as she is there. That's something that has to gradually wear away and the hard way at that.

I have to take your (our) radio down to have it checked again. I believe one of the tubes has blown as it did once before. It's a lot of company so I miss it very much when it won't play. Then I have to create my own music which isn't much.

I have to run over to the Hospital to see if I can get my diploma so I would better hurry before lunch.

All My Love,
Evelyn

September 2–

Dear Paul,

I'm sorry that I've had to wait so long to write you again. I can assure you that it could not be helped.

Last Friday evening I was in a car accident. We were driving along slowly and well on our side of the road, but the boys who were meeting us were zigzagging across the road. Of course, you know the rest as well as I for I didn't realize what had happened until they were helping me from the car. I have only slight injuries; in fact, just a few bruises and a black eye which will clear up in a few days. I did enjoy my ride in the ambulance. Thank Heavens, I didn't receive a fracture or any serious injury. Check wasn't injured at all. The boys who were meeting us were Ensigns and their car was really smashed. One was rushed to the Navy Hospital right away so I just wander what was the extent of his injury. Please don't worry about me for I'm O. K. My family doesn't know about this and I'm not going to tell them for they would only worry. I had to tell you for otherwise, you would wander why I haven't written sooner.

I like my new room so very much and Mrs. Chavers is very nice to me. She also has a school teacher who is renting the other room.

Doctor McLane is just wonderful to work for; in fact, they just don't come any better than he. He treats everyone the same and is jolly all the time.

I'll be so happy when you write me that you're on you way home. That will really call for a celebration. Of course, we shall celebrate together.

Oh yes, do you still have your "doggie"? I'll bet he is really a rounder after having stayed around you boys for awhile. We usually had some type dog around all the time that I was at Gadsden Street.

Its' getting rather late so I had better sleep a bit. Hope to hear from you again soon—

All My Love,
Evelyn

September 4–

Dear Paul,

Oh, but it's such a grand morning and I feel wonderful except for my black eye. The breeze makes it seem as though it were Autumn and it really won't be long before the Fall season. I do hope you can be home soon. Wouldn't it be wonderful to spend Christmas together?

Everyone has been so very nice to me and I appreciate their thoughtfulness so very much. A number of the Nurses and Doctors were in to see me when I was in the Hospital and since I'm at the house they call in to find out how I feel. Of course, I can't forgive them for kidding me about my black eye and you should see me. God must have been very close at the time for otherwise, I couldn't have come out of such a crash with such slight injuries. I can probably report on duty again in a couple of days.

Doctor McLane's wife just called in and said that she is going to have Doctor McLane stop in for me tomorrow night. She is having a barbeque for the Office crew and I think we'll have a very enjoyable time for they're such jolly people.

Mrs. Chavers treats me as if I were her daughter and I like it that way. She's really a swell person. Yesterday afternoon we rode almost to Milton and back. As you may know that gas isn't rationed anymore so we were out for a joy ride. Afterwards, I helped her prepare supper and we ate together. I just wish you could meet her. She knows all about you and is very interested about our engagement. I told her that we were going to be married so soon as you returned and I hope that we don't have to wait three extra days for a marriage license.

Oh yes, Mrs. Chaver's saw your camera and wants to buy some film in order to make some pictures. I think that's a good idea so maybe I can find some film some place. I'll send you the pictures in case we do make some.

How's the "doggie" and what did you name him? Oh yes, how are all the little doggies too?

Tell your room mates to take good care of you for I don't want you to be banged up as I am. The first black eye I ever had and I can't say I'm proud of it!

I'll get this letter in mail for it's almost time for the Postman.

All My Love Always,
Evelyn

September 5–

Dear Paul,

It's very early in the morning, but I was tired of sleeping so I decided to write some letters. Of course, as usual, I begin with writing to you first.

It is rather lonesome when I'm here alone for Mrs. Chavers has gone to visit her daughter. She always asks me to go along, but as you know I don't like taking advantage of someone's good nature all the time.

Later

Jancsik called over and wanted me to go along with her to town so we were shopping all morning. It is now two-thirty in the afternoon and I just returned home a few minutes ago. Mrs. Chavers is also home now.

I was so much in hopes that I would receive a letter from you, but was disappointed again.

Maybe I'll receive a letter tomorrow. The days seem so very long when I don't hear from you.

Smitty and Smitty are coming by to see me when she is off duty at three. They have an apartment on Davis Street, but are trying to find a place that will be nearer the Hospital. They are so cute together and are a lot of fun. They really have about the same type personality and even resemble each other a bit.

Haven't been home for some time so I may go over this week-end. I called Mr. Myers and talked with him for a few minutes yesterday. I didn't tell him about the accident for I knew he would tell Mother and she would only worry. Of course, there's no need for that for she has enough gray hairs already.

How's your Mother and Pauline? I haven't heard from them for such a long while.

I suppose I'll go to the barbeque tonight if Doctor McLane stops in for me. I do wish you were here to enjoy it too.

Love Always,
Evelyn

[Letter below is from Paul's friend, Leo.]

Sept. 6, 1945

Hi Fogel

Sure was glad you decided to write this old codger again. For I had began to think the slant eyes might have pulled a fast one. You asked my opinion of the war now. Well here it is, ship all of the lads home who wish to come, more quick than lightning and I do mean fast. If you disagree with me notify by return mail. You sound as if Iwo Jima might have been a lulu in the way of action. I expect you might have seen Mike by this time he was in the Pacific some where and still a going. He is on the hospital ship U. S. S. Sanctuary. If you do happen to run into him, get him to tell you about the blonde he thinks he has at his feet, who lives in Staten Island. I told him he was giving me some stuff about the gal. By the way in the last two letters I wrote you I asked you what happened to a certain little redhead. But you have not given me any facts or figures on the subject. None of my DM business huh! You said you had given up hope of me in regards to the ladies. I am much of that opinion myself, just ain't got what it takes I guess. Maybe when you Marines and sailors get home you will give me a few pointers on what gives. Speaking of Dewey he is in his glory he goes out hand lining every day. He goes out before day and gets home after dark. He is really burning the big trout up. Catching more than a hundred some days by himself. Speaking of haul [illegible], they are doing over there on the island, we used to use the same kind of method here until it got to be to hard work. You said you were learning to weld: Is it gas or electric or both. I used to do a little gas welding myself but I had to give it up on account of my eyes before I mastered it. Hope you have better success than I did. The folks sends their regards, for they were really glad to hear that the old boy was still in there pitching. Hoping to see you soon I remain the bachelor who don't seem to click.

Leonard Ward

P.S. Maybe you could find me a dark skinned one out there somewheres: No redheads though, (heap bad medicene)

September 7–

Dear Paul,

Remember last September at this date we had only been engaged a few days! I shall never forget the night (that special night) in the park opposite the house and then the night you gave me the ring. That was the happiest I had ever been. The next happiest moment of my life will be when I can be with you again.

I have only been home from duty a short while. I've had time enough to have my bath, polish my shoes, and set up my uniform for tomorrow. I was home from the office at seven-thirty and it's now nine o'clock. We only have duty until two o'clock tomorrow afternoon and also have off Sunday. You see, I just don't work any more, but it's lots of fun this way. While at the Hospital, it seemed that everyone was under such a great tension all the while, but working for Doctor McLane is such a pleasure. Everyone is so jolly all the time and never any arguments. He's always kidding us about something and you should hear the many things he has in store to tell you about me.

The barbeque was wonderful and I do wish you could have been present. Most of the girls had a date, but I was stag. Even so, I believe I had as grand a time as the others. Oh yes, Mrs. McLane said she would just love to meet you and wants the four of us to have a barbeque at her home when you return. Of course, she doesn't know that we don't plan to be here at that time. She asked so many questions about you that I don't remember any of them, although she seemed very much interested in our affairs.

I haven't seen Mother for some time, but I don't care to see her until I'm a bit more presentable. You know, I still have the black eye, although it has cleared up a great deal. Don't worry, for I think I shall even be back to normal one of these days.

It's so very quiet tonight for Mrs. Chavers is asleep and the school teacher who rooms here has gone out. Of course, I miss having the girls around.

There was the most beautiful sunset this evening. We just sat and admired the beauty for a long while.

It's quite early, but even so, I'm sleepy so I'll say "Good-night" until later.

All My love,
Evelyn

September 9–

Dear Paul,

You should join in on our conversation and see what "crazy nuts" we really are. Mrs. Chavers, our school teacher Danny and I really keep each other in the spot light all the time. You would rather think that this is an annex to Chattahoochee if you could be around for a while. Of course, we have lots of fun and I do like living here so very much.

It has been so very warm tonight, but looks as though it may rain before morning. We've had quite a bit of rain recently and I like it this way although I will be glad when Autumn begins.

Oh yes, I was out to the carnival last night and of course, I saw the usual things. The most interesting part of the show were the monkeys and they were so cute. I also visited the crazy house and felt quite at home. I did receive a few scares, but no gray hairs. I had to wash the dirt off by layers when I returned home.

You know, I was the first of our class to complete my training, but now most of my classmates are out. Pitts is going to do Supervision work at the Hospital and so is Hodges. I believe that they are the only two of the class who have decided to work for Sister. I wouldn't think of working for her as I'm really fed up on the dirty handout from those Sisters. Most of them are so two-faced, I'm sorry to say.

Do you ever go spear fishing anymore? You haven't mentioned going out for some time. It must be so much fun so you'll have to teach me the correct way to fish some day.

I'm so sleepy that I find myself dozing at intervals. I'll say "good-night" and I do hope to hear from you tomorrow.

Love Always,
Evelyn

September 11–

Dear Paul,

Dannie and I have just returned from the movie at our favorite theater, "The Strand." Of course, we saw a double-feature which were movies that played down town months ago, it seems. We saw, "Here Come The Waves," and "Dark Mountain." They were very cute pictures, but I can say I was a bit tired from sitting so long in one position.

It was about six-thirty when I returned from duty tonight, but Doctor McLane always drives us home which is very nice of him. You know he could very easily have us take the bus instead, but he is too wonderful than to have us wait for buses. Of course, there's no extra charge, and we would much rather ride in the car. He is going to Memphis, Tennessee tomorrow afternoon and night and will be there until Sunday night. You see, he has to be present at an annual meeting and he is also staying over for the horse show. While he's gone, we'll give the office and instruments an over-hauling and have them nice and clean when he returns.

Oh yes, would you like to know more about Dannie? She is a school teacher as I've told you previously and about thirty-two years of age. Her life history is rather interesting, but I'll only give you a sketch of it. While yet very young, she was married to some one whom she loved very much and of course, she thought he was truly in love with her. He was more or less a racketeer and also had a young girl in trouble. In order to prevent a great deal of conflict, Dannie divorced him. Then she fell in love with another guy and later found out he was no good so she has practically lost all faith, trust, and confidence in the whole of the opposite sex. I can't say I much blame her for she has surely gone through a great deal of discomfort. She is rather disappointed with life itself so I try to help her so much as I can, but there isn't much you can do in a case like that.

Just before we left the office, it began pouring down rain and by the time we ran across the street to the car, we were soaked. You know where Doctor McLane's office is, don't you? It's in the Brent building across from the San Carlos Hotel.

So you've been receiving letters from Iris, have you? Well, I just hope that she continues to write you. She is a "screwball"—the same as I. You certainly weren't too difficult to please when you chose me to be your wife.

I'm certainly sorry to hear the bad news about your Grandfather. I suppose you know that I've often thought of him and had been looking forward to meeting him for he must be a wonderful person.

I'll have to get some sleep so I'll say "Good-night."

Love Always,
Evelyn

September 13–

Dear Paul,

I feel like a new person now after having seen my Mother again after a period of about four weeks. I know that I should see her more often, but I have been quite busy getting settled at a new place and I'm still trying to get my other uniforms. I only have four and waiting to receive four more that I ordered at the same time.

I went along with Mr. Myers home last night so Mom and I visited Frank and Mamie after having eaten supper. I was quite surprised to hear that he is out of the service now and has been out about two weeks, I think. He didn't have to take a Medical discharge for he had enough points. Mamie said that she plans to write you, but she has been rather busy with her school work. You know, she teaches at school each year. Elizabeth taught for about eight years, but J. C. doesn't want her to teach anymore.

When I returned to Mrs. Chavers this morning, I decided I should wash my uniforms first. You should have seen me scrubbing those uniforms! Next time I think I'll leave them dirty. I hung them out back on a line and before they began to dry, it began raining. Oh boy, I ran out to get them and so much train smoke has blown on them that they were black! Trains are wonderful things, but not near the house. Pasty, the maid from Gadsden house came over and I gave the remains to her with my regards. I hope she can return them in good condition.

Mrs. Chavers and I had lunch and then I slept all afternoon—what a life! When I awakened, Jancsik called and asked me to go along with her to a movie tonight so here goes. Sure wish you could be along. You don't know how much I do miss having you in on the movies with me. I often think of the many things we did and how happy I was to have you near me. You soon will have been gone a year, but it seems like a lifetime almost.

Here's hoping that your Grandfather has improved and the rest of the family is O. K. I haven't heard from them in some time. Of course, you know I hope you're in perfect health.

All My Love,
Evelyn

September 16–

Dear Paul,

It's so very quiet here this morning and how I would like for something exciting to happen. We have been listening to the morning services by Rev. Thomas. You have probably heard him speak, but if you haven't, he is a wonderful man.

Dannie and I had so much fun preparing breakfast this morning and Mrs. Chaver's appreciated our help very much. You see, we buy our own food and prepare it as we want to so that helps Mrs. Chavers quite a bit. I bought some shrimp so we'll have fried shrimp for lunch along with some vegetables and an ice box pie that I made yesterday. You know, it's going to be so much fun to have a home of our own some day—don't you think? I enjoy my work and the people are so nice to me, but I wan't be completely happy until you return.

It has been reported for the past two days that we are to have a hurricane, but it is still off the coast and hasn't touched the Keys yet. We usually just get the remnants of such and that's enough.

Doctor McLane was still in Memphis, Tennessee over Friday and Saturday so we really did a cleaning up job at the office, but you should have seen us after having finished. I didn't think I would ever get my hands clean again for I cleaned the venetian blinds and they were black. We also cleaned and oiled all the instruments which was really a job.

Do you have any idea of when you may be sent to the States? Golly, I can hardly wait for you to return for I do want to see you so very much.

I took the radio down yesterday to have it repaired for I believe a tube has blown and I hope that is all that's wrong with it.

It's such a wonderful day and here I sit with nothing to do. I can't continue writing for there isn't enough to say for that. If I had some film, we could make some pictures, but haven't been able to find any yet. I'll say "so-long" until later.

All My love,
Evelyn

September 19–

Dear Paul,

I didn't return from duty until about seven-thirty last night and also tonight. We do have such long hours and I enjoy the work, but I always feel so tired when I do stop to relax. You see, the only time we're off during the entire day is the few minutes we take to have a sandwich. Of course, we're off all day on Thursday and have Saturday afternoon and Sunday off each week.

I had a letter from Elizabeth yesterday and she said she was going to write you the same day. It seems as though it had been so long since I last heard from her.

Your visits to the many outstanding spots of that Island sounds very interesting. How I would just love to be there with you! Couldn't we have lots of fun? It would make me very happy if such could be possible.

I'm all alone tonight for Mrs. Chavers is spending the night with her daughter and Dannie has a date and won't be home until late. I'm not afraid of being here alone except for one thing. I'll tell you of a couple of my experiences that shall never be forgotton sometime if I can get the courage to tell you. Those were the only times I have ever been very much afraid, but made me be a bit more cautious; In fact, there was a time when I would trust anyone, but after a few things happened, I found that I could really trust only a very few. It so happens that I always trusted you very much and still do.

I suppose I had better hush and get some sleep for I was practically asleep while writing this letter.

Love always,
Evelyn

September 20–

Dear Paul,

Was I happy to receive two letters from you today! One of which contained the post cards you sent of Hawaii. You know, that Island isn't as beautiful as I had pictured it in my mind, although the pictures were nice.

I'm very much in hopes that the rumors you're hearing are true. Just to think that it may not be much longer before I see you makes me very happy. You said that the rumors were that you may come in to Camp Davis. I've been try-ing to find out where that camp is and so far I still haven't found out. I have to give Doctor McLane a two weeks' notice before leaving so let me know as soon as you can if you do get to return right away. As you know, I want to see you as soon as possible after you reach the States. I can't help feeling quite excited over the news & I do hope it's true.

Oh yes, you were speaking of going in Mechanic business with the Marine friend in Connecticut. If he is the type you can depend upon, I think it's a very good idea. I believe you would accomplish a great deal at that type work for you seem to like it very much. Don't worry about my being so far away from home for as you know, I can't be with my Mother always. Just so I can be with you is all that really counts.

I had a letter from your Mother today. She is really a swell person and I look forward to receiving her letters very much. I'm just hoping that they (your family) won't be too disappointed in me upon personal appearance.

Mrs. Chavers has been gone all day and since I was not on duty, I've been here alone until Dannie came home this afternoon. I went to the Grocery Store this morning and bought vegetables for the afternoon meal. Dannie was very tired from having worked so hard so I prepared supper. Oh—it was lots of fun, but will be more fun when I have you help me. After having eaten, I had my bath and I'm ready for bed (with my pajamas on.) It's very warm tonight, but nevertheless, I always sleep well.

Elizabeth said that J. C. may be transferred at any time. She is rather upset about the news, I think. I don't know if she'll go along with him or not. You just wait until I can be with you for I won't let you out of my sight again.

I have a number of letters to answer, but I'm not going to answer them tonight. Instead, I'm

going to bed for it's nine-thirty and my bedtime.
Here's hoping I'll see you soon—

All My Love,
Evelyn

September 22–

Dear Paul,

Mrs. Chavers and I have just had supper and
now she is reading the newspaper. She treats me as
though I were her own daughter and I like it that
way. She wants to drive me over home sometime
which I think is a nice idea. She has a very pretty
car and of course gas isn't rationed anymore.

I was off duty at two this afternoon since
today is Saturday. We don't always get off on time
as it's just according to the number of patients
who register during the office hours. I did shampoo my hair and have had my bath so I feel very
much rested now.

Check works three to eleven o'clock every
day so she doesn't have a chance to get out much.
Nevertheless, she doesn't have to pick on me. She
just called and wants me to go along with her to
the midnight movie. Of course, I don't want to
go and told her so, but she won't listen to reason
so I finally told her I'd go. That girl can think of
some of the "craziest" things to do. I would much
rather stay home and enjoy my sleep.

Elizabeth said that Jimmie and Doris's baby
is so much like the one she had that it hurt to see
it. I believe I told you that she had a still born
once. If she had been taken care of properly she
would have had a normal child and both she

and the baby would have been well. She lived at Chipley at the time and the Doctor there wasn't an obstetrician. He did deliver the most of the babies there, but he was just a Doctor in general and in no special field. Elizabeth was very anemic and he didn't give her shots or extracts of any kind to build her up so the baby didn't get the proper nourishment and Elizabeth almost lost her life at delivery of the child. It was a nine month's baby and had only been dead a short while when born. It was the most beautiful baby I ever saw; in fact, it looked more like a big wax doll. It's really pathetic for they love children so very much and want a family of their own.

I'm still so much excited over the idea of your coming home. You know that's really going to be wonderful to be with you again and not have to worry about the War anymore and where you may be sent next. Oh yes, when you reach the States will you be discharged or do you have to complete the time you signed up for when you entered the service?

I saw Phiel and her husband last night and they seem to be very happy. You were speaking of his having money—I really don't believe that he has any too much. He just doesn't seem the type that would have much. I still say that I don't believe that marriage will last except for only a short period of time. I hope I'm wrong in my opinion.

We've had some of the most beautiful moonlight nights recently. Just wish you could be here to enjoy them too.

I'll hush for tonight.

All My love,
Evelyn

September 25–

Dear Paul,

Received two letters from you today and both contained very good news. I'm just hoping and praying that you are getting ready to return to the States instead of another Island. I know that you haven't really been overseas so terribly long, but it seems that it has been half of a lifetime; at least, you've been over there long enough.

As you say "I'm just not in the mood for writing tonight" applies here. I'm so very tired tonight for we haven't stopped all day except just long enough for a sandwich at about two o'clock this afternoon. It isn't hard work, but it's the long hours of standing that gets me down.

Just who do you suppose stopped by to see me Sunday? None other than David and Clara. Was I really surprised and happy to see them! And their baby is a beautiful child. Ronnie is as "cute" as can be, but was rather tired after the long ride from Kansas. They drove over since gas isn't rationed anymore. They were going over home so I told them that I would have Mrs. Chavers drive over Thursday for she has wanted to visit my Mother ever since I first came here.

You tell that room mate of yours that he shouldn't drink so much. I'm so glad that you don't care for intoxicating beverages for so much confusion can arise from such.

I've just had my bath and pressed my uniform for tomorrow so it's now nine o'clock and my bedtime. I'm not even going to take time out to dream for I'll sleep so soundly.

Hope to see you very soon.

All My love,
Evelyn

September 27–

Dear Paul,

Mrs. Chavers and I have just returned after having spent the day with my Mother. I believe she really enjoyed the trip and of course she said that she did.

David and Clara will be home until next Tuesday and he has to report back to the field by October the ninth. Their two children are really just as healthy and "cute" as can be. I'm going over again Sunday, but will probably see them again before then. They plan to come down tomorrow, I think.

We had a big parade for a Lieutenant General (formerly of Pensacola) who just returned from Overseas. The streets were so crowded and hot so we just watched from the office windows and could also see better from there. After the parade, he made a speech at the San Carlos Hotel.

I'm anxiously awaiting to hear that you're on your way home. I do hope that you are for I can hardly wait until I can see you. I'll just have to tell some of those people off if they keep you over there much longer.

Oh yes, Clara said that David received a letter from you sometime ago and had good intentions of answering it, but just hasn't. David doesn't write to anyone so far as I know so don't feel slighted. I could count every letter I've received from him on my fingers so you can see he never writes much.

Received a letter from Bennett today and she still cares a great deal for the boy who was once her patient. She said that he only has one leg, but she loves him just the same. I can understand that very well.

They're having a ball game down at the park as I can hear them hollowing. I can remember when I wouldn't miss a game for anything if I could possibly attend—

I do hope that you're on your way home. I love you very much.

Love Always,
Evelyn

September 29–

Dear Paul,

Dannie and I have just been discussing our daily problems, but haven't drawn any conclusions. She has been trying to find an apartment for she is so disatisfied here. She doesn't like Mrs. Chavers and visa versa, I think. Oh well, I'm just the "in-between."

We've really been having our share of rain today. I enjoy the rain once in a while and it has been some time since we've had a nice rain. It must have blown quite hard last night from the appearance of the surroundings this morning.

It's Saturday night again and Dannie wants to go to the midnight movie. Do I have your consent? I suppose I'll have to suffer the results if you disapprove. "Pride of The Marines" is playing so it must be good. I do get so sleepy when I go to a late movie so I don't go very often.

It's almost nine o'clock now, but at two o'clock tonight the time will be set back one hour. I really don't see anything wrong with the present War time, but some high officials must know the difference.

I'm going over home again tomorrow and spend the day. David and Clara asked me to go over for they're leaving Tuesday for Kansas. David expects to be out of the Army by November or December. You know, he has a home in Warrington so I suppose they'll live there when they return.

I just feel as though you will return to the States soon and I hope that I'm right. I've missed you so very much and will until I see you again. Maybe that will be soon.

All My love,
Evelyn

[Following letter is from Grace Fogel, married to Paul's brother, Charles]

Oct. 1, 1945.

Hello Paul:

Hold yourself or the shock might be too great for you to be receiving a letter from me after all this time. For all I know maybe you have dis-owned me as a sister. I hope you can find room for me on the family tree. How is your sweetheart Evelyn getting along? I bet she is anxious to hear when these Fogel's are being send home by Uncle

Sam. It was 2 years since Charles left Tatamy so you can't wonder that I'm mighty anxious to have him home. I suppose you know he is at Okinawa. I just finished my letter to Charles. It seems to take so long until I get an answer from him. It certainly will be swell when the Fogel's can have their reunion. How long does your enlistment call for yet? Buddy started school this year and likes it very much so Julia and I are all by ourselves during the day. Billy is in 8th grade now and I hope he will make the grade for High School. He is taller then I am and not quite as husky. He was picking potatoes on Saturday and of course then he was in the berries. I didn't see Mom Fogel for several weeks as I had been so very busy canning but now that is just about finished all except some pears. This year I raised quite an assortment of poultry. We have 1 goose (& 4 cats), 5 ducks, 60 chickens and two turkeys. If our turkeys keep healthy I'm planning to have a turkey for the grand home coming. Have you been hearing from your brothers? I had such high hopes for Xmas but according to the point system I guess it will be Spring before Charles can get home. The children we have don't build up points for Charles so you see his points are mighty few. It's time for Gabriel Heater so I hope he has good news for all of us. Paul are you close to Charles? I had hopes maybe you two would be able to see each other but so far I suppose you weren't so fortunate. It's been pretty cool the last two days making a person want to stay close to the stove. The time has been turned to Standard Time now again making the evenings pretty long being its dark by the time we finish our supper. The clock struck 9 so I must go to bed for my beauty sleep.

I'll say goodnight and will chat with you again soon. Billy has the Sears Roebuck Catalog and is on a wishing trip.

Lots of luck and here's hoping and praying you will be home soon.

Look again and make sure

<u>Grace</u>

P.S. My thoughts were with you right along, believe me.

Oct 2–

Dear Paul,

Received another letter from you that was addressed to Gadsden Street. Just so I get them, I don't mind. I still haven't really become reconciled to the fact that I'm out of training and free to be on my own. I'm very thankful that it isn't difficult for me to adjust to my surroundings.

Dannie and I were down to the "coffee cup" which is a cafe that has recently opened on Cervantes Street. We were walking through the park on our way back and did the sight of such a familiar place bring back many precious memories! When I saw the water fountain, I remembered the many times you stopped by for a drink.

I'm so glad that you may be home for Christmas. Just think, we'll spend our first Christmas together. Isn't that wonderful? I was hoping to see you before then, but I suppose Uncle Sam thought otherwise. If they keep you over there much longer, I'll just have to come over for you.

Oh yes, would you please tell me what my Mother has said to you that makes you think you have something to correct when you return? I would rather you would be as you were and I know of nothing that you need to correct.

You should have no complaints about not receiving letters. I'm so glad that you hear from such a number of friends. I can see that I'm not the only one who is very interested in your affairs.

I should have written you last night, but honestly I was so very tired when I finally came from the office. We had five operations yesterday and then saw all the patients who had registered at the office. I went on duty yesterday morning at seven-thirty and didn't get home until seven o'clock last night—almost twelve hours straight.

It's beginning to become a bit cooler for it's Autumn, you know. It's really wonderful to get out in the nice cool and refreshing breeze. Just seems to add an extra bit of energy of which I need a great amount.

I had better set up my uniform, have a bath and polish my shoes for it's about my usual bed time.

I love you very, very much.

Evelyn

Thursday Night
October 4–

Dear Paul,

Since I've had the day off duty, Mom came down to visit me. She came with Mr. Myers in the early morning so as soon as the stores were opened, we went shopping. When we returned, Mrs. Chavers had a very nice lunch prepared. She seemed to have enjoyed the visit and I was very glad to have her come. Her visits are so few and far apart.

Oh yes, I also had a nice surprise package arrive today. You told me you were sending some material, but you didn't tell me about the other articles. The material is beautiful even though it does have that Hawaian touch. I just wouldn't take anything for the beautiful little "hankie" holder and the two handkerchiefs. They must be hand painted. The pillow top is also nice. Oh, I've already showed them to a number of people so they want to become acquainted with you in order to receive some surprises too. You can bet that I'm very selfish though.

I've just written a letter to your Mother. At the time she wrote the last letter I received from her, your Grandfather was very ill. I do hope that his condition has much improved. I'm looking forward to meeting him in the near future and I know he is a wonderful person because of the many things you've said about him.

Phiel came over to see me which was the first time since I've been living here. Her name is Martin now, but I still call her Phiel from habit. She said that her husband plans to remain in service indefinitely. I can't understand why he would like that kind of a life, but there are people for all trades.

I'll say "Good-night" until later.

All My love,
Evelyn

October 7–

Dear Paul,

Sunday again and maybe it should have been a day of rest, but Dannie and I have been cleaning house. Mrs. Chavers hasn't been home for two days now so we run the place to suit ourselves. We're expecting her home this afternoon so she should really appreciate our cleaning house for her.

Check came by and asked me to go along with her to the beach, but as you know, I don't care about going there especially. I've enjoyed the day much more by just remaining home.

Oh yes, I prepared lunch and have had stomach ache ever since I ate. I wander if there could be any connections between the two—my "cooking" and the "stomach ache" after having eaten? We plan to go to a movie this afternoon and dinner in town tonight. I wish it were with you instead of her.

I just don't think it's right that you should have to remain overseas and especially since all your buddies may return. I do wish you could say you're on your way to the States instead of another Island. Oh well, it will at least make me that much happier to see you when you do return.

Doctor McLane is going to be gone for two whole weeks of next month and we will be free during that time. Of course, we'll give the office a good cleaning, but that will only take a couple or three days. We'll be paid the same as though we were working regular hours. He's really wonderful, don't you think?

Smitty was by to see me and she is still very happy.

I'm so sleepy so I believe I'll sleep for a while before going to a movie.

All my love,
Evelyn

THE END

IDENTITY OF NAMES MENTIONED

- Charles Fogel, Grace Fogel—Paul's brother, sister-in-law
- Dad / Leidy C. Fogel, Mother / Meda Lilly Fogel—Paul's father, mother
- David (W. D.) Wells, Clara Wells—Evelyn's brother, sister-in-law
- Elizabeth Brown, J. C. (John C.) Brown—Evelyn's sister, brother-in-law
- Frank (John Franklin) Wells, Mamie Wells—Evelyn's brother, sister-in-law
- Grandpa / Charles A. Fogel and Grandma / Helia Woodring Fogel—Paul's Grandfather and Grandmother Fogel
- Iris Wells—Evelyn's cousin
- Jimmie (James T.) Wells, Doris Wells—Evelyn's brother, sister-in-law
- Mom / Mrs. Ella Wells Myers—Evelyn's mother
- Mr. Myers—Evelyn's stepfather
- Pauline Fogel Acker, Earl Acker—Paul's twin sister, brother-in-law
- Sister Theodora—Head of Evelyn's Pensacola Hospital School of Nursing

[When Evelyn mentions going "over home," she is talking about the trek from the nurse's school in Pensacola to her home of origin, Holley, Florida, which is about a thirty-mile drive.]

AFTERWORD

So here's the surprise ending:

Paul was shipped back to the States in late 1945. In his own words,

> We were all set to go to Okinawa when we dropped the A-bomb...because I had more than enough points, I was discharged at the Great Lakes Naval Station in Michigan. I requested to go to Pensacola after discharge. After arriving in Pensacola, I contacted Evelyn, who had been working for an eye, ear, and nose doctor. After a day or so, she let me know she was not ready to marry.

Wait...what?

Turns out that Evelyn enjoyed working for that doctor and didn't want to leave him without proper notice. This just blew Paul's mind.

He continues,

> So I boarded a train and headed for Pennsylvania. This was just before Christmas, 1945. By Christmas, she had changed her mind and she came to Pennsylvania. I picked her up at the train station in Bethlehem. It had been snowing and on the way home, with my brother Francis' car, we slid into a snow bank. On January 6, 1946, we were married in the pastor's home in Bethlehem, Pennsylvania. It was a Sunday afternoon. My sister Pauline and brother-in-law Earl were present at the simple ceremony. The pastor's name was Rev. Herman.

The quotes above are from a short, autobiographical essay that my father wrote in October 1996. That was the year that he and Mom celebrated their fiftieth wedding anniversary.

This was Paul Fogel's postscript:

> I don't know how I will die or when I will die. I just want whoever reads this to know that I'm ready. Come what may, you can tell by what's in this report. My wife and I have had a good life together. We don't regret any part of it. Good times as well as bad. Don't think I've told you the whole story. I've purposely omitted some of the more trying years. The good by far outweighs the bad.

Paul & Evelyn Fogel's wedding picture
January 6, 1946

Paul & Evelyn Fogel's wedding certificate

Paul & Evelyn Fogel and children: Linda,
Larry, Debbie, and Kathy, 1956

Paul and Evelyn's children, 1956
Larry, Linda (standing), Kathy, and Debbie

ABOUT THE AUTHOR

Kathy Carroll shares a home with her daughter, son-in-law, and granddaughter in central Texas. This year, 2020, has been unusual and challenging because of the Coronavirus pandemic. Carroll's "new normal" in retirement has been to stay isolated as much as possible while reading good books and trying out new recipes in the kitchen. Carroll spent most of her career in office management, although she does hold an AAS in court reporting. She was involved with her husband in church music ministry and Christian education during the years they raised their children. Her interest in World War II was sparked when she and her sister came across their mom and dad's love letters that were written during the war.